THE ECONOMICS OF THE YACHT INDUSTRY

Liao Minsheng

1 Plus Books

San Francisco 2024

The Ecomonics of the Yacht Industry by Minsheng Liao
Paperback edition
First published in Chinese in China in 2024
Authorised by Minsheng Liao to publish in English
in the United States of America

ISBN: 978-1-949736-99-1
Library of Congress Control Number: 2024922202

Published by 1 Plus Books®
website: http://1plusbooks.com
email: 1plus@1plusbooks.com
San Francisco, 2024

Contents

Preface

The ocean is a treasure trove of rich resources, with proven marine minerals such a soil and gas resources 1000 times greater than those on land, so its impact on human future development is immeasurable. The ocean is also an important channel for the flow of global resources, as well as for opening up and cooperating with the outside world. The ocean is thus the new battlefield of modern technology and the birthplace of emerging industries. The ocean economy plays an important role in cultivating new momentum, giving birth to new business forms and leading new development.

To better develop marine tourism as part of this economy, and to meet people's demand for vacations on the ocean, a leisure industry oriented to the Chinese path to modernization is being built. During the 2021 Spring Festival, the head of the Hainan Free Trade Port Cruise and Yacht Research Base joined with the chief expert of the Maritime Silk Road Research Institute of Hainan Tropical Ocean University (a key think tank in Hainan Province) to lead a research team that carried out in-depth field trips and solicited opinions from domestic and foreign peers. They decided to write an academic monograph titled *The Economics of the Yachting Industry,* which has become a pioneering work in the academic field both domestically and internationally.

The author hopes to analyze the industry chain, supply chain, and value chain of the yachting industry from an economic perspective, and to study many relevant factors, including its brand connotation, technological innovation, financial support, talent supply and demand, consumer behavior and market patterns, future trends, and so on. This book is also a companion piece to *Cruise Economics* (published in Chinese by China Ocean University Press and in English by 1 Plue Books Press in the United States).

After nearly two years of writing and polishing, this book is now ready for publication. It focuses on analyzing and elaborating on the origin and development process of the yachting economy, including yacht design and building, yacht club development, yacht docks and destination cities, yacht sales and transactions, yacht brands and types, and yacht consumer markets and structures. Also discussed here will be promotion policies for the yachting industry as well as laws and regulations for yacht safety. The book also covers future trends in the yachting industry, such as high-level talent cultivation models and technology innovation.

This book is based on the multidimensional connotations of the yachting industry in the context of a digital economy. Starting from multiple factors such as the innovation chain, value chain, supply chain, and spatial chain of the yachting economy, it focuses on top-level design and overall planning, constructing a management system and mechanism for yachting economy development. This includes such factors as a comprehensive evaluation system, security governance system, talent cultivation, technological innovation, financial support models, and capacity building. It proposes new ideas, perspectives, and judgments involving the bottlenecks, shortcomings, and weaknesses encountered in the process of high-quality development.

Detailed introductions and explanations were made from the following aspects, proposing actionable countermeasures and suggestions:

1. High-quality development of the industry shall be achieved to meet the needs of the people. The yachting sector has a long industry chain and a significant driving force, which is of great significance for promoting the high-end transformation of the shipbuilding industry, improving the level of modern service industry, promoting the development of the marine economy, and meeting the growing needs of the people for a better life. In addition to automobiles, yachts are another high-end entertainment consumer product. As a carrier and tool of entertainment consumption, they are currently very popular in developed countries in Europe and America. With the rapid development of the Chinese economy, people's demand for high-end entertainment consumption is also increasing. In the near future, China's yachting industry will also catch up with developed countries and become an important component of the tourism industry. The innovative business model represented by yacht clubs will also become a new engine driving the vigorous development of the personal bulk consumer goods market.

2. The urban economic structure is going to be transformed and upgraded based on the development of the yachting industry. Major maritime projects will be introduced to promote the high-end development of advantageous marine industries throughout the entire industry chain and value chain. The manufacturing of large yachts is in line with China's active promotion of supply-side reform and consumption-side upgrading in recent years, which is a "dual circulation" strategy both domestically and internationally. It enhances the international competitiveness of China's yacht manufacturing industry and promotes its sustainable development. The international competitiveness of China's large-scale yacht manufacturing industry is currently at a moderate level. Currently, yacht manufacturing industries in Zhuhai, Xiamen, Wuhan, Shenzhen, Jiangsu, and Hainan provinces are closely following the model of yachting industry development in France, Italy, Germany, the United States, and other regions. We look forward to the overall breakthrough, surpassing, and development in the next golden decade, and propose strategies and suggestions to effectively enhance the international competitiveness of Chinese coastal cities.

3. China should adhere to green and innovative development to promote leapfrog development of the industry, aim for world-class industry and improve the design and manufacturing quality of yachts along the coast. As a high-end entertainment transportation vehicle,

yachts can be called luxury goods in the field of industrial products. In all aspects of the design process, yachts fulfill personalized needs for customer groups. The design of a yacht also needs to meet the requirements of its rationality in function and structure, safety in use, and convenience. From the perspective of design aesthetics, the shape of yachts also has strong contemporaneity, nationality, and regional characteristics. We should adhere to innovative and green development, strengthen the construction of independent innovation systems, accelerate the development of high-quality and efficient equipment, and promote the demonstration and application of new energy and clean energy technologies in yachts. The green transformation of the yachting industry is the general trend in the context of building a harmonious coexistence between human and nature in the Chinese path to modernization.

4. An ecological layout covering security governance, talent cultivation, and international cooperation around industrial upgrading shall be formed. After in-depth analysis of the root causes of yacht safety supervision problems, it is proposed that the functional transformation of yacht safety supervision, the construction of maritime service culture, public policy decision-making on yacht safety, electronic maritime construction, and the improvement of social participation abilities are feasible ways to solve the problems of yacht supervision.

We should strengthen the design and construction of various yachts, maritime technology and marine engineering, as well as the cultivation and construction of a full industry chain talent team in operation management, tourism services, legal consulting, etc. And gradually a new model for cultivating innovative and practical yacht talents that meets the needs of both international and domestic markets shall be built. Coastal cities shall be encouraged to hold high-level international and national yacht exhibitions, strengthen cooperation with internationally renowned yacht professional exhibitions, and build yacht technology exchange and cooperation platforms. We should create a favorable investment environment, create broad investment space, and attract global yacht research and development design, professional supporting equipment, and service enterprises to invest and cooperate in China.

This book was completed by the following: Professor Liao Minsheng from Hainan Tropical Ocean University is mainly responsible for the overall project design, planning, editing, and drafting. Professor Dong Zhiwen from Ocean University of China and Professor Huang Xuebin from Hainan Foreign Language Vocational College are responsible for comprehensive coordination and service. The team led by Associate Researcher Yin Xiangyu from the Water Transport Science Research Institute of the Ministry of Transport is responsible for researching materials related to yachts. Dr. Xue Rui from Hainan Tropical Ocean University served as the initial proofreader and reviewer for this book. The authors of each chapter in the book are as follows: Chapter 1: Huang Ying and Liao Minsheng; Chapter 2: Dong Zhiwen and Sun Wenqian; Chapter 3: Lu Xiaowen and Jiang Wenjia; Chapter 4: Huang Xuebin, Lin Shan, Zhang Wenjun, Liu Xiaomei, and Chen Sisi; Chapter 5: Song Hongjuan and Liao Minsheng; Chapter 6: Huang Xuebin, Liu Xinyue, and Jing Shaobo; Chapter 7: Liu Hongbing, Zhou Huaqiao, Song Zhen, and Wang Shengnan; Chapter 8: Song Danying; Chapter 9: Shen Sicong, Lu Shiwen, and Liao Minsheng; Chapter 10 Yin Xiangyu and Fang Yan; Chapter 11: Meng Yajun and Dong Zhiwen. The translation proofreaders are Guo Leting and Chen Qinbing.

In the process of its formation, this book used for references large amount of Chinese and foreign literature, and absorbed the ideological essence and insights of Chinese and foreign scholars and researchers. Though their names are not listed here, their contributions are accepted with gratitude and high respect. This book is suitable for teachers and students majoring in maritime disciplines in Chinese and foreign universities, government and enterprise personnel in the yachting industry, practitioners in the upstream and downstream of the industry, as well as enthusiasts of yacht tourism. Feedback from readers is welcome, and the editors look forward to a more diverse, meticulous, and comprehensive second edition.

It is said that the ocean is the cradle of life, the homeland of wind and rain, and the treasury of resources. It is the new territory of human development. Throughout history, the ocean has been a place for pursuing freedom, romance, and dreams, as well as containing infinite treasures and opportunities. Let's go to see the sea together, to listen to the crying and the joyful songs of the sea and view the unique flowers and plants, diverse marine creatures, geological structures, and wonders on the islands and reefs.

Here, let's have an intimate encounter with the sunshine and sea breeze. Lazy vacations always provide the best relaxation for both spirit and mood, especially for tourism enthusiasts who have intimate contact with the deep sea by riding on fast sailing yachts and experiencing the vastness, magic, and magnificence of the blue sea united with the sky. The sails are the peaks of the sea, while the heart is the shore. All will be immersed in the dreamlike scene of star journeys on the sea.

Minsheng Liao
May 1, 2022

Chapter 1

Introduction

China's National Development and Reform Commission took the lead in jointly revising and publishing The *Guiding Catalogue for Industrial Structure Adjustment* (2023 Edition) to encourage the development of technologies, equipment, and products that play an important role in promoting economic and social development. With a focus on economic development, the Commission accelerated the construction of an intelligent, green, and modern industrial system with integrated characteristics that are in line with the requirements of integrity, advancement, and safety.

Industry is the key to economic development and the foundation of a country's establishment. The 21st century has the potential to be the century of the ocean, and the yachting economy, as an important part of the development of the ocean economy and culture, is being hailed as a "business opportunity floating on a golden waterway." The yachting industry has become one of the global economy's growth points, offering enormous economic value and potential. The yachting industry involves not only manufacturing but also multiple fields such as tourism, sports, leisure, etc. It is thus a cross-disciplinary and cross-industry field.

The yachting industry has the characteristics of a long industrial chain and has high economic value. Internationally, many countries have regarded the yachting industry as a national strategic sector for cultivation and development. China has abundant marine tourism resources. Especially in recent years, with the improvement of people's living standards and the gradual maturity of leisure culture, the demand for the yachting industry in the domestic market is growing day by day, demonstrating enormous development potential. It can be concluded that the yachting economy plays an important role in the development of the marine economy. The marine economy is also one of the strategies for developing China into a strong country. Promoting the structural adjustment of the yachting industry and driving the rapid development of the yacht economy is an important measure to build a modern industrial system, enhance the core competitiveness of the industry, and promote the marine tourism industry to move towards the high-end of the global value chain.

However, there are also some difficulties and challenges in the development of the yachting industry. First, the technological strength of China's yacht manufacturing industry is relatively weak, especially in the field of high-end yacht manufacturing, which lags behind the international advanced level. Secondly, the large-scale development of China's yachting industry faces some difficulties, including contradictions in market demand, incomplete policy systems, and short funding chains. Therefore, we need to understand and explore yacht economics from both micro and macro levels. At the micro level, it is necessary to study the economic principles and business models of yacht manufacturing, sales, leasing, and maintenance processes. At the macro level, it is necessary to reveal the impact of the yachting industry on regional economy, employment, environment, and other aspects. Through such in-depth research, it helps us to have a deeper understanding of the development laws of the yachting industry, thereby providing theoretical guidance for the healthy development of the yachting industry.

Yacht economics is not only a scientific research on industrial economy, but also involves many issues in social and economic development, such as employment, ecological protection, and tourism industry development. In this context, the study of yacht economics has broad practical and theoretical significance. This book attempts to deeply analyze yacht economics from both theoretical and empirical perspectives. Firstly, this book will provide an in-depth analysis of the economic principles of the yachting industry, elucidating its development laws and economic dynamic mechanisms. Then, this book will conduct empirical analysis on the yachting industry in various countries and regions, revealing their development status, successful experiences, and existing problems, in order to provide useful insights for the development of China's yachting industry.

Section 1: The Origin of Yachts

1. The Origin of Foreign Yachts

(1) The Origin of Yachts

The origin of the yachting industry can be traced back to the prehistoric period, which marked the beginning of human civilization. Early primitive ships were mainly used for fishing and water transportation for human survival and livelihood. As early as the 4th century of the common era, yachts were called "boats" in what is now the Netherlands. The vessels originally used to hunt down pirates have now become synonymous with high-end leisure and entertainment. The term "yacht" originated from the Dutch word "jagen" ("hunting or chasing"). At first glance, Dutch yachts from the early 4th century had fundamental differences in design, size, and function compared to modern yachts.

Yachts were also the preferred means of transportation for 17th century explorers. The interiors of these yachts were spacious enough to accommodate several people and months of supply, including fresh food that helped prevent scurvy. Yachts thus became the perfect choice for exploring unknown waters because of their speed, flexibility, and seaworthiness. In 1606, the 60-ton small yacht *Duyfken* brought the first group of Europeans to Australia. Some 36 years later, a similar yacht led people to discover New Zealand.

In addition to being an ideal sea-exploration vessel, early yachts also played an important role in warfare. Armed by the Dutch for combat, *the Duyfken*, which is now famous all over the world, played an important role in a battle between Portugal and the Netherlands in 1601, thus determining the control of the spice trade in the Iberian Peninsula. With the increase of warship scale and the improvement of technology, yachts have been refitted as wartime mail ships, transmitting critical information through artillery fire with their extraordinary speed.

As the first inventor and manufacturer of yachts, the Netherlands brought yachts to the attention of world powers. At the same time, the complex waterways in and around the Netherlands was forcing this lowland country to actively find effective water transportation to quickly transport people and goods. It was by means of yachts that the Dutch went out into the wide world, established trade relations across the oceans that generated wealth thatin turn further stimulated them to see this magical water vehicle as a leisure product as well.

Evidence indicates that yachts have undergone a continuous transformation from functionality to entertainment in their development process. The role that yachts play is constantly changing in different social contexts. With the development of civilizations and technological progress, maritime navigation has gradually transformed itself into a high-quality leisure activity.

In light of these developments the yacht has evolved from a simple means of transportation to one of today's advanced leisure and entertainment vehicles. When King Charles II of England was crowned in 1661, the Dutch East India Company gifted him with a 74-foot-long, well-crafted royal hunting and fishing boat, called a "yachat", which gave birth to the term that is still in use. The original purpose of this ship was to pursue and fight pirates, but Charles II later used it as an entertainment ship. Charles II built more yachts and began racing them. He also established a yacht club called the "Royal James". The purpose of these activities was not just for entertainment, but to train naval officers and test the performance of new ship types.

(2) The Evolution of Yachts

The clear signs of this transformation appeared in Europe around 1800. With the advancement of the Industrial Revolution and the rise of capitalism, large numbers of people in the middle and wealthy classes began to emerge in society. Since they had both the time and economic resources to pursue higher-quality leisure activities, private ships called "yachts" became popular, emerging as status symbols for both the nobility and the nouveaux riches.

In the 17th century, boats were propelled by wind power, so early yachts were actually sailboats. After the First Industrial Revolution, steam-powered ships emerged that gradually replaced sailboats. Steam engines and propellers were retrofitted to yachts in the 19th century by the British and Americans. By 1913, the per capita GDP of the United States surpassed that of Britain, becoming the most developed country in the world at that time. At this time, the yacht economy of the United States also began to sprout, with 400,000 yachts in the country.

In the mid-20th century, after World War II, the modern yachting economy began to gradually develop, led by the United States, where the industry had integrated yacht manufacturing, sales, maintenance, insurance, and other systems, In Europe, companies like Bénéteau in France and Bavaria in Germany expanded their production scale with the widespread use of plastics and composite materials in the 1980s, enhancing the quality and performance of yachts. In some developed Western countries, yacht clubs have also emerged. To this day, the yachting industry in Western countries is still constantly developing. "Nowadays, the yachting industry has become a major pillar of Europe's industry, to the extent that every country and city is willing to invest in yachts," said Alan Jacob, General Manager of the KOEJAC Yacht Manufacturing Company in France.

2. The Origin of Domestic Yachts

Although most modern yachts are imported into China, similar yachting cultures have already developed there. *The Brief History of Yacht Development* points out that Chinese yachting culture can be traced back to painted boats and dragon boats. Japan and South Korea have been deeply influenced by Chinese culture, so they have similar yachting cultures.

Consider, for example, the Chinese vessel known as the Hua Fang, also known as the "boat house" due to its multiple towers and pavilions. In Japan, it is also known as the house-shaped boat. It is divided into a single-hull boat and a twin-hull boat with two ships side by side. The boat body embodies the essence of Chinese architecture: glazed tiles, flying eaves, pavilions, and towers. a veritabled water palace characterized by its delicacy. The Hua Fang dates back nearly two millennia: a depiction of one of them appeared in the painting "Luoshen Fu Tu" created by Gu Kaizhi, an artist who flourished in the Eastern Jin dynasty(266-420 CE).

The "Hua Fang" is commonly found in palace gardens and the private gardens of wealthy families. It can be used for recreation and can also be parked in a garden to form a unique scenery, complementing the landscaping. In addition to being used for sightseeing by nobles and wealthy individuals, commercial Hua Fangs have also emerged, with restaurants and hotels on board. In addition to boating around the lake, passengers also enjoyed drinking and singing to each other, which attracted many literati to linger there. Today, traces of these ancient yachts can still be found in famous gardens such as the Summer Palace and Beihai Park in Beijing.

In ancient Chinese culture, both the Hua Fang and the dragon boats were indispensable water-play vessels in palaces and wealthy courtyards. The development of China's modern yachting industry began in the 1950s. After the economic reforms of the 1980s, the yachting industry there began to develop slowly, about 30 years later than the development of the international yachting economy.

Section 2: The Development of Yachts

1. The Development of the World Yachting Market

(1) Development History

The modern yachting industry began after World War II. The United States, the United Kingdom, and Italy were all pioneers in yacht manufacturing. Since the 1950s, the world yachting market has gone through six important stages of development:

Early 1950s: Start-up stage. The annual sales volume of yachts in the world was about 3100, amounting to about US$52.7 million, of which 71% were small motor boats and sail boats with wooden structures, and a smaller amount being motor boats with aluminum structures.

Early 1960s: Developing period. In several years, the world's sales have reached US$1.6 billion, with fiberglass yachts accounting for 60% of the total. The Western yachting industry has developed into a more complete industrial system with comprehensive supporting facilities such as manufacturing, sales, repair, service, finance, and insurance.

Early 1970s: Four-level pattern. The yachting industry in the world has developed rapidly. The Asia Pacific region (Japan, Chinese Taiwan, Singapore, Hong Kong, South Korea) plus other countries or regions were the leaders. The international formation of the United States, Western Europe, Northern Europe and the Asia-Pacific region led the market.

Early 1980s: Unprecedented prosperity. In 1981, the total sales of yachts in the United States reached US$8.1 billion. By 1988, total sales had reached US$17.9 billion. At the same time, oil production and consumption were at high levels in many countries. By the late 1980s, due to two energy crises, the global yacht market began to weaken, and yacht and spare parts manufacturers sought to transform their production bases.

Early 1990s: Relative maturity period. While the yachting market in some countries was still sluggish, the markets in countries such as Japan, the United Kingdom, the Netherlands, Germany, Australia, and Sweden remained stable. Especially in Japan, the total amount of yachts imported from the United States alone reached US$163 million in 1990, an increase of 84% from US$88.549 million in 1989.

21st century: Highly centralized and highly concentrated markets. By the 21st century, the world yachting market was highly concentrated, forming two major markets: North America and Europe. In 2004, the combined market share of the two markets accounted for 94.3% of the world's revenues.

(2) Main Characteristics of Each Stage:

1. In the early 1950s, yachts were mainly small wooden motor boats and sail boats, with a small number of aluminum motor boats. Outboard motors provided most of the power for motor boats. In the United States, 642,000 outboard engines were sold in 1965, setting a yet-unbroken record. It can be seen that the sales of small motor boats were large at that time.
2. In the early 1960s, yachts made of fiber-

glass began to enter the market and developed rapidly. The Western yachting industry has evolved into a more comprehensive industrial system that includes manufacturing, sales and repair, services, finance, insurance, and other supporting facilities. At the same time, yachting exhibitions have emerged, along with yacht clubs and docks.

3. In the 1970s, the world yachting market consisted of four major groupings, mainly consisting of the United States, Western Europe, Northern Europe, and the Asia Pacific region. After the 1970s, the yacht-manufacturing industry in the Asia Pacific region entered a period of rapid development. Japan soon became the second largest yachting export country, and Taiwan became the third largest,with more than 20,000 yachts exported annually.
4. In the 1980s, with the recovery and development of the economies of Western countries, the demand for yachts significantly increased, propelling the industry into an unprecedented period of prosperity. In 1981, the total sales of yachts in the United States amounted to US$8.1 billion, growing to US$17.9 billion by 1988. In the late 1980s, due to various reasons, the world yachting market began to turn weak. The growth rate in countries such as Spain, Italy, Norway, Denmark, and the United States was slowing down, and some countries even showed a downward trend. Some production and sales companies mainly focused on yachts and spare parts, and sought markets with cheap labor to transfer production bases and improve product competitiveness. At that time, the Italian government also adopted a policy of reducing the value-added tax on yachts to encourage a rebound in the market.
5. In the 1990s, while the yachting markets in some countries were still sluggish, the markets in countries such as Japan, the United Kingdom, the Netherlands, Germany, Australia, and Sweden remained stable. Especially in Japan, the total amount of yachts imported from the United States alone reached US$163 million in 1990, an increase of 84.0% from the previous year's figure of US$88.549 million. In 1997, yacht sales in the United States reached 595,700 units, a decrease of 3.7% from 1996, though sales revenues reached US$19.345 billion, a 9% increase from US$1775.3 billion in 1996.
6. After entering the 21st century, the world yachting market has maintained a rapid development trend, and the original market pattern has gradually been broken. The market share of yachts in Asia Pacific countries continued to decrease, resulting in two major yacht markets; North America and Europe. In 2006, the sales of yachts in the United States (including yachts, accessory sales, and maintenance services) reached US$39.5 billion, making it the world's largest yacht consumer and the largest yacht market. Its sales accounted for more than half of the world's yachting market share.

According to international experience, when the per capita GDP of a region reaches $3000, the yachting economy begins to sprout, and when the per capita GDP reaches $4,000, the yachting economy will grow rapidly. According to statistics from the National Bureau of Statistics of China, in 2012, China's per capita GDP exceeded US$6,100, and the per capita GDP of eastern and other coastal areas exceeded or approached US$8,000. Shanghai, Beijing and other places even exceeded US$13,000. There is still a lot of room for the development of the yachting economy in China, since its yachting industry is not yet perfect, and various systems and regulations have not been well formulated. With the development of China's economy, the yachting industry there can expect a promising future.[1]

2. The Current Development Status of the International Yachting Industry

The global yachting market size in 2022 amounted to US$8.91 billion, and it is expected to grow at a compound annual growth rate (CAGR) of 5.8% from 2023 to 2030, reaching US$1.39 billion. Due to the increase in personal disposable income and the tendency towards leisure or entertainment activities, the demand for yachts has gradually increased in the past few years. The increasing preference of travelers for luxury travel, personalized services, and exclusive travel is the main factor driving yacht sales.

The yachting industry is growing in the United States, which is the most representative developed country in the industry, . In 2021, it achieved a revenue of US$2.6 billion, and by 2022, it added US$100 million to this total. Experts predict that from 2023 to 2030, the yachting economy in the United States will continue to maintain a yearly growth trend.

(Data source:
https://www.grandviewresearch.com)

(1) The Impact of COVID-19

During the COVID-19 pandemic in 2019 and beyond, the demand for yacht rentals decreased, severely hindering market growth. The emergence of the pandemic and subsequent lockdowns imposed by governments around the world, coupled with strict travel restrictions, led to a decrease in the number of tourists visiting tourist destinations, resulting in a decline in the growth of the tourism sector in 2020. The COVID-19 has seriously affected the tourism industry, especially the yacht-leasing industry. Due to the rapid spread of the virus worldwide, the industry has stagnated. As it is impossible to predict the recovery of the yacht-leasing business, the COVID-19 pandemic brought huge uncertainty to the industry and panicked all members of the value chain of related industries. Supply-chain disruption has become the main obstacle to yacht construction. Industry participants are taking measures to overcome the uncertainty brought about by the pandemic, including implementing safety and preventive measures in charter flight contracts. However, people are optimistic that once the pandemic eases, the chartering market will soon recover. After prolonged isolation,

[1]World yachting industry Development Report

people are now more inclined to engage in leisure activities. Therefore, with the relaxation of restrictions, the market has begun to recover, and with a significant increase in the number of tourists willing to travel with their families, the number of new yacht orders from manufacturing companies has also increased.

After experiencing stable growth over the past two years, yacht sales in the United States began to normalize in 2022. In that year, consumers began shifting their consumption patterns from yacht activities to other accessible activities, such as tourism, concerts, and sports events. In Europe, Asia Pacific, Latin America, the Middle East, and Africa, the growth of yacht leasing slowed down in 2020 due to uncertain factors. However, the market has returned to normal and promises to show strong growth in the coming years. Therefore, in view of the impact of the COVID-19 epidemic, in order to improve the current situation of the European yacht market, the EU offers the following two comments:

- Favorable trends related to ocean tourism and private island resorts help expand the market.

Marine tourism has a positive impact on economic growth in several aspects. It also earns foreign exchange and contributes to government revenue. It has created employment opportunities and made significant contributions to the local economy. In addition, it also provides various social and cultural benefits, such as strengthening communities and promoting sustainable tourism. Due to climate change and environmental degradation, many countries around the world are formulating policies to strengthen the coastal tourism sector.

- The European Union's ocean policy supports the growth of coastal tourism and marine economic activities.

For example, in January 2021, the National Oceanic and Atmospheric Administration (NOAA) of the United States finalized the *2021-2025 Blue Economy Strategic Plan* to accelerate the growth of the US blue economy. This strategy focuses on five sectors: marine exploration, tourism and entertainment, maritime transportation, water sports competitiveness, and coastal resilience. India also plans to develop 78 marine tourist attractions in the coming years. These measures will encourage future growth in the marine tourism industry, thereby supporting market growth.

(2) The Driving and Constraining Factors Affecting the Development of the Yachting Industry

1. Driving factors - The increasing popularity of leisure yachts and marine tourism activities helps to expand the market.

   The increase in disposable income of consumers, as well as their increasing preference for marine tourism and leisure activities such as navigation, are contributing to the expansion of the market. In the past few years, leisure boating has become increasingly popular, paving the way for yacht rental services. In addition, advanced booking systems allow customers to rent yachts while booking flights, ultimately driving market growth.

   Governmental favorable measures and

plans to promote marine tourism are expected to stimulate market growth. For example, the Indian government will develop infrastructure and services, support local tourism and port city tourism, encourage cruise tourism, and increase sea tourists to 1.5 million by 2030-31. The Indonesian government has also updated its maritime tourism policy and canceled the CAIT license (authorized by Indonesian territorial customs). The policy expects a significant increase in the number of yachts traveling to Indonesia, bringing in over US$500 million in revenue.

2. Constraints - High yacht-rental costs hinder market growth.

   Yachts are typically rented for a basic or weekly rate. The cost of renting a yacht depends on several factors, such as the type of yacht, crew requirements, rental destination, local taxes, and basic expenses. Therefore, the basic rates for chartering vary greatly. In addition, the rental fees for small sailboats and catamarans range from $10,000 per week to $150,000 per week for the most luxurious super yachts. In addition, implicit costs such as taxes and value-added tax (VAT), insurance, crew remuneration, and meal prepayments are not mandatory, but they account for approximately 15-30% of the basic ticket price and are collected before chartering.

   For example, the Bahamas announced a 10% value-added tax on all charter ships flying foreign flags. This is being enforced in all charter flight contracts signed after July 1, 2022. In addition to the 4% charter flight fee, this additional cost will increase by a total of 14%. This is similar to the expense account that a captain can use during the charter period. This cost is an obstacle for many customers in developing countries, further suppressing the growth of the yacht rental market.

(3) Market Segmentation of Yacht Rental

Geographically, the market is divided into Asia Pacific, Europe, North America, and other parts of the world. Due to its well-established tourism industry, and the short distance between its member countries, Europe dominates the market for yacht rentals.

Europe: Europe holds the largest market share in yacht rental. The income contribution in 2022 exceeded 35%. The high share can be attributed to the increase in yacht sales in the region. Due to the high growth of maritime tourism and the increase in the number of tourist destinations, the region may dominate the market. Croatia, Greece, France, Spain, and Italy are the main tourist destinations. The increasing popularity of fishing and water sports, as well as the increase of upper-class members, are expected to drive the development of the market in the region. European flight booking, online demand cooperation with charter service providers, and the issuance of more aircraft licenses are expected to drive market growth. The affluent population in the region may also drive market growth.

In addition to scuba diving, free diving, and snorkeling, investment in coastal areas and recreational activities such as fishing, sailing training adventures, whitewater rafting, kayaking, and one-day rowing adventures will also increase. More and more trade exhibitions and leisure rowing events organized by manufacturers have supported market growth in the region.

North America: North America holds the second most important position in the market due to its diverse coastline and excellent cruise destinations. The United States ranks first in this regional market because it has a major charter center.

Asia Pacific Region: The Asia Pacific yacht-rental market is expected to achieve the highest compound annual growth rate in the coming years. This growth is attributed to the rapid development of urbanization, improvement in living standards, and increase in disposable income, which has led to the evolution of personal taste. In Thailand, Malaysia, Singapore, China, Japan, and Australia, recreational activities such as fishing and water sports are becoming increasingly popular, and maritime tourism is also increasing, providing excellent opportunities for yacht-rental companies. In addition, the government's vigorous development of the maritime tourism industry, especially in countries such as China and India, is expected to drive market growth.

However, countries facing economic crises, political instability, and strict foreign direct investment policies are expected to experience a negative impact on growth. On the other hand, in countries such as Singapore, Thailand, China, and Australia, as people increasingly participate in ocean entertainment activities, the demand for these activities is expected to surge, which is also expected to promote regional market growth.

(4) Market Division of Yacht Preference

1. The most popular types of yachts

The two main types of yachts are motor yachts and sailing yachts, each with different styles, sizes, hull shapes, and materials. Super yacht manufacturers offer a certain degree of customization, ranging from customization and semi customization to production series.

Motor yachts dominate the global yacht market, with a market share of over 82% in 2022. The high market share in this segment can be attributed to the advantages provided by these yachts, including high speed and power, as well as long-distance coverage. In addition, these yachts are highly favored due to their advanced systems and equipment. Modern equipment is a key driver of high sales of yachts in the global market. In addition, it is expected that this segment will also become the fastest-growing part during the forecast period.

Sailing yachts use sails as their propulsion system, thus relying on wind speed for movement. Although sailboats can cover long distances, the design, deck space, and onboard facilities of motorized yachts make them more attractive to buyers. The increasing attention to entertainment activities and the continuous improvement of technology are expected to further drive the growth of motorized yachts in the global market.

2. Popular sizes for yachts

In 2022, the 20 to 50 meter yachts dominated the global market with over 57% revenue share. It is expected that they will continue to dominate the segmented market during the forecast period.

Due to the afford ability of small yacht leasing, the sub-market of less than 40 meters will occupy the largest market share. According to the size of yachts, the market is divided into below 40 meters, 40 to 60 meters, and over 60 meters. These yachts can be used for both personal competitive activities and leisure rowing activities. A 40-meter charter ship has many advantages, including wind navigation ability, ensuring wind direction, and fuel savings. End users also prefer yachts up to 4,000 meters in length because they are reasonably priced, have low maintenance costs, are fixedly installed in shallow water areas, are easy to use, and have low mooring costs.

Rapid urbanization, improved living standards, increased disposable income, and an increase in the upper-class population have enhanced individuals' purchasing power for luxury goods and leisure activities. Therefore, in recent years, the demand for yacht services in the market has also shown significant growth. The observed trend in yacht construction indicates that the average length of yachts increases by 3 centimeters per year. This is due to the increasing demand for super yachts and large yachts in most developed countries, as well as the overall surge in tourism in these regions. Therefore, it is expected that the 40-60m yachts will experience significant growth, while the yachts above 60m will have the fastest growth rate during the forecast period.

Currently, 165 yacht manufacturers from 28 countries are building at least one yacht over 24 meters tall . Every year, about 400 yachts over 24 meters are delivered to owners, built by shipyards specializing in yacht categories or product segmentation, which sets them apart from other commercial shipyards. Yacht manufacturing is a global industry. Some countries and regions specialize in producing yachts of a certain style, which is usually determined by their naval history or maritime traditions. Other shipyards position themselves in niche product categories with growth or high demand.[2]

(5) The Major Yacht-Rental Companies in the World

1. Dream Yacht Charter is a world leading expert in yacht management, brokerage, and private yacht ownership. Loic Bonnet founded the company in 2000, headquartered in Maryland, USA. The company is a pioneer in providing easy and worry-free rental, expert advice, and customized solutions. The company is renowned for providing new sailing destinations and a wide range of charters, including captains, bare boat crew, vacations, crew, and cabins. The company currently has over 1,000 yachts in approximately 60 locations worldwide. The company owns some of the world's largest yacht manufacturers, including Dufour, Aquila, and Fontaine Pajot. In 2019, the company launched the "More Women At Sea" campaign to encourage more women to go out to sea and receive sailing education. In February 2020, the company announced a partnership with inland cruise expert Les Canalous to expand and promote boat va-

[2] https://iyc.com/yacht-builders/

cations on canals across Europe.

32, List of major companies:

- Global Boat Company Limited (USA)
- Dream Yacht Group (France)
- Northrop Johnson & Johnson (USA)
- Cerro Corporation (Monaco)
- Camper & Nicholsons (UK)
- Ocean Independence (Switzerland)
- Burgess Yacht (UK)
- The Moorings Limited (USA)
- Boatbookings (UK)
- Liz Shipping Company Limited (USA)

(6) Shipyards Around the World (by region)

1. Northern Europe

Nordic countries are particularly famous for building fully customized and semi-customized motorboats and sailboats. The Netherlands and Germany rank first in the yachting industry, delivering yachts larger than50 meters in large quantities and at high value. German builders Lürssen, Abeking & Rasmussen and Nobiskrug offer fully customized yacht projects, while Dutch builders Amels/Damen Yachting, Heesen, and Moonen build high-end semi customized yachts based on model platforms. In the fully customized category, Feadship, Oceanco, and Royal Hakvoort focus on the construction of fully customized motor yachts, while Royal Huisman offers tailor-made sailing yachts. Customized and semi-customized yachts built in Nordic countries often maintain higher resale value in the brokerage market. Due to their high-quality completion and extreme customization level, it can be said that these yachts are like floating artworks.

In the production-series shipyards in Nordic countries, the Sainte, Princess Yacht, and Pearl Yacht companies offer motorized yachts ranging from 17 meters to 40 meters. These companies compete directly with yacht manufacturers in southern Europe. Among Mediterranean countries, Italy and Turkey are the two main producers of semi-customized and production series of yachts, with a maximum length of 50 meters.

2. Italy

Most Italian-made yachts are made of fiberglass and are usually part of the shipyard brand series, such as San Lorenzo, Custom Line, Ferretti, Benetti, Acadia yachts, Myola, Falcon yachts, and Amir yachts. When it comes to speed, Italian shipbuilders such as AB Yachts, Tecnomar, Azimut, Mangusta, Leopard Yachts, Riva, and Pershing have performed well in planning and opening up ships. But in the past decade, a large number of new yacht manufacturers have entered the market, offering larger yachts and more customizable options while competing with traditional yacht manufacturers such as Baglietto, Codecasa, and ISA yachts. Perini Navi remains one of the most unique sailing yacht manufacturers in terms of performance and style, but when it comes to innovative design solutions, the revival brought by Columbus Yachts, Tankoa, Cantiere delle Marche, and Admiral has stood out.

3. Turkey

Turkey has a long marine heritage and is famous for building boats with wooden cabins. But Turkey's shipyards are now turning their attention to building motor vehicles and sailboats out of fiberglass and steel. At present, the most famous yacht manufacturers in Turkey include Turquoise Yachts, Bilgin Yachts, Alia Yachts, Mengi Yay, Numarine, AvA Yachts and Bering Yachts. In the Middle East, Gulf Craft, a shipyard in the United Arab Emirates, has gained reputation and success with its extensive semi-custom and production series of yachts.

4. North America

It is not surprising that the North American market is driven by shallow draft boats and sports brands, as American yacht owners enjoy cruising in the Bahamas and Caribbean. Production is mainly concentrated in semi-customized motor yachts by famous shipyards, such as Westport Yacht, Palmer Johnson, Viking Yacht, Hatras Yacht, Jarrett Bay, Merritt's boat and Jim Smith's racing boats. In larger markets, American-made super yachts have a higher degree of customization, with Christensen Yachts and Delta Marine offering motor yachts over 37 meters in length. Crescent Custom Yachts in Canada has also adopted a similar approach.

5. Asia

Asia is the production center of GRP series motor yachts. Most of the facilities of well-known brands such as Horizon yachts, Ocean Alexander, Cheoy Lee, Heysea, Johnson yachts and Nordhavn are located in Chinese Mainland, Hong Kong and Taiwan.

6. Other parts of the world

The remaining yacht manufacturers are in Oceania, South Africa, and Brazil. SilverYachts and Echo Yachts are located in Australia, matched by McMullen & Wing and Yachting Developments in New Zealand. Brazilian shipyards INACE and MCP rank last for South America.

3. The Current Development Status of Yachts in China

The yachting economy in mainland China started relatively late, developing only after the 1980s. Despite this, the continuous growth of international economic exchanges, the integration of global markets, and recent transformations in industrial structure have contributed to the gradual development of the industry.

(1) The Development of the Yachting Industry Started Late

Compared to the development process of the international yachting market, the modern market in China has a relatively short history, dating back to the 1970s and 1980s, while the yachting market in Taiwan began in the 1950s. At that time, the quality of yachts was not a factor for yacht manufacturing companies to consider; instead, price was the main factor that truly facilitated the development of the yacht manufacturing industry. Pricehas also played a good role in promoting the development of the yacht market in Taiwan. Similarly, although China's yacht economy developed relatively late, with the improvement of Taiwan's economic level, the labor cost in Taiwan no longer has an advantage. Therefore, various foreign-funded enterprises have shifted their focus to China's mainland, investing in building factories there.

(2) Significant Advantages in the Development of the Yachting Industry

China has more than 90,000 lakes, 65,000 islands, and 18,000 kilometers of coastline, but it is difficult to see a beautiful and luxurious yacht in any of these locations. The number of yacht clubs is even rarer. The reason behind this is that China lacks yacht-related infrastructure, and many wealthy Chinese have purchased luxury yachts that can only be parked in Hong Kong, Monaco, Miami and other places with great difficulty. Therefore, it is urgent for the Chinese national and local governments to introduce some supportive policies as soon as possible, vigorously developing yacht infrastructure and planning a number of yacht-supporting industrial parks. Taking advantage of the 2008 Beijing Olympics and the 2010 Shanghai World Expo, the Chinese began this effort in recent years. According to data, many cities in China have started to develop their own yachting industry facilities in their respective regions. For example, Zhoushan in Zhejiang will "create a paradise for yachts at sea" and Zhuhai in Guangdong will emerge as a new yachting industry zone, Shanghai plans to build 9-10 yacht terminals on both sides of the Huangpu River, including public yacht ports, private membership ports, commercial yacht ports, and yacht port communities. In a similar vein, Xiamen in Fujian will build China's largest yacht terminal.

At the same time, Chinese governments at all levels, plus real estate developers, and boat manufacturing companies are also trying to invest heavily in the yachting industry, hoping to form a virtuous cycle. Thus, China's yachting industry has gone from being cautious in the past to investing heavily in the future. It is still difficult to predict the size of China's future yacht market, but investment and enthusiasm offer every reason to believe that the time has come for China to develop the leisure yacht market. Many industry experts also strongly believe that China's yachting industry has a huge labor advantage and latecomer advantage in participating in international competition, and also possesses very attractive market development prospects in yacht entertainment, services, and industrial development.

In the 1990s, many international entrepreneurs came to China to invest in the yachting industry. By 2003, the number of yacht-producing enterprises in China's mainland had exceeded 300. According to the 2012-2013 China yachting industry Report, as of the end of April 2013, there were 440 yacht manufacturers, 46 yacht clubs, 54 yacht sports and leisure service institutions, and more than 6,000 berths built in China. On April 18, 2011, the China International Yacht Exhibition concluded in Shanghai, with yacht sales exceeding ¥1 billion in just four days. In 2012, the overall market size of China's yachting industry reached 1.75billion yuan, of which the sales revenue of the luxury yacht market is approximately 7,800 million yuan, accounting for 44.6% of the entire yachting industry. According to the 2012-2013 China yachting industry Report, in 2012, an average of 430,000 people in China owned one yacht. By 2020, the total consumption of domestic yachts will reach 100,000, with a total market value of 50 billion yuan. It can be seen that the development trend of yacht sales is very optimistic.

(3) Current Development Status of the Yachting Industry

The Chinese yachting industry is currently on the eve of an explosive period. The period from 2000 to 2012 was a period of rapid development, with commercial yachts as the main focus. Later, it entered a bottleneck period, and the commercial yacht market was basically saturated. However, fishing yachts and other products showed signs of budding development. The present period is one of transformation in the industry, shifting from a focus on commercial yachts to a mainstream development of popular yachts. A series of actions such as the "Guiding Opinions on Promoting Yacht Tourism" issued by the government are also guiding and supporting the development of popular yachts. In recent years, with the improvement of yacht production technology of domestic enterprise, production capacity has been continuously expanding, and domestic yacht production has grown rapidly. According to statistics, as of 2022, China's yacht production is about 1,958, with a demand of about 2,122.

(4) Supporting Policies and Regulations for China's Yachting Industry

In August 2022, the Ministry of Industry and Information Technology and five other departments jointly issued the Implementation Opinions on Accelerating the Development of Cruise and Yacht Equipment and Industry (hereinafter referred to as the Implementation Opinions). According to the development goals proposed in the Implementation Opinions, by 2025, China will initially establish an industry system of cruise and yacht equipment, complete and deliver domestically produced large cruise vessels, accelerate the promotion of medium-sized cruise vessels, and achieve mass construction of small cruise vessels. The cruise and yachting industry has a long chain and a significant momentum, which is of great significance for promoting the high-end transformation of the shipbuilding industry, improving the level of the modern service industry, promoting the development of the marine economy, and meeting the growing needs of people for a better life. In recent years, China's cruise and yacht development has achieved positive results, but compared with advanced countries in the world, there is still a gap in equipment industrialization, market maturity, and consumer popularization.

(5) The Development Trends of China's yachting industry

The yachting industry in China is about to experience explosive development. The Implementation Opinions document cited in (4) above clarifies the active guidance and support for the upgrading and innovation of the yachting industry, and supports the development of popular yachts that use clean energy. The current research on yachts will focus on yacht design, materials, manufacturing, and accessories. In the future, small and medium-size yachts as well as domestic yachts, will become the main types purchased in China. Yacht leasing will become an important way for China to promote mass yacht consumption. The innovation and development trend of yacht technology will put forward new requirements in research and development and design, green energy application, and intelligence.

Section 3: Theoretical Development of the Yachting Industry

1. Research on Yacht Economy

(10 The Supply and Demand Relationship of Yachts

The supply-demand contradiction is the main factor in the development process of the yachting economy, and it is also the driving force for the development of the yacht market. The degree to which these yachting supply and demand contradictions are resolved directly affects the overall development of the industry. As an emerging sector, the yachting economy has unique requirements for the supply and demand of yacht products, as well as the development of the market. Therefore, it is necessary to conduct detailed and sufficient research on products, market participants, and market segmentation in order to formulate unique economic development strategies for yacht products and lay the foundation for adjusting the supply and demand imbalances.

(2) Yachting Market

The yachting market is a place where buyers and sellers gather to deal with the industry's supply and demand contradictions. In principle, the development of the market directly decides the development of the yachting economy as a whole Therefore, research on market competition, market division, and market order is particularly important for the development of the yachting economy. Studying the yacht market offers a clearer understanding of its development, direction, laws, and status, thus prompting appropriate strategies for its future development.

(3) Yacht Consumption

Yacht consumption is the ultimate goal of yacht production and the driving force behind the development of the yachting economy. According to the economic conditions and development status of the yachting economy in different countries or regions, the nature of yacht consumers varies, and the nature of yacht consumption also varies, such as self-purchased yacht consumption, yacht rental consumption, and yacht tourism consumption that currently exist. Yacht consumption is also a factor driving yacht production. With the development of personalized customized yachts, different special requirements have been put forward for yacht production based on the consumption intentions and preferences of different consumers. In addition, yacht consumption usually cannot be separated from yacht clubs, which tend to be service-oriented consumption. Therefore, yacht operators must have a full understanding of yacht consumption tendencies, preferences, consumption structures, and other aspects in order to organize the production of yacht products that meet the needs of yacht consumers.

(4) Yacht Investment

According to different yacht consumption patterns, yacht investment is usually divided into two aspects: yacht manufacturing enterprise investment and yacht club investment. Yacht consumption is usually divided into two aspects: yacht consumption in itself and yacht club consumption. The investment of yacht manufacturing enterprises is the investment in yacht products themselves, which provides the basic means to expand the yacht market structure and meet the consumption willingness and preferences of yacht consumers, Yacht club investment is an investment in yacht services, which is a guaranteed measure to improve the quality of yacht consumption services and promote sustainable development of the yachting economy.

(5) Yacht Economic Management

The development of the yachting economy is a dynamic process of mutual influence and promotion between yacht supply and demand. Due to its instability, it is easily disturbed by other market factors. Yacht economic management involves the analysis of the total supply and demand and its operation in the yacht market. The purpose of such analysis enables managers to regulate and manage the yacht market reasonably, formulate reasonable planning strategies for economic development, and ultimately promote the balanced development of the yacht economy.

2. Theoretical Research on the Development of the Yachting Industry

This refers to the theoretical study and exploration of the overall laws, characteristics, trends, and Influencing factors in the development process of the yachting industry. Its main content includes:

(1) Market demand theory:

The development of the yachting industry is highly dependent on market demand, considering factors such as consumer demand for yachts, types, and changing trends. The yacht market demand theory mainly studies the various factors that affect yacht market demand and their relationships. These factors usually include consumer income levels, consumption habits, leisure culture, social status, consumer expectations and understanding of the entertainment lifestyle. In addition, the yacht market demand theory also focuses on the impact of market environments on demand, such as the economic environment, policy environment, cultural environment, etc. For example, in regions with rapid economic development, people's income levels are higher and their demand for yachts may also be greater. In addition, the yacht market demand theory, through the study of demand, helps enterprises better understand the market and formulate products and marketing strategies that are more suitable for the market, thereby improving the competitiveness of enterprises and driving the development of the yachting industry.

(2) Corporate competition theory:

This theory focuses on the competitive strategies between yacht manufacturing enterprises, such as how to obtain, maintain, and improve competitive advantages.

This theory mainly studies and analyzes how yacht manufacturing and sales companies compete, how to obtain competitive advantages through various strategies and methods, and how to maintain and strengthen this competitive advantage.

The theory of corporate competition involves internal and external factors, including but not limited to product quality, design innovation, brand image, marketing strategy, service quality, enterprise scale, economic strength, and management efficiency. These factors collectively determine the position of yacht companies in the market, affecting their ability to successfully attract and retain consumers. For example, a yacht company can gain a competitive advantage by providing high-quality products and services, establishing a unique brand image, and implementing effective marketing strategies. To maintain this advantage, they need constantly to offer innovative products and services, to be sensitive to market trends, and to be monitor competitors.

Corporate competition theory also involves the structure of the yacht market, such as the number of competitors in the market, their size, and market share. These factors have a significant impact on the company's competitive strategy and market behavior. Overall, the competition theory of yacht companies helps them understand the market competition pattern, formulate and implement effective competitive strategies, and thus achieve their business goals and long-term development.

(3) Technological innovation theory:

This emphasizes the driving role of technological progress in the development of the yachting industry, including technological innovation in new materials, new processes, new designs, new equipment, and other aspects.

The theory of technological innovation mainly studies new technologies, methods, and concepts in yacht manufacturing and design, as well as how to improve product quality, reduce manufacturing costs, enhance service quality, and enhance industrial competitiveness through technological innovation. This theory mainly includes the following aspects:

1. **Innovation in manufacturing technology:** This mainly involves new processes, materials, and equipment used in the design and manufacturing process of yachts. The application of these new technologies can improve manufacturing efficiency, enhance the performance and safety of yachts, and reduce manufacturing costs.
2. **Design innovation:** This mainly refers to the introduction of new design concepts and methods in yacht design, such as environmental protection design, humanized design, and intelligent design. Such innovations can improve the comfort and convenience of yachts and enhance the user experience for consumers.
3. **Service technology innovation:** This mainly refers to improving the maintenance and upkeep services of yachts through new service technologies and methods, thus enhancing service quality and efficiency.

Companies can gain a competitive advantage through technological innovation and strive for more market share. At the same time, technological innovation can also promote the development of the entire yachting industry, promoting the upgrading and optimization of the industrial structure. Therefore, the theory of technological innovation emphasizes promoting the development of the yachting industry, improving the quality of yachting products and services, and reducing manufacturing and service costs through technological innovation.

(4) Industry chain theory:

This theory emphasizes the division of labor and cooperation between the upstream and downstream of the yachting industry, mainly focusing on supply chain management, industrial chain layout, and industrial chain upgrading. The industry chain theory of yachts mainly involves the upstream supply chain, midstream manufacturing links, and downstream sales and service links of the yacht manufacturing industry. This theory emphasizes how to improve the efficiency and competitiveness of the entire industry chain by optimizing each link of the industry chain.

1. Upstream supply chain includes raw material supply, component production, and other links. For example, companies can improve product quality and reduce production costs by selecting suppliers of higher quality and lower cost raw materials or components.
2. Midstream manufacturing process mainly includes the design and production of yachts. Companies can improve the performance of yachts, shorten production cycles, and reduce production costs through technological innovation, process improvement, and efficiency enhancement.
3. Downstream sales and service include yacht sales, maintenance, leasing, insurance, and other services. The company can increase its market share by providing high-quality sales and after-sales service, enhancing both brand influence and customer satisfaction.

In addition, the industry chain theory emphasizes the collaboration and integration between various links so as to achieve seamless integration of various links in the industrial chain through horizontal and vertical cooperation, thus improving the collaborative efficiency of the entire industrial chain. Overall, the industry chain theory is an important concept in yachting industry management, which is crucial for improving the core competitiveness of yacht companies and achieving sustainable development of the industry.

(5) Sustainable development theory:

This emphasizes the environmental protection and social responsibility aspects of the yachting industry, such as how to achieve efficient resource utilization, how to reduce environmental pollution, and how to contribute to society. The sustainable development theory mainly applies the concept of sustainable development to the yachting industry, including three dimensions: economy, society, and environment. It mainly considers how the yachting industry should comprehensively consider and balance environmental protection, resource conservation, and social equity while growing and developing.

1. Environmental sustainability: This includes the production process of yachts, which requires minimizing energy consumption and environmental pollution, using environmentally friendly materials, and achieving the recycling and disposal of discarded yachts. At the same time, during the operation of yachts, pollution should also be minimized as much as possible, as by reducing the noise and greenhouse gas emissions generated by yacht operations.
2. Economic sustainability: The development of the yachting industry must ensure economic benefits and growth. However, in order to achieve long-term development, manufacturers cannot excessively pursue short-term profits and should consider long-term investment, including product innovation, technology research and development, and talent cultivation.
3. Social sustainability: The development of the yachting industry should serve society and contribute positive value to it. This includes providing employment opportunities, improving people's quality of life, and promoting the development of related industries.

   Overall, the sustainable development theory of yachts advocates the implementation of economic, environmental, and social sustainable development policies and strategies in order to achieve long-term healthy development of the yachting industry.

The above theories are not independent of each other but complement each other. Studying and understanding these theories can help manufacturers better grasp the development trends of the yachting industry.

3. A Study of the Characteristics of Yachting Economics

Yachting economics is a sub field of industrial economics, based on modern economic theory. Its main characteristics are as follows.

(1) Yachting Economics is an Emerging Discipline

Yachting economics emerged from the formation and development of the modern yachting economy. Yachts first appeared in the mid-17th century and developed in the 20th century. Strictly speaking, the modern yachting economy originated in the mid-20th century so it has a history of only about 100 years, making it a relatively new emerging discipline. In terms of disciplinary content, many issues related to system construction, basic content, basic concepts, research methods, have been triggering extensive academic discussions and improvements.

(2) Yachting Economics is an Applied Discipline

Yachting economics is based on modern economic theory, which studies various economic phenomena, relationships, and development laws. Its basic principles and content originate from the practice of yachting economy activities. In the process of perfecting the disciplines, theories have been formulated about regional yacht economy resource development and utilization, development strategies, and reasonable development and distribution of yacht products and income.

(3) Yachting Economics is a Discipline of Industrial Economics

Yachting economics studies economic activities within a certain industry sector, in order to reveal various relationships, contradictions, and inherent laws in that sector. Yachting economics mainly studies the interaction, contradictions, and inherent laws of various economic phenomena generated in economic activities, guiding them with the theory of industrial economics, and promoting the development of the yachting industry.

(4) Yachting Economics is a Marginal Discipline

Yachting economics is also based on economic principles and theories, combined with theories and methods from tourism, aesthetics, psychology, geography, resource science, statistics, leisure science, and other disciplines. It comprehensively examines the interrelationships, contradictions, and internal laws between yachting economic activities and other economic phenomena. It is a highly comprehensive marginal discipline.

Chapter 2

Design and Manufacturing of Yachts

Section 1: Design Organizations of Yachts

Yacht design organizations mostly exist in the form of studios where several yacht designers work together to create. At the same time, yacht design studios cooperate with yacht manufacturing organizations to jointly create unique yachts. Yacht designers are the soul of yacht design, and the formation of their yacht design styles is closely related to the ideological trends and regional characteristics of the era in which they live. Both domestic and foreign yacht design organizations are committed to creating, innovating, and meeting the personalized needs of customers. In terms of exterior design, they focus on the integration and development of shape, color, and quality while taking into account practicality and economy in order to design a yacht that integrates comfort, beauty, and safety. In their interior designs, they integrate art and technology, and achieve a balanced development between aesthetics and operability from the perspectives of harmony, safety, and practicality.

1. Overseas Yacht Design Laboratories

The design of yachts outside China started earlier, with a more mature system and numerous yacht design studios, including Banneberg & Rowell, Zuccon International Project, Nuvolari & Lenard, and Winch Design.

(1) Banneberg & Rowell

In the early 1960s, Jon Banneberg, the recognized father of modern yacht design, founded his own company and began designing yachts. The sailing yacht *Tiawana* was the first project. Over the next decade, he designed more than 10 yachts as well as the iconic modern yacht *Carinthia VI*. By the 1980s, the company's position in the yachting industry had significantly improved, and it began designing yachts for world-renowned individuals. For example, the company collaborated with the Oceanfast shipyard in Western Australia to design a series of groundbreaking yachts including *Moecca* and *Thunder.* Subsequently, Dickie Bannenberg and Simon Rowell continued the founders' original intentions and visions, leading the design team in a new direction: collaborating with all major shipyards to design residences for private clients and real estate developers, and collaborating with furniture designers and developing other creative partnerships. At the same time, the company is the exclusive design company for the superyacht manufacturer Feadship. The company is outstanding or its interior design. With the advent of the 230-foot *Feadship Joy*, the company showcased its fully designed work. The 46-year-old creative director also designed the interiors of *Lurssen Pacific* and *Heesen Galactica Star*. Led by the founder Jon Banneberg, the team has invested in multiple top-notch superyacht projects. At the same time, it creates unique and non-mainstream layouts at the request of ship owners, such as the 322-foot Aviva with an internal tennis court. Banneberg & Rowell is committed to treating the process of building a yacht as a unique, customized, and intimate experience. Pursuing creative, groundbreaking design combined with long-term team-based progressive design, they created a modern yacht that integrates creativity, innovation, and efficiency for customers.

(2) Zuccon International Project

Giovanni Zuccon and his wife Paola Galeazzi, who have been working as yacht designers since 1976, founded Zuccon International Project in 1984 as a family-owned company. The company is committed to innovation in different design fields and has architecture and industrial design studios. From office and civil architecture to yachts and automobiles, it is active in several traditional fields and successfully applies multidisciplinary methods to them, which has become the core advantage of the company's development. In terms of home, office, and yacht design, the company adheres to the cultural affinity and long-term commitment to its customers to create products that meet their requirements. The company's mission is based on the fundamental principle of "project as the core of understanding reality itself and research as an important source of new ideas." At the same time, the company believes that "combining technology with in-depth understanding of customers, including their values and backgrounds, enables designers to support any architectural plan." By understanding customers' values and backgrounds, a continuity is created, allowing designers to interpret and express customers' cultures and identities in their products. Design plays an important strategic role in seeking and maintaining corporate image and serves as a productivity tool that coordinates all other elements. Currently, the company is managed by the new generation of Martina and Bernardo Zuccon. The key to the company's success lies in its ability to establish long-term relationships with customers, aiming to represent their corporate image and striving to achieve continuous product development. The company's projects include Sanlorenzo, Bluegame, Perini navi, Ferretti yachts, Custom line, CRN, and I.C. yachts. In 2021, together with Sanlorenzo, the company researched and designed 72 Steel, a super yacht with a total load of 1,850GT that spans five decks. It is expected to be launched in 2025 and become the new flagship project of the Italian shipyard. It is also the largest steel-aluminum structure ship ever built by the shipyard

(3) Winch Design

Winch Design was founded by Andrew

Winch. He received a degree in 3D design from Kingston College of Art and furthered his studies in the Caribbean to obtain a captain's qualification. He then studied under renowned yacht designer Jon Banneberg, and his love for yachts continued into adulthood. In 1986, he and his wife Janes (who is also a designer and company manager) established Andrew Winch Design. The company's first project was to design the interior and exterior of the *Swan 36-foot* sailboat, which successfully delivered the project and earned it larger projects, including the interior design of the 140-foot *Cyclos III* and the 160-foot *White Rabbit* powerboat. For nearly three decades, the company's design scope has included yachts, castles, villas, resorts, and private aircraft. Its founder is also a designer of aircraft exteriors and interiors who worked with Lufthansa's commercial aircraft company to convert Lufthansa's civilian aircraft into private planes. Its most famous aircraft design was Russian billionaire Roman Abramovich's Boeing 767-33A/ER, which cost an estimated USD$300 million in 2016 and has the same air defense missile system as Air Force One. Winch Design and Philippe Briand jointly designed the *Jeanneau Yacht 64*, which is the largest sailboat built by Arnold. Super yachtslike *Dubai, Madame GU, Avanti, Dilbar* (interior) and other well-known examples are all designed by Andrew Winch. Winch Design is a multidisciplinary, fully integrated design studio that always insists on creating dreams for its clients, staying honest, daring to innovate, and enjoying the fun of work

(4) Nuvolari & Lenard

In 1990, Carlo Nuvolari and Dan Lenard established Nuvolari & Lenard in Venice, Italy. This is an Italian super yacht design studio that specializes in designing luxury yachts. The company has worked with Palmer Johnson, Perini Navi, and CRN, and its most famous work is the 269-foot *Oceanco Alfa Nero* (Figure 2-3). The first *Alfa Nero* was launched in 2007, and its open deck design at the stern broke the conventional concept of yacht design, making the overall appearance of the yacht more fluid and incorporating a 7-meter-long and 3.5-meter-wide super pool. At the same time, the pool can be covered to accommodate helicopters, creating a precedent for embedding a pool at the stern of a yacht. The two principals have more than 20 years of design experience in the luxury yachting industry. They have built yachts for the former world's richest man Carlos Slim. Hollywood director Steven Spielberg's yacht *Seven Seas* also comes from this studio. With their outstanding design talent, the two have become famous in the luxury yacht design industry. Currently, the *Monte Carlo* yacht series designed by them includes MCY 66, the new MCY 70, the new MCY 76, MCY 80, MCY 86, MCY 96, and MCY 105.

(5) De Basto Designs

De Basto Designs is a Miami-based studio founded in 1995. Luiz de Basto, the president and chief designer, is from São Paulo, Brazil, and has been engaged in the field of yacht design for decades. This studio mainly engages in the design of luxury yachts, residential buildings, and unique merchant ships. From preliminary concepts to space planning, styling, and interior design, creativity and excellence are the main considerations, all while maintaining a constant awareness of functionality. The company designs boats with the philosophy that "the path is the destination: each project and each customer is a world in itself, and the result must be perfect." The *Dar* yacht designed by the company won the Best Exterior Design and Best New Superyacht Award at the Monaco Yacht Show in 2018. The themes of the Dar yacht are nature, flowers, feathers, fish, and waves. The designer integrates extraordinary appearance and interior design to create extraordinary yachts, such as *Amer 41M Explorer*, which perfectly integrates elegant design and complete functionality. Likewise, he exterior design of its *Seafair* yacht integrates aesthetics and functionality to form a high-end luxury yacht. Passion, vision, and insight are the cornerstones of De Basto Designs' success and progress in design (Figure 2-3).

(6) Others

Redman Whiteley Dixon (RWD) was founded in 1993 by Justin Redman and Mark Whiteley, who were joined by Tony Dixon in 2001, each contributing the first letter of their last names, Their *Vava II* and Como are both important projects in the industry. Initially, the studio worked on interior projects for sailing and powerboats, and then began to produce exterior designs for yachts, such as the 239.5-foot *Audemars Piguet Ilona* launched in 2004. The famous 188.65-foot superyacht *Twizzle* (Figure 2-4) is also one of RWD's works.

Espen Oeino is a Norwegian company whose studio is located in the Monaco Yacht Club in the super yacht center of that principality. The company has designed projects In six countries and regions, including the 460-foot *Ocean Victory*, the 312-foot *Kismet*, the 292-foot *Infinity*, and the 253-foot *Silverfast*. *Skat* and *Silverfast* are of a rugged style (exterior design), whilethe Octopus, built by Paul Allen (one of the founders of Microsoft), is currently the world's largest expedition yacht. It uses a diesel-electric hybrid system, and its main facilities include a spa center, library, cinema, gym, basketball court, and a dedicated recording studio on the flybridge deck. It can accommodate two helicopters and has landing gear on the stern deck and front deck. The stern deck also has an airplane hangar, which can store helicopters. The supporting facilities on the yacht include an 8-person submarine named *Pagoo* and a manned submarine that can be remotely submerged to two miles.

2. Yacht Design Laboratories in China

There are relatively few Chinese companies specializing in yacht design most of which are in their infancy. In the context of economic globalization, domestic yacht design and manufacturing companies are committed to seeking similarities and differences with international market demands in order to explore opportunities for the development of domestic yacht design and manufacturing companies and enhance their competitiveness.

(1) UID Yacht Design Co., Ltd.

UID Yacht Design Co., Ltd. (UID) was incorporated in Hong Kong, China in 2012. Its predecessor was UID Yacht Design Studio, which was established in cooperation with the British yacht design company RMD and the Italian yacht design studio A.M YACHT DESIGN. It is the first company in China specializing in yacht customization and design, mainly engaged in design and development, interior design, and product improvement, It focuses on the overall design of 20-164-foot power yachts, yacht interior design, yacht supervision, yacht purchase consultants, as well as yacht equipment and ship submissions. UID integrates the latest design concepts and ideas from Italy into the conceptual design of yachts, striving to present the best design to yacht builders and owners. Every yacht and yacht design from UID embodies the concept of "good creativity, good yacht." UID integrates the philosophy of "excellence," the wisdom of "emperor," and the trend of "elegance" into all aspects of yacht design. The wisdom of "excellence" is reflected in the fact that the designers of UID Yacht Design regard meeting the strict requirements of customers as the glory of their work's success. The wisdom of "emperor" is reflected in the pursuit of a utopian world inside the yacht, which is the dream of every UID yacht designer. Constantly pursuing the balance between art and technology and finding their intersection point on every yacht embodies the wisdom that UID advocates. "elegance" is another goal that UID pursues in the interest of good taste.

(2) DN Yacht Design Company

DN Yacht Design Company (Dawn), is a relatively new professional yacht design company in China. The company has hired Italian, French and other foreign designers to form a professional design team. Dawn Design has rich experience in the overall design of luxury custom yachts and catamaran super yachts (including fiberglass boats under 131 feet as well steel, tempered glass and steel-aluminum super yachts above 131 feet) that are greater than 44 feet. At the same time, it also engages in product management, process optimization, marketing strategy, and other pursuits. Some of their classic designs include the Aquitalia 95', 85' and the Sea Stella 63', 53'. The world-renowned yacht factories that have cooperated with Dawn Design include Molinari, Azimut, and Benetti. In cooperation with Yihong Yacht, Dawn Design has designed various types of yachts including the Sea Stella series, Aquitalia series, sports yachts, and sightseeing yachts.

Section 2: Major Yacht Manufacturers in the World

1. Foreign Yacht Manufacturing Enterprises

(1) Overview of Global Yacht Manufacturing Enterprises

The world's earliest yacht manufacturing enterprises were founded in Europe. In 1660, the first royal hunting and fishing boat was manufactured in the UK, and "yacht" became synonymous with top luxury and was favored by the upper class in Europe. After the first industrial revolution, the British installed steam engines and propellers on yachts, and yacht manufacturing gradually became industrialized. In the 19th century, the number of shipyards specializing in yacht manufacturing increased. Some century-old factories are still active in the yacht manufacturing industry today. The Riva shipyard of Ferretti Group in Italy, which began in 1842, is one of the few shipyards that insist on handmade yachts. The Lürssen shipyard in Germany, which was founded in 1875, built the world's first motorboat in 1886, and built the world's longest giant yacht Azzam (590 feet long) in 2013.

At present, among the 230 countries and regions in the world, the enterprises that occupy a significant place in the yacht manufacturing market are mainly distributed across the traditional industrial powers of North America, Western Europe, Northern Europe, and emerging economies in the Asia-Pacific region. The enterprises that can manufacture super sailboats and power boats with a length of 24 meters (78 feet and 8 inches) or more are concentrated in the United States, Italy, Britain, Germany, France, the Netherlands, China, Japan, Turkey, Poland and a few other countries (see Table 2-1 for details).

Table 2-1 Top 30 global yacht manufacturers (ranked by the total length of super yachts in orders)

Ranking in 2015	Company	Country	total length (meters)	total length (feet)	New project	Average length (feet)	New Project in 2014	YRanking in 2014
1	Azimut/ Benetti	Italy	2555	8383	66	127	79	1
2	Sanlorenzo	Italy	1690	5545	48	116	39	2
3	Ferretti Group	Italy	1551	5089	49	104	32	3
4	Sunseeker	United Kingdom	1082	3550	36	99	26	5
5	Lürssen	Germany	878	2881	9	320	7	6
6	Amels/ Damen	Netherlands	793	2602	12	217	10	7
7	Feadship	Netherlands	724	2375	12	198	8	8
8	Princess Yachts	United Kingdom	708	2323	25	93	30	4
9	Heesen Yachts	Netherlands	565	1854	11	169	10	13
10	Horizon	China	514	1686	16	105	16	11
11	Gulf Craft	United Arab Emirates	468	1535	13	118	15	10
12	Fipa Group	Italy	442	1450	12	121	9	16
13	Overmarine	Italy	430	1411	12	118	14	9

14	Alexander Marine	United States	428	1404	15	94	11	22
15	Oceanco	Netherlands	392	1286	4	322	5	12
16	Christensen	United States	360	1181	8	148	8	15
17	Cerr-Baglietto	Italy	303	994	7	142	9	17
18	Palmer Johnson	France	294	965	5	193	4	28
19	Sunrise Yachts	Germany	285	935	5	187	5	26
20	Privilege	France	277	909	2	454	2	25
21	Abeking & Rasmussen	Germany	277	908	4	227	3	30
22	The Italian Sea Group	Italy	272	892	6	149	10	14
23	Mengi Yay	Turkey	263	863	7	123	4	--
24	Oruçoglu	France	260	853	7	122	8	20
25	Heysea (Sea Star)	China	256	840	8	105	9	27
26	Mondo Marine	Italy	253	829	5	166	6	21
27	Dream Ship Victory	Turkey	238	781	3	260	3	29
28	Perini Navi	Italy	228	748	4	187	5	23
29	Hatteras	United States	213	699	8	87	3	--
30	Oyster Marine	England	209	686	8	8	8	--

Source: American magazine *ShowBoats International (now known as Boat International).*
Note: Some large yacht manufacturers do not provide order data to the magazine every year, so the ranking is for reference only.

The financial crises in 2008 and 2014, the COVID-19 pandemic in 2019-20, and the geopolitical warsand other factors have brought major challenges to the world yachting industry, and many giant yacht enterprises have been affected. The global yacht manufacturing industry has entered a period of contraction due to insufficient orders. Some traditional yacht manufacturing giants have gone bankrupt and disappeared or have been reborn through mergers and acquisitions. For example, the Italian Ferretti Group, known as the "Rolls-Royce of the yachting industry", was acquired by the Chinese Weichai Group in 2012 to avoid bankruptcy.

(2) Ferretti Group

1. Company Profile

Ferretti Group, an Italian yacht manufacturing company with a history of hundreds of years, is an important part of the world's luxury yacht and leisure ship design, manufacturing. and sales. It owns a number of world-renowned brands with unique characteristics and complementary advantages: Ferretti Yachts, Pershing, Riva, Bertram, Itama, Mochi Craft, Custom Line, Wally and CRN.

Ferretti Group focuses on the management of product technology, personnel structure, environmental protection, sales service, and group development. In terms of product technology, based on traditional Italian craftsmanship combined with advanced industrial production technology, it creates high-quality power yachts. In terms of sales service, it has six modern shipyards in Italy and nearly 60 distributors, which enables it to provide customers with quality services. In terms of personnel structure, it adheres to the "people-oriented" business philosophy and provides employees with a good working environment. In terms of environmental protection, it focuses on innovation and develops environmental protection projects to achieve the sustainable development of the group. Based on quality, innovation and uniqueness, Ferretti Group strives to move towards higher levels of yacht design through technological innovation, sustainability and economic achievements, adhering to the concept of "creating greatness, striving for innovation, and creating value," and further building itself into the most influential luxury yacht manufacturing group.

2. Development History

(1) Initial Expansion Stage (1968-1995)

The brothers Norberto and Alessandro founded Ferretti Group in Forlì, in the north-central region of Italy, in 1968. They obtained the agency rights for a US powerboat company, Chris Craft, and began their yacht marketing.

In 1971, the first wooden sailing yacht equipped with sails and engines was launched by the Ferretti Group. In 1982, the Group launched the first yacht powered entirely by engines and began to build sea fishing boats, open yachts, and flybridge yachts. In 1989, in order to seek synergies in the field of advanced technology, an engineering department, focused on new yacht design and new material research and development, was established, marking the beginning of Ferretti Group's participation in offshore championships.

The expansion of product scale and continuous success in sports events have promoted the internationalization process of Ferretti Group. In 1993, Ferretti Group established Ferretti America, which is responsible for product marketing in the United States, Canada, Mexico, Venezuela, and the Caribbean. Ferretti America cooperated with the original dealer networks in Greece, France, Spain, Germany, and the United Kingdom to strengthen the sales influence of Ferretti Group abroad. From 1994 to 1997, the Ferretti team won the championship of the World Class Offshore Rowing Championships twice and the European Championship once, and applied the technological achievements originally developed for the competition to yacht construction. In 1994,

Ferretti Group began its globalization process by creating a strategic dealer network outside Europe.

(2) Merger and Acquisition Development Stage (1996-2011)

In the late 1990s, with the help of institutional investors, the Ferretti Group's outer expansion strategy was launched, and it began to acquire some top powerboat construction companies. In 1996, Ferretti entered the 92- to 132-foot glass-reinforced plastic flybridge yacht market by acquiring the Custom Line. In 1998, Cantieri Navali dell'Adriatico (CNA S.r.l.), which specializes in the production of open-powered yachts, joined the group with the well-known brand Pershing. Its yachts are a model that combines excellent performance, comfort, and design.

In 1999, the Group acquired CRN Limited, a shipyard specializing in the construction of large composite yachts, as well as giant luxury yachts with steel hulls and aluminum superstructures over 98 feet in length.

In 2000, the Group fully acquired Riva Limited, one of the world's most famous and prestigious shipyards.

In May 2001, Ferretti Group parent company Ferretti Limited acquired part of the assets of the Oram shipyard in La Spezia, and subsequently Riva Yachts' new production base was established here. In November of the same year, the Group completed the acquisition of the Mochi Craft shipyard in Pesaro.

In 2002, the Group took over the Diesse Arredamenti company, acquiring its new technologies in the field of marine decoration, further improving its proprietary technology in yacht construction. Based on this strategy, the Group acquired the Mario Morini shipyard in Ancona in 2002, which increased CRN's production capacity.

In 2004, the Itama shipyard, which specializes in the construction of open powered boats, joined the Group.

In 2008, Ferretti Group acquired the assets, brands, and businesses of Allied Marine, a US company that specializes in after-sales, marketing, and intermediary services for new and used powerboats.

(3) Chinese Capital Entered the Group and Went Global (2012)

In 2012, the Weichai Group of China acquired 75% of the Ferretti Group. In August of the same year, Tan Xuguang, Chairman of Weichai Group, also became board chair of the Ferretti Group. Alberto Galassi, CEO of the Ferretti Group, led a new management team, committed to research and development and product innovation, and promoted the Group's yacht as the ambassador of "Italian-built" technology and style to a new market area. Over the years, the Group has made tremendous investments in public welfare, products, communication and activities.

In February 2016, Ferretti's FSD division was established. The new division is dedicated to the design, development, and construction of a series of state-of-the-art vessels, satisfying the needs of international waters and inland coastlines for security, patrol, and defense through exquisite product features and ambitious goals. FSD195, Ferretti's first high-speed patrol vessel certified by RINA FPV and CE, is a 66-foot high-performance vessel with a speed of over 50 knots and a range of over 500 nautical miles.

Based on its existing performance, the Group has received further investment from Weichai Group. Ferretti Group's listing on the Asian stock market provides opportunities for further expansion of its business and integration within the Group to achieve sustainable development. The expansion of its shareholder base enables the Group to obtain the support needed to pursue innovation and development.

In 2021, the Ferretti Group generated a total economic value of over €900 million, an increase of 42% compared to 2020 and 30% compared to 2019. In the economic value created, about 90% was allocated to various stakeholders, including suppliers (operating costs), employees, capital providers, the public sector, shareholders, and local communities (see Table 2-2).

Table 2-2 Benefit Distribution Table (in thousands of Euros)

	2021		**2020**		**2019**	
Economic value generated	100%	908092	100%	638864	100%	698642
Economic value assigned	89.4%	811875	90.5%	578445	91.3%	638122
Operating costs	75.1%	681972	74.2%	473726	75.6%	528387
Value assigned to employees	12.4%	112417	14.5%	92454	13.8%	96446
Value allocated to capital providers	0.7%	5940	1.1%	6897	1%	6608
Value assigned to shareholders	0.7%	6707	0.5%	3510	0.9%	6582
Others	0.5%	4839	0.3%	1858	0.0%	99

Economic value of reservation	10.6%	96217	9.5%	60419	8.7%	60520

3. Major Shipyards

Advanced construction bases and excellent teams are the prerequisites for high-quality yacht construction. The exquisite craftsmanship, efficient production efficiency, and attention to detail of the craftsmen at Ferretti Group shipyards have made great contributions to ensuring the high quality of each yacht. The Group has established shipyards with high-tech equipment and advanced production systems, including Forlì, Cattolica, Mondolfo, Ancona, Sanico, and La Spezia.

(1) Forli

The total area of the Foley shipyard is 39,000 square meters, which is used for the construction of yachts of brands such as Ferretti Yachts, Itama and Mochi Craft. It is also the location of the headquarters of the group.

(2) Cattolica

The Cattolica Shipyard was established in 2001, covering a total area of 12,000 square meters, including a construction area of 6,800 square meters and 14 berths. The shipyard meets the latest productivity standards and can build 14 powerboats up to 66 to 98 feet in length simultaneously. In particular, the layout of the production line located in Cattolica is an "island" construction system, where each "island" can independently complete the construction of a yacht. This means that any yacht can be completed and leave the factory without having to interrupt the operations being carried out at other berths. In addition, the advantage of offshore can also achieve rapid testing and trial navigation, and all the purchased shipbuilding materials are accepted and strictly inspected by the acceptance department.

(3) Mondolfo

The total area of Mondolfo shipyard is about 45,000 square meters, of which the construction area is over 13,000 square meters. It is not only a construction center, but also a complex integrating beauty and function, technology, and dreams. Every detail is designed to meet the requirements of Ferretti Group's production development in terms of continuous expansion of product series and yacht size, and for all water experiments related to yachts (engines, drainage devices, navigation bottom and generators) and watertight testing. The gantry with a load of 130 tons is used for the transportation and hoisting of yachts in the test pool.

(4) Ancona

The ship center in Ancona covers an area of about 80,000 square meters, including a construction area of 31,000 square meters, which can build yachts up to 312 feet. It is a "multi-brand" construction base, specializing in the construction of all CRN yachts, some customized Ferretti series, and vessels in the new Riva superyacht department. The

Ancona shipyard faces the Adriatic Sea and is strategically located with a small private dock on the coastline.

(5) Sarnico

The shipyard was founded in 1842 and has produced many classic Riva yachts. The yachts built include: Iseo, Aquariva Super, Rivamare, Rivarama Super, Rivale, 56' Rivale, 63' Vertigo and 63' Virtus. The shipyard covers an area of about 43,000 square meters, with a construction area of about 17,000 square meters. It includes10 berths, 2 cantilever cranes, 4 painting rooms and a 50-ton electric crane for carrying finished boats and other large components.

(6) La Spezia

The shipyard in La Spezia was established in 2004 and plays a strategic role in industry, society, and the environment. It is the main base for the Ferretti Group to provide technical, logistics and sales support in the Ligurian Sea and Tyrrhenian Sea. The plant covers an area of over 47,000 square meters and has a construction area of 14,000 square meters, including industrial facilities, office buildings, and a 400-meter dock and quay for the main plant, equipped with a 400-ton tire-strength gantry.

(3) Azimut-Benetti Group

1. Group profile

Azimut-Benetti, founded by Paolo Vitelli, is the largest private enterprise group in the yachting industry. Over the years, the group has achieved fruitful results by pursuing product excellence and continuous investment in new technologies, with the aim of expanding product categories and service scope. Behind its achievements lies a lasting passion for the ocean, sailing, work, and future challenges. The group pays special attention to research and development, with its core business being the design and construction of the most beautiful, reliable, technologically advanced, and innovative yachts and luxury mega yachts. Also, it is striving to provide customers with quality services. In addition, the group organizes recreational activities, arranges test sailings, and allows ship owners to enjoy the elegance and unique environment in Italian style.

The Azimut-Benetti Group constantly strives for excellence in technical services, environmental protection, and production and operation. In terms of technical services, the Group established a strategic department dedicated to service (Yachtique - Elite Yachting Services) in 2008 to provide excellent services to shipowners. The Group provides advanced technical assistance centers for owners, with all types of maintenance provided by Lusben, including planned services, modifications, and reorganizations. The Group implements an environmental management system aimed at limiting air pollution, energy consumption, and the use of chemical products. It is the first company in the industry in Italy and in the world to obtain ISO 14001 certification, which is a milestone in promoting safety and responsibility. In terms of production and operation, the Azimut-Benetti Group operates six shipyards and produces more than 40 models of products.

2. Development History

(1) Initial development stage (1969-1985)

In 1969, Paul Vitelli, with his love for the sea and sailing, established Azimut from the funds he accumulated in college.

In 1970, at the Genoa Yacht Show, Paul Vitelli won the agency rights for a large Dutch shipyard in Italy with his own booth. Since then, he has signed agency agreements with other important shipyards. Subsequently, he expanded his business scope to the production field. He formed a joint venture with the Dutch Amerglass shipyard to combine Dutch experience and Italian craftsmanship to build the first AZ 43' Bali, which was one of the largest fiberglass yachts produced at the time. In 1977, the smallest yacht AZ 32' Targa came out, known as the "Ford Model T on the sea".

From 1977 to 1985, Azimut never stopped expanding, and through constant challenges and self-improvement, it achieved success after success. It adhered to the design of yachts to meet the high demands of market demand and taste and created the first 98-foot yacht in yacht history, the Failaka, which was completely built of fiberglass materials. With this huge yacht, it entered the American market.

(2) Internal construction stage (1985-2001)

In 1985, Azimut took over the Fratelli Benetti shipyard in Viareggio, forming the Azimut-Benetti Group. In 1988, the Azimut-Benetti Group began its adventure to win the Blue Ribbon Trophy, crossing the Atlantic Ocean without refueling. The group became the focus of international fashion and sports media. In the early days of its history, Azimut entrusted the yacht design work to British professionals, but by the end of the 1980s, Italian style became unique, so it began a cooperative journey with the dynamic young designer Stefano Righini, whose revolutionary style created a trend and established Azimut design as the standard in the world yachting industry.

With Righini's contributions, Azimut yachts were redesigned, liberating their shape. At the same time, processing technology was also applied from the automotive industry, which remains a feature of Azimut-Benetti companies around the world: glued glass panels, electric windows and seats, as well as authentic heather wood roofs. At the same time, marketing and sales were also reconsidered. The brand began to move towards the peak of international reputation.

(3) Stage of development and growth (2001-)

In 2001, the company acquired the Gobbi shipyard, which now produces open-engine yachts ranging from approximately 33 to 59 feet in length under the new Atlantis series. A major shipbuilding center will be developed around the shipyard, covering an area of approximately 200,000 square meters. When the shipyard is fully operational, it will produce approximately 100 yachts per year. In 2003, Azimut Benetti took over Fraser Yachts.

In 2007, the group was awarded the "Growth Champion" and "Best Performer" prizes by the Italian Federation of Industries, indicating that the company had the best performance in terms of quality and quantity among many Italian companies in the five years from 2001 to 2006. However, the success of the group far exceeded the business field in Italy. According to the authoritative ranking of the American ShowBoats International magazine, Azimut-Benetti became the world's largest giant yacht manufacturing company, and it has been ranked first for 12 consecutive years. Under the management of Paolo Vitelli and managers, the Azimut-Benetti Group has gained worldwide recognition.

In April 2007, Azimut entered China and set up an office in Shanghai. The establishment of the Shanghai Representative Office demonstrates its confidence in exploring the Chinese market and its desire to become a market leader. As a leading luxury yacht brand in the world and a representative of top-notch Italian yachts, Azimut Yachts is deeply loved by yacht enthusiasts and successful people around the world. Whether it is a classic flybridge yacht or a stylish sports yacht, its design and production represent the global trend and is one of the best-selling brands in Europe, America, and Asia.

Azimut's after-sales service is also outstanding. The yacht's after-sales warranty is extended to 3 years, including 2 free maintenance services at any distribution network worldwide. Azimut also designs a 5-star 24-hour assistance policy for yacht owners, including parts replacement, technical problem tracking service, network interaction, hotel accommodation, medical consultation, item storage, return or continuous diagnosis, and even free emergency yacht service.

3. Major shipyards

The total area of the Azimut=Benetti Group's production facilities in Italy and abroad exceeds 500,000 square meters, of which nearly 161,000 square meters are enclosed. Technological innovation and extensive professionalization of personnel ensure high standards of quality. Creativity, technology, and experience provide the foundation for the production of Azimut-Benetti products by shipyards. These shipyards have obtained BS OHSAS 18001 certification, which is an international standard for occupational health and safety management systems. The Azimut-Benetti Group is the first large shipping company in the world to have obtained this important certification. In order to better meet the increasingly professional and advanced market requirements, the brand has organized its production into five different series that are produced in six shipyards. The shipyards in Italy include Avigliana, Viareggio, Livorno, Fano, and Savona; the Itajai shipyard is located in Brazil and mainly produces yachts under 100 feet.

4. Beneteau

1. Company Profile

In 1884, Benjamin Beneteau, a French shipbuilder, founded Beneteau in Saint-Gilles-Croix-des-Bouquets on the west coast of France to build sailing and fishing boats. The company is the world's first sailing boat manufacturer and one of the world's largest powerboat manufacturers. It offers a full range of sailing and powerboat models to meet the sailing dreams of different people. From the first fishing boat launched in 1910 to the most advanced digital interface for boat control, Beneteau development history is full of innovation. In the 140-year history of Beneteau, innovation has always been embedded in construction, design, technology, materials, processes, production, and service. From high-performance unified design sailing boats to top-level racing boats and comfortable and elegant leisure boats, Beneteau's sailboats and powerboats are renowned worldwide for their many innovative achievements. As the world's leading shipbuilder, the Beneteau Group has been active in the Chinese market since 2005. The Group established its Asia-Pacific headquarters in Shanghai and is committed to promoting the popularization of sailing and powerboat sports in China while promoting its own brands. Its Beneteau and Lagoon brands offer more than 60 different models of sailing and powerboats ranging from 20 to 60 feet. The Group's Monte Carlo Yachts produces luxury powerboats over 60 feet in length, while CNB is a brand of super custom yachts.

2. Development History

(1) The starting stage (1884-1962)

In 1884, Benjamin Beneteau founded the Beneteau company in Saint-Gilles-Croix-des-Vents on the west coast of France, to build sailing ships and fishing boats. Benjamin Beneteau vowed to build the first powered fishing boat in France regardless of cost, and successfully launched the first powered boat in 1912. The outbreak of the First World War caused the dock to stop operating, and it did not operate again until 1928. Subsequently, André Beneteau, Beneteau's only son,, took over at the age of 21 At the end of World War II, the original employees of the shipyard gathered together again. With the decline of the fishing industry, Beneteau began to experience the end of its prosperity as a shipbuilder. In 1963, it began selling a sardine fishing boat that was made of polyester fiber, a new material. This created a market for recreational fishing boats.

(2) Growth and expansion stage (1965-2003)

In 1965, the First series of yachts was displayed at the Paris Boat Show and well-received by dealers. Subsequently, sales were conducted through a network of dealers, and customer requirements were continuously met through the design and manufacture of new products.

In 1972, a new factory was built in Commequiers, France, with the aim of producing the largest-sized production boats that met market demand. At the same time, the Antares series of powerboats was born.

1976 was a crucial year. The company redesigned the sails, keels, interior layout, and roof shape of the First yachts, which were widely exported.

In 1980, the powerboat department of the shipyard produced an improved catamaran, which won the "Paris Six-hour" race. Subsequently, the first in the Flyer series of yachts were exhibited at the Paris Boat Show. The most popular competition in the sailing world is the "Admiral's Cup" regatta, an event promoted by Beneteau and its partner Corum, the Swiss watchmaking company. The two companies collaborated on new hulls, giving birth to the prototype of the First Evolution series of boats. The First Evolution combines the most traditional craftsmanship with the most cutting-edge technology and concepts, becoming a milestone in the modern yachting industry.

At this stage, the Beneteau began to enter the US market, not only to establish its brand but also to understand the tastes of American consumers. This included the birth of Idylle, which reflected the basic characteristics of cruising boats, and the rebirth of the First series, which regained its former vitality in the US market after collaborating with designer Philippe Starck.

(3) Steady development stage (2004-)

Since 2004, Beneteau has built many new shipyards and expanded its market share.

In 2008, Beneteau Group merged with the Italian company Monte Carlo Yachts. Monte Carlo Yachts completely subverted the concept of luxury yachts, introducing what it called "timeless classics, inherent quality, and unique value.". On July 23, 2010, 18 months after the completion of the shipyard, Beneteau Group Monte Carlo Yachts debuted a 75-foot flybridge yacht in Venice, reflecting its tremendous value. In addition to yachts, Beneteau Group also created new important brands.

In 2014, Beneteau implemented a new external growth initiative. As part of the Group's development strategy in the North American powerboat market, Beneteau acquired Rec Boat Holding LLC, adding four American yacht brands to the Group: Four Winns, Glastron, Wellcraft, and Scarab.

2. Major yacht manufacturing enterprises in China

(1) Overview of Chinese yacht manufacturing enterprises

In the early days, yacht manufacturing enterprises in China were all state-owned enterprises, mainly producing boats for official purposes. The earliest yacht manufacturer was Changzhou GRP Shipyard, which was financed and built by the state in 1970 and is now affiliated with Changzhou Lanxiang Machinery Co., Ltd. of the China Aviation Industry Group Corporation. Dongwuan GRP Shipyard, founded in 1976, is also a state-owned enterprise that produces GRP yachts in China. Since its establishment, it has produced various types of motorboats, high-speed passenger ships, and yachts.

China's professional yacht manufacturing enterprises emerged after the economic reforms of the early 1980s. Seeing the prosperity of overseas water leisure activities and fitness tourism, coupled with the vigorous development of domestic tourism, a number of professional yacht manufacturers emerged in coastal areas such as Jiangsu, Zhejiang, Guangdong, Fujian, and Shandong. These enterprises prospered through the introduction of foreign advanced technology, and joint ventures with foreign companies, and began to produce a variety of vessels including luxury yachts. In September 1981, Jianghui GRP Shipyard, China's first luxury yacht factory, was completed and put into operation in Shekou Industrial Zone, Shenzhen. In April 1982, the first 22-foot luxury yacht Gypsy Island Man was produced and sold to the United States.

In the 1990s, the number of yacht manufacturers in China increased rapidly, and the design and construction level of yachts also improved to some extent. In 1994, Guangdong Dongwuan GRP Shipyard built four 40-foot catamaran sailboats for France.

Other factories, such as the Qingdao Beihai Yacht Factory, the Dongfang High Speed Boat Factory, the Nanhua Yacht Factory, the Gaohua Yacht Factory, the Changzhou GRP Shipyard, and the Xiamen GRP Shipyard also produced various motorboats, workboats, sports boats and luxury yachts of different specifications and models to meet domestic needs and exports. During this stage, the overall quality of China's yacht products was relatively low, and the main sales targets were domestic public administration departments, tourism departments, fishery departments, and passenger transport departments. The export volume was relatively small.

According to the statistics of the Ship and Boat Branch of the China National Shipbuilding Industry Association, by the end of 2007, China's yacht manufacturing enterprises had grown to number about 374, mainly distributed in economically developed and coastal (river) areas such as Jiangsu, Zhejiang, Shanghai, Guangdong, Fujian, Shandong, Liaoning, Beijing, and Tianjin. Guangzhou, Shenzhen, and Changzhou are the areas with the most yacht manufacturing enterprises. After several years of effort, a flourishing situation has now emerged. In addition to foreign-funded enterprises such as Xianli, Shenzhou, Donghai Ship, Raffles, Benson, Alpha, Sunshine, and Oulun, which have successfully established production bases in mainland China, national enterprises such as Sunbird, Hongshuangxi, Hansheng, Xiongda, Duoyang, Haixing, Baoda, Minhua, Yunhui, Yihong, Aopulan, Xingma, Xingnuo, Jinhaiwan, Haite, Zhunei, Zouzhi, and Xinhe have become the backbone of China's yacht manufacturing industry. In particular, Sunbird ranked first among domestic national enterprises with its boat sales of more than ¥200 million.

Since the financial crisis in 2008, the global yacht manufacturing industry has entered a stage of fluctuating development. In order to promote economic transformation and expand domestic demand, the central and local governments at all levels have issued a series of policies to support the development of the yachting industry, and domestic yacht manufacturing enterprises have developed. With the gradual rationalization of domestic yacht consumption, yacht manufacturing enterprises have begun to compete in product positioning, service quality improvement, technology upgrading, brand building, and other aspects. By the end of 2022, according to the author's incomplete statistics, there were more than 120 domestic yacht manufacturing enterprises, including Yaguang Technology (formerly Sunbird 300123), Yihong Group (835558), and Jianglong Boat (300589). Some groups have implemented diversified development strategies and engaged in yacht manufacturing businesses, such as the yacht subsidiary of Shuangyi Technology (300690), which mainly manufactures fishing boats.

At present, Shenzhen, Zhuhai, Dongwuan and Guangzhou in Guangdong Dawan District, Shanghai, Changzhou, Wuxi and Suzhou in Yangtze River Delta, Sanya and Haikou in Hainan, Jiaodong Peninsula city cluster centered on Qingdao, Xiamen in Fujian have initially become important bases of yachting industry in China.

(2) Heysea Yacht Group

1. Group Profile

The Heysea Yacht Group was formally established in 2007 with its headquarters located in Hong Kong. It was founded by several overseas returnees in the yachting industry, with the founders and management having rich and professional experience in yacht research and development, design, and construction. The company's production base is located in Xinhui District, Jiangmen City, with a well-established modern yacht production plant, launching ramp, and berth. Adhering to the concept of "quality is the core competitiveness," the Heysea Yacht Groupworks diligently to open up and build factories to "build ships behind closed doors". It places "design" at the forefront and "quality" at the core.

After years of hard work, Heysea has been recognized by the global yachting industry. According to the statistics of international authoritative institutions in 2015, for the sales and delivery of yachts over 80 feet, Heysea was number one in China and number 25 worldwide. Heysea is also the only yacht manufacturing enterprise in mainland China to be listed among the globe's top 30 super yacht manufacturing enterprises. In 2017 and 2018, it ranked 16th in the global order book for two consecutive years, becoming the only mainland Chinese yacht manufacturer to rank in the top 20. In 2019, the internationally renowned Boat International Media released its 2020 Global Order Book, in which Heysea Yacht jumped to 12th place in the ranking of global super yacht (over 80 feet orders orders, the only manufacturer in mainland China to enter the top 15.

2. Development history

(as shown in Table 2-3)

Table 2-3 Development History

Time	Representative events
Initial development stage (2004-2007)	In 2004, Heysea Yacht Company was established. From 2004 to 2007, the company mainly produced houseboats for Hong Kong. These boats had an interior that met yacht standards, but an ordinary exterior and a very low speed. Heysea were the main supplier of houseboats in Hong Kong.

Rapid promotion stage (2008-2015)	Heysea abandoned traditional ship manufacturing and successfully transformed into a professional manufacturer of medium-sized yachts. In 2008, Heysea Yacht launched a 60-foot yacht; in 2009, Heysea was named one of the Top Ten Yacht Manufacturing Brands in China Heysea launched a 78-foot yacht and an 82-foot yacht. In2011, Heysea Yacht was named the best selling yacht brand made in China, and launched a 70-foot yacht. The 82-foot yacht won 12 orders within one year and won the 2011 China Power Boat Single Yacht Sales Award. In 2012, Heysea was awarded the title of Outstanding Contribution Person in Chinese Yacht Design and Best Yacht Manufacturer in China; its 82-foot yacht won the only "2012 Best-selling Power Boat in China Award" with a total of 18 orders; its 108-foot yacht won the only "2011-2012 China Power Boat Single Yacht Sales Award" with 4 orders from domestic enterprises. In 2013, Heysea was awarded the title of Pioneer of Chinese Yacht Manufacturing and Best Yacht Manufacturer in China; he also won the Best Design Award for National Yacht; the Asteria 108-foot yacht was named "China's Best-Selling Domestic Power Yacht of 2013"; and the Asteria 108-foot yacht was named "China's Most Highly Regarded Domestic Yacht of 2013". In 2014, Heysea was awarded the Best Yacht Manufacturer in China and the Best Yacht Brand in China, and passed the ISO9001:2008 quality management system certification. In 2015, Heysea was awarded the Best Yacht Manufacturer in China and the Best Yacht Brand in China. It was also named as the "Star of Innovation and Entrepreneurship" by Guangdong Province, a national high-tech enterprise.

Steady development stage (2016-)	In 2016, Heysea was awarded the Best Yacht Manufacturer in China and the Best Yacht Brand in China. 2017 Top 5 Most Craftsman Spirit Award, Top 5 Yacht Brands in China Market, Top 10 Meritorious Figures in Promoting the Development of China's yachting industry (Leng Xuehua, one of the founders of Heysea Yacht); Vice Chairman of the International Organization for Standardization (ISO) Technical Committee for Marine and Ocean Technology (TCB) Subcommittee for Large Yachts (SC12) (Leng Xuehua); Guangdong Engineering Technology Research and Development Center; 2017 Third Prize of Xinhui District Science and Technology Award (Zoom 72); 2017 Third Prize of Xinhui District Science and Technology Award (Asteria 108); passed ISO9001:2015 Quality Management System Certification in 2017. In 2018, Heysea was awarded the title of "Asia-Pacific Best Super Yacht Manufacturer"; 2018 China Yacht Brand Annual Top 20; 2018 China Yacht Brand Annual Contribution Award; 2018 Most Potential Manufacturer Diamond Award; 2018 OHSAS18001 Occupational Health and Safety Management System Certification.

3. Main product series

Asteria super yacht series As a highly personalized custom yacht, from the atmospheric main cabin to the luxurious lower cabin, the living facilities and entertainment equipment are made of superior materials; the presentation of art and craftsmanship, even in the smallest details, is exquisite, making it an ideal yacht for many customers. Super yachts are Heysea's highly personalized custom yachts, with distinctive streamlined shapes that are extremely dynamic. The huge hull is specially treated to provide superior seaworthiness and seakeeping. The ingenious space and functional design evokes the unforgettable blue ocean luxury art and the transcendence of private leisure.

Zoom Panorama series Aseamless combination of fluid mechanics and structural mechanics. The rigid body and elegant style evoke symbols of masculinity and dominance. The external lines are smooth and fresh, and the elegant curvature is perfectly combined with the strong hull. The space layout is very exquisite. The design concept of spaciousness and practicality creates a large comfortable space, and the details reveal luxury and charm. It can meet the needs of customers of all ages, and through the combination of spaciousness, high-quality materials, comfort and performance, it can make life on the boat meet the ideal standards.

Heysea Starfish Series The classic streamlined shape and smooth space of the starfish are predominant here. After careful sculpting, it is luxurious, bright, and avant-garde, and its momentum is unstoppable. The rigid straight lines and smooth curves of the hull are both tough and soft, making it extremely stylish and dynamic. The interior space layout is unique, from the main salon to the dining room, the bar counter, and even the VIP room and master bedroom in the lower cabin, all of which reflect the depth and clarity of function and radiate the beauty of wisdom and craftsmanship. The portholes provide more natural light, and the warm and noble atmosphere of home prevails. In terms of power, Heysea82 is equipped with two super-performance main engines, with surging power hidden under the fluid shape. Heysea82 quickly became popular in the industry since it was introduced to the market in 2008; for yachts above 80 feet, it won honors such as "China's Best-Selling Power Yacht" and " China's Single Power Yacht Sales Award." It is a classic best-selling ship type that is highly sought after by yacht players and yacht clubs.

Other series of Seastar yachts, such as the Seaview double-sail series, Heysea CAT catamaran series, Vista full-custom superyacht series, all with super high quality and exquisite craftsmanship. The success of the products has mirrored the growth of the company.

(3) Sunbird Yacht Co., Ltd. (Yaguang Technology)

1. Company Profile

Sunbird Yacht Co., Ltd., founded in 2003, adheres to the concept of "being the best yacht manufacturer" and focuses on the research, development, production and promotion of high-performance composite-material boats. With yachts as the leading product, it has three major series of products: 15 specifications and 40 models of private yachts (about 21 feet-164 feet); 18 specifications and 55 models of business yachts (about 32 feet-197 feet); and 16 specifications and 30 models of special yachts (about 19 feet-328 feet). It is one of the largest composite-material boat manufacturing enterprises in China. Its products are sold in more than 30 provinces, municipalities. and autonomous regions across the country, and its self-owned brand products have successfully entered the international market via exports to the United States, Britain, Spain, Southeast Asia, Africa, and other countries and regions.

Table 2-4 Classification of Sunbird Products

Classified by yacht use	Private yacht
	Business yacht
	Special purpose vessel (mainly for official business)
Divided by yacht material	Composite boat
	Multi-mixed vessel

Sunbird Yachts upholds the concept of "transmitting emotions and creating beauty." After years of development, Sunbird is one of the largest composite-material shipbuilding enterprises in China with the highest level of design and R&D technology and the most complete variety structure. Its composite-material ship production has ranked first among domestic enterprises for many years. The Sunbird Technology Center - Hunan Modern Yacht Technology Research and Industrial Design Center is a domestic yacht R&D and design platform, with a postdoctoral workstation for yachts. The company has a total of 169 patents, including 3 invention patents, 66 utility model patents, and 100 design patents. The company's products have won various international and domestic design awards many times. In 2010, the company successfully developed the "multi-mix design, multi-mix materials and multi-mix technology" processes jointly with the National University of Defense Technology and Huazhong University of Science and Technology. The design and construction of the "Green" luxury catamaran yacht of the Sea Bird series 42M broke the world record of the series 40M composite-material super yacht. In May 2011, Sunbird Yachts was recognized as a national well-known trademark by the Trademark Office of the State Administration for Industry and Commerce. In August 2011, Sunbird Yachts won the award of Best Yacht Manufacturer in Asia, and in 2012 it again won the Red Star Gold Award for Chinese Innovative Design. Sunbird Yachts is now the vice chairman unit of China Shipbuilding Industry Association, the member unit of China Composites Association, the expert unit of China Professional Standardization Technical Committee, the deputy director unit of China Small Boat Standardization Committee, the member unit of American Yacht Association, the national small boat equipment mobilization center, the national large yacht key project undertaking unit, and the national Torch Plan key enterprise .

2. Development History

(1) Financing and development stage (2003-2010)

In 2002, Sunbird Yacht Co., Ltd. passed ISO9001-2000 and UKAS international quality management system certification. The company aims to be the largest yacht manufacturer in Asia, and constantly promotes yacht culture in China. At the end of April 2009, Sunbird received an investment of ¥31 million from Shenzhen Dachen Venture Capital Co., Ltd. At the same time, it planned to establish a 4S store for yachts (like cars), so that yachts can truly enter people's lives. With the development of the middle class, the market for Sunbird is gradually expanding. After opening up the capital channel, Sunbird will fully establish its leading position in the domestic market and become an internationally competitive brand. In 2003, Sunbird produced the Qingdao Olympic Sailing Regatta reception yacht, andthe Shengshi Feiyang luxury yacht for Qingdao Shengshi Feiyang Marine Tourism Co., Ltd. It also built yachts of different levels for Huawei Group, Jinmao Group, CITIC Pacific, UK Dennis Company, and Shanghai World Expo. In 2009, a yacht exported to Seattle, USA, won praise from foreign yacht enthusiasts. On September 28, 2010, Sunbird Yacht Co., Ltd. was listed on the Growth Enterprise Market of Shenzhen Stock Exchange, becoming the first yacht company in China to go public for financing (stock code: 300123).

(2) Rapid expansion stage (2011-2012)

On May 27, 2011, the Trademark Office of the State Administration for Industry and Commerce announced on China Trademark Online that 289trademarks were identified as well-known trademarks in China. These included the company's "Sunbird and Figure" (categories and goods/services used: Class 12, yachts).

From 2011 to 2012, Sunbird's sales scale ranked first in the industry, completing its leap from an industry-wide brand to a nationwide brand. After 2012, the company integrated the supply and service chain, created competitive advantages at both ends of the value chain, and became an international new type of integrated solution provider for boats and watercraft.

(3) Steady improvement stage (2012-2016)

Sunbird has always adhered to the concept of "synchronizing with the world" and adhering to world-class standards to build its core competitiveness. In terms of design and research and development, it has established design centers in the United States and Italy, recruited world-renowned designers to participate in product design and research and development, and established long-term cooperation with Huazhong University of Science and Technology, Wuhan Shipyard, Hunan University, and National University of Defense Technology to develop products. It also created the first yacht design center in China. Sunbird has gathered global yacht technology and always keeps the design concept and innovative products in sync with the world's advanced level.

Alarge-scale multi-material energy-saving and environmentally friendly intelligent boat newly developed by Sunbird has been listed as a key project by China's the National Science and Technology department and has been invited to participate in the development of the 150-foot luxury yacht, a national key project of the Ministry of Industry and Information Technology. This boat has several original technologies (multi-material design, multi-material components, and multi-material processes), and has nearly 30 national patents.

In the manufacturing process, Sunbird also uses world-class standards to manufacture yachts. For example, the first 58-foot luxury yacht Jianxing in Hunan, which is the first of its kind in China, is made of polymer materials and basalt fiber and other aerospace materials and fabrics using advanced vacuum infusion molding (aircraft manufacturing) technology. It not only has the advantages of light weight, high strength, high speed, low fuel consumption, corrosion resistance, no maintenance, no pollution, low cost, and a service life of 100 years, but also integrates world-class brand configuration, intelligent depth measurement, satellite positioning, automatic steering, automatic monitoring, and automatic switching of internal functions. It is a new generation of intelligent yachts/

The other side of "synchronizing with the world" is "creating luxury yachts that the public can afford." In Europe and the United States, yachts are the second largest consumer goods after cars, with 18 million people owning yachts in the United States, most of which are low-end products. In China, the yachting industry has just started, and the consideration of cost-effectiveness is the key to measuring the success of a company. Sunbird Yachts integrates world-class design technology, world-class configuration, and top-quality products from Europe and the United States, but the price is only one-third to one-quarter of similar products in Europe and the United States. This is mainly due to strict process management and excellent cost control, and it is also a concrete example of Sunbird's core concept of "moving the world"

Due to Sunbird's entrepreneurial and management team's long-term involvement in the research, development, production, and sales of new materials boats, their deep understanding of the industry, and their rich practical and enterprise-management experience, their business model has taken the lead over most domestic similar enterprises. Sunbird has a first-class management team that has adopted scientific management methods, established a strict quality and cost control system and spare parts supply system, and that has innovatively applied the concepts of variable batch production and strong design capabilities. Sunbird has successfully designed and manufactured a variable production line for boats, which has gradually resulted in standardization, programming, simplification, and mass production for the complex discrete manufacturing of the ship industry. This has created a new precedent for variable production of boats worldwide, greatly improving the comprehensive competitiveness of Sunbird.

(4) Diversified development stage (2017)

After experiencing rapid development in 2008, China's shipbuilding industry has entered a relatively slow stage of development. Due to the impact of the economic crisis in 2014, the domestic and international yacht market has experienced slow growth, and the contradiction between overcapacity and insufficient demand in the yachting industry has become increasingly acute. The efficiency of domestic yacht manufacturing enterprises has generally declined. Sunbird Company's business began to shrink in 2014. Although the company has extended its industrial chain through multiple mergers and acquisitions in the industry, it hopes to rapidly expand the market for large yachts and high-speed passenger ships, enhance the production capacity of official ships, and enrich the product variety of the company. However, due to the sustained downturn in the industry, the overall effect is not obvious, and the company urgently needs to overcome difficulties through reform.

Table 2-5 Operating income and profit margin of Sunbird (Yaguang Technology) (2014-2022)

Project year	Before the merger (Sunbird)			After the merger (Yaguang Technology)					
	2014	2015	2016	2017	2018	2019	2020	2021	2022
Total operating revenue (CNY 100 million)	3.862	4.416	5.871	10.47	14.12	22.06	18.13	15.88	16.86
Net profit margin (%)	5.46	3.33	2.61	9.86	10.96	12.72	1.66	-74.81	-70.99

Source: Annual Report of Sunbird (Yaguang Technology)

In September 2017, Sunbird completed the cross-industry acquisition of Chengdu Yaguang Technology by issuing shares, becoming one of the largest listed companies in China making military microwave RF chips, components, modules, and microsystems, and one of the main production fixed-point manufacturers of military microwave integrated circuits in China.

On January 24, 2018, the listed company changed its name to Yaguang Technology Group Co., Ltd. The original yacht business of Sunbird continued to develop. As a military-civilian integration enterprise, it further expanded the business boat market by consolidating the private yacht and business yacht markets.

3. Main products

The Sunbird series is the company's main product, with three main models: 45-foot, 48-foot, and 55-foot. The 45-foot Sunbird has a white exterior, making it more agile and lightweight compared to the larger size of this series of yachts. The interior is decorated with wooden accents and white furniture, which creates a unique aesthetic. The imported satellite positioning system and dual control system of the yacht enhance the performance of the entire boat, while the imported engine allows the yacht to reach a cruising speed of 18 knots. The kitchen facilities are complete, allowing for the preparation of food at any time, and the bedroom is spacious and focuses on comfort in every detail.

The 48-foot Phoenix Bird has a simple white exterior, allowing the owner to enjoy the refreshing sea breeze at the top. The interior design continues to use the white interior and wooden furniture combination of this series to create a stylish and elegant lool. The FRP hull is made using high-precision "mirror" molds, providing excellent views from the front observation portholes. White curtains are hung on both sides of the cabin walls, slightly covering the portholes on both sides. A exquisite circular wooden table is placed in front of the S-shaped sofa, creating a relaxed and casual atmosphere.

The exterior design of the 55-foot Phoenix Boat still follows the pure white style, incorporating a little black to highlight the refined and elegant style of the product. The interior is spacious, with excellent views from the forward porthole. The flesh-colored curtains on the cabin walls blend seamlessly with the teak deck and wooden furniture, with white pear-shaped sofas and straight-line sofas on either side, perfectly fitting the furniture contours. The master cabin features a comfortable king-size bed in the center, with slanted cabinets on either side and a wooden wardrobe below (Figure 2-7).

(4) Fujian Yihong Yacht Co., Ltd.

1. Company Profile

Fujian Yihong Yacht Co., Ltd. (hereinafter referred to as "Yihong Yacht") was founded in 2005. It integrates R&D, manufacturing, planning and design, operation management and other business segments with yachting and waterfront leisure industry as the entry point. Yihong Yacht is the first domestic yacht brand shortlisted for the Best Yacht Brand in Asia. The firm adheres to the business philosophy of "taking the world standard as the starting point" and is committed to building high-end equipment through its attention to product design, R&D, production, sales and operations. Its research and design innovation ability has made Yihong Yacht a leading enterprise with core competitiveness in the industry. Its market share is 21%, the company's registered capital is ¥125.358974 million. Zhangzhou Yihong Boat and Yacht Industrial Park serves as its production base and R&D center, with a total area of 275 acres and a production land area of 670,000 square meters. It also has a coastline of more than 1,400 meters and a sea area use right of 29.37 hectares. The facility has an annual production capacity of 300 yachts and 3,000 caravans, with an annual output value of about ¥1 billion. In terms of human resources, it has a professional design team that includes many Italian yacht designers and interior architects. Yihong's strong production capacity and professional design team laid the foundation for providing customers with high-quality services covering design planning, high-end equipment and supporting output, destination operation and characteristic IP creation, waterfront tourism business operations, management and service output.

2. Development history (see Table 2-6)

Table 2-6 Development History of Yihong Company

Time.	Representative events
Year 2005	On June 8, Fujian Yihong Yacht Co., Ltd. was established, with its address in Zhangzhou, Fujian Province;
Year 2011	2011 Best Contribution Award for Domestic Yacht Enterprises;
Year 2012	Won the 2012 National Science and Technology Progress Award;
Year 2013	Yihong Yacht's Sea-stella brand was awarded the title of Famous Trademark of Fujian Province. Xiamen Sea-stella Club was officially established and took the lead in introducing advanced foreign operation models.
Year 2014	Yihong Yacht was selected as a Class I yacht manufacturing enterprise by the China Classification Society;
Year 2015	Set-up of the Yihong Yacht Sanya branch and completion of the construction of the high-end Xishi Club at the end of the year;
Year 2016	Yihong Yacht was listed on the New Third Board, stock code: 835558;
Year 2017	Fujian Yihong Yacht Co., Ltd. was listed as one of the top 100 yacht R&D and production companies in China's New Third Board Innovation Brand; Yihong Yacht won the Best Yacht Brand award at the SIBEX2014 Golden Sail Awards;

Year 2018	Yihong Yacht won the Golden Horn Award as the 2018 Most Growth New Third Board Company;

Yihong Yacht Group integrates yacht research and development, design, production, sales, after-sales service, accessories, and yacht club operations. It has obtained CE certification and CCS certification and is one of the four major A-class yacht manufacturers in China. Its products mainly include the Sea Stella and Aquitalia series. The Aquitalia series is a private customized yacht, including the Aquitalia46/53/63/68/7285/95 models; the Sea Stella series includes the Sea Stella40/42/53/56/72/78 models (Figure 2-8).

Yihong Yacht manages a wide range of businesses, including water villas and boat houses In addition, it has an experienced team of operators and managers for waterfront tourism destinations and provides standardized and systematic operation and management services for waterfront tourism destinations with advanced industry management and marketing experience.

(V) Jianglong Boat Technology Co., Ltd.

1. Company Profile

Jianglong Boat Technology Co., Ltd. and Jianglong Boat Co., Ltd. (hereinafter referred to as "Jianglong Boat") was established in 2003 and headquartered in Zhongshan City, Guangdong Province. It includes the Zhuhai Branch, Aolong Subsidiary and the Hong Kong Subsidiary. Jianglong Boat has a registered capital of ¥377.667,996 and mainly engages in the design, research and development, production, and sales of public-service law-enforcement boats, tourism leisure boats and special operation boats. It is a small and medium-size high-performance boat enterprise with the ability to research, develop and produce steel, aluminum alloy and composite-materials boats in China.

In the field of law-enforcement, it has built several high-performance boats for the Ministry of Transport, the Ministry of Agriculture and Rural Affairs, the Ministry of Ecological Environment, the Ministry of Emergency Management, the Ministry of Public Security, the General Administration of Customs of China and other agencies, and has participated in many national key projects and national strategies such as the "the Belt and Road".

It is one of the first domestic boat companies to realize the industrialization of new energy boats, having built pure electric, diesel-electric, and methanol-fueled boats and has begun to study the construction of hydrogen-fueled boats., It has also designed and built many high-end and luxury tourism and leisure boats.

In the field of special operation boats, Jianglong has independently developed a number of advanced ship types such as fire-fighting operation boats, navigation-mark maintenance boats, scientific examination and testing boats, and pilot boats, having introduced world-leading design concepts and construction technologies.

Jianglong Boats is led by technological innovation, has a rich database of ship design and professional talents, and has Class A ship design qualifications and 277 patents. It has been recognized as a "steel-aluminum ship research and development production base" by national industry associations nd has won many honors and qualifications making it a National High-tech Enterprise, a National Green Factory Demonstration Enterprise, and a National Postdoctoral Research Station.

2. Development history (see Table 2-7)

Table 2-7 Development History of Jianglong Boats

Time	Representative events
Initial development stage (2003-2008)	In 2003, the company was established and a performance boat construction base was planned in Pingsha Yacht Industrial Zone, Zhuhai. In 2008, it undertook the patrol-boat project for the Ministry of Fisheries of Angola, and its products were exported to the so-called "Belt and Road" countries.
Steadily improving stage (2009-2016)	In 2010, the construction of the special sightseeing ship for the Shanghai World Expo opened a new era of building large-scale multi-material composite ships. In 2011, Zhongshan Company was established and Jianglong Boat Science and Technology Park was established in Zhongshan City. In 2014, a major breakthrough was made in the field of clean-energy-powered boat construction, and the Pearl River Crystal was delivered, a boat of 54.5 meters with fully connected diesel electric power. In June 2016, Jianglong Boat and the international brand Austal established a joint venture: Austal Jianglong Boat Technology Co., Ltd.

Development and expansion stage (2017-)	In January 2017, the company was successfully listed on the Shenzhen Stock Exchange (stock code: 300589). In January 2019, Aolong Shipbuilding Co., Ltd. undertook the construction of a 71-meter/1,200-passenger/34-speed all-aluminum alloy catamaran high-speed passenger ship; In January 2020, new energy ships such as the Prince of the Pearl River, a 486-passenger pure electric cruise ship were to be delivered, leading the upper reaches of the Pearl River into a new era of green, environmentally friendly and low-carbon travel. In March 2021, the Jiuzhou Bay No. 1, the first near-shore mini cruise ship in the Guangdong-Hong Kong-Macao Greater Bay Area, together with many other designated ships and boats, boosted the development of the region. In January 2022, the subsidiary Aolong Boats signed a contract with South Korea for the construction of an 80-meter aluminum alloy high-speed passenger roll-on/roll-off vessel. In May 2022, the construction of the first 500kw hydrogen fuel cell-powered vessel in China began. In November 2022, part of the 1,000-ton marine advanced ship intelligent manufacturing base was put into use.

3. Main products

Jianglong Boats' products cover three major categories: official boats, leisure boats, and special boats, as shown in Table 2-8.

Table 2-8 Main types of Jianglong boat products

Product Classification		Product introduction
Classification by purpose	Official law-enforcement boats	Widely used in various types of boats for law enforcement and patrols in public services such as the coast guard, maritime affairs, customs, maritime surveillance, port and shipping, fishery administration, public security border defense, water police, water administration, flood prevention, and anti-smuggling activities.
	Tourism and leisure boats	Widely used in various types of boats for passenger transport, sightseeing, business and leisure activities between rivers, seas, lakes and islands, such as passenger ships, inter-island transport ships, sightseeing cruise ships, luxury yachts, and sea fishing boats.
	Special operation vessels	Special operation vessels refer to the types of vessels that provide services and safety guarantees for special operations and work scenarios. Special operation vessels include fireboats, scientific research vessels, wind power operation and maintenance vessels, pilot boats, car passenger ferries, tugs, engineering vessels, ro-ro passenger ships, dredgers, and barges.

Classified by power	New energy boats	The main forms of new energy boats include battery power (such as lithium batteries, fuel cells), alternative fuels (such as LNG, methanol, ammonia, hydrogen), wind energy, nuclear energy, and hybrid power (diesel-electric).
	Traditional energy boats	Driven by traditional fuel oil

Source: Annual Report of Jianglong Boat Technology Co., Ltd. in 2022

(6) Yantai CIMC Raffles Marine Science and Technology Group Co., Ltd.

1. Company Profile

On May 24, 2022, CIMC and Yantai Guofeng Group jointly funded (with each party holding 83.3% and 16.7% of the shares respectively) the establishment of Yantai CIMC Raffles Marine Technology Group Co., Ltd. The company says it is "people-oriented" with a strategic foundation of "large ocean and new offshore engineering". It has nearly 4,000 employees, including about 1,000 R&D and technical personnel, providing favorable talent support for the development of its business. The company's business interests include offshore oil and gas facilities, marine fisheries, marine clean energy, marine tourism, and asset operation and management. The group's many subsidiaries include Yantai CIMC Raffles, Haiyang CIMC Raffles, Longkou CIMC Raffles, CIMC Marine Engineering Research Institute, CIMC Blue, CIMC Jiguang, and Jihai Innovation. Through CIMC Marine Engineering Co., Ltd. located in Shenzhen, the group has invested in the establishment of subsidiaries such as Jinghai Fisheries, Jifeng New Energy, CIMC Jidian, and the Shenzhen Intelligent Marine Engineering Innovation Center. The group has two marine engineering design companies in Europe, forming a research and development nexus of interaction between China and Europe. In terms of yacht manufacturing and design, the company is committed to the research, design, manufacturing, marketing, management, and service of super yachts. The company's headquarters is located in Hong Kong, and its manufacturing base is located in Yantai, Shandong. It builds exclusive office, manufacturing and warehousing facilities for yachts in accordance with international standards. CIMC Raffles Group has always been committed to providing innovative equipment and solutions for the sustainable development of marine resources through independent innovation and lean management.

2. Development History

Table 2-9 Development History of CIMC Raffles Marine Technology Group Co., Ltd.

Development Stage	Major Events
Initial Development Stage (1977-2007)	In 1977, Yantai Shipyard was established. In 1978, China's first submersible drilling platform Shengli No.1 was delivered In 1994, Yantai Shipyard established a joint venture with Singaporean enterprises to establish Yantai Putai Shipbuilding Co., Ltd.
Stage of Development and Expansion (2008-2015)	In 2008, CIMC officially acquired Yantai Raffles In 2010, Yantai Raffles Offshore Engineering Co., Ltd. was renamed Yantai CIMC Raffles Offshore Engineering Co., Ltd. In 2013, CIMC Raffles became a wholly-owned subsidiary of CIMC. In 2015, CIMC Raffles became one of the first seven enterprises in China to enter the "white list" of marine equipment enterprises approved by the Ministry of Industry and Information Technology.

Steady Improvement Stage (2016-)	In 2016, CIMC Raffles delivered the first offshore fish farm platform Sixty Li No. 1 in China, ushering in the sixth wave of China's marine fishery industry led by equipment. In 2017, CIMC Raffles delivered the world's most advanced ultra-deepwater semi-submersible drilling platform Blue Whale 1 In 2019, the Brazilian state oil company P71FPSO hull was delivered, achieving a new breakthrough in the field of offshore oil and gas production. In 2020, CIMC's Blue Whale 2 helped China achieve success in the second round of flammable ice test-mining, setting two world records. In 2021, the world's first 100,000-ton semi-submersible production and storage platform Deep Sea No. 1 energy station was delivered In 2022, Yantai CIMC Raffles Marine Science and Technology Group Co., Ltd. was created. Delivery of the first domestically developed semi-submersible offshore photovoltaic power generation platform, independently developed by CIMC Raffles in 2023

3. Main products

The group has a wide range of business modules, including drilling platforms offshore wind power equipment, production equipment, deep-sea fishery equipment and special ships and equipment Other modules deal with maintenance and transformation, decommissioning and dismantling, and marine tourism. The marine tourism business module mainly produces super yachts, high-end cruise ships, cruise liners, ro-ro ships, marine complexes and other marine leisure equipment.

(1) Fantasy series super luxury yacht - Fantasy

The 88.5-meter super luxury large yacht Fantasy is designed according to the highest European standards. It has a luxurious master room, VIP room, and 2 swimming pools. The exterior design of the yacht comes from RSD, a well-known yacht design company in the UK, and the interior design is completed by the world-renowned Dutch interior design company Sinot. The basic design was completed by the Dutch Azure design company. The streamlined hull with a straight bow makes it unique. The ship is equipped with Rolls-Royce diesel engine electric propulsion and a stable system with continuous power positioning capability. Delivered in 2018.

(2) Super luxury yacht - Asean Lady

The 88-meter steel luxury yacht Asean Lady was designed by Ian Mitchell, and the entire interior design and construction was completed by CIMC Raffles. It was delivered in 2003. The unique feature of the ship is its asymmetric double hull design, which provides more space, better stability, and reduces cabin noise. Asean Lady won the Most Creative Yacht Award at the 15th annual ShowBoats magazine awards in Monaco in 2004.

(3) Classic luxury yacht - Nero

Nero is a 90-meter long superyacht that can accommodate 12 guests and 20 crew members. The interior panels are made of traditional oak and ash wood, and the sun deck is equipped with a large water jet Jacuzzi. The front deck is equipped with a swimming pool. With an advanced anchoring stability system and a maximum speed of 17 knots, the speed and stability of the hull are improved. The vessel was delivered in 2008.

(4) Nanhai shellfish, a marine complex

Based on the blueprint of semi-submersible living platforms and catamarans, CIMC Raffles announced plans to create floating islands on the sea to support multiple tourism functions. The upper part of the semi-submersible floating island can be designed in any shape according to customer needs, while the lower part consists of columns and buoys, similar to a semi-submersible platform.

(7) Xiamen Hansheng Yacht Co., Ltd.

1. Company Profile

Xiamen Hansheng Yacht Co., Ltd. (hereinafter referred to as Hansheng Yacht) was founded in 1984. The company is committed to research and development, manufacturing and exporting luxury yachts, and providing a series of services such as yacht consulting, maintenance, management. It is a comprehensive national high-tech enterprise. The company provides sailing yachts, rowing boats for large-scale competitions, and has developed more than ten series of products including the Flying Tiger Competition Sailboat, Gallop Luxury Yacht, Sailiner Leisure Sailboat, Jieneng Pure Solar Power Boat, Chi Yi Catamaran Yacht, Fishing Boat. Its Pearl 62, Pearl 80, Pearl 95 vessels have been internationally recognized and have won many international best boat awards.

2. Development history (see Table 2-10)

Table 2-10 Development History of Hansun Yacht

Development Stage	Events
Initial Development Stage (1981-2002)	In 1981, Xiamen Aquatic Shipyard and the American/Hong Kong Xilai Xue Company established a Sino-foreign cooperative company, Xilai Xue Company, which mainly produces luxury yachts. In 1983, the company manufactured China's first luxury yacht, Celestial 48, which was launched for testing and exported to the United States the following year. In 1984, Xiamen Xilai Xue Yacht Company was changed to a wholly foreign-owned enterprise. In September of the same year, Xiamen GRP Yacht Factory was established to collaborate with the Fujian Provincial Water Center and the State Sports Commission to develop windsurfing and sailing products. From 1990 to 1995, the company developed speedboats and transport boats for fishery administration, which became the main economic growth point of the company at that time. In 1995, it acquired Xiamen Xilaixue Yacht Co., Ltd. In 1997, it undertook the OEM business of the US Passport Yacht Company. In September 2002, the company successfully restructured and was renamed Xiamen Hansheng Yacht Co., Ltd.

Stage of Development and Expansion (2003-2015)	Since 2003, the company has collaborated with the American Stevens Yacht Company. In September 2004, the Stevens mold was designed by the American side and produced by the company. On November 5 of the same year, the first Steven53 yacht was officially launched. In 2008, the company's own brand Gallop 48#01, designed by British designer Bill Dixon, was completed. In 2011, Xiamen Jieneng Marine Technology Co., Ltd. was established as a holding subsidiary. In early 2012, it successfully developed China's first pure solar yacht. It also handles maintenance and repair of world-renowned yachts such as Azimut 95, Sunseeker88, and Ferretti84. The Han Sheng Gallop62.8 luxury powerboat was widely praised by industry insiders at the Sea and Sky Feast yacht exhibition. In early 2012, the first pure solar-powered sightseeing business yacht in China was successfully developed, and the company participated in the formulation of industry standards for the yacht while obtaining several national patents. The Sailiner Zongheng 46 also obtained IRC coefficient certification, making it more professional in large-scale sailing competitions. The Gallop series Chi Yee 52.8, the first luxury business catamaran yacht in China, was unveiled at the fifth China (Xiamen) International Yacht and Sailing Exhibition. In December 2013, construction began on the British brand Pearl series luxury 65-foot powerboat, and it was successfully exported in 2014, debuting at one of the world's most famous yacht exhibitions, the 2014 Cannes International Yacht Show in France. In 2014, the company produced the Gallop 48 "Integrity and Innovation" yacht to test the waters at Jinmen, opening up a new era of direct cross-strait yacht travel. In 2015, the company began to develop and construct a 24-meter super luxury leisure fishing yacht, and Hansheng Yacht ranked first in the domestic yacht market.

Steady Improvement Stage (2016-present)	In November 2016, the luxury leisure racing yacht Sailiner 46 obtained the first CE certificate for yachts issued by the China Classification Society. In 2017, construction began on an 80-foot luxury powerboat in the British brand Pearl series, , and it was exported in September. In 2018, a luxury powerboat was completed in the British brand Pearl series and unveiled at the Cannes Yachting Festival in France.

3. Main products

The business modules of HanSun Yacht include: sailing boats, luxury power boats, fishing boats, OEM ocean cruising sailboats, pure solar power boats, and fiberglass-reinforced plastic auto parts and products. Among them, luxury power boats are the Chiying 52.8 and Gallop 62.8. OEM ocean cruising sailboats include Passport 545, Passport 615, Outbond 46; pure solar power boats include pure solar catamaran -480L, pure solar catamaran -600L, pure solar catamaran -600S,and pure solar catamaran -Mini400.

The Chi Yee 52.8 is China's first luxury catamaran business yacht, mainly used for business reception, private leisure, and friends' gatherings. It has an all-round function with a living room, a meeting room, a salon area, a leisure area, and bar counter/ kitchen (as shown in Figure 2-11).

(2) The Gallop62.8 luxury yacht is from the UK and designed by British designer Bill Dixon. Its smooth lines and elegant appearance reflect British elegance and nobility. It has three bedrooms, two living rooms, three bathrooms, and one kitchen

Section 3: Production and Manufacturing of Yachts

(1) Production Steps of Ships

1. Yacht design

The first step in yacht manufacturing is design. Yacht design includes two main aspects: exterior design and interior design. Exterior design analyzes shape, color, and quality, adhering to the characteristics of applicability, safety, and economy. Interior design starts from the harmony and safety of yachts in connection with nature and people, integrating elements such as space, color, light, shadow, and furnishings to present different styles and genres.

As they work, designers develop schemes for the exterior shape, dimensions, body structure, power systems, electronic equipment, and other aspects of yachts based on customer needs and construction standards. Like fashion and handicrafts, yachts—especially luxury yachts—are symbols of consumer identity and status, and thus have high design requirements. Many yacht manufacturers hire world-renowned yacht designers (or purchase designs from them) to enhance the visibility and competitiveness of their vessels.

Yacht design documents include a complete set of creative design elements for yachts, including conceptual design, space design, preliminary technical conditions, and 2D graphic displays.

2. CAD modeling

After the yacht design is completed, it is necessary to use computer-aided design software (CAD) for 3D modeling. CAD software can quickly and accurately generate 3D models of yachts, helping yacht designers better understand the structure and performance of yachts, in order to effectively optimize the structure and improve performance.

3. Model making

After the modeling work is completed, it is necessary to make a scale model of the yacht. Various tools and materials are required for molding, such as aluminum plate, wood plate, or foam plastic. At present, 3D printing technology is used for yacht molding. Compared to traditional CNC technology, 3D printing is simpler, faster, better, and cheaper. For yachts with high aesthetic requirements, designers need to test many different options to determine the ideal design, and the advantages of 3D printing are even more pronounced.

The CAD file created by 3D design software, is then imported into printing software to set print parameters and determine how to assemble all the different parts. Then, all the individual parts of the hull structure are printed using PLA consumables. Finally, all the parts are glued together using adhesive, and the 3D modeling process is complete.

4. Material cutting

In the process of yacht manufacturing, it is necessary to cut materials such as aluminum plates, steel plates, and fiberglass. Cutting can be done using machines or by hand. After cutting, some materials need to be polished and trimmed to ensure their flatness and accuracy.

5. Welding

The manufacturing of yachts requires a lot of welding work. Welding can be done using manual welding, gas shielded welding, and other methods. After welding is completed, the welds need to be polished and painted.

6. Outfitting

In the process of yacht manufacturing, various assembly work is required. Outfitting refers to the installation of all equipment, devices, and facilities outside the hull of the yacht, including the installation of power systems, electronic equipment, cabin equipment, fire-fighting equipment, pumps, steering gear, and other components. After assembly, various tests are required to ensure the normal operation of the yacht.

7. Coating

After the yacht is completed, it needs to be painted. Painting protects the yacht from corrosion caused by seawater, sunlight, and other factors, and also makes the yacht look more beautiful. Painting usually uses spraying technology, which requires multiple coats and sanding.

8. Debugging

A process of self-inspection in which manufacturers conduct systematic debugging of various indicators for the constructed yachts according to relevant national, industrial, and local standards as well as the yacht's own design standards. Only after passing the debugging stage can the yacht be inspected by the ship inspection agency.

9. Inspection

As a non-conventional vessel, yachts do not have uniform safety and pollution prevention requirements specific to them, and their inspection management is governed by domestic laws of each country. The Ministry of Transport of the People's Republic of China implemented the Regulations on the Safety Management of Yachts (hereinafter referred to as the "Regulations") on January 1, 2009. Article 4 of the Regulations clearly stipulates that yachts shall be inspected in accordance with the yacht inspection regulations and specifications approved by or recognized by the Ministry of Transport before obtaining corresponding ship inspection certificates.

With the advancement of yacht production technology and the innovation of ship production modes, the entire process is constantly optimized and re engineered, resulting in continuous improvement in the construction speed and quality of yachts.

(2) Evolution of the yacht construction model

With the advancement of technology, the mode of shipbuilding has also been constantly developing. From the era of building riveted ships to the present, the development of shipbuilding mode has gone through four stages.

1. Phase I: the mode of organizing production according to function (system)

This is the oldest mode of shipbuilding, characterized by:

(1) Ship design and production organization for hull construction are based on structural functions, while outfitting is based on usage functions.

(2) Vessel assembly is carried out according to the ship's design functions/systems, with the hull first and outfitting later. Each phase is carried out separately on the slipway and outfitting dock according until the hull is completed.

2. Phase II: Organize production by region

This is a shipbuilding mode that was formed in the early stages of constructing fully welded ships. The application of welding technology in shipbuilding has pioneered the construction of ship segments. With the development of segmented construction technology, the construction of ship hulls can be divided into segments and components according to their structural characteristics, creating the possibility of performing flow operations by region, while also providing the possibility of pre-outfitting in segmented regions. Product tasks can be divided according to the structural areas of the hull construction, while for outfitting, the expanded pre-outfitting can still be organized according to its use function (system) to organize shipbuilding production.

Although ship design is still carried out according to functions (systems), the decomposition and combination of shipbuilding tasks can be planned and embodied through the use of hull production design through lofting.

3. Phase III: Organize production according to the model of "region-phase-type"

Due to the application of group technology in shipbuilding and the sharp increase in demand for large ships, this shipbuilding model has been promoted, which is characterized by:

(1) The decomposition and combination of product tasks are based on the principle of dividing areas according to the spatial locations of ship products and decomposing and combining them in stages and types.

(2) The decomposition and combination of product tasks are planned and embodied through the production design of the hull and outfitting.

(3) The product operation method is based on the division of the hull into different areas and the outfitting of the areas according to the region. The completed various operation areas are then combined to form a complete ship product.

4. Phase IV: Organize production according to the model of "regional-phase-type integration"

The main motivation for the formation of this shipbuilding model is that the increasing number of large-scale ship coating projects and their continuous improvement have prompted the separation of coating from outfitting operations, resulting in a unique coating production system. The characteristics of this model are:

(1) The decomposition and combination of product operation tasks not only follow the principles of decomposition and combination by region/stage/type, but also reflect the integration of the three major operation systems of hull construction, outfitting, and painting.

(2) The decomposition and combination of product operation tasks are planned and embodied through the production design of hull, outfitting, and painting.

(3) The combination of ship design, shipbuilding production and production management, and the integration of production design.

The above four shipbuilding modes can be divided into two types with essential differences. The first two belong to the system-oriented shipbuilding mode, collectively referred to as traditional shipbuilding mode, while the latter two belong to the product-oriented shipbuilding mode, collectively referred to as modern shipbuilding mode.

The traditional shipbuilding mode of the system-oriented type is essentially a shipbuilding process that decomposes and combines product tasks according to functions (systems), divides process stages according to ship, machinery, and electrical disciplines, and subdivides each process item as a process link in the shipbuilding process, organizing production in the form of a process.

The product-oriented modern shipbuilding model, on the other hand, essentially divides and combines product tasks by region from the perspective of integration of hull, outfitting, and painting, and divides various types of tasks by region to form a shipbuilding model in which the hull is segmented and the outfitting is organized by pallets (or units) as the basic production unit for ship construction.

The modern shipbuilding mode and traditional shipbuilding mode are two completely different procedures, which are not only different in the basic principles and methods of organizing shipbuilding production, but also completely different in terms of design methods, production methods, management methods, and the nature of shipyards.

Chapter 3

Sales and Trading of Yachts

This chapter clarifies the definition of yacht sales and introduces the channels and customer structure of yacht sales. Yacht sales channels include both direct and indirect sales channels. Direct sales channels include offline sales and online sale; indirect sales channels include yacht wholesalers, yacht retailers and yacht agents. Yacht customers mainly include private customers, commercial customers, government customers, and other social organizations. This chapter underscores the importance of selecting appropriate sales channels based on actual situations, providing reference for yacht manufacturers and sellers to choose appropriate sales channels and customer groups.

Section 1: Sales of Yachts

The phrase "yacht sales" refers to the commercial activity in which yacht manufacturers or operators initially provide customers with various information, technical data, and production knowledge to enable them to make informed purchasing decisions. At the same time, the sales company also needs to provide customers with a series of after-sales services such as installation and commissioning, training. and maintenance.

In the yacht manufacturing industry, sales companies undertake a series of tasks, including providing after-sales services and training to customers. Through these tasks, yacht manufacturers and operators will be enabled to convey information about the safe and reliable operation of their vessels, giving full play to the functions and roles of yachts so as to achieve the maximum economic benefits of their products.

1. Sales Channels

(I) Direct Sales Channels

Direct sales channels refer to the direct sales and promotion of yacht manufacturers to consumers, mainly including the following:

1. Direct Offline Sales

This phrase efers to the direct sales and promotional activities of yacht manufacturers or dealers with potential customers and yacht enthusiasts in real life. It usually requires yacht manufacturers to invest a large amount of funds and resources to establish exhibition venues and carry out marketing and promotional activities.

Yacht offline sales is a very important sales method, because yachts are high-value, high-investment consumer goods, and potential customers often need to see, touch, and experience the performance and luxurious appearance of yachts before making a decision to purchase. During the offline sales process, yacht manufacturers can communicate yacht design, technology, and performance to potential customers and yacht enthusiasts, provide professional advice on yacht purchase and maintenance, and establish long-term partnerships with them.

The direct offline sales of yachts include the following methods:

(1) Establishment of a professional sales department. Small-scale enterprises may only need to set up a number of full-time sales positions; medium-sized enterprises can set up an independent sales department; and large yacht enterprises can establish independent sales subsidiaries. For example, Yihong Group established a wholly-owned subsidiary, Xishi Club Yacht Club Co., Ltd., for the sale of itsyachts. Relying on the resources of Yihong Yacht, this subsidiary provides comprehensive business development such as member reception, yacht experience, yacht sales, maintenance and repair, dock management, island and sea tourism development member services for the elite circle. Yihong group has established these Xishi Clubs in Xiamen, Shanghai, and Sanya, which are relatively developed in the domestic yacht market. This move has played a huge role in yacht sales and corporate culture promotion.

(2) Participation in yacht exhibitions. Yacht exhibitions are an important component of the yacht sales industry, providing a platform for yacht manufacturers, distributors, and related companies to showcase products, conduct business, and exchange cooperation. At the yacht exhibition, exhibitors can showcase the latest yacht designs, technologies, and products to attract the attention and interest of potential customers, industry experts, and the media.

Yacht exhibitions are usually held in major yacht markets and tourist destinations around the world in Europe, America, Asia, and the Middle East. Some of the most famous yacht exhibitions include the Denver International Boat Show,.one of the longest-running yacht exhibitions in the United States, held annually in Colorado; the Miami International Boat Show, one of the largest yacht exhibitions in North America, held annually in Florida in February; and the Monaco Yacht Show, the largest yacht exhibition in Europe, held annually in Cannes, France, in May. Exhibitors usually include yacht manufacturers, yacht dealers, yacht brokers, ship equipment and accessory suppliers, and yacht repair and maintenance service providers. Yacht exhibitions also attract yacht enthusiasts, wealthy consumers, industry experts, media and investors. These shows provide an important platform for the yacht sales industry, and can promote exchanges, cooperation, and development within the sector.

(3) Establishing a yacht brand showroom: A yacht brand showroom is a display space built by yacht manufacturers or dealers to showcase their yacht brands and products. It is usually a space with a modern and high-tech look, used to display yacht design, technology, performance, and luxurious interior decoration. The design and layout of the yacht brand showroom aims to attract the attention and interest of yacht enthusi-

asts, wealthy clients, and people working in the yachting industry.

In the yachting brand exhibition hall, yacht manufacturers usually showcase their latest yacht designs and technologies, including various models and sizes of sports yachts, luxury yachts, super yachts, among others. The exhibition hall is usually equipped with luxurious furniture, lighting, audio systems, and decorations to showcase the luxury and high-end quality of the yacht. The yacht's bridge, deck, cabin, and supporting facilities are also displayed to showcase the comfort and practicality of the yacht.

Yacht exhibition halls are not only important places for yacht manufacturers to display their brands and products, but also an important sales and promotional platform. In the process of visiting the exhibition hall, yacht manufacturers can establish connections with potential customers and yacht enthusiasts, understand their needs and requirements, and introduce them to the design, performance, and advantages of their yachts. In addition, yacht brand showrooms are also an important way for yacht manufacturers to carry out marketing and brand promotion, which can enhance brand image and popularity, attracting more customers and business partners.

The brand exhibition halls are not limited by space, as they can be displayed both physically and using virtual reality technology. The location of brand exhibition halls is usually in public yacht ports, yacht clubs or bustling areas of a city.

In short, offline sales of yachts are an important way for yacht manufacturers to directly sell and promote their yachts. It allows potential customers and yacht enthusiasts a place to more intuitively understand the true performance and luxury of yachts, establish trust and cooperation, while allowing manufacturers an opportunity to enhance the brand image and market position of their yachts.

2. Online Sales

Yacht manufacturers can also sell yacht products directly to consumers through online sales channels, such as through the official websites of yacht brands. Online sales can achieve global coverage, allowing more consumers to understand and purchase yacht products. Many well-known yacht brands have their own official websites for direct sales, such as Azimut Yachts, Sunseeker, Princess Yachts, and Ferretti Yachts. These official websites usually provide detailed product descriptions, pictures, specifications, prices, and other information, which make it convenient for consumers to choose and purchase. At the same time, yacht brands also provide online customization services, where consumers can customize their purchases to meet personalized needs.

(2) Indirect Sales Channels

Indirect sales channels refer to the sales and promotion of yacht manufacturers and sellers through intermediary channel providers or agents, mainly including the following:

1. Traditional offline dealers

(1) Yacht wholesalers. Wholesalers refer to companies or individuals responsible for providing yachts to yacht dealers or retailers. Yacht wholesalers usually work directly

with yacht manufacturers or yacht owners to acquire yachts and sell them to retailers at lower prices, so that they can earn higher profits when selling the vessels.

In the yachting industry, many manufacturers have their own sales channels and distribution networks. However, some yacht manufacturers may not have their own sales channels or want to expand their sales network. In this case, yacht wholesalers will play an important role.

Yacht wholesalers may work with several yacht manufacturers to provide more choices and better prices for dealers or retailers. They may also provide consulting services on market trends, sales strategies, and marketing support for yachts to help dealers or retailers improve their sales performance.

It should be noted that the existence of yacht wholesalers is not required for all yacht transactions but depends on the sales strategy of the yacht manufacturer and market demand.

The online sales of wholesalers rely on self-operated yacht sales (rental) websites and app online stores, such as: Blue Sea Yacht app, Yacht Butler app, Yacht Life app, among others. The offline channels of wholesalers are similar to the offline sales channels of manufacturers, except that the former sells multiple brands of yachts, while the latter sells only its own brand.

(2) Yacht retailers. Yacht retailers are businesses that specialize in selling yachts. They usually purchase yachts from yacht manufacturers or wholesalers and then retail them to consumers at a higher price. The business of yacht retailers includes the sales of yachts and their accessories, as well as pre-sales and after-sales services. They usually provide services such as yacht repair, maintenance, storage, insurance, and financing, to ensure the good operation of the yacht and maintain its value.

Yacht retailers can be divided into two categories: local yacht retailers and international yacht retailers. Local yacht retailers are usually professional yacht sellers with a good reputation in the local community. They usually have close partnerships with local yacht manufacturers and distributors. International yacht retailers are large companies that sell yachts worldwide. They have extensive sales networks and channels and cooperate with yacht manufacturers and distributors around the world.

Some well-known yacht retailers include MarineMax, Galati Yacht Sales, HMY Yachts, Fraser Yachts, Northrop & Johnson, and Ocean Independence. These yacht retailers are an important part of the yacht sales industry, typically operating globally and providing a wide range of yacht products and services.

(3) Yacht operators. Intermediaries who do both wholesale and retail business of yachts are called yacht operators.

(4) Yacht agents (yacht brokers). Yacht agents refer to companies or individuals that represent yacht manufacturers or yacht owners. They are responsible for selling, promoting, and managing the sale and rental of yachts. Unlike retailers who earn profits by obtaining sales margins, agents mainly rely on a commission system, where the seller of the yacht pays a certain percentage of the sales amount to the broker. Agents connect with potential buyers or renters in the

market, provide information about yachts, coordinate transactions, and provide after-sales services. Yacht agents need to have professional knowledge and experience, understand the design, construction, and maintenance of yachts, and work with yacht manufacturers, repair service providers, and other relevant parties to ensure that customers receive high-quality products and services. In addition, they need to understand local and international regulations to ensure the legality and compliance of yacht transactions. The work of yacht agents includes but is not limited to: understanding market demand and trends, finding new customers and maintaining existing customer relationships, providing customers with detailed information and advice on yachts, assisting customers in selecting yachts that suit their needs and budgets, handling transaction documents and contracts, and arranging yacht delivery and maintenance.

The representative type of yacht agents is yacht brokerage companies, which have a team of yacht brokers. Yacht brokers in European and American countries must be certified by their respective yacht brokerage associations and obtain a qualification certificate before taking up their positions. China's CETTIC Yacht Broker certification program was launched in 2012, and the first batch of yacht brokers obtained their qualification certificates on November 4 of that year. This is also a landmark event for China's yacht sales industry to standardize and professionalize the sales process.

In general, there are various channels for yacht sales, including direct and indirect channels. Different channels are suitable for different yacht manufacturers and sellers, so it is very important to choose the right combination of sales channels based on the actual situation of the enterprise.

2. Customer Structure of Yacht Sales

(1) Private Customers

This is one of the main customer groups for yacht sales. They are usually wealthy individuals or families who have a passion and pursuit for yachts. From the perspective of yacht purchase motivation, private yacht customers can be divided into the following two categories:

1. Investment-oriented private clients

Investment-oriented private clients purchase yachts to increase their wealth and purchase luxury yachts within their financial capabilities. Such private clients usually have a deep understanding of yachts and have many connections, as well aa strong financial resources to purchase yachts. They invest in luxury yachts on a long-term basis to preserve and increase their assets.

2. Leisure private customers

Leisure-oriented private clients purchase yachts mainly to improve their quality of life, show their personal taste, leisure and recreation, and reflect their social status and economic strength, thus satisfying their social communication and identity identification needs that can be fulfilled via water activities, small banquets, and travel and leisure on yachts. Such clients usually require personalized customization of yachts to meet their various requirements around the appearance, interior space, facilities, and functions of the yachts.

Private clients usually have high financial resources and can afford the high cost of yacht purchase and maintenance. They usually establish long-term partnerships with yacht manufacturers or yacht brokers to receive better services and support in all aspects of yacht design, manufacturing, delivery, and maintenance. For yacht manufacturers and brokers, private clients are an important customer group for whom new yacht products and services must constantly be developed.

(2) Commercial Customers

Commercial customers for yacht sales can be various types of businesses or organizations, including hotels and resorts, tourism companies, and other enterprises.

1. Hotels and resorts

Hotels and resorts are one of the important business customers for yacht sales. They often use yacht rentals as part of their customers' leisure and tourism activities, providing customers with a unique and luxurious experience. These companies usually look for high-quality, unique-looking, and luxurious-equipped yachts to provide the best yacht rental services to their customers. At the same time, some hotels and resorts also purchase yachts to expand their services and provide a broader range of tourism experiences.

2. Travel agents

Tourism companies are also important business customers for yacht sales. These companies can provide tourists with yacht rental and charter tourism services, offering customers sea sightseeing and fishing experiences. Yacht rental services usually include a captain and necessary crew members to ensure the safety and comfort of tourists.

3. Other enterprises

Some companies may use yachts for business meetings, entertainment events, or corporate incentive programs. Yachts can provide a unique venue for hosting meetings, events, and entertainment. Companies and organizations often seek high-quality, luxury yachts to showcase their brand and provide a unique experience. Yacht sellers can provide suitable yacht options and services based on customer needs and budgets.

In summary, the business customers of yacht sales are diverse, with different needs and budgets. Yacht sellers need to understand their customers' needs and provide professional advice and services to meet their requirements and establish long-term partnerships.

(III) Government Customers

Government customers for yacht sales usually include departments or agencies such as customs, maritime management departments, and maritime rescue agencies. These government customers require official yachts to support their public services and duties.

1. Customs

Customs agencies are one of the main government customers for the sale of official boats. Customs agencies need yachts to perform tasks such as maritime patrol, border control, and smuggling suppression. These official yachts need to be fast, stable, and adaptable to different sea conditions, so that customs personnel can respond quickly and carry out their tasks. In addition, various monitoring and communication equipment needs to be deployed on the yachts to help customs personnel achieve their mission objectives.

2. Maritime administrative departments

These departments are responsible for the supervision of maritime shipping, port management, fishery management, among others. Boats can be used to perform maritime monitoring, security patrols, and rescue missions. Maritime official yachts need to have high performance and reliability to meet the requirements of maritime administrations for safety and efficiency.

3. Maritime rescue agencies

These agencies are responsible for carrying out various maritime rescue missions, such as maritime search and rescue andemergency medical rescue. Yachts must have the characteristics of high speed, adaptability to different sea conditions and weather so they canhelp rescue agencies respond quickly and carry out missions.

When working with government clients, yacht manufacturers and sellers need to comply with government procurement regulations and standards to ensure that the yachts meet government requirements and specifications. In addition, yacht sellers also need to provide necessary training and support to ensure that government clients can safely operate and perform tasks on the yachts. Finally, yacht manufacturers and sellers also need to provide necessary after-sales service and maintenance support to ensure the reliability and performance of the official yachts.

(4) Other Social organizations

Other social organizations refer to non-profit organizations designed to achieve specific social, cultural, educational, environmental, and other public welfare goals. From the perspective of yacht purchasers, these other social organizations mainly fall into two categories:

1. Schools

Schools can purchase yachts for teaching purposes. Secondary or tertiary institutions offering majors related to yacht design, manufacturing, and service can purchase yachts for practical teaching, which can enhance teaching effectiveness and improve the quality of talent cultivation.

Many universities in coastal areas around the world have set up sailing majors or courses, formed sailing teams to participate in sailing competitions at various levels at home and abroad, and purchased sailing boats for daily training and competition. Among universities in Qingdao, for example, the following have sailing teams:China Ocean University, China University of Petroleum (East China), Qingdao University, Naval Submarine Academy, Qingdao University of Science and Technology, Qingdao University of Technology, Qingdao Ocean Shipping Vocational College, Qingdao Vocational and

Technical College, Shandong University of Science and Technology, and Qingdao Port Vocational and Technical College. As one of the first universities in China to recruit professional sailors, China Ocean University first participated in the Olympic Sailing Games on behalf of the country in 2008. In 2013, it took the lead in offering sailing majors in China. In 2021, it first opened a Sailing Driving Foundation course and a tourism management professional sailing internship training course in a Sino-foreign cooperative education program, further increasing the demand for sailing.

In addition to universities, primary and secondary schools that focus on marine-themed education purchase yachts (sailboats) for students' marine-themed research and sailing competitions.

2. Charitable and public welfare organizations

Large charitable and public welfare organizations at home and abroad generally have their own full-time staff, office space, and specialized agencies. After purchasing (donating) yachts, they are mainly used for public welfare activities and charitable donations.

Figure 3-1 The training of the sailing team of Ocean University of China

(Photo source: provided by Professor Chang Xiaofeng, the coach of the sailing team)

With the miniaturization of yacht specifications and the popularization of prices, the customer profiles will become more diversified. It is necessary to provide different types and specifications of yachts according to different market demands and customer groups to meet customer needs.

Section 2: Yacht Exhibitions

1. Well-known Yacht Exhibitions in China

(1) China (Shanghai) International Boat Show (CIBS)

1. Introduction to the exhibition

China (Shanghai) International Boat Show (CIBS) was founded in 1996 and is held annually. The exhibition organizers are China National Shipbuilding Industry Association, Shanghai Shipbuilding Industry Association, Shanghai UBM Sinoexpo International Exhibition Co., Ltd. and Shanghai Science Exchange and Technology Center. CIBS is the oldest comprehensive yacht event in Asia, with exhibits covering real ships, boat equipment and accessories, boat services, and water sports. It provides an efficient, high-quality, all-in-one business exchange platform for yachting industry brands and global high-quality buyers. CIBS, one of the platinum members of the International Federation of Yacht Show Organizers (IFBSO), has greatly promoted the development of the Asian yachting industry.

2. Review of Representative Exhibitions

On April 8, 1996, the first China International Boat Show and Shanghai International Yacht Show (CIBS) was held at the Portman Hotel in Shanghai.

In 2005, CIBS moved to the Shanghai Exhibition Center, with a exhibition area of over 15,000 square meters and more than 240 exhibitors, making it the largest in Asia. There were also four national pavilions from France, Italy, New Zealand and Australia.

In 2012, CIBS moved to the World Expo Exhibition & Convention Center, with a booth area of nearly 40,000 square meters, attracting 450 exhibitors, nearly 500 actual ships, and an additional 3,000 square meters of water exhibition area. The number of visitors reached 31,825 for the first time, facilitating a transaction volume of about ¥2.2 billion and establishing its status as the flagship exhibition of the whole industry chain in Asia.

In 2018, the Lifestyle Shanghai Show derived from CIBS was held at the same time and place as CIBS, and was composed of a number of themed exhibitions that met the needs of high-net-worth individuals, including water sports, lure fishing, RV camping, theme tourism, Expo lifestyle, amusement facilities, and outdoor sports. The show revolutionized traditional concepts, integrated high-quality resources, crossed the boundaries of land and sea, and combined multi-dimensional space with cross-border exhibits.

The 2019 Shanghai Yacht Show and Lifestyle Shanghai Show moved to the National Exhibition and Convention Center (Shanghai), with an exhibition area of 55,000 square meters, more than 600 exhibitors, and over 36,000 visitors from 85 countries and regions. More than 100 immersive experience activities were held on site, showing the audience a complete display of contemporary high-quality life and fashion leisure styles.

The 2021 Shanghai Yacht Show and Lifestyle Shanghai Show returned to the Shanghai World Expo Exhibition & Convention Center, with an exhibition area of over 44,000 square meters and nearly 600 exhibitors. The exhibits covered the entire industry chain, including yachts, yacht equipment and accessories, yacht clubs, yacht-related services, and water sports. A total of 185 in-depth experience activities and professional forums were held, and 108 KOLs gathered together, attracting a total of 37,000 visitors.

On March 31, 2023, the 26th China (Shanghai) International Boat and Technical Equipment Exhibition and the 2023 Shanghai International Yacht Show (hereinafter referred to as "CIBS2023") came to a successful conclusion at the Shanghai New International Expo Center. The exhibition covered an area of over 40,000 square meters, with more than 400 exhibitors and more than 100 domestic and foreign exhibiting brands. More than 150 events were held on-site. CIBS2023 was one of the first exhibitions of the Shanghai Tourism Industry Expo. As one of the three major representative activities of the "Shanghai Tourism" peak construction project during the "14th Five-Year Plan" period, the Shanghai Tourism Expo is a comprehensive tourism industry expo cluster with the world's leading scale and concept, consisting of a number of exhibitions for vertical industries. This year's exhibition was divided into two phases. The first phase of the exhibition covered the Shanghai International Hotel and Commercial Space Expo and the Shanghai International Yacht Show and Lifestyle Shanghai Show.

3. Exhibition evaluation

As a flagship exhibition of the entire industry chain of boats and ships, CIBS is committed to serving the waterfront leisure industry, integrating high-quality resources in the boat and ship industry, providing a high-quality trade negotiation environment for people in the boat and ship industry chain, actively promoting the integration of China's yachting industry and equipment manufacturing industry with the international community, and discussing the new future of the boat and ship industry. Through offline exhibitions, forum exchanges, on-site activities and other means, the organizers hope to continue to strengthen theyachting industry exchange platform, while linking the form of "Internet plus" to effectively serve the industry. Bohua Youxuan is a digital platform integrated by offline physical exhibitions and online e-commerce platforms, which has entered the 4.0 stage after more than ten years of high-quality development. Relying on the CIBS offline exhibition, the online B2B platform for boat leisure tourism (XIUGLE) has a large number of industry resources, and has successfully held a number of online business matching meetings and a series of online activities, matching suppliers with high-quality partners and gaining a good reputation from suppliers and buyers.

(2) China (Shenzhen) International Boat and Equipment Exhibition (SIBEX)

1. Introduction to the exhibition

China (Shenzhen) International Boat and Equipment Exhibition (SIBEX), also known as Shenzhen Boat Show, was founded in 2007. It is supported by the Shenzhen Administration of Qianhai, a pilot free-trade zone in Guangdong Province, and hosted by the Shenzhen Bay Yacht Club. It adopts the water and land exhibition mode in line with international standards and displays high-end consumer goods such as yachts and sailboats, yacht equipment and supporting services, and luxury cars and mansions According to the records of the Shenzhen Bay Yacht Club's ship and boat industry trading platform and the bonded port, Shenzhen is currently the port city with the largest import and export trade volume of ships and boats in China, and is also the preferred city for foreign investment and development of related industries. Shenzhen Bay International Boat Show is the largest and most influential boat show in South China. In addition, the Shenzhen Bay Yacht Club is currently the yacht club with the largest number of super luxury yachts, the longest size and the largest number of international famous brands in China. In order to better promote the development and prosperity of the yacht industry, it makes full use of the successful operation of the yacht Guangdong-Hong Kong-Macao free travel and the yacht bonded port policy permission conditions, and is planning to build a Bay Area yacht free port, a maritime sports competition center, and a national demonstration port for yacht tourism, to promote the development of Shenzhen as a global ocean center city.

SIBEX is the stage for the world's yachts to enter China. Every year, brands from more than 20 countries and regions including the United States, Britain, France, Italy, Germany, Australia, Canada, Denmark, Sweden, Poland, and Japan. participate in the exhibition. The world's most famous first-line yacht brands are all present, showcasing the grand occasion of hundreds of luxury yachts gathering in Dameisha Bay. The main visitors include potential buyers and owners of yachts, brand yacht operators, manufacturers of boats and accessories, boat builders, architectural and interior designers, operators of yacht clubs and water clubs, yacht agents and distributors, yacht clubs and neighboring real estate developers, water sports enthusiasts, wealthy celebrities, business executives, business elites, and cultural celebrities who advocate high-end consumption of water life.

2. Review of representative exhibitions

In 2009, the third Shenzhen International Yacht Show achieved two-level leaps: first, it was approved and officially upgraded to a national-level yacht show; second, it was held for the first time in cooperation with the organizer of the largest European water yacht show, France GPO, which doubled its scale and greatly improved its internationalization.

The fourth Shenzhen International Yacht Show in 2010 was another brilliant achievement, winning three national firsts in the core data that determines exhibition efficiency.

The sixth Shenzhen International Yacht Show in 2012 was held at the Dameisha Bay

Yacht Club in Yantian District, Shenzhen, maintaining the growth momentum of previous years. All booths were sold out, with a land area of 15,000 square meters and 3 water piers. The overall scale increased by 30% compared to 2011. A total of 208 brands and 120 actual ships from more than 20 countries and regions participated in the exhibition, and the water scale continued to maintain the position of "China's first water exhibition". In addition, the strong rise of domestic yacht manufacturers, competing with foreign brands at the Shenzhen Yacht Show, the proportion of domestic yachts and foreign brand yachts participating in the exhibition has soared from 1:6 to 1:1 since 2011.

The 15th China Shenzhen International Yacht and Equipment Exhibition (Yunbo) in 2021 specially set up an online exhibition website homepage, starting from the perspective of users, drawing on the offline yacht exhibition model, setting up numerous product theme exhibition areas, and building a powerful platform for transaction display, communication and cooperation for major yacht exhibitors. It accomplished this through the innovative model of "website homepage + theme zone + exhibitor homepage + product detail page + video display. This exhibition not only showcased the latest and various top yachts and their equipment in China, but also invited international innovative and advanced yachts and their equipment to be exhibited. These boats included powerboats, fishing boats, sports boats and sailing ships, some of which had a strong sense of technology, future and design, while others displayed have strong fashion trends that advocated the unity of function and aesthetics. From design, manufacturing to marketing, these yachts and equipment represented the latest development achievements of the international yachting industry.

3. Exhibition evaluation

The economically developed Hong Kong-Zhuhai-Macao Greater Bay Area is the biggest advantage for SIBEX. The exhibition is committed to creating the largest luxury event in South China, interpreting the charm of high-end fashion and spreading the culture of marine life by creating a fashionable water carnival, with nearly 100 yachts exhibited on the water every year, ranking first in China and known as the'first exhibition of yachts on the water in China.'

(3) Sanya International Yacht Show

1. Introduction to the exhibition

The annual Sanya International Boat Show is hosted by the Sanya Municipal People's Government, the Hainan Provincial Department of Commerce, and the Hainan International Economic Development Bureau. It was first held in 2007.

2. Review of representative exhibitions

In 2010, the fourth Sanya Yacht Show was themed "Building Hainan International Tourism Island and Gathering in Sanya Marine Culture Month." It included a series of activities devoted to water motorcycling, windsurfing, and sea fishing. The exhibition area of the yacht show was nearly 7,000 square meters, exceeding the sum of the previous three exhibitions. The exhibitors comprised

25 companies including domestic and foreign yacht brands and yacht machinery equipment companies, as well as high-end yacht real estate companies on the island, exhibiting 15 yachts and speedboats over 5 meters. They were accompanied by many different brands of motorboats, speedboats and mountain bikes. It attracted nearly 6,000 visitors, including nearly 2,000 professional visitors. From the analysis of the registration data of the professional visitors, the proportion of people with purchasing intention was as follows: : real estate developers 35%, hotels and tourist attractions 22%, entrepreneurs 20%, yachting industry personnel 14%, and others 9%.

Themed "Sailing Sanya, Cheers to the World", the 2023 Sanya International Yacht Show was held at the Sanya International Yacht Center, which was opened for the first time as the main venue. The total exhibition area is 125,600 square meters, including 105,000 square meters of water display. Nearly 600 brands of well-known yachts, water-friendly equipment, new energy boats, art, wine, and daily necessities were be displayed on site. In addition, the organizers planned a series of activities such as the "Wonderful Sailing Night" and the "Sanya Wind and Wave Electric Carnival" at three venues, namely Sanya Hongzhou International Yacht Marina, Sanya Banshan Peninsula Sailing Port, and Sinopharm China Service Duty Free Sanya Store. The exhibitors included the main domestic yacht agents, shipyards, and water equipment sellers, with a wide range of highlights. There were 12 new product launches and premieres, including the global launch of the Seaview 56-foot catamaran by Starfish Yacht, the domestic launch of the Dufour 56-foot monohull by O'Neill Yacht, the domestic launch of the Mastercraft X24 water skiing boat, the global launch of the ROCK XL, the national launch of the FG-57 fishing boat by Haoyun, and the national launch of the JY700E fishing boat by Jinyun. The numerous premieres and debuts demonstrated the importance of the Sanya International Yacht Show in the hearts of various brands and exhibitors.

3. Exhibition evaluation

The Sanya International Yacht Show has policy, geographical, market and venue advantages. Focusing on the construction of a yachting industry reform and development innovation pilot zone, Sanya has established a number of key projects, , implemented a number of core policies represented by the "zero tariff" yacht, formed a number of institutional innovation achievements represented by the "multiple certificates in one" for yachts, and expanded a series of yacht tourism scenarios represented by the night navigation of rental yachts. The yacht economy has become a new growth point for Sanya's economic development. Sanya's goal is to build a full industrial chain of yachts integrating research and development, design, maintenance, operation, and training, and to create itself as the Asia-Pacific yacht capital.

The Sanya International Yacht Show, which integrates many advantages, is positioned as the top-tier and internationally renowned yacht show in Asia.

(4) China International Consumer Goods

Fair Yacht Show

1. Introduction to the exhibition

The China International Consumer Goods Fair (hereinafter referred to as "CICGF") was proposed in the overall plan for the construction of the Hainan Free Trade Port and is the first national-level exhibition with the theme of consumer goods in China. The organizers are the Ministry of Commerce of the People's Republic of China and the People's Government of Hainan Province. It has been held for three consecutive years since its debut in 2021. CICGF is divided into different themed exhibition areas, with the yatch exhibition area being an important component.

2. Review of representative exhibitions

In 2021, the first CICGF Yacht Show was held at the public dock of the National Sailing Base in Haikou City; it was organized by the Haikou Municipal People's Government and Nan Guang (Group) Co., Ltd. The total area of the water and land exhibition area of the yacht show was about 80,000 square meters, attracting 107 boats and 58 well-known brands from 12 countries and regions. The total number of visitors was nearly 30,000. During the exhibition, six new products were launched in Asia and the country, two overseas yachts on the Qionggang Macao Yacht Freedom Tour set sail from the port for the first time, and the transaction and intentional investment amount of yachts exceeded ¥500 million. During the show, there were more than 20 theme activities, which helped the CICGF to build an international consumer goods global display and trading platform.

The public dock exhibition area of the first CICGF yacht exhibition has a total of more than 100 water berths covering an area of 70,000 square meters, and the onshore exhibition area covers an area of 10,000 square meters. A total of 107 boats representing 58 well-known brands from Australia, Poland, Germany, France, Finland, the United States, Sweden, New Zealand, Italy, the United Kingdom, and China were unveiled together. A total of six new product launches were made at this yacht exhibition, including the first appearance in Asia of a 42-foot ship from Bavaria, Germany, in Asia, and the first appearance in China of a 43-foot ship from Azimut, Italy. Four overseas super yacht brands made their Asian debuts through ship models and videos, including Australia's Selway, Italy's Arcadia, Italy's Benetti, and Germany's Le Shun. During the yacht exhibition, the organizers also organized nearly 40 yachts and sailing boats of various types to conduct a maritime display outside the Hainan International Convention and Exhibition Center, showing the casual cultural atmosphere of Hainan and Haikou to global visitors.

In 2022, the second China International Consumer Goods Fair Yacht Show was held in Haikou City. For the first time, four special exhibition halls for Italy, the United States, Germany, and the Netherlands were set up in the onshore exhibition area, further demonstrating the investment achievements of the yachting industry and yacht tourism products and helping the Hainan yachting industry enter the fast lane of development and achieve high-quality development. The total area of the main production area of the second China International Consumer Goods Fair Yacht Show was 180,000 square meters, and the exhibition area increased by 125% year-on-year. The exhibition attracted more than 200 boats and ships, with the number of exhibitors increasing by nearly 90% year-on-year, and the number of overseas brand boats accounted for about 45%, which was a significant increase over previous years. In addition to the onshore water exhibition area, this year's exhibition launched a series of live events for exhibitors and audiences, including the Yacht Show Launch Ceremony, the Brand Yacht Debut Show, and the International Yacht Forum, to create a platform for international yacht boutique global display, exchange, and transaction for domestic and foreign exhibitors and audiences. This show was attended by nearly 50,000 people, including buyers, industry insiders, and citizens and tourists. A number of yacht transactions were reached, with a total intention to sell of ¥500 million.

In 2023, the third China International Consumer Goods Fair Yacht Show as well as the China (Haikou) International Boat and Lifestyle Exhibition were held in Haikou. The exhibition gathered many well-known domestic and foreign yacht brands and focused on the lifestyle and experience of boats and ships in the "exhibition + conference + competition" mode. Ten water and land series activities helped create a yacht event combining professionalism and popularity. The third CICGF Yacht Show attracted many well-known domestic and foreign yacht brands to participate, such as the American yacht brands RIG and Chris, the British yacht manufacturer Princess Yacht, the French yacht brands Perlee and Arno, the Italian yacht manufacturers Ferretti and Azimut, the German yacht brand Bavaria, and the Finnish yacht brand. Also participating were well as domestic yacht brands Far East Boat, Shangyuan and Coincidence, with more than 200 boats on display. During the exhibition, the organizers held a variety of exhibition activities, including the 2023 Hainan Free Trade Port International Yyachting industry Development Forum, the Hainan Free Trade Port International yachting industry Promotion Conference and Project Centralized Signing Ceremony, the Water Sports Performance Show, the Boat and Ship Food and Wine Show, the Hundred-person Sea Fishing War, the Coffee and Food Culture Festival, to build a close communication platform for exhibitors, professional audiences, and the public, showcasing a luxurious water life experience.

3. Exhibition evaluation

The exhibition adhered to the "fine-quality route" positioning, highlighting the world's first launch, first show and first exhibition of new products, and strove to become an important platform for promoting high-level displays, facilitating the connection between domestic and foreign markets, smoothing the domestic and international cooperation, promoting consumption upgrading and global consumption fashion.

2. Internationally renowned yacht exhibitions

(1) Famous exhibitions in Europe

1. Cannes Yachting Festival

The annual Cannes Yachting Festival

Figure 3-2 Yacht Exhibition of the 3rd China International Consumer Products Expo

was first held in 1978. It is the largest water yacht exhibition in Europe and the opening exhibition of the boating season, serving as the world's first stage for the global debut of many new yachts. The organizer is Reed Exhibitions International Convention & Exhibition Company, UK. It is held in September every year in the Port of Cannes, France. The total exhibition area of the Old Port (Vieux Port) and Port Pierre Canto is 150,000 square meters. The vessels exhibited at the Yacht Festival include powerboats, super yachts, catamarans, auxiliary boats and sailing boats. As the opening station of the European Yachting Festival, the Cannes Boat Show is highly favored by major yacht manufacturers around the world due to its unique and superior water exhibition area and good yachting culture atmosphere. It has been committed to providing a good exhibition environment for new models and technologies and has set new records every year. Due to COVID-19 pandemic, the exhibition in 2020 was suspended.

The 2021 Cannes Yacht Festival was held in two famous ports (Old Port and Cantor Port) from September 7 to 12, with 560 ships (lower than the average of 600 ships before COVID-19) and 430 exhibitors participating, and more than 140 ships debuting. Ferretti Group unveiled a luxurious fleet of 23 yachts on the charming Côte d'Azur, including five world premieres from Riva, Pershing, Ferretti Yachts and Wally brands: Riva 68' Diable, Riva 76' Perseo Super, Pershing 6X, Wally WHY200 and Ferretti 1000. The Azimut Benetti Group showed 18 yachts,, including the first public display of four highly anticipated new vessels: the Giant Series Trideck, the Azimut 68, the Azimut 53, and the new Magellan 66. Princess Cruises displayed 8 yachts, debuting the Princess Y72. Kadier yachts brought 6 yachts for on-site display, introducing the Galeon 325 GTO.

In 2022, the Cannes Yacht Festival surpassed the pre-pandemic exhibition in 2019. Nearly 650 ships and 600 exhibitors appeared, including Treasure class ships and 135 world premiere ships, as well as the latest water equipment and countless innovative achievements, attracting 54,000 visitors from France and around the world. Another highlight of this exhibition was the attention paid by the organizers to ecology via a "green" theme, where 60 exhibitors showcased a series of concepts that benefitted the environment. To thank exhibitors and partners and let Cannes citizens experience the charm of the yacht show together, the exhibition cooperated with the Cannes Town Hall to create a spectacular drone show. In 15 minutes, 400 drones illuminated the sky over Cannes without causing any pollution to the ocean.

2. Boot Düsseldorf, Germany

Boot Düsseldorf, founded in 1969, is the world's first indoor exhibition for water sports. It is a global exhibition recognized by the International Federation of Boat Show Organizers (IFBSO). Every year, visitors from all over the world gather here to find suppliers, meet customers, and understand the latest developments in the industry. The exhibition covers all aspects of boats, yachts, and their components also while showcasing various water sports and entertainment facilities with distinctive themes. In particular, the diving exhibition is the largest diving consumer goods exhibition in Europe, and has become a hot spot for many professional buyers.

The 2023 Düsseldorf Boat Show has 16 exhibition halls with a total exhibition area of 220,000 square meters. It attracted nearly 237,000 registered visitors from more than 100 countries and more than 1,500 exhibitors from 68 countries, displaying motorboats, luxury yachts, sailing boats or diving equipment, and trendy sports and resorts. Many manufacturers and potential buyers from the United States, South America, and Asia once again traveled to Düsseldorf, and enriched the industry event with innovative products, inspiration, and in-depth knowledge.

The 2023 German Yachting Show launched a new sustainable development forum, "Blue Innovation Dock", where policymakers and international associations held high-level dialogues and exchanges. It proved the great success of the trade fair and opened a fascinating new perspective for the sustainable future of the boating industry. From CEOs to political decision makers, more than 110 high-quality speakers emphasized the importance of sustainability in water sports. Key decision makers from the political and business sectors discussed the current political situation and the necessary steps to achieve sustainable market development Via this new platform, the industry focuses on sustainability, promotes innovation, introduces next-generation technologies, discusses new methods, encourages politicians and industries to take action, and motivates tourists to get involved.

Since its inception, Boot Düsseldorf has been the home port and engine of international water sports. It provides a full range of boating services. Sailors and motorboat drivers will find a wide range of boats here, from entry-level boats and dinghies to luxury yachts. Diving, surfing, rowing and fishing have also become a focus of attention. With the innovations and technologically advanced products of exhibitors.

3. Fort Lauderdale International Boat Show

The Fort Lauderdale International Boat Show (FLIBS) was founded in 1959. Itis owned by the South Florida Marine Industries Association (MIASF) and hosted by Informa Exhibitions. Widely recognized as the world's largest water yacht show. FLIBS covers an area of nearly 90 acres and has a 900,000 square meter exhibition area neat the beach that is connected by a complex network of water and land transportation services.

The Fort Lauderdale International Boat Show has long been an important component of the city's economy. Each year, FLIBS attracts people and businesses from around the world, generating unprecedented economic impact and showcasing Fort Lauderdale as an exciting, vibrant, and growing community.

In 2021, travel restrictions of the COVID-19 pandemic prevented overseas exhibitors and visitors from going to the site. The exhibition still created more than US$1 billion of economic output for Florida, attracting more than 100,000 visitors.

From 26 to 30 October 2022, the five-day exhibition attracted more than 100,000 attendees and 1,000 exhibitors from 52 countries, exhibiting more than 1,300 boats. More than 20 new boats made their world or American debuts. The exhibition set up seven exhibition areas, including Bahia Mar Yacht Center, Las Olas Yacht Marina, Hall of Fame Marina, Super Yacht Village at South Pier 66, Pier 66, Hilton Fort Lauderdale Marina, and Broward County Convention Center. As the transportation hub of the exhibition, the convention center provides affordable parking, free air-conditioned shuttle buses, and seamless water taxi transfers. The Super Yacht Village, an exclusive yacht marina, showcases the most amazing boats at the exhibition. Guests can shop on world-famous boats or meet with famous yacht manufacturers to discuss their next sea trip. The luxury component showcases the luxury of the entire industry, providing VIP club guests with a unique experience centered on five-star cuisine, as well as an exclusive bar.

Over the past 63 years, the exhibition has become a world-class event and a valuable platform, attracting tourists from all over the world to appreciate Fort Lauderdale and consolidating the city's position as the world's yacht capital.

4. Grand Pavois, La Rochelle, France

The Grand Pavois, founded in 1973, is organized by the Grand Pavois Association of La Rochelle, France. It is held annually and includes yachts, inflatable boats, sailing boats, steamships, amphibious boats, shipbuilding equipment, ship repair equipment, ship parts, engines, motors, propulsion equipment, consumer services, boat-related accessories, lifeboats, and other water sports equipment. The exhibition venue is located in the port of La Rochelle, covering an area of 35,000 square meters. On average, there are more than 600 exhibitors and 90,000 visitors per exhibition. It is one of the largest and most influential yacht and marine equipment exhibitions in the world.

La Rochelle is known as the city with a beautiful sea view. It is located on the coastline of western France and is the capital of Charente-Maritime. La Rochelle has been an excellent natural harbor since ancient times.

From September 27 to October 2, 2022, a six-day exhibition took place in this French "city of chocolate" where more than 800 international brands and 750 yachts were exhibited, including about 110 new yachts and products. The exhibitors mainly came from China, Spain, the United States, the United Arab Emirates, Japan, Finland, the United Kingdom, Australia, and Russia.

5. Singapore Yacht Show

The annual Singapore Yacht Show, which was first held in 2011, has become a leading yacht and luxury yacht show in Asia. It has made a significant contribution to the development of the fast-growing ASEAN maritime and luxury lifestyle market through innovation, creative opportunities, and glamour.

The Singapore Yacht Show is held at the ONE°15 Yacht Harbour Club in Sentosa Cove, providing exhibitors with a first-class platform to meet potential customers and yachting professionals from the Asia-Pacific region and beyond. In addition to impressive exhibits, the Singapore Yacht Show also hosts a four-day yacht lifestyle celebration, featuring a variety of interactive activities, live demonstrations, dinners, and glamorous parties to maximize the experience of exhibitors and visitors. Elegant yacht parties, exciting water sports experiences, gourmet restaurants, bustling bars, and showcased supercar parades are part of the experience.

As the only large-scale yacht show in Asia, the Singapore Yacht Show provides strategic business networking opportunities for industry professionals. The SYS gala and Asian Rowing Awards have become a fixture on the social calendar in the region.

ONE°15 has been the venue for the Singapore Yacht Show since its opening, equipped with world-class facilities including a beach front hotel, luxury spa and fitness center. The venue was built according to the 5 Platinum Anchor standard (out of approximately 250,000 marinas worldwide, only 9 are listed as 5 Platinum Anchor marinas). Since its inception in 2007, it has been rated as the Best Asian Marina of the Year eight times. The marina has 270 berths with a maximum draft depth of 4.5 meters, which can accommodate super yachts, and is the permanent residence of some of the world's most famous ship dealers.

Appendix 1: List of Internationally Renowned Yacht Exhibitions

Serial number	Exhibition Name	Exhibition Cycle	Exhibition Venue	Organizer
1	Cannes Yachting Festival	Once a year	Cannes Port	Reed Exhibitions International
2	Boot Düsseldorf - The Boat, Yacht and Water Sports Show	Once a year	Düsseldorf Exhibition Center	Organizer Alliance of International Boat Show, Messe Düsseldorf GmbH
3	Fort Lauderdale International Boat Show FLIBS	Once a year	Bahia Mar Yacht Center, Fort Lauderdale	Informa Exhibitions
4	La Rochelle Yacht Show, France Grand Pavois	Once a year	La Rochelle Expo Center	Grand Pavois Association of La Rochelle
5	Monaco Yacht Show	Once a year	Grimaldi Pavilion	Informa Exhibitions
6	EURASIA Boat, Istanbul Yacht Show, Turkey	Once a year	Istanbul Exhibition Center	Turkey Yacht Association, CNR Exhibition Company
7	Australian Ship and Yacht Show	Once a year	Sydney International Convention and Exhibition Center	Boat Industry Association Limited BIA
8	Cruise Shipping Miami	Once a year	Miami Beach Convention Center	Informa Exhibitions
9	Brazilian Rio de Janeiro Maritime and Shipping Exhibition Marintec	Once a year	Rio de Janeiro International Convention and Exhibition Center	Informa Exhibitions
10	Singapore Yacht Show	Once a year	Singapore One 15 Yacht Club	Singapore Yacht Events Pte Ltd
11	Russian Moscow Yacht Show MIBS	Once a year	Moscow Crocus Expo International Exhibition Center	Russian Yachting Association
12	Dubai International Boat Show	Once a year	Dubai International Yacht Club	Dubai World Trade Centre (DWTC)

13	Marine Equipment Trade Show	Once a year	Amsterdam Exhibition Center	RAI International Exhibition Company, Amsterdam, Netherlands
14	Boatica Cape Town, South Africa	Once a year	V & A Waterfront, Cape Town, South Africa	Messe Frankfurt GmbH
15	INMEX SMM, Mumbai, India	Every two years	Mumbai Exhibition Center	Informa Exhibitions
16	Korea Ocean Expo	Once a year	Incheon Exhibition Center	Reed Exhibitions International Ltd.
17	UK Maritime & Yacht Show	Once a year	Southampton Mayflower Park	International Exhibition Company of London, UK
18	London Boat Show	Once a year	Excel International Convention and Exhibition Center, London, UK	British Maritime Federation
19	Barcelona Yacht Show Salon Nautico	Once a year	Port Vell, Barcelona, Spain	Barcelona Exhibition Center, Spain
20	Salon Nautic, the Paris Yacht and Water Sports Exhibition	Once a year	Paris Pavilion, Porte de Versailles, Paris, France	Reed Exhibitions France
21	São Paulo Boat Show	Once a year	Expo São Paulo Exhibition Hall	Brazilian Shipbuilders Association, Grupo Náutica
22	Palm Beach International Boat Show	Once a year	Palm Beach, Florida, USA	American Shipbuilding Industry Association
23	Genoa Boat Show	Once a year	Genoa Palazzo della Meridiana	Italian yachting industry Association and its subsidiary I Saloni Nautici
24	SCIBS, the International Yacht Show in Sanctuary Cove, Australia	Once a year	Yacht marina of Fairy Bay Resort, Gold Coast, Australia	Mulpha Events

25	Japan International Boat Show	Once a year	Yokohama Convention Center, Japan	Yokohama Exhibition Corporation
26	Warsaw Boat Show, Poland Warsaw Yacht Salon	Once a year	PTAK International Exhibition Center, Warsaw, Poland	Ptak Warsaw Expo
27	Korea International Boat Show (KIBS)	Once a year	Korea International Exhibition Center	Korea Trade and Investment Promotion Agency
28	Lebanon Beirut Yacht Show Beirut Boat Show	Once a year	Lebanon Beirut dock	IFP Group
29	Adelaide Boat Show	Once a year	Adelaide Convention and Exhibition Centre, Australia	Boat Industry Association Limited BIA
30	Helsinki Boat Show, Finland Helsinki International Boat Show	Once a year	Helsinki Exhibition Center, Finland	Finnish Fair Corporation

Appendix 2: List of Yacht Shows in China

Serial number	Exhibition name	Exhibition cycle	Exhibition Venue	Organizer
1	Shanghai International Boat Show (CIBS)	Once a year	Shanghai New International Expo Center	China National Shipbuilding Industry Association, Shanghai Shipbuilding Industry Association, UBM Sinoexpo International Exhibition Co., Ltd.
2	Shenzhen International Boat and Technology Equipment Exhibition GBIBS	Once a year	Shenzhen International Convention and Exhibition Center	Shanghai UBM Sinoexpo International Exhibition Co., Ltd.
3	China International Consumer Goods Fair Yacht Show	Once a year	Haikou National Sailing Base Public Pier	Ministry of Commerce of the People's Republic of China, Hainan Provincial People's Government

4	Sanya International Boat Show	Once a year	Sanya International Yacht Center, Nanbianhai International Yacht Dock	Sanya Municipal People's Government
5	China Dalian International Yacht Show	Once a year	Dalian Xinghai Bay Yacht Port	China Institute of Pacific Relations, China Recreational Fishing Association, Liaoning Shipbuilding Industry Association
6	China (Xiamen) International Yacht Show	Once a year	Xiamen Wuyuan Bay Yacht Port	Xiamen Municipal People's Government
7	Taiwan International Boat Show (TIBS)	Once a year	Kaohsiung Exhibition Hall, Taiwan	Kaohsiung City Government
8	Asia Yacht Show - Guangzhou Yacht Show	Once a year	Guangzhou Changzhou Wharf	Guangdong yachting industry Association, Guangdong Economic Investment Promotion Association
9	China (Qingdao) International Boat Show	Once a year	Qingdao Olympic Sailing Center	China Council for the Promotion of International Trade

Chapter 4

Brands and Types of Yachts

Yachts are a luxury watercraft that come in many different brands and types around the world. The brands described in this chapter represent the top level of yacht manufacturing. Whether they fall into the category of luxury yachts, sports yachts, or sailing yachts, these brands embody a focus on innovative design, superior performance, and comfort. This chapter will detail the development history and characteristics of relevant yacht brands, providing a reference for consumers as well as manufacturers to understand the diversity of the yachting market.

Section 1: European yacht brands

Europe is one of the birthplaces of yachts. Yachts originated in the Netherlands in the 17th century, initially used for royal and aristocratic cruises and leisure activities, and later used as gifts between European royal families. Until the 18th century, the nobility and wealthy individuals in European maritime countries competed to convert sailing ships into yachts, which gradually became a trend. Yachts were also used for military and exploration purposes, such as the Dutch using armed yachts in battles with the Portuguese , and the Americans using yachts to convey wartime information. Later, the British added propellers and steam engines to yachts in the 19th century, resulting in power yachts. The modern yachting industry began after World War II. From the 1950s to the present, the world yachting industry has developed according to standard business models, undergoing a classic inheritance and germination period, a growth period, a high-speed development period, and a diversified development period. In the development history of the world yachting industry, many long-established European yacht brands have emerged. This section will briefly introduce six representative yacht brands in Europe.

1. Ferretti

Ferretti is the largest luxury yacht design and manufacturing company in Italy; Founded in 1968, it is one of the most influential and prestigious yacht companies in the world. It has several well-known brands, such as Riva, Pershing, Bertram, and others.

(1) Development History

In 1968, the brothers Alessandro and Norberto Ferretti founded Ferretti Yachts, initially focusing on the design and manufacture of sailing boats. Later, they turned to the market for powerboats and launched a number of popular wooden motor yachts. During the period from 1980 to 2000, Ferretti Yachts began to acquire and integrate other yacht brands, such as Riva and Pershing, forming a multi-brand group company that covers yacht product lines of different lengths and styles from 8 meters to 95 meters. Ferretti Yachts has also been constantly innovating in technology and design, such as introducing the ARG anti-tilt system and ZEM noise reduction system. Since 2000, Ferretti Yachts has undergone a major crisis and restructuring. In 2012, it was acquired by China's Weichai Group, which provided financial and resource support to restore its performance and market share. Ferretti Yachts has also entered the field of business boats and super yachts, enhancing its brand image and profitability. In 2022, Ferretti Yachts was listed on the Hong Kong Stock Exchange, becoming one of the few Italian companies listed there in the past decade.

(2) Brand Features

Ferretti is known for its exquisite craftsmanship, advanced technology, and elegant style. Its brand philosophy is "The sea is a natural studio," which means it constantly draws inspiration and innovation from the ocean. The interior design of Ferretti Yachts highlights Italian style and craftsmanship, as well as the concept of "Just Like Home." The cabin and public areas are equipped with high-end furniture, decorations, and facilities, allowing guests to feel the warmth and happiness of home. Its performance and safety are also first-class, using advanced technologies and solutions such as FSEA technology (Ferretti's advanced sustainable technology), which improves navigation efficiency and environmental performance. The ship is also equipped with various navigation, communication, and entertainment systems, providing convenience and fun for guests.

2. Riva

Riva is a top luxury yacht brand under the Italian Ferretti Group. Founded in 1842, it has a reputation as the "Rolls-Royce on the Water" and is a world-renowned yacht legend. Its representative works include Aquarama, Racer, Corsaro, Scoiattolo, and others.

(1) Development History

The founder of Riva Yachts, Piero Riva, opened the first shipyard on the shores of Lake Iseo in Italy in 1842, mainly engaged in repairing and renovating fishing boats and transport ships. In 1870, Piero's son Ennio Riva took over the shipyard and began manufacturing sailing ships and steamships, also participating in the Italian Unification War and World War I. In 1920, Ennio's son Sperello Riva inherited the shipyard and began producing sports yachts, such as Racer, Corsaro, and Scoiattolo, which won several championships. Later, Sperello's son Carlo Riva became the head of the shipyard in 1950 and was also the founder of the golden age of Riva Yachts. He designed many classic wooden yachts, such as Aquarama, which were favored by celebrities around the world. In 1969, Carlo Riva sold the shipyard to the Whitaker Group of the United States, but remained as the design director, launching a number of fiberglass yachts during the period. In 2000, Ferretti Group acquired Riva Yachts, bringing it back to the hands of Italians and investing heavily in technological innovation and market expansion. In 2004, Riva Yachts established a second production base in La Spezia, specializing in the manufacture of luxury yachts over 60 feet. In 2010, Riva Yachts established a third production base in Ancona for the manufacture of superyachts. Riva Yachts launched the new Riva 88' Folgore (Lightning) series in 2020, showing its vision for the future of yacht design.

(2) Brand Features

Riva's yachts are renowned for their elegant lines, exquisite craftsmanship, and unique style. They have been the first choice of many celebrities and royalty. With a century of accumulated design concepts, as well as a commitment to traditional craftsmanship and continuous innovation, Riva has become synonymous with luxury, comfort, and elegance in the yachting industry. Riva yachts are divided into four categories: open, cool, flybridge, and steel yachts. Open yachts range in length from 8-68 meters, with a streamlined appearance and distinctive personality, suitable for cruising at sea; cool yachts range in length from 27-43 meters, combining the advantages of open and flybridge styles, with both dynamic and comfortable; flybridge yachts range in length from 56-110 meters, are fully customized luxury products, providing spacious space and high-end facilities; steel yachts range in length from 50-100 meters, are drainage-type yachts with innovative appearance and style, and allowing owners to customize interior and home furnishings as they wish.

3. Wally

Wally, a luxury yacht brand in Monaco, is one of the world's leading composite luxury yacht and sailing brands. Established in 1994, it is known for its innovative design and superior performance. Its representative works include Wallypower 118, WHY 58x38, Wallytender X, among others.

(1) Development History

The history of Wally Yachts is a story full of innovation and challenges, which also reflects avant-garde concepts and excellent performance. In 1994, Wally Yachts was founded by Italian businessman Luca Bassani in Monaco, initially focusing on the design and manufacturing of sailing boats. It gained attention for its innovative styling and efficient power. In 1998, Wally Yachts launched its first powered yacht, the Wallypower 60, which was praised for its minimalist style, excellent performance, and comfortable space. In 2003, Wally Yachts launched its most famous yacht,the Wallypower 118, which is a super yacht integrating technology, aesthetics, and environmental protection. It was featured in the movie *Escape from Clonel* and and is known for its unique wedge-shaped appearance, powerful jet propulsion system, and luxurious interior. In 2009, Wally Yachts partnered with French luxury brand Hermès to establish Wally-Hermès Yachts, aiming to create a new way of living on the sea. The company launched a series of conceptual yachts named Why, such as the Why 58x38 and the Why 200, reflecting the emphasis on space, nature, and sustainability. In 2019, Wally Yachts was acquired by the Italian Ferretti Group, becoming a brand under its umbrella, which provided more resources and support, enabling Wally to continue to develop its innovative and avant-garde yacht products. In 2020, Wally Yachts launched its new Wallytender X series, a power yacht designed for high-speed navigation, with a top speed of up to 69 knots. The series includes models of different sizes, such as Wallytender 43X, Wallytender 48X, and Wallytender 58X, all of which use lightweight materials and advanced technology to provide excellent maneuverability and stability.

(2) Brand Features

Wally's yacht combines technology, comfort, and environmental protection, embodying the aesthetics of minimalism. Wally is committed to providing customers with superior performance, safety and reliability, ease of operation, and a perfect product that combines form and function through unique design and technological innovation.

4. Princess

Princess is one of the top yacht manufacturers in the UK. Founded in 1965, it has extensive shipbuilding experience and excellent engineering technology. It is known for its high quality, high performance, and high taste, meeting the needs and preferences of different customers. Its representative models include the Y85, F45, V40, among others.

(1) Development History

Princess Yachts, formerly known as Marine Engineering Limited, was founded by David King in 1965 in Plymouth, England. It initially produced and rented the first "Type 31" yacht. In 1970, Princess Yachts launched the first yacht using glass fiber reinforced plastic shell molding technology, the Princess 32, which sold over 1,200 units and established Princess as a major player in the world yacht market. In 1981, Princess Yachts was acquired by British car manufacturer Rolls-Royce and became a division of the company, beginning to produce larger luxury yachts such as the Princess 37 and Princess 41. In 1987, Princess Yachts was acquired by American investment company Vickers PLC and became a subsidiary, continuing to expand its product line and market share. In 1994, Princess Yachts launched the first fly bridge series yacht, the Princess 45, which was popular for its elegant lines, spaciousness, and high performance. In 2001, Princess Yachts launched the first super yacht, the Princess 95, a luxurious masterpiece measuring 29 meters long and 7 meters wide, with four cabins and five bathrooms. In 2008, the company was acquired by LVMH and became a brand under its umbrella, enjoying more resources and support. In 2016, Princess Yachts launched its M series with the Princess 30M, a modern style yacht that integrates design, craftsmanship, and technology.

(2) Brand Features

The yachts produced by Princess are characterized by their elegant and graceful lines and luxurious interior decoration, giving people a maximum aesthetic experience. Princess perfectly combine modern shipbuilding technology with traditional handicrafts. The hull designed by world-class designers embodies pure British style. Princess Yachts offer has five categories of products: X, Y, F, S and V. The X series adopts the design concept of the super flybridge, providing a new standard for yacht living space. X95 and X80 are representatives of this series, both with spacious flybridge decks and flexible layouts. The Y series is Princess's customized series, with each yacht in the series being uniquely designed and built according to customer needs and preferences. Y95 and Y85 are two classic products in this series, both with exquisite interiors and excellent performance. The classic F series is Princess's flybridge yacht series, with models ranging from F45 to F65, featuring advanced technology, spaciousness, and beautiful styling. The S series is Princess's sports yacht series, with models ranging from S62 to S80, featuring cool and charming design, balanced layout, and comfortable space. It is Princess yacht's fashion choice. The V series is Princess's sport cruise yacht series, with models ranging from V40 to V65, featuring powerful power, beautiful lines, and agile control.

5. Bénéteau

Bénéteau is the largest yacht group in France, founded in 1884. It mainly produces sailing and power boats, as well as powerboats, catamarans, and luxury yachts. Its representative models include Oceanis 51.1, First 53, Swift Trawler 48, among others.

(1) Development History

The history of Bénéteau Yachts dates back to 1884, when Benjamin Bénéteau Founded a small shipyard in Saint Gilles Croix de Vie, mainly providing sailing and power boats for local fishermen. Until 1982, Yachts gradually developed from a small family business into an international group company, constantly innovating and expanding its product line. During this period, Bénéteau Yachts launched many classic ship types, such as the First series, Oceanis series, and Antares series, among others. From 1982 to 2000, BénéteauYachts entered a period of rapid growth, expanding its business to Europe, the United States, Asia, and other regions through acquisitions and partnerships, and acquiring numerous well-known sub-brands such as Arnaud, Lagoon, CNB, among others. During this period, Bénéteau Yachts also launched some Innovative services, such as second-hand boat trading, loan services, and custom services. Since 2000, Bénéteau Yachts has entered a mature and stable period, maintaining its leading position in the sailing and power boat market, constantly improving the quality and performance of its products while also focusing on environmental protection and sustainable development. During this period, Bénéteau Yachts also launched some new ship types, such as the Swift Trawler series and the Bénéteau One design series. (II) Brand Features

Bénéteau is widely acclaimed for its innovative design, reliable performance and reasonable price, and is one of the most popular yacht brands in the world. Its yachts are known for their diverse product lines, innovation and sailing performance, satisfying different customers' imagination of the marine lifestyle. Bénéteau sailing boats are suitable for leisure travel, short trips, cruises or competitions, with an elegant and practical design style that combines advanced technology and traditional craftsmanship, providing owners with a comfortable and safe sailing experience; Bénéteau's powerboats are suitable for fast movement, exploration or enjoying life at sea, with a design style that focuses on performance and innovation, using efficient power systems and intelligent space layouts, providing owners with a flexible and convenient sailing experience. The CNB super custom yacht is a sub-brand of Bénéteau, founded in 1987, specializing in the production of luxury custom yachts over 60 feet, suitable for owners who pursue extreme quality and personalized customization. Its design style reflects high-end and unique features that, combine the expertise of top designers and engineers, providing owners with an extraordinary and unique sailing experience.

6. Lürssen

Lürssen is a German yacht brand with a history of more than 140 years of shipbuilding. It is one of the world's oldest yacht manufacturing companies and is known for producing super luxury yachts and mega yachts. Its representative models include Azzam, Dilbar, Octopus, Tis, Carinthia VII, among others

(1) Development history

Founded in 1875 by Friedrich Lürssen, the company initially engaged in the manufacturing of wooden boats. In 1886, it built the world's first motorboat, demonstrating its hallmark of originality and high quality. In 1925, Lürssen launched its 10,000th ship, a 14-meter-long wooden motor yacht. In 1994, Lürssen developed the "frameless window" technology, which adheres the side windows directly to the fiberglass hull without any steel frame through a special elastic adhesive material. This research design is unprecedented, featuring sleek and complex curves. In 2001, it established a modern comprehensive yacht factory with a total area of 100,000 square meters, of which about 44,000 square meters are dedicated to the manufacturing of yachts over 68 feet. In 2006, Lürssen established a joint venture with cruise ship manufacturer Fincantieri SpA to meet the manufacturing demand for a new generation of mega yachts. In 2013, Lürssen launched the world's longest yacht, the Azzam, with a total length of 180 meters and a speed of 32 knots, known as the "mini-sun." Subsequently, in 2016, it created the world's heaviest yacht, the Dilbar, with a total tonnage of over 15,900 GT and an internal swimming pool with a capacity of 180 cubic meters, which is currently the largest swimming pool installed on a yacht.

(2) Brand Features

Lürssen focuses on innovation and quality, constantly introducing new designs and technologies to provide customers with high-end customized services. Lürssen yachts have unique styles and personalities, each reflecting the preferences and needs of the owner. Its yachts have won numerous world awards and hold a very high position in the industry.

Section 2: Yacht Brands in the Americas

As the world's two major yachting markets today, the Americas and Europe account for more than 90% of the world's yachting market share. In the Americas, the United States is the world's leading yacht consumer, with its yachting sales accounting for more than half of global sales. American yacht companies have experienced significant growth over the past few decades, gradually growing from small family businesses to globally renowned yacht manufacturers. These companies continue to innovate, introducing new technologies and designs to meet customers' constant pursuit of luxury, quality, and performance.

As one of the largest, most dynamic and diverse yacht markets in the world, the Americas are home to many well-known brands such as Four Winds, Chris-Craft, Regal, Sea Ray, and Westport, as well as Grady-White, Monterey, Leopard, and Chaparral, among others.

1. Development History

The American yacht manufacturing industry has undergone a transformation from traditional wooden boat manufacturing to industrialized production, and from small sailing ships to luxury yachts. Technological innovation, performance improvement, and changes in customer demand have all been driving forces for the sustainable development of the industry. With the pursuit of luxury and comfort, American yacht manufacturers continue to play an important role in the global market and are committed to providing innovative designs and superior quality.

(1) The Initial Stage (from the Early 20th Century to the 1940s):

In the early 20th century, the yacht manufacturing industry in the Americas was mainly concentrated in North America. Early yacht manufacturers mainly focused on small sailing ships and wooden yachts, which were mainly used for entertainment and leisure activities. At that time, most yacht manufacturers were small family-owned businesses with relatively traditional production processes.

(2) Technological Innovation and Industrialization (1950s-1970s):

In the 1950s and 1960s, with the development of new materials, ship design, and manufacturing technology, the yacht manufacturing industry underwent significant changes. The use of glass fiber reinforced plastic (FRP) made yacht production more efficient, allowing manufacturers to produce more and larger yachts. At the same time, more powerful engines and ship systems were introduced, improving the performance and reliability of yachts.

(3) The Rise of Luxury Yachts (1980s-1990s):

In the 1980s and 1990s, American yacht manufacturers began to focus on the development of the luxury yacht market. The growing demand for high-end, customized yachts by the wealthy population prompted manufacturers to launch larger and more luxurious yachts to meet customer needs. The design and craftsmanship of yachts further innovated, focusing on comfort and optimization of internal layout.

(4) Innovation and Diversification (2000s to present):

Entering the 21st century, the American yacht manufacturing industry continues to pursue innovation and diversification. The application of new materials, the advancement of ship design, and technological innovation in ship systems have improved the performance and energy efficiency of yachts. At the same time, yacht manufacturers continue to introduce new products to meet customers' demand for personalized and customized services. Electric and hybrid yachts have become an emerging trend, and environmental awareness has gradually gained attention.

2. Market Positioning

The American yachting market has a diverse positioning worldwide, aiming to meet the needs and preferences of different consumers. Whether it is luxury super yachts, medium-sized to large yachts, sports yachts, family entertainment yachts, or low- and mid-price yachts, consumers can find a suitable option for themselves.

(1) Luxury Super Yachts

The Americas are an important market for the manufacture and sale of luxury super yachts. These yachts often exceed 100 feet (30 meters) in length, equipped with luxurious facilities and spacious interiors. They represent the highest level of manufacturing technology, innovative design, and unparalleled luxury experience in the world.

(2) Medium-sized to Large-size Yachts

The medium-size to large-size yacht market is also active in the Americas. Yacht sizes range from 40 feet (12 meters) to 100 feet (30 meters), and typically include sports boats, pleasure boats, and sailing boats. These yachts feature versatility, comfort, and performance, attracting consumers who seek more flexibility and adaptability to different activities and sailing needs.

(3) Sports Yachts and Water Sports Yachts

The yacht market in the Americas also focuses on sports yachts and water sports yachts. These yachts emphasize speed, maneuverability, and sporting performance, and they are suitable for water sports enthusiasts and consumers seeking a sense of excitement. They often use lightweight materials, equipped with powerful engines and advanced technology, allowing for rapid acceleration and flexible maneuvering.

(4) Family Entertainment and Leisure Yachts

The American yacht market also includes boats for family entertainment and leisure. These yachts are usually smaller, providing comfortable interior space, fully equipped kitchens, bedrooms, and seating areas, suitable for family vacations and leisure activities.

(5) Low- and-medium-priced Yachts

In addition to the high-end market, the American yacht market also offers a variety of mid-price and low-price yachts. These yachts are more affordable and suitable for beginners and intermediate yacht enthusiasts, as well as consumers who want to own their own boats but have limited budgets.

3. Characteristics and Development of Yacht Brands

(1) FOUR WINNS

Four Winns Yachts is a yacht manufacturing company headquartered in the United States, founded in 1962. It stands out in the yachting industry for its superior craftsmanship, stylish appearance, and good sailing performance. Their yachts represent quality, comfort, and reliability, providing owners with a luxurious and satisfying water experience.

1. Development History

Four Winns was founded in 1962 in Michigan, USA, and quickly became an important player in the yacht manufacturing industry. In the 1970s, it began producing larger sport and luxury yachts and achieved success in the market. In the 1990s, it introduced advanced hull design and construction technology to improve the performance and quality of yachts. In the 21st century, it launched a series of popular light and leisure boats, including the H series, HD series, RS series and V series. The yacht sizes range from 18-foot speedboats to 38-foot yachts. Four Winns enjoys a high reputation worldwide and is always committed to continuously improving product quality and customer satisfaction to meet the needs of different boat owners.

2. Brand Features

The characteristics of Four Winns yachts are: exquisite craftsmanship, using advanced shipbuilding technology and high-quality materials to ensure that each yacht has excellent craftsmanship and durability; stylish appearance, focusing on innovative design, attracting the eye of the owner with a stylish, modern, elegant appearance. The yachts have spacious interiors, providing a comfortable living and entertainment environment for the owner and passengers, emphasizing functionality while taking into account comfort and practical functions. With a focus on ship design and hull shape, Four Winns vessels provide excellent navigation performance, stability, and controllability.

(2) Chris-Craft

Chris-Craft is a yacht manufacturing company headquartered in Sarasota, Florida, in the southern United States. Established in 1874, it is known as one of the oldest and most influential yacht brands in the world, with 72 agents worldwide. With its unique combination of classic and modern styles, as well as its exquisite craftsmanship and superior ship performance, it has always been popular among boat owners.

1. Development History

Chris-Craft was founded in Michigan, USA in 1874, initially manufacturing wooden boats. From the 1920s to the 1950s, it began to manufacture high-quality wooden sports and leisure boats worldwide, becoming a representative of the era. From the 1960s to the 1970s, it began to use new glass fiber composite materials and shifted to the production of fiberglass yachts,constantly introducing more new models. Since the 1980s,, it has launched more luxury yacht and sports boat series, including the Corsair, Launch, Catalina, and Calypso series, with sizes ranging from 20 feet to 36 feet.

2. Brand Features

Chris-Craft yachts are known for their classic design and unique appearance style, inheriting the elegance and luxury of traditional wooden yachts; exquisite craftsmanship, focusing on the perfect presentation of every detail; and handmade and exquisite craftsmanship. In terms of innovative technology, the company constantly adopts new shipbuilding techniques and advanced materials to improve the performance and reliability of the vessel, as well as comfort and luxury. Chris-Craft is committed to providing comfortable and luxurious interior spaces for owners, providing high-quality customized configurations and marine accessories.

(3) REGAL

REGAL Yachts is a high-end yacht manufacturing company founded in 1969 in the United States. Headquartered in Orlando, Florida, it is now a family-owned business run by the third generation of heirs. REGAL Yachts has won the American Marine Manufacturers Association's Customer Satisfaction Award for five consecutive years. Its products are known for their streamlined design, superior quality, power, safety and durability, fuel economy, and cost performance.

1. Development History

In 1969, REGAL was founded in Orlando, Florida, USA, starting with the manufacturing of small fiberglass boats and speedboats. From the 1970s to the 1980s, the product line was gradually expanded, and different types and sizes of yachts were launched, including maintenance boats, sports boats, and luxury yachts. In the 21st century, REGAL is committed to technological innovation and product development, launching more luxury yacht and sports boat series, and expanding their market share worldwide. Their product series include the LX series, the LS series, the SX series and the Fastrac series. Today, REGAL yachts enjoy a high reputation in the industry for their excellent design, high performance and overall quality. They constantly pursue innovation and excellence, with the aim of providing owners with a pleasant sailing experience and luxurious marine life.

2. Brand Features

The characteristics of REGAL yachts mainly include: innovative design, focusing on the balance between practicality and aesthetics, providing comfortable and luxurious yacht experiences; high performance, focusing on marine technology and engineering, committed to providing superior performance, maneuverability and fuel efficiency. REGAL also uses advanced propulsion systems and hull designs to enhance navigation performance and comfort; the yachts are built with spacious and well-designed internal layout, providing comfortable and luxurious living and entertainment space for owners and passengers. The firm is committed to providing reliable and high-quality yachts for owners, using high-quality materials and strict manufacturing standards to ensure that each yacht has durability and reliability. REGAL yachts attach importance to customer satisfaction, providing comprehensive pre-sale and after-sales services to ensure that owners receive good support and experience in the process of purchasing, using and maintaining their yachts.

(4) Sea Ray

Sea Ray is the world's largest high-end yacht manufacturer, founded by C.N. "Connie" Ray in Tennessee in 1959. Producing more than 40 models of yachts ranging from 17 to 60 feet, Sea Ray vessels are widely acclaimed for their luxury, comfort, and reliability. They continue to introduce industry-leading products and provide comprehensive after-sales service and support, providing owners with an exceptional yacht experience.

1. Development History

In 1959, Sea Ray Yacht, founded in Tennessee, USA, initially produced sailing boats and finished toys. In the 1960s, Sea Ray gradually turned to yacht manufacturing and became a well-known brand for high-quality sports yachts, achieving breakthroughs in appearance and functionality. In the 1970s, Sea Ray continued to expand its product line, introducing more styles and sizes of yachts to meet the needs of different markets and customers. Currently, Sea Ray enjoys a high reputation worldwide and continues to provide innovative, luxurious, and reliable yachts for boat owners. Their yachts continue to make progress in design and functionality to respond to changes and demands in the market and industry.

2. Brand Features

Sea Ray yachts are known for their luxury and comfort. The company is committed to creating vessels with exquisite interior spaces, equipped with high-quality decorations and facilities, providing comfortable and elegant yacht experiences. Sea Ray integrates innovative technology into the design and manufacturing process, constantly introducing new products and features to provide advanced marine technology and optimal navigation performance. Its product lines are diverse, including sports yachts, speedboats, and luxury yachts, all featuring high-end materials and carefully assembled components to ensure quality and durability.

(5) Westport

Westport yachts are known for their high quality, luxury, and sailing performance. These factors make them one of the world's top yacht brands. Not only do they manufacture yachts, but they also provide after-sales service and attentive support for boat owners.

1. Development History

In 1964, Westport Yachts was founded in Washington State, USA. Initially, it mainly engaged in the construction of commercial ships and fishing boats. In the 1980s, it began to turn to the manufacture of luxury yachts, and at this time began to receive recognition and appreciation. In the 1990s, it launched a series of luxury yachts ranging from 98 feet to 130 feet in length, expanding its influence in the yacht market. Currently, Westport Yachts continues to grow and develop, and has been committed to providing yachts for high-end boat owners. Westport Yachts is committed to continuous improvement and innovation to adapt to market demand and provide customers with superior products and services.

2. Brand Features

Westport Yachts prides itself on customized manufacturing, designed to create unique yachts that meet the tastes of the owners based on their individual needs and preferences, making each Westport vessel unique and reflecting a sense of dignity and luxury. The company's yachts also focus on navigation performance, striving to provide excellent stability, maneuverability and fuel efficiency. Westport's yachts are equipped with advanced hull design and propulsion systems to ensure excellent performance under different navigation conditions.

Section 3: Chinese Yacht Brands

1. Background and Development History of Chinese Yacht Brands

Yachts originated in China relatively early, and the original styles of yachts there are completely different from those in the West. For example, the painted boat and dragon boat are ancient Chinese yachts. During the 12th Five-Year Plan period, the yachting industry was listed as a strategic emerging industry with a focus on development, so it received strong support from national policies. At the same time, with the rapid development of China's economy, people's living standards are constantly improving, and the demand for leisure tourism is also increasing. Against this background, Chinese yacht brands are gradually emerging.

The development history of Chinese yacht brands can be traced back to around 1992, when some Taiwanese and American yacht manufacturers began to consider developing in the Chinese Mainland due to the devaluation of the US dollar, the rising price of foreign labor, China's reform and opening up, and other factors. During this period, only a few foreign-funded factories in coastal areas of Fujian and Guangdong began to build yachts, and the size of the boats was only 30-40 feet.

After nearly 20 years of hard work, China's yachting industry has developed rapidly. By 2008, Chinese yacht exports had expanded from the United States to Italy, France, and other places, and the market price of a typical vessel rising from more than US$100,000 to more than US$1million, with the size of the ship exceeding 60 feet. By 2018, the Chinese-made luxury yacht Fantasy was launched, currently the largest super yacht in Asia.

In general, the development history of Chinese yacht brands is a history of gradual maturity and growth. Although there were many difficulties and setbacks in the early days, the rapid development of China's yacht manufacturing industry in recent years has proved the strength and potential of Chinese-made yachts.

2. Characteristics of Chinese Yacht Brands and Product Design

(1) Yi Hong - Xiamen Yi Hong Group Investment Co., Ltd.

Yi Hong Yacht is a Chinese yacht brand. Its product line includes the luxury yacht business platform, SeaStella flagship class business yachts, and the ultimate business travel car known as the land yacht, Kaijun RV. These products focus on quality, innovation, and practicality in design. For example, the SeaStella flagship business yacht combines technology and comfort, with spaciousness and top-level configuration to meet the needs of high-end business people.

(2) Sunbird - Yaguang Technology Group Co., Ltd.

Sunbird has three major product lines: yachts, business yachts, and special yachts.

In terms of its design, the appearance of the Sunbird Yacht is smooth and elegant, while paying attention to practicality to adapt to the diverse needs of today's market. Its internal layout is reasonable and comfortable, focusing on space utilization and functional design, so that tourists can enjoy the best travel experience on board. Sunbird yachts use high-quality, with attention paid to environmental protection and sustainable development. Sunbird Yacht's power systems are strong and stable, ensuring the safety and comfort of tourists on the sea. Their vessels are equipped with various entertainment facilities such as KTV and swimming pools. Sunbird Yachts are also equipped with various safety facilities and equipment to ensure the safety of tourists on board. Comfort is one of its main qualities, with every detail from seats to beds carefully designed to provide the best travel experience.

(3) Allegro- Fujian Allegro Yacht Industrial Co., Ltd.

Allegro Yacht is a yacht brand that focuses on first-time boat buyers and yacht operating companies as its main target markets. TheAllegro Raider35 is its main product. This is a small yacht for family experience, sea fishing, business activities, and youth parties. Known as the "King of Space," it is compact in shape but rich in functions, Its unique combination of axe-shaped bow and glider makes it a stable, low-resistance, and energy-efficient vessel during navigation. In addition, its simple design style highlights the simplicity and fashion style of Northern Europe. As for design features, the Allegro Raider35 is very modern. Its exterior design is elegant, with smooth and dynamic lines, which conforms to modern aesthetic concepts. Its interior design is also very exquisite, with luxurious details. The design focuses on the needs of guests' comfort and business social functions, which makes the Allegro Raider35 yacht not only beautiful in appearance, but also very practical.

(4) Pride Yacht - CIMC Raffles Yacht Co., Ltd.

Pride Yacht is a high-end brand from CIMC Raffles Yacht Co., Ltd., a company that focuses on the design, manufacturing, and marketing of large luxury yachts. Since its launch in 2013, the brand has delivered a number of large luxury yachts, including the 88.5-meter-long Fantasy.

The design style of Pride Yachts is very modern, focusing on streamlined design, emphasizing rounded curves and curved structures, which is not only reflected in the appearance of the hull, but also space and layout inside the boat. Its design aims to give passengers a smooth and comfortable feeling. Pride Yacht pays great attention to the exquisite design of space and height in the design process, creating a spacious and comfortable space experience through clever layout and design. Pride Yacht also pays great attention to functionality in the design process as well as to the unity of details and integrity in the design process.

(5) Jingsui - Chongqing Jingsui Ship Manufacturing Co., Ltd

Jingsui Yacht Manufacturing Co., Ltd. is a company dedicated to providing high-quality and diverse boats for domestic and foreign customers. It mainly produces and operates various types of fiberglass boats, such as high-speed boats, leisure boats, fishing boats, passenger ships, assault boats, sanitation boats, and other series.

Jingsui Yacht's products integrate modern design and exquisite production techniques. Specifically, the company will use targeted design and production based on different boat uses and functional requirements. For example, for business boats that require fast navigation and good maneuverability, the company will adopt streamlined hull design and high-performance propulsion systems.

The business yacht is one of the representative products of Jingsui Yacht. This yacht has excellent hull lines and has been verified by the National Marine Laboratory of the United States through towing model tests, with excellent speed and seakeeping performance. Its hull structure is made of high-strength fiberglass materials and is produced using advanced methods of vacuum bag forming.

Jingsui Yacht also focuses on improving the comfort and safety of its products. For example, the official yacht is equipped with German-made elastic shock-absorbing seats for super-speed boats and high-speed driving helmets with a radio communication system, which facilitate the driving of the yacht and improve the safety of navigation.

(6) Huaying - Hangzhou Huaying Yacht Co., Ltd.

The product line of the Huaying Yacht brand includes flybridge yachts, sports yachts, leisure yachts, and work yachts. The design and manufacturing of these yachts comply with the latest technical standards of the international shipbuilding industry.

In the design of Huaying yachts, a focus is made on integrating aesthetics, ergonomics, and performance to create yachts that are both beautiful and practical, while meeting the individual needs of customers.

For example, Huaying's flybridge yachts are designed with full consideration for comfort and wide views. The flybridge area is spacious and can accommodate several passengers to enjoy the sea view. The cockpit of the flybridge yacht is also designed to be very spacious, providing a good driving environment for the driver.

Huaying's sports yachts use advanced waterjet propulsion systems and high-horsepower engines, which can provide strong power and excellent handling performance.

(7) Hongshuangxi - Shanghai Hongshuangxi Yacht Co., Ltd.

The product line of the Hongshuangxi brand covers a variety of types and styles of yachts, including the classic series, fashion business series, and large luxury series. he design concept of Hongshuangxi yachts focuses on innovation and practicality. Among the classic series of Hongshuangxi, the Alaska 42-65-foot single-station and double-station medium-size yachts are favored by customers for their stability and power. These yachts adopt modern hull design and high-quality materials, providing a comfortable, safe, and durable sailing experience.

Hongshuangxi Yacht also focuses on fashionable and elegant design. In the fashion business series, the 45- and 48-foot Gianetti yachts have attracted much attention for their unique shape and elegant interior design. The exterior lines of these yachts are smooth and dynamic, showing a modern and stylish atmosphere. At the same time, their interior spaces are spacious and comfortable, providing a luxurious sailing experience.

Hongshuangxi Yacht also committed to building large luxury series yachts, such as Navetta 80-foot and Cortenzo 86-foot yachts. These large yachts fully reflect the high quality and unique taste of Hongshuangxi Yacht in their design. They have spacious space, luxurious interiors, and advanced functional facilities, such as large living rooms, separate master suites, and spacious storage space. In addition, these yachts also pay attention to details, such as exquisite furniture, elegant lighting, and high-quality decorative materials.

In short, the product and design features of Hongshuangxi Yacht can be summarized as innovative, practical and luxurious. In the design and manufacturing process, Hongshuangxi Yacht focuses on details and quality control, and is committed to providing customers with a unique, high-quality, comfortable and elegant sailing experience.

In addition, China's yacht brands also include Shengshi, Ouren yachting industry, Shenzhen Yacht and so on, all of which have unique design features.

3. Market Performance and Competitiveness of Chinese Yacht Brands

Although the development of China's yachting industry has experienced ups and downs in the past few decades, in recent years, with the economic development and the increasing consumption demand of consumers for yachts, the market performance and competitiveness of China's yacht brands have gradually improved.

The market size of China's yachting industry in 2022 was about CNY¥2.716 billion, including CNY¥1.123 billion for private yachts and CNY¥1.593 billion for institutional and corporate yachts. This figure indicates that China's yacht market has considerable scale and potential.

In terms of market performance, Chinese yacht brands such as Dongji Guanglian, Chariot, Seaflo, Yinglang, Hangkai, and Yili, have achieved a certain visibility and competitiveness in the market. These brands cover different types and price ranges of yachts, ranging from inflatable rubber yachts, to luxury yachts.

In terms of competitiveness, Chinese yacht brands are also gradually improving. On the one hand, with the improvement of domestic enterprises'yacht production technology and the continuous expansion of productivity, the domestic yacht production has grown rapidly, and the price advantage has gradually emerged. On the other hand, Chinese yacht brands are also gradually attaching importance to brand building and service improvement, constantly improving product quality and after-sales service level, which enhance consumer trust and loyalty. At present, the competitiveness of China's large yacht manufacturing industry in the international market is at a low-medium level, and the competitiveness and market share of China's large yacht brands in the market need to be further improved. Although the market size and potential are huge, Chinese yacht brands still need to increase investment in product innovation, brand building, and talent cultivation to enhance their core competitiveness and better meet the needs of consumers and market changes.

4. Development Trends of Yachts in China

The yachting industry in China is gradually transforming towards mass yachts. With the progress of society and the increase of people's consumption level, the demand for mass yachts is also increasing. A series of policies such as the Guiding Opinions on Promoting Yacht Tourism issued by the state are also guiding and supporting the development of mass yachts. The yachting industry in Hainan is also developing rapidly. According to the Hainan Provincial yachting industry Development Plan Outline (2021-2025), by 2025, the yacht infrastructure service network will be further improved, and the number of yacht dock berths (including dry berths) will break through 3,394. At the same time, with the improvement of domestic yacht production technology and the expansion of production capacity, domestic yacht production is growing rapidly, and market demand is also increasing. It is expected that in the next few years, the demand for China's yacht market will continue to maintain a growth trend.

In the future, the yachting industry, especially the rental service, will become an important way to promote mass consumption of yachts in China. With the improvement of relevant laws and regulations, the prospects for yacht rental in China are promising.

In the future, it is expected that with the continuous optimization of the yacht consumption structure, small- and medium-size yachts and domestic yachts will become the main development direction of yacht consumption in China. Atthe same time, with the upgrading of consumption, the yacht market will be further subdivided, and yacht products such as fishing boats and sailing boats will play an inestimable fundamental role in cultivating the yacht consumption market Yacht leasing will also enable more urban white-collar workers to make contact with yachts, understand them, and enjoy the life on the sea, while stimulating domestic demand, forming economies of scale, and promoting the promotion of yachts in China.

5. International Market of Chinese Yacht Brands

The performance of Chinese yacht brands in the international market is gradually improving. Although there is still a gap between Chinese yacht brands and some internationally renowned brands in terms of technology and quality, domestic manufacturers are gradually increasing their investment in research and development and brand building, improving product quality and competitiveness.

Some Chinese yacht brands such as Dongji Guanglian, Chariot, Seaflo, Yinglang, Hangkai, and Yiliare also selling and servicing in the international market, where they have some visibility and market share. The products of these brands are not only competitive in price, but also recognized and praised by consumers in terms of performance and quality. In addition, some domestic yacht companies have invested in the international market and have exchanged and cooperated with foreign yacht brands in terms of technology and management, which has also enhanced the international competitiveness of Chinese yacht brands.

Of course, Chinese yacht brands still need to further enhance their brand awareness and image in the international market, strengthen product innovation and technology research and development, and meet the international market's demand for high-quality and high-performance yachts. At the same time, it is also necessary to strengthen management and marketing in the international market, improve after-sales service levels, and enhance customer satisfaction and loyalty.

Section 4: Yacht Brands from Other Countries

In addition to the cruise brands from Europe, the Americas, and China, the yacht brands of other Asian countries and some Arab countries have also emerged in recent years. These countries, with their unique geographical locations and cultural backgrounds, have injected new vitality and innovation into the yachting industry. Asian countries such as Japan, South Korea, Singapore, and Oceania countries such as Australia, with their rich manufacturing experience and technological strength, have gradually become important forces in the yacht manufacturing industry. Some of the world's most luxurious yachts are being manufactured in the United Arab Emirates, and yachts made in Australia have also begun to enter the international market, competing with traditional European and American brands. This section will briefly introduce representative yacht brands in Japan, South

Korea, Singapore, Australia, and the United Arab Emirates.

1. Yacht Brands in Japan

As an island country, Japan has abundant marine resources and a culture of water sports, and yachting projects are becoming increasingly popular, with many well-known yacht brands.

(1) Development History

The development history of Japanese yacht brands can be traced back to the early 20th century, when yachts were mainly purchased and used by wealthy businessmen and aristocrats. However, after the outbreak of World War II, the yachting industry in Japan almost stagnated. After the war, with the recovery of the economy and the increased demand for leisure activities, the yachting industry began to gradually recover. From the 1950s to the 1960s, some small yacht brands began to emerge, mainly producing small sailing boats and rowing boats. These brands mainly targeted wealthy amateur maritime enthusiasts and club members. By the 1970s, Japanese yacht brands began to emerge. Some well-known brands such as Matsushita Yacht, Japan Shipbuilding, and Japan Yacht Association began to produce and promote various types of yachts. During this period, the yachting industry in Japan received government support and encouragement, and the yacht market gradually expanded. After entering the 21st century, Japanese yacht brands continued to develop. As people's demand for luxury yachts increased, some high-end yacht brands began to emerge in the Japanese market. At the same time, innovative products such as Japanese electric yachts also began to materialize.

(2) Brand Introduction

1. Yamaha: Yamaha is a company with more than 50 years of shipbuilding history. Since the second half of the 1950s, Yamaha has started to research and develop the new material FRP (glass fiber reinforced plastic) that was highly regarded at the time. In the 1960s, Yamaha began to produce and sell a variety of marine products such as yachts and fishing boats made of FRP. Through continuous research and development combined with market demand, especially in the field of marine engines, Yamaha has continued to grow and develop. Today, Yamaha yachts are widely recognized for their luxury and high performance and are widely used in more than 180 countries and regions around the world. Yamaha's yacht design emphasizes comfort and sports performance. The company has also introduced new products, such as water motorboats.
2. Mitsubishi Heavy Industries Yacht (Mitsubishi Heavy): Mitsubishi Heavy Industries Yacht,a brand of Mitsubishi Heavy Industries Co., Ltd., focuses on designing and manufacturing high-quality yachts. Its yacht product line is very rich, including luxury yachts, sports yachts, business yachts and other types, to meet the needs of different customers. The luxury yacht series is Mitsubishi Heavy Industries' flagship product, famous for its

exquisite craftsmanship, high-standard quality, and personalized design. These luxury yachts use the most advanced shipbuilding technology and materials, focusing on details and interiors, to provide spacious and comfortable interiors and an excellent navigation experience. Mitsubishi's sports yachts are also highly sought after. These yachts are fashionable in design and excellent in performance, suitable for high-speed navigation and marine sports. Business yachts are characterized by practicality and comfort, suitable for various purposes such as business meetings and team activities.

2. Yacht Brands in South Korea

Although the yachting industry in South Korea started late, its brands have gradually emerged with their own unique styles and manufacturing technologies through continuous exploration and research and development, becoming an important part of the global yacht market.

(1) Development History

The development of Korean yacht brands began in the early 1980s, when the Korean government began to encourage and develop the yachting industry. Many shipbuilding companies and private enterprises have participated. In the early days, Korean yachts mainly imported technology and design from Europe and the United States, using materials such as glass fiber and vinyl fiber, with beautiful appearance and luxurious interior configuration. After entering the 21st century, the Korean yachting industry gradually matured and began to develop independently. Some Korean yacht brands began to explore their own design and manufacturing styles, gradually breaking away from the imitation of European and American yachts. These brands began to focus on research and development and innovation, and more yacht products with Korean characteristics were introduced. Today, Korean yacht brands have become an important part of the global yacht market, with product lines including large luxury yachts, small recreational yachts, high-speed boats, and other models. Well-known Korean yacht brands include those from Hyundai Heavy Industries and Samsung Heavy Industries, LG,. These brands continue to innovate in design and manufacturing, driving the sustainable development of the Korean yachting industry.

(2) Brand Introduction

1. Hanjin Heavy Machinery (HHM): As a subsidiary of South Korea's Hyundai Heavy Industries, Hanjin Heavy Machinery was established in 1972. It has become a leader in the yacht manufacturing industry in South Korea. HHM offers various types of yachts, including large luxury yachts, sports yachts, and high-speed yachts. The company has extensive experience and technology in yacht manufacturing, and constantly introduces new designs and technologies to meet market demands.
2. Daewoo Shipbuilding & Marine Engineering (DSME): Founded in 1977, DSME is a subsidiary of South Korea's Daewoo Shipbuilding & Marine Engineering Co., Ltd. The company is a globally renowned manufacturer of ships and marine engi-

neering equipment, providing various types of vessels and marine engineering equipment, including yachts. DSME's yacht product line includes large luxury yachts, high-speed passenger ships, and sailing ships, which are known for their high-quality materials and exquisite craftsmanship.

3. Samsung Heavy Industries (SHI): Established in 1972, Samsung Heavy Industries is a well-known manufacturer of ships and marine engineering in South Korea and around the world, providing various types of vessels and equipment, including yachts. SHI's yacht product line includes large luxury yachts, small- and medium-size yachts, sports yachts. The companyis known for its advanced technology and innovative design.

3. Yacht Brands in Singapore

(1) Development History

Singapore's yachting industry dates back to the early 20th century, when some international yacht brands began setting up branches there and began promoting and selling their products locally. At that time, British and European aristocrats and other wealthy individuals began purchasing yachts in Singapore for entertainment and business travel. Over time, Singapore gradually became one of the luxury yacht centers in Asia. For example, Singapore's Rendition Yacht Company has supplied many super yachts to Asian royalty and wealthy individuals, and Singapore has gradually become an important yacht manufacturing center in Southeast Asia. In recent years, the development of the Singapore yachting industry has received strong support from the government and has won the favor of tourists. The first Singapore Yacht Festival was held in 2019 and it has become one of the important events in the Singapore yachting industry, which is of great significance for promoting the development of the Asian yachting industry in general. The Nirup Island yacht marina under construction is expected to provide up to 70 new berths upon completion, aiming to provide more convenient facilities to meet the increasing demand for yachts.

(2) Brand Introduction

Singapore is a vibrant and innovative yacht manufacturing center with some excellent local yacht brands:

1. Grand Banks Yachts: Established in 1966, this is one of the most famous yacht brands in Singapore, with a focus on manufacturing high-quality long-distance ocean yachts, including luxury sailing boats and classic-style motor boats. Vessels produced by Grand Banks Yachts are known for their excellent navigation performance, exquisite craftsmanship, and classic design. Their yachts are made of high-quality materials, providing luxurious interiors and comfortable living spaces, while also focusing on energy conservation and environmental protection.
2. Megaway Engineering & Trading Pte Ltd: Megaway is a comprehensive yacht manufacturing and service company headquartered in Singapore. They provide one-stop services such as yacht manufacturing, maintenance, upgrade,

and management. Megaway has its own yacht brand, focusing on quality and innovation, to provide customers with high-quality yacht products. Their yacht design is unique, focusing on details and comfort, while also incorporating modern technology and environmental protection concepts.

3. Sealion is a Singapore-based yacht brand founded in 2005, specializing in the manufacture and sales of luxury yachts. Its yachts are popular for their innovative design, high-quality materials, and excellent craftsmanship. Sealion's yacht product line includes sailing and power boats ranging from 38 to 68 feet, suitable for family use and marine activities. Sealion's designers focus on functionality, comfort, and safety, while pursuing simplicity and modernity. Its ts yacht product line includes models such as the 370, 430, 500, and 600, as well as customized private yachts. In addition to manufacturing and selling yachts, Sealion also provides yacht rental and maintenance services, providing customers with a full range of yacht experience and support.

4. Yacht Brands in Australia

(1) Development History

Yacht manufacturing in Australia dates back to the early 20th century, and it has gradually emerged and grown with the continuous development of the marine environment and maritime tradition. In the early days, the focus was mainly on the manufacture of sailing boats, but after World War II, Australian designers began to use advanced technology and materials to produce high-performance yachts. Well-known brands such as Riviera and Maritimo focus on navigation performance, luxurious interiors, and innovative design, which have won the favor of customers both at home and abroad. In the second half of the 20th century, multi-hulled boats gradually emerged, such as the ones produced by Seawind Catamarans. Multi-hulled boats have the advantages of navigational stability, optimum space utilization and overall performance, which are popular among customers. Australian yacht manufacturers have also made significant achievements in technological innovation, focusing on developing new hull designs, navigation systems, and deploying materials to improve the performance and comfort of yachts. Australian yacht brands have performed well in international competitions and have won several awards, further enhancing their reputation and popularity.

(2) Brand Introduction

1. Riviera: For more than 30 years, Riviera has been luxury yacht manufacturing brand in Australia, headquartered in the Gold Coast. Its facilities boast of more than 300,000 square feet of manufacturing space. This brand is famous for manufacturing high-quality and high-standard yachts and providing quality services. Their product line is very rich, including a flybridge series, a sports yacht series, and a sports speedboat series. Riviera focuses on personalized design, and each yacht is carefully designed and manufactured to provide customers with the best sea experience. Over the years, Riviera's

products have won numerous awards.

2. Ocean Master: Ocean Master Boats in Melbourne was founded in 2002. It has always adhered to the concept of "handmade and rigorous craftsmanship" to create boats. Ocean Master boats are made of raw materials, which greatly ensures the integrity and robustness of the hull. In the interests of maintaining and improving quality, Ocean Master's fiberglass yachts are all customized products. Its 7-year warranty for the quality of the boat is rare in the yachting industry.

5. Yacht brands in Dubai, United Arab Emirates

(1) Development History

The yachting industry in Dubai originated in the 1960s, when Dubai's economy began to rise as it became an important commercial and tourism center. With the increase in oil revenue, the wealthy class in Dubai began to seek more luxurious and unique transportation vehicles, and yachts became their first choice. Initially, the yachting industry in Dubai mainly relied on imports, from shipyards in Europe, the United States, and other places. However, with the development of Dubai's economy, the country began to establish its own yacht manufacturing industry. In 1974, Dubai established its own shipyard, Dubai Marina Yacht Services, marking the official start of the yachting industry there. In the 21st century, with the increase in oil revenue and the general prosperity of the global economy, Dubai has become an important player in the global luxury yacht market. Many world-renowned yacht brands have established branches or agencies in Dubai to provide customized, high-quality yacht services for the wealthy.

(2) Brand Introduction

Gulf Craft: Established in 1982 with its headquarters in Dubai, Gulf Craft is one of the most well-known yacht manufacturers in the UAE. It focuses on manufacturing high-quality motor boats and luxury yachts. Its Nomad series includes luxury long-distance yachts with spacious interiors and high-quality luxury decoration, providing a comfortable living experience. The Oryx series features yachts that use advanced hull design and power systems, with excellent acceleration performance and stability. The Silvercraft series includes family and leisure yachts that are compactly designed, suitable for day cruising, entertainment, and water sports.

Gulf Craft employs some of the world's top yacht designers to integrate modern style and luxury elements into the appearance and interior of the vessels. Gulf Craft's yachts have a streamlined shape, large glass windows, spacious deck space, and luxurious interior decoration. Its yachts have been favored by customers worldwide for their superior design, high-quality craftsmanship, and reliable performance. Their products have won multiple awards and recognition on the international stage. Through continuous innovation and by meeting customer needs, Gulf Craft has achieved an important position in the yacht manufacturing industry in the UAE and around the world.

Chapter 5

Yacht Consumer Market and Market Structure

Although the history of pleasure boats can be traced back to ancient Egypt, the term "yacht" originated in the Dutch language as jaght (modern Dutch: yacht) in the 14th century. In those days, the Dutch used small boats to hunt pirates, while wealthy ship owners began to use their small boats for pleasure. Since then, our understanding of the difference between boats and yachts is its purpose: pleasure (American Sailing Association, 2020). Since the 14th century, many European aristocrats, monarchs, and nobles have owned and used yachts. Later, the industrial revolution made it possible for the first non-royal but wealthy upper classes to spend their leisure time on yachts, which by then were stronger, better, and more advanced.

Over the past 150 years, several important factors have changed the landscape of the yachting industry, Lighter synthetic materials such as fiberglass and steel have replaced wood as the primary component, and the source of power has also shifted from mainly wind power to steam engines and internal combustion engines. Yacht racing, also known as regattas, has become more accessible for people from different social classes. Since the end of World War II, more and more privately owned luxury yachts have entered the market. These luxury superyachts include the Savannah owned by Swedish-Canadian entrepreneur Lukas Lundin in Geneva; the Predator owned by Russian entrepreneur Iskander Kakhramonovich Makhmudov; and the Aquarius owned by American real estate tycoon Steve Wynn.

China's yachting industry is currently in a stage of rapid growth. With the continuous development of domestic tourism there, the ownership of yachts in China continues to rise, increasing to 26,500 in 2022. It is expected that with the continuous increase in per capita disposable income in China and the post-pandemic recovery of the overall tourism industry, the ownership of yachts in China will continue to grow. Hainan, the largest special economic zone and the only tropical island province in China, possesses unique resources and policy advantages for the development of the yachting industry. By the end of June 2023, Hainan province has built and operated 13 yacht marinas and 2,286 berths. Hainan has also successively published an Implementation Plan for the Construction and Development of the Innovation Pilot Zone for the Reform and Development of the yachting industry in Hainan Province and the Development Plan Outline for the yachting industry in Hainan Province (2021-2025).

By 2025, the yachting industry chain system in Hainan will be basically formed. The level of yacht manufacturing and service will be in line with international standards; the consumption scenario of yachts will be more diverse; the safety, green and intelligent development level of the yachting industry will be at the top in China; and internationally renowned yacht brands will gradually enter Hainan. Yacht consumption will become a new growth point of urban consumption asthe yachting industry will become the leading industry in the construction of Hainan Free Trade Port. Hainan will become the most attractive yacht consumption location in China

Section 1: Yacht Tourism

In the early 21st century, yacht tourism has developed greatly and begun to play an important role in leisure activities worldwide It has provided more income for the overall economy and created new employment opportunities. More and more people are willing to invest in buying their own yachts or renting yachts in order to spend leisure time on the sea.

The development status of yacht tourism can be viewed from the following aspects:

Expanding market size: The market size of yacht tourism is constantly expanding, attracting more and more tourists and investors. Many countries and regions are actively developing the yacht tourism industry, providing relevant facilities and services to attract tourists.

Diversified destinations: The destinations for yacht tourism are also becoming more diverse. In addition to traditional seaside resorts, some emerging destinations such as the Caribbean, the Mediterranean, and Pacific islands have also become popular choices for yacht tourism.

Professional services: With the development of yacht tourism, related services and facilities have also been upgraded and professionalized. Yacht tourism companies provide a variety of customized services, including yacht rental, crew services, and route planning to meet the needs of tourists.

Sustainable development: Yacht manufacturers and tourism operators have begun to pay attention to environmental protection and resource management, taking measures to reduce the impact on marine ecosystems and promote sustainable yacht tourism development.

However, yacht tourism also faces some challenges. These include high costs, environmental impacts, and safety issues. In order to promote the sustainable development of yacht tourism, it is necessary for the government, business, and academic sectors to work together to formulate relevant policies and regulations, and strengthen supervision and management.

Overall, yacht tourism, as a unique form of tourism, is receiving increasing attention and development worldwide. With the advancement of technology and the maturity of the market, yacht tourism is expected to continue to grow and bring new opportunities and challenges to the tourism industry.

1. Concepts of Yacht Tourism

Yachts are vessels designed for travel and sports purposes. They can typically accommodate up to 36 people. Yachting is a free-spirited activity and a relatively expensive pastime. However, with the improvement of a country's standard of living, yachting has taken its place in the field of marine tourism. The difference between yachting and cruise tourism is that yachting does not require regular transportation between ports

Due to different research parameters, the definition and concept of yachting tourism may differ. Mikulic believes that although there is no universally accepted definition of yachting tourism it should be viewed within the broader concept of nautical tourism. Diakomihalis believes that the main function of yachts is to provide users with opportunities for tourism and leisure, which is mainly reflected in the crew's ability to provide sufficient services for yacht users, such as food and water sports guidance. In addition, according to the research of Sariisik, yachts, as medium-sized ships for tourism and sports purposes, can carry up to 36 passengers, and the tourism activities they provide are of great significance to the economy and the creation of employment opportunities. Since the yacht marina is the service provider of yachts, it can be evaluated as the main locus of yacht tourism.

Yao Yunhao (2017), a Chinese scholar, analyzed the concept of yacht tourism, writing that it is "a new form of tourism that integrates sports, navigation, entertainment, leisure, and social interaction. Yacht enthusiasts can control the ship themselves or hire professional drivers, involving yacht cruising, sailing, sports, rowing, kayaking, motorboating and other ocean-friendly activities."

To sum up, yacht tourism refers to a form of tourism that uses yachts as a means of transportation for travel and exploration. Yacht tourism typically involves travel on waters such as oceans, lakes, or rivers, aiming to provide a luxurious, comfortable, and unique travel experience.

Yacht tourism can include various forms, from short-term day trips to long-term sailing adventures either on private yachts or inorganized yacht tourism activities, including such diversions as swimming, diving, fishing, bird watching, or island exploration.

The definition of yacht tourism is also related to luxury and comfort. Yachts are usually equipped with high-end facilities and services, such as luxury rooms, restaurants, spas, and entertainment facilities to ensure that passengers enjoy the highest level of comfort and convenience during their travels. Yacht tourism also provides opportunities for intimate contact with the natural environment, where passengers can enjoy the magnificent scenery of the ocean, feel the freshness of the sea breeze, and the gentle lap of the waves.

Yacht tourism is also connected with environmental protection and sustainable development. In yacht tourism, it is crucial to protect the marine ecosystem and reduce the impact on the environment. Many yacht tourism companies are committed to adopting sustainable business practices, such as using clean energy, reducing waste emissions, and protecting coral reefs and marine life.

2. Characteristics of Yacht Tourism

The temptation of the ocean has been calling for at least 4,000 years since navigators from Taiwan moved south and east to Polynesia and beyond to find new islands. At first, their travels were designed to locate better food sources, more suitable climate and easier living areas—as well as adventure—but now, thousands of people spend their hard-earned money every year to travel. Why do some people choose cruise ships while others choose yachts? In order to better understand yacht tourism, this section focuses on the differences between yacht tourism and cruise tourism.

(1) Personalized Yacht Tourism Services

One of the main differences between these two industries is scale. The size of the boat determines the number of guests and crew, as well as the quantity, quality, and exclusivity of the available facilities on board. Luxury yachts are much smaller in size and have higher prices after economies of scale. They have more expensive per capita features, including salaries, employee-to-guest ratios, and food. This means that their appearance in terms of interior details of space is very high-end, and the ratio of yacht guests to staff is usually 1:1, so the service level is higher and more personalized. According to industry insiders, some luxury yachts have a ratio of 1:2.

Luxury cruise ships are much larger in size, so they are generally more cost-effective overall. The ship is usually designed to be elegant, but also durable enough to withs and use by a large number of passengers. The ratio of guests to crew ranges from 1:1.5 to 1:0.3 for some major cruise ships. However, on average, luxury cruise companies usually offer a ratio of 1:1 to 1:0.4, which means that there is approximately one crew member for every one or two guests (Cruisewatch, 2021). Considering these points, luxury yachts usually cost more than their cruise counterparts, as they offer more exclusivity, privacy, accessibility, and higher levels of service and food quality. Cruise ships also offer other attractive elements that yachts cannot provide due to their size, one of which is the on-board entertainment. The larger the ship, the more choices guests have. Other major desirable options include food and social options.

(2) Identity Prominence

Luxury yachts are usually more expensive than luxury cruise ships. Exclusivity, accessibility, privacy, and higher levels of service come at a price, so a luxury yacht tour affirms one's status. However, taking a luxury cruise ship can also affirm and indicate high status. Cruises have various levels of cabins to choose from, with more expensive and larger cabins offering more facilities and a more "luxurious" experience, which can be experienced through additional spending, such as more attentive cabin attendants and in-cabin perks, priority access to the ship's yachts for disembarkation, and free meals at specialty restaurants.

Most cruise ships offer special concierge

lounges, which provide free facilities only for suite guests. These lounges typically include barista-grade coffee, sparkling water and non-sparkling bottled water, soft drinks, wine, spirits, and other beverages; In the morning, there may be croissants and other fresh cakes; in the afternoon, there may be hand-made smoked salmon sandwiches and mini egg cakes, as well as the chef's specially made macaroon, which are not found anywhere else on the ship. The lounges may also offer the latest high-end magazines, newspapers, and books as well as travel books and elegant coffee-table art books. The staff in the concierge lounges are always trained to the highest level and are capable of meeting any requirements of guests. For example, they will help arrange for guests to have private consultations with the onboard cruise consultant to facilitate booking their next trip. Such lounges provide an opportunity for guests to meet and form social relationships with other high-income guests.

(3) Younger Consumer Groups

Cruises have always been a popular vacation destination for the older generation, but this trend is changing. Currently, different cruise lines cater to different age groups, with elderly guests aged 65 and above preferring to sail on Holland America Line, Cunard Line, and Silversea Line. Couples aged between 40 and 65 mainly enjoy Princess Cruises and Viking Cruises. Royal Caribbean Cruises and Disney are popular with families because they are very suitable for children. Carnival usually does not cater to the luxury crowd, but provides a "party cruise" experience for younger people in the 30-40 age group. This may vary from country to country, but the overall trend is that luxury yachts cannot be stereotyped as to a specific age or nationality, and the only condition for entry is afford ability. Luxury travelers are becoming younger and younger.

(4) High Exclusivity

Due to the space limitations of yachts, few people can stay on luxury yachts. Cruises are much larger and can accommodate more people. The cost of cruises depends on the cabin category. Regardless of the cabin category, most of the vacation experience outside the cabin is the same, as everyone can choose to eat, have entertainment, and use the main lounge on board (except for the lounge reserved for suite guests). By contrast, the experience on a luxury yacht is very unique. Many yachts offer butler-level services, with more one-on-one attention and personalized services, rather than offering a range of services for everyone to choose, as on cruise ships. Yachts tailor personalized services for their guests, which enhances exclusivity. Crew members are expected to meet the wishes of guests, including preparing meals in the middle of the night or arranging for parties at the last minute. Crew members must be experienced to be hired, and they usually participate in additional marine survival and silver service courses to become a steward.

Luxury cruise ships can provide multiple ways to experience exclusivity in a larger ship environment. For example, guests staying in suites can use private cabanas (tent-like seating areas that typically accommodate up to four people) in a specially designated area on the ship, which regular guests cannot use. However, these areas can be accessed by any guest prepared to pay the per-cruise fee, typically \$300 per person per week.

Many cruise lines offer additional perks that are automatically included in the suites, but also charge additional fees to any guests who want to experience these suites. This means that additional exclusive access can be arranged for an additional fee. These services include professional restaurants that offer higher levels of service, usually with an additional fee, as well as on-board hot spring suites, which typically cost around \$200 per couple for a week-long cruise. For some guests in cheaper cabins, these additional luxuries provide a much more exclusive experience than they would receive by booking a suite.

Another factor to consider is the docking location of the ship. Cruises are larger and therefore cannot dock at every port. Due to their smaller size, yachts are usually able to dock in very small ports that are inaccessible to ships. For guests on yachts and cruise ships, the onshore experience is basically the same. Any onshore tours in any port are limited to the services provided in the area. Luxury yachts may receive more exclusive travel by paying additional fees, but cruise ships also offer different levels of travel. For example, passengers can choose to take a bus tour of a nearby city with 40 other guests, or they can choose a private car tour with a driver guide for 2-4 people.

(5) High Privacy

Luxury yachts provide more privacy than luxury cruise ships because the latter are larger and can accommodate more people. Traditionally, luxury yachts provide privacy away from other vacationers and the public, which is highly valued by those in the spotlight. There is also evidence that wealthy tourists prefer to vacation with other wealthy tourists (Batabyal & Yoo, 2020), which can help explain the popularity of renting luxury yachts as well as small cruise ships. The social need to be with one's own elite "tribe" may be significant

3. The Role of Yacht Tourism

With the growth of social wealth, the types of activities related to waterways have also increased significantly. As a product with high economic and social value, yachts can not only provide a new leisure experience, but also promote employment and economic development in tourist destinations. At present, yacht tourism is an entertainment activity that combines leisure, competition, and timeliness. Leisure yachts allow tourists to freely sail to different destinations and enjoy an entertaining lifestyle. The huge economic influence of yacht tourism has gradually been recognized by many governments. Turkey, Greece, Italy, Scotland, Australia, China are among the countries and regions that have developed yacht tourism to create more employment opportunities.

In China, with the continuous increase in disposable income of its citizens, the yacht tourism lifestyle has gradually entered the public's field of vision. In recent years, the Central Government and the State Council have issued a number of policies and regulations on the development of yacht tourism, such as Several Opinions of the State Council on Further Promoting Tourism Investment and Consumption and the newly revised Maritime Traffic Safety Law of the People's Republic of China in April 2021. China's yachting industry has a history of several decades, mainly developing in coastal cities such as Xiamen, Shenzhen, Sanya, Shanghai, Qingdao, Dalian, and Tianjin. After years of fluctuations, the Chinese public's understanding of yachts has become more predictable, and the development and promotion policies issued by the government are gradually being implemented.

As a part of the marine industry, yacht tourism plays an important role in tourism activities and provides important resources for the overall economy. Recognizing the huge potential, the government and private sector are investing heavily in yacht tourism. Many new yacht marinas, both private and state-owned, have been built or are under construction. Tourism companies are investing heavily to increase berths. As a result, yacht tourism in China is expected to expand rapidly in the near future.

(1) The Promotional Function of Yacht Tourism in a Regional Economy

The economic benefits of yacht tourism can bring huge profits to the tourism industry. With the improvement of people's living standards and the continuous expansion of the tourism market, more and more people are willing to choose to travel on water, and yacht tourism emerges as a result. The rental income from yacht tourism mainly includes rent, service fees, and parking fees, all of which play an important role in the development of the tourism industry.

Yacht tourism can also create employment opportunities. The development of yacht tourism requires professional operation management and service teams, thus providing employment opportunities for local residents. In addition, related industries such as yacht manufacturing, repair, and maintenance will also be stimulated, further promoting employment and economic growth.

Finally, yacht tourism can also promote the diversification of local tourism. Traditional tourism resources are often limited to natural landscapes or cultural heritage, but the emergence of yacht tourism brings new elements and vitality to the industry. The promotion of yacht tourism can attract more visitors to the local area, thereby promoting the development of other local industries.

(2) Yachts Improve the Core Competitiveness of Tourism Products

Since the beginning of the 21st century, countries have been promoting yacht tourism to shape a differentiated image of their resources. The tourism industry in various countries currently needs diversification, so yacht tourism is an important project in national industrial planning. Yacht tourism is considered to be a niche product of the tourist sector, so its development must be seen as a necessary strategy to overcome the negative factors of seasonality and spatial intensity on the coast. Developing niche tourism forms such as yacht tourism is also a key factor in coping with the spatial agglomeration of mass tourism. Kalemdaroglu et al. believe that yacht tourism has great potential for development because it meets the needs of freedom while allowing proximity to nature and history, sports and adventure Nowadays, tourists' needs are more complex: they prefer to actively participate in vacations that are sensitive to nature and give them an opportunity to experience adventure. Yacht tourism products are quite suitable for these needs.

Firstly, yacht tourism provides unique experiences and luxury services. Visitors can enjoy luxurious accommodation, food, and entertainment facilities on private yachts, while also enjoying magnificent sea views and marine activities. This luxury experience attracts consumers who seek unique, high-quality tourism experiences.

Secondly, yacht tourism provides personalized and customized services. Visitors can choose different types and sizes of yachts, as well as routes and itinerary arrangements according to their own needs and preferences.

In addition, yacht tourism also provides unique ways of exploring destinations and attractions. Visitors can travel by yacht to some remote islands, beaches and marine protected areas to explore places that are rarely visited. This unique travel style provides visitors with a distinctive experience, allowing them to get close to nature and feel the charm of the ocean.

However, yacht tourism also faces some challenges. The high cost of yacht tourism limits the participation of some consumers. In some cases, yacht tourism has had a negative impact on the environment, especially in terms of marine protection and sustainable development. Therefore, measures need to be taken address these concerns.

In summary, yacht tourism, as a form of high-end tourism, has certain competitive advantages in the market. Its personalized service, and unique way of exploring destinations attract consumers who seek luxury, personalized, and distinctive travel experiences. However, yacht tourism also needs to face challenges such as cost and environmental sustainability to maintain its competitiveness and achieve sustainable development.

(3) Cultural Effects of Yacht Tourism

Though it is often seen as merely a recreational activity, yacht tourism can also be a carrier of cultural communication and interaction.

Cultural exchange: Yacht tourism provides opportunities for people from different cultural backgrounds to communicate and interact. Visitors can learn about the lifestyle, traditions, and values of local residents through contact with them. This cross-cultural exchange helps promote awareness and understanding of cultural diversity.

Cultural preservation: Yacht tourism often involves destinations with historical and cultural value, such as ancient port cities and seaside villages. The preservation and maintenance of these destinations require funding and attention, and the development of yacht tourism can bring economic benefits to these places, thus promoting the protection of cultural heritage.

Cultural innovation: The development of yacht tourism can also promote cultural innovation. When tourists interact with local residents, they may be inspired by the local culture, resulting in new ideas and thoughts. This cross-cultural exchange can help promote cultural innovation and artistic development.

Cultural education: Yacht tourism can also provide opportunities for cultural education. Visitors can visit museums, art exhibitions, and historical sites to learn about the local history, art, and culture. This cultural education helps to improve visitors' cultural literacy and cognitive level.

However, it is important to note that the cultural effects of yacht tourism may also have some negative impacts. For example, excessive commercialization and tourism development may lead to commercialization and standardization, weakening the uniqueness and authenticity of local culture. Therefore, in developing yacht tourism, it is necessary to balance the considerations between economic interests and cultural protection and adopt appropriate management and planning measures to ensure that yacht tourism maximizes its positive impact on culture.

(4) Environmental Protection Functions of Yacht Tourism

Yacht tourism has the potential to influence environmental protection in several ways, such as the following.

Promoting awareness of marine protection: Yacht tourism brings people closer to the ocean, enhancing their understanding and respect for the marine ecosystem. By allowing tourists to experience the beauty and fragility of the ocean firsthand, yacht tourism can stimulate people's awareness of marine protection and promote more environmental protection actions.

Advocating sustainable development: The yacht tourism industry is increasingly focused on sustainable development. Many yacht companies have adopted environmental protection measures, such as using clean energy, reducing waste emissions, and promoting recyclable materials. These initiatives help reduce the negative impact on the marine ecosystem and set an example for other industries.

Protecting marine biodiversity: The development of yacht tourism can promote the establishment and management of marine protected areas. Restricting yachts from entering sensitive areascan protect the habitats of marine organisms and maintain marine biodiversity. In addition, yacht tourism can also provide financial support for research and conservation work in marine protection projects.

Education and research: Yacht tourism can provide valuable opportunities for scientists and researchers to conduct research and monitoring of marine ecosystems. Passengers on board can also participate in scientific research projects that increase their understanding of the marine environment and contribute to the protection of marine ecosystems.

Despite these benefits, there are still some challenges and problems. For example, over-development and overuse of yachts may lead to marine pollution, damage to coral reefs and marine habitats, and other issues. Therefore, the yacht tourism industry needs to strengthen supervision and self-discipline, adopt more environmental protection measures, and ensure sustainable development.

Overall, yacht tourism has a positive role in environmental protection. By raising awareness of marine conservation, promoting sustainable development, protecting marine biodiversity, and promoting scientific research, yacht tourism can contribute to the protection and sustainable use of the marine environment. However, in order to maximize its potential, it requires the joint efforts of all parties in the industry to ensure that yacht tourism is aligned with environmental protection goals.

The COVID-19 epidemic in the past three years has had a significant impact on yacht tourism and the global tourism industry overall, as in the following:

Reduced tourism demand: Due to the restrictions of the pandemic and people's concerns about traveling, the demand for yacht tourism has plummeted. Many people have canceled their planned yacht trips, choosing to stay at home or choosing other safer forms of tourism. This has resulted in a significant reduction in revenue for yacht tourism companies.

Travel restrictions and epidemic prevention measures: In order to control the spread of the epidemic, countries have implemented travel restrictions and epidemic prevention measures, including restrictions on international travel, the closure of ports and maritime borders, and other things. This has had a serious impact on the yacht tourism industry, with many yachts unable to freely navigate and with travel routes restricted.

Economic dilemma: The COVID-19 epidemic led to a global economic recession, which affected the economic situation of many people. This makes yacht tourism a luxury, and more people cannot afford the high cost. This further reduced the demand for yacht tourism.

In conclusion, the COVID-19 epidemic has had a negative impact on yacht tourism. However, with the popularization of vaccines and the gradual control of the epidemic, the yacht tourism industry is expected to gradually recover.

Section 2: Yachting Events and Activities

Yachting activities refer to various activities and events related to yachting, including yacht exhibitions, yacht competitions, yacht leasing, and yacht travel. These activities are usually designed to showcase, promote, and facilitate the development of the yachting industry, attracting the participation of yacht enthusiasts, industry insiders, and potential customers. The definition of yachting activities can vary depending on the specific type and purpose of the activity but can generally be understood as a collection of various social, commercial, and recreational activities related to yachting.

Such yachting events and activities have a positive role in promoting economic development and tourism. They attract a large number of participants and spectators, bringing direct and indirect economic benefits to the local economy. Hotels, restaurants, transportation and other service industries around the competition venue can benefit from the hosting of yachting events, which can attract domestic and foreign tourists, promote tourism development, and enhance the local reputation and image.

Yachting events and activities are of great significance in promoting the development of the yachting industry. They bring business opportunities to related industries such as yacht manufacturers, yacht leasing companies, and yacht repair and maintenance service providers. Such events and activities can increase the exposure of yacht products, increase sales volume, and promote innovation and development of the yachting industry.

In addition, yachting events and activities can also have a positive impact on environmental protection by emphasizing environmental awareness and advocating sustainable development. Organizers can develop relevant environmental policies and measures to ensure that the impact of the competition and activities on the marine ecosystem is minimized. At the same time, yachting events and activities can also raise public awareness of marine environmental protection and promote protection of the marine ecosystem.

In summary, yacht events and activities play an important role in economic development, yachting industry development, and environmental protection.

1. Yachting Racing

(1) Definition of Yacht Racing

Yacht racing refers to sports events that use yachts as the racing vehicles. These events usually include various types of yacht races, such as sailing, motorboat racing, and rowing. Yacht racing is a popular sports activity that attracts many participants and spectators.

Yacht racing events are usually held in waters such as oceans, lakes, or rivers. Competitors compete for speed and skill by operating yachts using propulsion forces such as wind, engines, or human power. These competitions can be divided into different categories and levels, based on the size, type, and rules of the yachts.

Yacht racing is attractive to both competitors and spectators. For competitors, yacht racing provides a platform to showcase their skills and competitiveness, as well as an opportunity for communication and learning. For spectators, yacht racing provides an opportunity to watch the competition and appreciate the excitement of yachting.

In yacht racing, participants need to possess certain skills and experience. They need to be familiar with the control and operation of yachts and understand the impact of natural conditions such as wind and water on the competition. In addition, they also need to possess teamwork and tactical strategies to gain an advantage in the race.

Yacht races are held worldwide, some of which have significant international influence, such as the America's Cup, the Tour de France, and the Olympic Regatta. These events attract top-level athletes and teams, as well as significant media attention and sponsorship support.

Overall, yacht racing is a popular sports event that is attractive to both competitors and spectators. These events not only showcase technical and competitive abilities, but also promote the development and promotion of water sports.

(2) Types of Yacht Racing

Depending on the nature and scale of the event, yacht racing can be divided into various types. Here are some common types of yacht racing:

Sailing racing: Sailing racing is one of the most common yachting events. Depending on the size and design of the boats, sailing racing can be divided into multiple levels, including Olympic-level sailing competitions, the International Sailing Federation World Cup series, and the Volvo Ocean Race. Sailing events are usually held on oceans, lakes, or rivers, where the competitors use the wind to maneuver their boats.

Power yacht racing: Unlike sailing racing, power yacht racing uses engine-driven yachts in competition. Such events typically include high-speed rowing competitions, yacht rallies, and yacht cruises. Power yacht racing emphasizes speed and technology, with competitors required to quickly navigate their yachts along a predetermined route to complete the race.

High-end yacht racing: High-end yacht racing refers to those competitions involving luxury yachts and super yachts. These events are usually held in famous seaside cities or resorts around the world, attracting the attention of wealthy individuals and yacht enthusiasts. For example, the America's Cup in the United States and the Saint-Tropez Regatta in France are prestigious high-end yacht racing events.

Multihull Yacht Racing: Multihull yacht racing refers to races that use yachts with multiple hulls. The most famous of these is the America's Cup multihull sailing race, where the participating yachts are typically composed of multiple hulls, providing high speed and maneuverability.

Active yacht events: In addition to formal competitions, yacht events also include yacht exhibitions, yacht cruises, and yacht parties. These events aim to provide social and entertainment experiences, attracting yacht enthusiasts and spectators to participate.

(3) Value of Yacht Racing

As an elite sport and social activity, yacht racing has multiple values:

Economic value: Yacht racing can drive the development of related industries, including yacht manufacturing, maintenance, sales, and leasing. The venue of the event usually attracts a large number of tourists and participants, driving the prosperity of local tourism, hotels, catering, and other industries. In addition, yacht racing can also promote related brands and attract the participation of sponsors, bringing direct and indirect benefits to the economy.

Tourism promotion value: Yacht races are usually held in scenic waters or coastal cities, providing opportunities for the local tourism industry to promote and publicize them. The races attract domestic and foreign tourists and media attention, enhancing the popularity and image of the host location.

Social value: Yacht racing is an important

social platform that attracts the participation of wealthy individuals, entrepreneurs, and political figures from different countries and regions. During the event, participants can establish new business connections, exchange experiences, and share resources, promoting international cultural exchange and cooperation. In addition, yacht racing also provides participants with opportunities to showcase their personal taste and social status, enhancing the cohesion of their social circles.

Sports value: Yacht racing is a high-level sports event, and participants need to possess professional skills and rich experience. The hosting of the event promotes the development of yachting, improves the level and skills of the participants, and promotes the popularization and promotion of yachting worldwide. At the same time, yacht racing also provides spectators with opportunities to watch exciting competitions and increases the choices of sports entertainment.

2. Yacht Exhibitions

(1) Definition of Yacht Exhibitions

Yacht exhibitions are dedicated to showcasing and promoting yachts and related products and services. They are usually one of the most important events in the yachting industry, attracting yacht manufacturers, dealers, owners, designers, suppliers, and yacht enthusiasts from all over the world.

The main purpose of the yacht show is to promote the development and promotion of the yachting industry, provide a platform for yacht manufacturers to showcase their latest products and technologies, and also provide an opportunity for yacht enthusiasts to learn about and purchase yachts. The yacht show usually displays various types and sizes of yachts, including sailing yachts, power yachts, and luxury yachts.

(2) Types of Yacht Exhibitions

Yacht exhibitions can be divided into the following types:

International yacht exhibitions: These exhibitions are usually held in major port cities or tourist destinations around the world, attracting yacht manufacturers, dealers, owners, and yacht enthusiasts. These exhibitions are large-scale, showcasing the latest yacht designs, technologies, and innovations, while also providing related services such as yacht purchase, rental, and maintenance.

Regional yacht exhibitions: These exhibitions are usually held in specific regions or countries, attracting yacht manufacturers, dealers, and consumers in the region. These exhibitions may be more focused on the needs and characteristics of the local yacht market, showcasing the products and services of local yacht manufacturers, and providing information and opportunities related to the local yachting industry.

Themed yacht exhibitions: In addition to general yacht exhibitions, there are also exhibitions that focus on specific themes or market segments. For example, luxury yacht exhibitions, sailing exhibitions, fishing yacht exhibitions, among others. These exhibitions attract participants and audiences interested in specific fields.

Commercial yacht exhibitions: These exhibitions are mainly targeted at professionals in the yachting industry, such as yacht manufacturers, dealers, designers, shipowners, and shipping companies. These exhibitions provide a platform for business exchanges and cooperation, showcase the latest yacht technology, equipment, and services, and promote cooperation and development within the industry.

(3) Value of Yacht Exhibitions

The value of yacht exhibitions is mainly reflected in the following:

Promoting business development: The yacht show provides an opportunity for yacht manufacturers and dealers to display and promote their products, attracting potential buyers and partners. Through the exhibition, they can establish new business connections, expand market share, and increase sales.

Enhancing brand image: Participating in the yacht show can enhance the popularity and image of the yacht brand. Yacht exhibition showcasing the latest designs and technologies, as well as high-quality yacht products, can help establish a professional image and high-end positioning for the brand.

Promoting technological innovation: The yacht show is a platform for yacht manufacturers to showcase the latest technologies and innovations. Exhibitors can display their innovative achievements in yacht design, hull materials, power systems, and other aspects, promoting technological advancement in the entire industry.

Promoting tourism and economic development: Yacht events and exhibitions often attract a large number of tourists and participants, bringing direct and indirect economic benefits to the local economy. Yacht events can also enhance the tourism image of the destination and attract more tourists to visit and experience the local offerings

(4) Representative Yacht Exhibitions

According to the information collated by IBI International yachting industry magazine, post-pandemic yacht exhibitions and activities have included:

1. Miami International Boat Show

The Miami International Boat Show was held from February 16-20, 2022, with approximately 100,000 visitors attending the five-day event.

2. Dubai International Boat Show

The Dubai International Boat Show was held from March 9-13, 2022. This is the first time the show has returned after the pandemic, attracting many well-known yacht brands.

3. Korea International Boat Show

The 2022 Korea International Boat Show was held from March 11-13, bringing together 152 exhibitors and 55,031 visitors.

4. Australia Fairy Bay International Yacht Show

The 2022 Australian Fairy Bay International Yacht Show was held from May 19-22, with over 330 exhibitors attending, including 30-40 new exhibitors. The scale of this exhibition has expanded by 30% compared to last year, and is considered to be the largest since the global financial crisis in 2008.

5. Venice International Boat Show

The 3rd Venice International Boat Show ended successfully on June 5, 2022. The nine-day exhibition gathered about 30,000 visitors and 200 exhibitors, with 300 yachts on display, including 240 on the water. During the period, there were more than 50 in-depth cultural events.

6. Sydney International Boat Show

The 53rd Sydney International Boat Show will be held from July 28 to August 1, 2022 this year, with a total of 190 exhibitors and about 60,000 visitors.

7. Cannes International Boat Show

The 2022 Cannes International Boat Show was held from September 6 to 11 in Cannes, France. Nearly 600 exhibitors displayed more than 650 yachts, attracting more than 50,000 visitors.

8. Southampton International Boat Show

The Southampton International Boat Show 2022 was held at Mayflower Park from September 16 to 25, with more than 250 powerboats on display. Many products were unveiled at the show for the first time in the UK and around the world.

9. Sao Paulo International Boat Show

The 2022 Sao Paulo International Boat Show was held from September 23rd to 28th, with approximately 100 different brands on display.

10.Genoa International Boat Show

The 2022 Genoa International Boat Show was held from September 22 to 27, showcasing 998 brands and more than 1,000 yachts, including 168 world premieres. The Genoa International Boat Show is constantly growing and expanding. This year's water exhibition area increased by 5.2%.

11. Monaco International Boat Show

The Monaco International Boat Show 2022 was held from September 28 to October 1, with more than 550 exhibitors and 118 yachts ranging in length from 23 meters to 115 meters (75-378 feet).

12. Fort Lauderdale International Boat Show

The 63rd Fort Lauderdale International Boat Show opened on October 27, 2022. This year's exhibition had favorable conditions, with an exhibition area of nearly 3 million square feet, connected by a complex network of water and ground transportation services. The scene was crowded and bustling.

13. METSTRADE Yacht Equipment and Accessories Exhibition

The 2022 METSTRADE Yacht Equipment and Accessories Exhibition in the Netherlands has been upgraded and returned, held from November 15th to 17th at the RAI Exhibition Center in Amsterdam. The three-day visitor flow was 26,480, receiving a total of 17,417 registered independent visitors from 126 countries, as well as 6,175 exhibitors.

14. Abu Dhabi International Boat Show

The 4th Abu Dhabi International Boat Show was held from November 24 to 27, 2022. 548 brands from 44 countries participated in the show, an increase of 55% over last year, with the number of foreign exhibitors increasing by 400% compared to last year.

Section 3: Yacht Vacation and Leisure

In the 18th century, many aristocrats and wealthy people in European maritime countries regarded luxury yachts as a symbol of wealth. By the mid-20th century, as the social strata in developed countries gradually changed yacht culture, which represents status, wealth, and identity, moved beyond the narrow boundaries of the wealthy class and entered the lives of the middle class in Europe and the United States.

For many people, yacht tourism has become a more popular and high-end consumption method than car tourism. Yachts yearn for the freedom of the sea, and personality and freedom are increasingly valued by people.

1. Definition of Yacht Leisure

Yachting vacations can be defined as a way to relax, entertain, and enjoy the natural environment through yachting activities. Yachting vacation usually involves renting or owning your own yacht and sailing and engaging in activities in waters such as oceans, lakes, or rivers. This vacation style can provide a unique experience that allows people to escape from the hustle and bustle of the city and enjoy the tranquility and beauty of the ocean.

The definition of yachting leisure can be considered from the following aspects:

Yacht: A yacht is a vessel used for water activities, typically with large dimensions and comfortable facilities that can be used for entertainment, sports, and travel. Yachts vary in type and size, from small sailing ships to large luxury yachts that can be used for yachting leisure activities.

Leisure activities: Yacht leisure activities include but are not limited to yacht cruising, fishing, diving, swimming, beach vacations, and sea parties. These activities aim to bring people away from the hustle and bustle of the city and allow them to enjoy the beauty and tranquility of nature.

Luxury and high-quality lifestyle: Yachting leisure is often associated with a wealthy and high-quality lifestyle. Owning and using a yacht is seen as a symbol of status and prestige, and requires a certain level of financial resources to maintain and operate. Yachting leisure activities provide a luxurious and comfortable experience, including high-end facilities, food, entertainment, and services.

2. Yacht Leisure Culture

(1) Definition of Yacht Leisure Culture

Yacht leisure culture refers to a specific leisure style and cultural phenomenon centered on yacht activities. Yacht leisure culture involves the ownership, use, and related social activities of yachts, as well as the values, behavioral norms, and lifestyles associated with these vessels.

Firstly, yacht leisure culture is closely related to the ownership and use of yachts. Owning a yacht is seen as a symbol of status and wealth, so yacht leisure culture is often associated with the wealthy and high-income groups. The use of yachts includes cruising, entertainment activities, and water sports that provide a unique leisure experience and enjoyment.

Yacht leisure culture also involves social activities related to yachts. Yacht clubs, yacht exhibitions, and yacht resorts have become important places for communication and interaction among yacht enthusiasts. These social activities not only provide opportunities to meet like-minded people, but also provide a platform for yacht enthusiasts to share experiences, display their yachts, and participate in competitions.

In addition, yacht leisure culture is also related to a series of values, behavioral norms, and lifestyles. Yacht leisure culture emphasizes respect for and protection of the marine environment, and advocates sustainable development and environmental awareness. Yacht enthusiasts usually focus on quality and detail, and they pursue a comfortable, luxurious, and high-quality lifestyle.

(2) Regional Differences in Yacht Leisure Culture

There may be some differences in yacht leisure culture depending on different regions and cultural backgrounds.

Firstly, the differences in yacht leisure culture can be reflected in the way yachts are used. In some regions, yachts are regarded as luxury goods, mainly used for entertainment and social activities by the wealthy. In this cultural context, yacht leisure focuses more on showing off and socializing, and yacht exhibitions also focus more on displaying luxury and high-end yacht products.

In other regions, the yacht leisure culture places more emphasis on closeness to nature and relaxation. Yachts are seen as a way to explore nature and enjoy the ocean as people pursue harmony with nature through yacht vacations. Against this cultural background, yacht exhibitions may focus more on displaying environmentally friendly and sustainable yacht products, as well as activities related to nature conservation. In Western developed countries, some people's interest in weekends and vacations has shifted from land to sea, and yacht tourism has become a more popular and high-end consumption method than car tourism. Due to the popularity of the consumption combination of"small yacht + yacht trailer + pick-up car" among many middle-class families, many families own low-end private small yachts. Taking the United States as an example. there are more than 25 million yachts of various types in the country, 70% of which are not docked on the water, but parked in garages and yards, and are towed to the waterfront or dock for launching when used. Yachts with a length of less than 9 meters account for 80% of the annual number of new yachts, while yachts with a length of more than 13 meters account for only 5% of the annual number of new yachts.

The differences in yacht leisure culture can also be reflected in the content and purpose of yacht activities. In some regions, yacht leisure focuses more on water sports and recreational activities, such as rowing, sailing competitions, and fishing. In other regions, yacht leisure focuses more on navigation and exploration, and people use yachts to explore unknown seas and islands. The world yacht leisure industry has matured in Europe, the United States, Canada, Australia. Yacht culture has entered the consumption choice category of the middle class as a way of life and tourism and has become the mainstream choice for people to relax and vacation. In Europe and the United States, yachting is very fashionable and popular. Canada has 5.5 million yachts, with an average of fewer than 6 people owning a yacht. In countries such as Norway, Sweden, and New Zealand, the per capita ownership of yachts is as high as eight to one. On weekends, it is a very common scene for a family to go out on a yacht for fun. The thrill of breaking wind and waves, the speed and freedom of driving, can only be experienced by personally driving a yacht. Leisure activities related to yachting include surfing, diving, swimming, fishing and even doing nothing but sunbathing on the deck in a bikini. The existence of yachts allows people to have intimate contact with water and experience a new and novel way of life.

Yacht communities in various regions may have different values and codes of conduct that reflect local cultural characteristics and social customs. Some yacht communities in certain may focus more on social interaction and organize various social activities and gatherings, while others may focus more on individual independence and adventure/ Understanding and analyzing these differences helps us better understand and appreciate yacht leisure culture in different regions and promote cross-cultural exchange and cooperation.

3. Yachting Vacations and Yacht Leisure Motivation

The types of yacht leisure motivations can be divided into the following categories:

1. Exploration and Adventure Motivation

Some people choose yachting for leisure to explore new seas and destinations. They pursue adventure and excitement, hoping to discover unknown ocean landscapes and cultural heritage through yachting vacations.

2. Comfort and Luxury Motivation

Yacht leisure also attracts those who pursue luxury and comfort. They hope to enjoy high-quality services and facilities on the yacht, immerse themselves in a luxurious environment, and pursue relaxation and enjoyment.

3. Social and entertainment motivation

Yachting vacations provide a platform for socializing and entertainment, attracting those who enjoy spending time with family, friends, or peers. They can host parties, gatherings, and other social activities on the yacht, enjoying the fun of interacting with others.

4. Self-actualization and personal growth motivation

Some people choose yachting for leisure in order to pursue self-realization and personal growth. They may participate in training courses or activities on the yacht to learn sailing skills or other related knowledge in order to enhance their abilities and skills.

5. Environmental and sustainability motivation

With the increasing awareness of environmental protection, some people choose yachting as a way to experience harmony with nature. They are concerned about environmental protection and sustainable development and may choose to use environmentally friendly yachts or participate in marine conservation projects. These types of motivations are not mutually exclusive, and a person may have multiple motivations for choosing yachting leisure. An individual's motivations may also change over time and experience. Therefore, understanding different types of yachting leisure motivations helps us better understand people's motivations and purposes for participating in yachting vacations.

4. Demand for Yacht Leisure by Chinese Consumers

According to market research, wealthy Chinese people prefer golf, swimming, spas and yoga as leisure activities, as these pursuits are well-known for their health benefits in Chinese culture. On the other hand, in the traditional Chinese context, yachts do not provide similar physical benefits. These cultural premises are relevant in considering the gap between target customers and industry culture. Considering all factors, it is not impossible for Chinese consumers to change their views, as China's shopping habits and tastes are rapidly changing due to the increasing number of high-net-worth individuals. Tastes may change and may be shaped. Given this phenomenon, he lack of brand familiarity and recognition on the part of consumers may actually provide opportunities for brand pioneers.

In the past three years, the central government's desire to stimulate consumption and encourage tourism (including yacht tourism) has created unprecedented potential for the yachting industry in the near future at least for small and medium-sized vessels. The formation of the Hainan Free Trade Port and the development of new ports may make the island the center of China's yacht culture. In the past decade alone, the number of registered yachts in Sanya has increased from 10 to more than 1,000. Yacht rental services have become increasingly popular in China, and yacht culture has been promoted among the middle class and high-income classes.

On August 18, 2022, China's Ministry of Industry and Information Technology joined with other ministries in issuing a report titled the *Guiding Opinions on Accelerating the Development of Cruise and Yacht Equipment Industry*. The report recommended that , the yachting industry should achieve four development goals by 2025: improving design and construction capabilities, consolidating the foundation of the equipment industry, expanding consumer market demand, and strengthening cooperation and talent cultivation.

In this context, Sanya is expected to transform into an international cruise home port, one of several international first-class cruise tourism destinations. The Chinese government is focusing on the development of water tourism resources in several regions, including the Bohai Rim Economic

Zone, Guangdong Hong Kong Macao Bay Area, Guangdong Fujian Zhejiang Coastal City Cluster, Hainan Free Trade Port, Yangtze River Economic Belt, the Pearl River Xijiang Economic Belt, Grand Canal Cultural Belt. At the same time, Hainan is being encouraged to develop a pilot yacht leasing business. The report also requires the construction of a disciplined and professional talent team in the whole industry chain, including the design, construction, navigation, operation, management, repair, and maintenance of cruise ships, yachts, and tourist passenger ships; as well as other related tourism services and legal consultations.

As China's yacht culture is still in its infancy, yacht manufacturers are being encouraged to focus on meeting the expectations of Chinese customers, from emphasizing the design of the entertainment room to making it easier for short-term rental of super yachts. On the other hand, the absence of proficient Mandarin experts and Chinese designers among European and American yacht manufacturers has to some extent stifled the growth of the shipbuilding industry in the Chinese market. Foreign shipbuilding companies need to tailor their products according to the needs and preferences of Chinese buyers, taking into account lifestyle and cultural preferences. For example, Chinese yacht owners rarely spend the night on board, and they prefer boats with leisure and entertainment facilities such as KTV (karaoke). Meeting this special demand of Chinese customers is an important part of challenging cultural differences so Chinese yachts can achieve a place in such a promising market.

Section 4: Yacht Rental and Distribution

The world yacht rental market is rapidly developing, with its scale expanding continuously and expected to continue to grow in the coming years. This is mainly attributed to the increase in the wealthy class and the demand for luxury travel and unique experiences. The yacht rental market has a significant presence worldwide, but it is particularly popular in some regions. With their rich coastlines and beautiful beaches, the Mediterranean, Caribbean, and Southeast Asia regions have become the most popular destinations for yacht rental. The yacht rental market offers a variety of rental options, including luxury yachts, sailing boats, fishing boats, canoes, and similar vessels. Luxury yachts are the most popular choice because they provide the highest level of comfort and luxury.

1. Yacht Rental

(1) Definition of Yacht Rental

From the perspective of scholars, yacht rental is a special form of leisure activity that combines elements of marine tourism, water sports, and luxury vacations.

Yacht rental provides consumers with a unique leisure experience. As a high-end entertainment facility, yachts have luxurious facilities and comfortable spaces, providing users with a distinctive way of vacationing. Renting a yacht allows people to escape from the hustle and bustle of the city, get close to nature, and enjoy the beauty and tranquility of the ocean.

Yacht rental also meets people's demand for luxury and unique experiences. Yachts are usually equipped with high-end facilities, such as helicopters, luxury rooms, swimming pools, bars, gyms and so on, to provide users with a luxurious holiday experience. Renting a yacht also allows people to experience the feeling of owning a private yacht first-hand, satisfying some consumers in their pursuit of unique experiences.

In addition, yacht rental also provides an ideal platform for water sports enthusiasts. Yachts are usually equipped with various water sports products, such as water skis, snorkeling equipment, or fishing gear, allowing people to enjoy the fun of water sports to the fullest. Renting a yacht can also lead users to explore different seas and discover new water sports venues.

However, yacht rental also has some problems and challenges. For one thing, he high cost of yacht rental limits the participation of some people. The impact of yacht rental on the environment also needs to be addressed, including issues such as marine pollution and ecological damage. Therefore, experts need to pay attention to the sustainable development of marine ecology in yacht rental and propose corresponding management and supervision measures.

(2) Characteristics of the Yacht Rental Market

The yacht rental market refers provides yachts for consumers to engage in leisure and entertainment activities on a short-term basis. The following is an analysis of some important aspects of the yacht rental market:

Market size: The yacht rental market has shown a steady growth trend over the past few years. As consumer demand for luxury leisure experiences increases, yacht rental has become a popular choice. According to market research, the size of the yacht rental market is expected to continue to expand.

Geographical distribution: The geographical distribution of the yacht rental market is mainly concentrated in coastal cities and tourist hotspots. These areas often have abundant marine resources and attractiveness to attract tourists and yacht enthusiasts. For example, the Mediterranean coast, the Caribbean region, and the Pacific Islands are all popular areas for the yacht rental market.

Rental model: The yacht rental market usually adopts different rental models to meet the needs of different consumers. These models include short-term rental, long-term rental, and shared rental. Short-term rental is suitable for consumers who only want to engage in weekend leisure activities, while long-term rental is suitable for those who want to enjoy yacht life for a longer time. The shared rental model allows several consumers to jointly rent a yacht to reduce costs.

Consumer groups: The consumer groups in the yacht rental market are diverse. In addition to the wealthy class and high-net-worth individuals, an increasing number of middle-class and tourists have also joined the ranks. These consumers are fueling a growing demand for luxury leisure experiences, which has driven the development of the yacht rental market.

Continuous innovation: The yacht rental market is constantly innovating and developing. In order to attract more consumers, rental companies not only provide high-quality yachts and comfortable facilities, but also offer various value-added services such as private chefs, tour guides, marine life experts, and water activities facilities. Some companies have also launched sustainable yacht rental models to reduce the impact on the environment.

Overall, the yacht rental market is a dynamic and promising market. With the pursuit of luxury leisure experiences and the development of tourism, the yacht rental market is expected to continue to grow and create more business opportunities. However, it is important to note that the market is highly competitive, and charter companies need to constantly innovate and improve service quality to meet ever-changing consumer demands.

(3) Yacht Rental Process

The yacht rental process is as follows:

Booking: Customers book yachts through online platforms, by phone or directly at yacht rental companies. They can choose different types and sizes of yachts based on their needs and budget.

Negotiation and signing of contract: After booking, the customer negotiates with the yacht rental company to discuss the rental period, fees, insurance, and other related matters. After reaching an agreement, the two parties sign a rental contract.

Payment and deposit: Customers need to pay the rental fee and a security deposit. The deposit is usually refunded to the customer at the end of the rental period, provided that the yacht is not damaged or in default.

Yacht delivery and inspection: At the beginning of the lease period, the yacht rental company delivers the yacht to the customer. The customer and the company representatives conduct a joint inspection of the yacht to ensure that the yacht is delivered to the customer in good condition.

Use and return: Customers can use the yacht for sailing and leisure activities during the lease period. At the end of the lease period, customers return the yacht to the rental company for final inspection and liquidation.

Evaluation and feedback: After the end of the rental period, customers can evaluate and provide feedback on the yacht rental service to help the rental company improve and enhance service quality.

Overall, the yacht rental market provides a luxurious and unique way to vacation. The rental process is relatively simple but requires cooperation and negotiation between both parties to ensure a good rental experience. As people's demand for luxury tourism increases, the yacht rental market is expected to continue to grow and develop.

(4) Yacht Rental Fees

Yacht rental fees usually consist of the following factors:

Basic rental: Basic rental refers to the basic cost of renting a yacht, usually determined by the the length of the rental period and the type of yacht. Different types of yachts may have different basic rental standards, and in general, the basic rental for luxury yachts will be higher.

Insurance fee: Yacht rental usually requires the purchase of insurance to protect against risks during the lease period. The insurance premium depends on the value of the yacht and the length of the lease. Generally speaking, higher-value yachts require higher insurance premiums.

Fuel costs: Fuel costs during the yacht rental period are borne by the renter. These costs depend on the fuel consumption of the yacht and the length of the rental period. Luxury yachts typically consume more fuel, so fuel costs will increase accordingly.

Food and beverage expenses: In some yacht rental services, it is common to provide food and beverages. These expenses are usually not included in the basic rental fee, but are additional charges. The cost depends on the renter's needs and the level of service provided on the yacht.

Additional costs: During the yacht rental process, there may be additional costs, such as docking fees, crew fees, or cleaning fees. These costs vary depending on the rental location and the policy of the service provider.

It is also important to note that the calculation of yacht rental fees varies depending on the region and service provider. In some high-end tourist destinations, the rental fees for yachts may be higher, while in some ordinary tourist destinations, the fees may be relatively lower. In addition, the rental fees for yachts may also be affected by factors such as season, holidays, and market supply and demand. Therefore, when choosing a yacht rental service, lessees should consider the above factors comprehensively and compare with different service providers to obtain the most cost-effective rental plan.

2. Yacht Distribution

(1) Definition of Yacht Distribution

Yacht distribution can be defined as the process by which yacht manufacturers or suppliers sell yacht products to end consumers through different channels. This process involves sales, distribution, logistics, and after-sales services of yachts.

The definition of yacht distribution can be further subdivided into the following aspects:

Channel selection: Yacht manufacturers need to choose suitable channels to sell their products. These channels can include direct sales to consumers, sales through distributors or agents, or sales through online platforms. Selecting the right channel can help manufacturers better reach their target markets and provide better sales and after-sales services.

Channel management: Yacht manufacturers can establish partnerships with distributors or agents to conduct channel management. This includes developing contracts, pricing policies, sales targets, and sales training. Through effective channel management, manufacturers can ensure the widespread distribution of products in the market and provide consistent brand image and service quality.

Logistics and delivery: Yachts are large and expensive products, so logistics and delivery are important aspects of the distribution process. Manufacturers need to ensure that the yachts can be safely transported to the destination and provide necessary insurance and tracking services. At the same time, manufacturers also need to consider aspects such as assembly, installation, and after-sales service of the yachts to ensure that consumers can have a smooth purchasing experience.

Marketing and promotion: Yacht distribution also requires marketing and promotional activities to attract consumers' attention and motivate them to purchase. This includes increasing brand awareness and product recognition through advertising, exhibitions, social media, and public relations activities. Manufacturers can also collaborate with relevant tourism agencies, resorts and yacht clubs to expand market share and increase sales.

From a scholarly perspective, yacht distribution is a complex process that involves channel selection, channel management, logistics and marketing. Manufacturers need to successfully bring yacht products to market through effective distribution strategies and partnerships and provide quality sales and after-sales services to meet consumer needs.

(2) Channel Selection of Yacht Distribution

The channel selection of yacht distribution also refers to the process and method by which yacht manufacturers or suppliers distribute yacht products to end users. The selection of yacht distribution channels includes the following factors:

Direct sales by manufacturers: Yacht manufacturers can choose to directly sell yacht products to end users. This approach can help manufacturers establish direct connections and relationships, understand user needs, and provide personalized services. Direct sales by manufacturers can also reduce intermediate links to improve sales efficiency and profits.

Dealer channels: Manufacturers can choose to sell wholesale yacht products to dealers, who are then responsible for sales and distribution. Dealers usually have a wider sales network and customer resources and can provide better market coverage and after-sales service. Manufacturers can expand their sales range and market share by working with multiple dealers.

Agent channels: Manufacturers can choose to work with agents who represent them in selling and distributing yacht products. Agents usually have rich industry experience and customer resources and can provide professional sales and consulting services. Manufacturers can further expand their market share and brand influence by working with multiple agents.

Online channels: With the development of the Internet, online channels are playing an increasingly important role in yacht distribution. Manufacturers can directly sell yacht products to users by establishing their own official websites or online platforms. In addition, manufacturers can also use online channels such as e-commerce platforms and social media to promote and sell their products.

Partnerships: Yacht distribution channels can also include establishing partnerships with other related industries to jointly promote and sell yacht products. For example, manufacturers can collaborate with travel agencies, luxury hotels, and resorts to provide yacht rental services and provide users with a one-stop luxury travel experience.

In general, the channel structure of

yacht distribution is diverse, and manufacturers can choose suitable channel strategies based on market demand and their own resources to achieve sales growth and improve their market share. Establishing good partnerships and providing quality after-sales services are also key factors for the success of yacht distribution.

(3) Channel Management of Yacht Distribution

Channel management for yacht distribution refers to the process of effectively organizing, coordinating, and controlling yacht sales channels to achieve sales goals. The goal of yacht distribution channel management is to ensure that yachts are sold in the best way possible while meeting the needs of consumers.

In the channel management of yacht distribution, the following factors need to be considered:

Channel selection: Selecting channels suitable for yacht sales, including direct sales, agents, or dealers while considering the coverage of channels, market influence, sales ability, and other factors.

Channel cooperation: Establishing good cooperative relationships with channel partners, including developing cooperation agreements while providing training and support. Stability and mutual trust in the partnership are keys to channel management.

Channel incentives: Incentives are used to stimulate the enthusiasm of channel partners, including providing rewards, sales support, and marketing materials. Incentives need to be aligned with the interests of channel partners to achieve a win-win situation for all.

Channel monitoring: Monitoring and evaluating the sales performance of channel partners, including such factors as sales data analysis and market feedback collection. Through such monitoring, problems can be identified in a timely manner and corresponding measures can be taken.

Channel optimization: Optimizing and adjusting the channel according to market demand and sales situation. Adding new channels, adjusting channel structure and improving channel management can be considered as strategies to improve sales effectiveness.

In short, the channel management of yacht distribution requires a comprehensive consideration of market demand, the characteristics of channel partners, and sales goals. By selecting appropriate channels, establishing good partnerships, motivating channel partners, monitoring sales performance, and optimizing channel structure, the best results can be achieved in yacht sales.

(4) Logistics and Delivery of Yacht Distribution

Logistics and delivery are very important for yacht distribution. Since yachts are a high-value and large-scale commodity, the logistics and delivery process requires careful management to ensure smooth and efficient delivery to customers.

The logistics process begins when yachts are purchased from manufacturers or suppliers and then transported to the warehouses or display centers of distributors or retailers. During this process, it is necessary to consider the size, weight, and special requirements of the yachts and choose the appropriate mode of transportation, such as sea, land, or air. At the same time, it is also necessary to ensure that the yachts are properly protected during transportation to prevent damage or loss.

The delivery process next involves delivering yachts from distributors or retailers to end customers. This may involve arranging professional logistics companies or transportation teams to ensure that the yachts can be safely transported to the customer's designated location, such as a harbor, dock, or private marina. During the delivery process, route planning, traffic conditions, and safety measures need to be considered to ensure the safety and timely delivery of the yachts.

In the logistics and delivery process of yacht distribution, it is also necessary to consider related procedures and documentation work, such as customs clearance, insurance, and transportation contracts. These procedures and documents require a professional team to ensure compliance and smooth progress.

(5) Market Promotion of Yacht Distribution

The marketing promotion of yacht distribution should consider the following factors:

Target market positioning: Yachts are a high-end luxury product, so market promotion should target consumers with purchasing power and demand for luxury goods. Through market research and analysis, yacht distributors can determine the characteristics and needs of the target market, ao as to carry out targeted promotional activities.

Brand building: Yacht distributors should focus on brand building and create a unique brand image and values. Through carefully designed brand logos, promotional materials, and websites, they can convey the high quality, luxury, and uniqueness of yachts, attracting the attention and recognition of target consumers.

Multi-channel promotion: Yacht distributors can use multiple channels for market promotion, including online and offline channels. In terms of online channels, they can increase brand exposure and promote the spread of promotional activities through social media platforms, search engine optimization, email marketing, and other methods. In terms of offline channels, they can participate in yacht exhibitions and other industry events to engage in face-to-face communication and promotion with potential customers.

Personalized marketing strategy: For the particularity of yacht distribution, personalized marketing strategies can be adopted. For example, customized promotional materials and gifts can be customized according to the needs and preferences of potential customers, increasing attractiveness and uniqueness. By collaborating with high-end tourism agencies and luxury hotels, etc., yacht experience activities or packages can be provided to attract target customers to participate.

Reputation marketing: Yacht distributors can establish a good reputation by actively managing customer relationships, providing quality after-sales service and maintenance, and communicating well with customers. Satisfied customers often become loyal supporters of the brand, and promote the brand through word-of-mouth communication, attracting more potential customers.

In short, the marketing of yacht distribution needs to focus on brand building, multi-channel promotion, personalized marketing strategies, and word-of-mouth marketing. Through effective market promotion, it can enhance brand awareness, attract target customers, and promote the sales and distribution of yachts.

Section 5: Research on Yacht Consumer Experience

Yacht consumer experience refers to the feelings, emotions, and satisfaction that yacht consumers gain during the process of purchasing, using, and enjoying yacht services. Yacht consumer experience research focuses on several aspects:

Consumer needs and expectations: Scholars have found that yacht consumers have different needs and expectations for yacht experiences. Some consumers focus on luxury and extravagance, hoping to enjoy high-quality services and facilities on the yacht; while others focus more on the natural environment and sailing experience, pursuing intimate contact with nature. Understanding consumer needs and expectations can help yacht distributors provide products and services that better meet consumer expectations.

Service quality and satisfaction: Scholars have studied yacht consumers' perceptions and satisfaction with yacht service quality. Service quality includes yacht facilities, crew service attitudes, navigation safety, and other aspects. The study found that yacht consumers' satisfaction with service quality directly affects their consumption decisions and willingness to purchase again. Therefore, yacht distributors should focus on improving service quality to enhance consumer satisfaction and loyalty.

Emotional experience and emotional value: Scholars have studied the emotional experience and emotional value that yacht consumers gain during their yachting experience. Yacht consumers often experience luxurious, relaxing, and free emotional experiences on the yacht, which play an important role in their sense of satisfaction and happiness. The provision of emotional experience and emotional value can enhance yacht consumers' emotional connection to the yacht, thereby promoting consumer loyalty and word-of-mouth communication.

Personalized customization and differentiated experience: Scholars have studied the demand of yacht consumers for personalized customization and differentiated experience. Yacht consumers hope to customize the design, route, and service of their yachts according to their preferences and needs. Personalized customization and differentiated experience can increase consumers' sense of participation and satisfaction and enhance the experiential value of yacht consumers.

In summary, research on yacht consumer experience can help yacht distributors better understand consumer needs and expectations, improve service quality and satisfaction, create emotional experiences and value, and provide personalized customization and differentiated experiences, thereby enhancing yacht consumers' satisfaction and loyalty.

1. Research on Yacht Consumers' Needs and Expectations

The demand and expectations of yacht consumers are one of the important topics in yacht market research. Scholars explore the needs and expectations of yacht consumers through surveys and research on yacht consumers, so that yacht manufacturers and dealers can better meet consumers' expectations and provide better products and services.

Some scholars study the needs and expectations of yacht consumers by using qualitative and quantitative research methods, such as in-depth interviews, questionnaire surveys, and market research. Through these research methods, scholars can understand the needs and expectations of yacht consumers in terms of yacht function, design, performance, quality, and service. Research has shown that the needs and expectations of yacht consumers can be divided into multiple aspects.

Yacht consumers have high requirements for the functions and performance of yachts. They expect yachts to have good navigation performance, stability, and safety, and to be able to meet the needs of different waters and climatic conditions. In addition, yacht consumers also have high expectations for the comfort and convenience of yachts, including the design and configuration of cabin space, facilities and equipment, entertainment systems, kitchens, and bathrooms.

These consumers also have high requirements for the appearance and design of yachts. They expect that yachts have unique exterior design and exquisite interiors, which can show their personal taste and style. Yacht consumers also have certain requirements for the materials and craftsmanship of yachts, pursuing high quality and fine manufacturing process.

In addition, yacht consumers attach great importance to after-sales service and support. They expect yacht manufacturers and dealers to provide comprehensive after-sales services, including maintenance, parts supply, technical support and training, to ensure the normal operation and maintenance of their yachts.

2. Research on Yacht Service Quality and Satisfaction

The quality of service for yacht consumers refers to the level of service provided by yacht companies or service providers during the purchase and use of yachts. Scholars' research on the quality of service for yacht consumers mainly focuses on the following factors:

Service quality categories: Scholars have proposed several categories to measure the quality of yacht services through consumer surveys and research. These categories include reliability, responsiveness, assurance, credibility, and personalization. These factors can help yacht companies understand consumers' expectations for service quality and provide corresponding improvement measures.

The relationship between service quality and satisfaction: Research has shown that there is a close relationship between yacht consumers' perception of service quality and their satisfaction. High-quality services can enhance consumers' satisfaction, thereby increasing their loyalty and word-of-mouth approval. Therefore, yacht companies should focus on improving service quality to meet consumers' needs and expectations.

Service quality improvement strategies: Scholars have also proposed some service quality improvement strategies that yacht companies can adopt. For example, strengthening employee training to improve the professionalism and skills of service personnel; establishing effective communication channels to respond to consumer needs and complaints in a timely manner; and optimizing service processes to improve service efficiency.

The relationship between service quality and loyalty: Studies have also found that there is a positive relationship between yacht consumers' perception of service quality and their loyalty. High-quality services can enhance consumers' trust and loyalty towards yacht companies, making them more inclined to purchase yachts again or recommend them to others. Therefore, yacht companies should focus on improving service quality to promote consumer loyalty and word-of-mouth communication.

3. Research on Emotional Experience and Emotional Value of Yacht Consumers

The emotional experience and emotional value of yacht consumers are one of the important research areas being studied in the yachting industry. From the perspective of scholars, the following research directions and findings are related to the emotional experience and emotional value of yacht consumers:

The components of emotional experience: Research has shown that the emotional experience of yacht consumers is composed of multiple components, including the environmental atmosphere, the attitude and skills of service personnel, and the comfort of yacht facilities. Consumers' perceptions and evaluations of these factors directly affect their emotional experience.

The influencing factors of emotional value: The emotional value of yacht consumers refers to the degree of emotional satisfaction they feel from the yacht experience. Research has found that emotional value is influenced by multiple factors, including the degree of personalization of yacht services, the consistency between consumers' expectations and actual experiences, and the brand image of yachts.

The relationship between emotional experience and loyalty: Research has shown that there is a positive relationship between the emotional experience of yacht consumers and their loyalty. Consumers who experience positive emotions during their yachting experience will enhance their loyalty to the yacht brand, thereby promoting repeat purchases and word-of-mouth communication.

Emotional experience management strategy: In order to enhance the emotional experience of yacht consumers, yacht companies can adopt a series of management strategies. For example, providing personalized services and paying attention to consumers' emotional needs; training and motivating employees to provide quality service experiences; and designing and improving yacht facilities to provide a comfortable and pleasant environment.

Measurement and evaluation of emotional experience: In order to gain a deeper understanding of the emotional experience of yacht consumers, scholars have conducted a large number of measurement and evaluation studies. They have used various methods such as questionnaire surveys, in-depth interviews, and observations to understand consumers' emotional reactions and evaluations during yacht experiences.

Overall, research on yacht consumers' emotional experience and emotional value is of great significance for the development of the yachting industry as it struves to enhance consumer satisfaction. By deeply understanding consumers' emotional needs and expectations, yacht companies can provide more personalized and quality services, thereby enhancing consumers' emotional experience and loyalty.

4. Research on Personalized Customization and Differentiated Experience of Yachts

Yacht personalized customization and differentiated experience are important aspects of yacht consumers' needs and expectations and are also one of the key factors in the strategies of the yachting industry.

Personalized customization is at the core of yacht consumers' needs. Yacht consumers usually want to own unique and distinctive yachts to show their taste and identity. Therefore, yacht manufacturers need to provide personalized customization services to meet consumers' personalized needs in terms of exterior design, interior layout, and equipment configuration. Scholars can study the characteristics of yacht consumers' personalized needs, the implementation methods of personalized customization, and the impact of personalized customization on consumer satisfaction and loyalty.

Differentiated experience is also an important aspect of yacht consumers' expectations. Yacht consumers not only pursue the quality and performance of the yacht itself, but also hope to gain unique experiences and values through the use of the yacht.

In addition, there is a close relationship between personalized customization and differentiated experience. Personalized customization can provide unique differentiated experiences for yacht consumers, meeting their needs for personalized experiences. Research on yacht personalized customization and differentiated experience mainly includes the following factors:

Consumer needs and expectations: Yacht consumers often have highly personalized needs and expectations. They hope to customize their yachts according to their preferences and needs, including hull design, interior layout, and equipment configuration. Relevant research uses survey questionnaires, in-depth interviews, and other methods to understand consumers' needs and expectations, so that yacht manufacturers can provide personalized customization services that better meet consumer requirements.

Implementation of personalized customization: Yacht manufacturers need to conduct relevant research to determine how to implement personalized customization. This includes determining the scope and types of customization options, developing a customization process and timetable, and establishing effective communication channels with consumers. Research explores different personalized customization strategies and evaluates their impact on consumer satisfaction and loyalty.

Creating differentiated experiences: In order to provide unique yacht experiences, manufacturers need to focus on creating differentiated experiences. This can be achieved through innovations in yacht design, improved comfort, personalized services, and other methods. Relevant research can explore different elements of differentiated experiences and assess their impact on consumers' emotional experiences and satisfaction.

Section 6: Big Data Analysis of Yacht Consumers

With the development of the Internet and wireless technologies, tourism, as an information-intensive industry, has been profoundl affected. The ever-changing communication technology and network technology are profoundly changing people's life concepts and lifestyles. Especially with the popularity mobile phones, all tourism needs can be quickly and easily solved through the Internet, thus generating new transaction modes and consumer habits. Tourism enterprises are facing the challenges of changing marketing environment, multilateral market competition, and the shift from offline to online.

The competition among yacht brands in the future will be multi-dimensional. Brands need to keep up with the evolving trends of consumers, changes in the competitive landscape, and the speed of the evolution of the digital ecosystem, actively building an end-to-end consumer value chain, and truly achieving "consumer-centricity".

1. Characteristics of Yacht Consumer Demand in the Big Data Era

In the era of big data, the characteristics of yacht consumer demand have undergone some changes, mainly in the following areas:

Data-driven decision-making: The development of big data technology enables yacht consumers to more accurately understand market trends, product features, and competitors. They can make more informed purchasing decisions by analyzing big data and selecting the yacht products that best suit their needs.

Increased demand for personalized customization: The application of big data technology enables yacht manufacturers to better understand the personalized needs of consumers. Consumers hope to customize their own yachts to make them unique and meet their unique preferences. Therefore, yacht manufacturers need to use big data analysis to understand consumer needs and provide personalized customization services.

Experience-oriented consumption: Yacht consumers in the era of big data are more focused on the experience brought by purchasing products. They hope to gain joy, relaxation, and luxury through the use of yachts. Therefore, yacht manufacturers need to provide differentiated experiences, such as comfortable interior design, high-quality services, and innovative technology applications, to attract consumers and enhance their satisfaction.

Social media influence: Yacht consumers in the era of big data rely more on social media to obtain information and share experiences. They will learn about the comments and suggestions of other yacht consumers through social media platforms, which will affect their own purchasing decisions. Yacht manufacturers need to pay attention to the influence of social media, actively participate in and guide consumer discussions, and enhance brand image and reputation.

2. Yacht Consumers' Data-driven Decision-making in the Big Data Era

In the era of big data, yacht consumers' decision-making is increasingly influenced by data-driven factors. Here are some key aspects of analysis:

Market trend analysis: Through big data analysis, we can understand the trends of the yacht market and changes in consumer demand. Consumers can use data analysis to understand the development direction of the yacht market, making more informed purchasing decisions.

Personalized recommendation: Big data analysis can help yacht consumers obtain personalized recommendations and suggestions. By analyzing consumers' preferences, needs and behavioral data, the industry can provide them with yacht choices that match their preferences and improve their purchase satisfaction.

Price optimization: Big data analysis can help yacht consumers understand market price changes and trends. Consumers can use data analysis to find the best purchase opportunity to gain better price advantages.

User feedback analysis: Big data analysis can help yacht consumers understand the evaluations and feedback of other consumers. By analyzing users' reviews and rating data, consumers can better understand the performance, quality, and service of yachts, making for more informed purchasing decisions.

Marketing strategy optimization: Big data analysis can help yacht consumers understand market competition and competitors' marketing strategies. Consumers can use data analysis to understand the strengths and weaknesses of different brands and choose the yacht brand that best suits them.

3. Personalized Customization

Demand of Yacht Consumers in the Big Data Era

In the era of big data, data-driven decision-making for yacht consumers is becoming increasingly important. By collecting analyzing, and utilizing large amounts of consumer data, yacht manufacturers and sellers can better understand consumers' needs and preferences, and thus provide personalized customization and products and services that better meet consumers' expectations.

Studying big data can help yacht manufacturers understand consumers' preferences and needs. By analyzing consumers' purchase history, behavioral data, and social media activities, it is possible to gain insight into consumers' preferences, interests, and lifestyles. These data can reveal consumers' preferences for yacht size, design, features, and accessories, as well as their concerns about navigation performance, comfort, and safety. Manufacturers can use this data to guide product development and design, ensuring that yachts can meet consumers' individual needs.

Big data can also help yacht manufacturers to conduct accurate market positioning and marketing strategies. By analyzing consumers' geographical location, income level, purchasing power, and consumption habits, manufacturers can identify target consumer groups and customize promotions and marketing campaigns based on their specific needs and preferences. In addition, by monitoring consumers' social media activities and feedback, manufacturers can obtain real-time information about consumers' product evaluations and feedback, enabling them toadjust marketing strategies and product positioning in a timely manner.

Finally, big data can also help yacht manufacturers conduct predictive and predictive analysis. By analyzing historical sales data, market trends, and consumer behavior patterns, manufacturers can predict future market demand and trends, adjusting production plans and supply chain management accordingly. By monitoring and analyzing consumer data in real time, manufacturers can detect market changes and changes in consumer demand in a timely manner, enabling them to adjust products and services in a timely manner to maintain a competitive advantage.

4. Experience-oriented Demand of Yacht Consumers in the Big Data Era

In the era of big data, the experience-oriented consumption demand of yacht consumers presents the following characteristics:

Personalized customization: Big data technology can collect and analyze a large amount of consumer data, including their preferences, interests, behaviors, and other information. Yacht consumers hope to customize their yachts according to their personalized needs, to meet their pursuit of unique and personalized experiences.

Customer participation: Big data technology can enable real-time interaction and feedback with consumers, and yacht manufacturers can communicate and exchange ideas with consumers through online platforms, social media, and other channels. Consumers hope to participate in the design and decision-making process of yachts, and offer their own opinions and suggestions, in order to achieve a better personalized experience.

Personalized service: Big data analysis can help yacht manufacturers understand consumers' preferences and needs and provide more personalized services. For example, recommending suitable routes, destinations, activities, and providing customized travel experiences based on consumers' preferences. Consumers hope to enjoy distinctive and unique services and enhance the comfort and satisfaction of yacht travel.

Social interaction: Social media platforms in the era of big data provide yacht consumers with more opportunities for social interaction. They can share their yacht experiences, exchange ideas, and connect and interact with other yacht enthusiasts through social media. Consumers hope to obtain more information and inspiration through social media platforms where they canshare their preferences and experiences with other yacht consumers.

5. The Influence of Social Media on the Decision-making of Yacht Consumers

In the era of big data, social media has a significant impact on yacht consumers. Here are some possible areas of influence:

Brand promotion and awareness creation: Social media platforms have become an important channel for yacht brand promotion and publicity. Yacht manufacturers and dealers can showcase their products and services by posting beautiful pictures, videos, and stories. This direct brand promotion can increase consumers' awareness and interest in yacht brands.

Consumer opinions and reputation communication: Social media platforms provide a platform for consumers to share their yacht experiences and opinions. Consumers can post photos, videos, and reviews of their yachts on social media, communicating and sharing their views with other consumers. This user-generated content has an impact on the purchasing decisions of other potential consumers, and word-of-mouth communication plays an important role in the yacht consumer community.

Personalized recommendations and customized needs: Social media platforms can provide personalized recommendations and customized needs by analyzing users' interests and behavior data. Yacht consumers can obtain relevant information and suggestions through social media platforms based on their preferences and needs, thereby better meeting their expectations.

Fashion and design trends: Social media platforms have become an important channel for yacht consumers to learn about the latest fashion and design trends. Consumers can follow yacht brands, designers, and related social media accounts to obtain the latest design inspiration and trend information. This information acquisition can help consumers better understand market dynamics and make more informed purchasing decisions.

Chapter 6

Developmental History of Yacht Clubs

The yachting industry involves all aspects of economic activity, from consumption (marketing and sales) to service and post-sale assistance and support Yacht travel is a very complex experience, covering such things as renting, and maintenance, participation in club activities, acquiring necessary facilities, receiving professional training, and purchasing insurance. There are two pillars of the yachting tourism industry: to provide high-quality services for tourists, and to provide convenient transportation and parking places for yacht enthusiasts.

Yacht clubs are committed to providing a variety of yacht-related services, from early design to later maintenance, requiring professional management and operation. Yacht clubs not only have well-established parking facilities, but also provide opportunities for a wealth of water sports training, leisure vacation, maintenance, business meetings, hotel services, and other functions. These services provide tourists with a more convenient way to travel, promote the widespread development of marine leisure activities, and play a vital role in promoting the economic development of the yachting industry.

This chapter will describe the developmental history of yacht clubs. The first section will detail the emergence and rise of yacht clubs. The second section will introduce the history of yacht clubs in Western countries. The third section will introduce yacht clubs in China, including their overall size and general distribution, the factors affecting their layout, an overview of large-scale and well-known clubs there, the conditions for the development of yacht clubs there,, the reasons for restricting their development and the countermeasures to promote the development of yacht clubs in China.

Section 1: Developmental History of Yacht Clubs

In 18th-century Britain, navigation was an important tool for the country's diplomacy, trade, and colonization. The shipbuilding industry also developed to a considerable degree. With the continuous accumulation of wealth, the pleasure demand of the upper-class aristocrats gradually diversified the functions of ships from transportation and combat to the emergence of private small sailing ships with entertainment as the main function. In order to provide berthing, supply, and repair services for these aristocrats' small sailing ships, small docks were built, which were the early yacht clubs.

With the increasing number of upper-class aristocrats who loved boats, the number and scale of docks continuously expanded, and the level of decoration and decoration gradually increased. At this time, many docks have specialized names and their functions have been enriched. Yacht clubs have become another important gathering place for upper-class aristocrats, in addition to gentlemen's clubs and societies.

After World War II, yacht clubs grew rapidly. In the 1950s, the prosperity of the global economy and the continuous improvement of yacht technology made the number of yacht owners rise sharply, and yachting activities became more popular. They became not only high-end leisure and entertainment projects, but also symbols of personality and noble status, together with luxury cars and private planes.

The global yachting industry generates tens of billions of dollars in economic revenue every year, with the United States leading the way. Sales in the US yacht market account for more than half of the world's total sales. These revenues include sales of new and used boats, engines, trailers, accessories, safety equipment, fuel, insurance, maintenance, docking, launching, storage, club fees, and other expenditures. The development of the US yachting industry can be divided into four stages.

The first stage: Before the 1970s, the per capita GDP of the United States had been leading the world, even surpassing the United Kingdom, making it one of the richest countries in the world. During this period, the yachting industry in the United States developed rapidly. In 1913, the number of yachts owned in the United States reached 400,000. By the 1960s and 1970s, this industry had developed into a complete industrial system, covering manufacturing, sales, maintenance, service, and insurance. It made important contributions to the economic development of the United States. In 1970, the yacht market in the United States developed rapidly, with sales reaching US$3.44 billion, and the number of yachts exceeding 8.81 million, which meant that one in every 23 Americans owned a yacht.

The second stage: From the late 1970s to the mid-1980s, the US yacht market developed rapidly, with more than 1,300 yacht clubs and more than 4,000 yacht marinas serving a total of 12 million yachts, accounting for almost one-third of the total global yachts at that time. Vy 1988, the US yacht market achieved total sales of up to US$17.9 billion, and the number of yachts also exceeded 15 million, with an average of one in 16 people owning a yacht.

The third stage: From the late 1980s to the early 1990s, the global yacht market experienced a significant decline, with the United States experiencing a particularly significant downturn. In 1992, sales of the yachting industry in the United States declined to US$10.3 billion.

The fourth stage: Since the 1990s, the yacht market in the United States has experienced a second boom, including a total of more than 17 million yachts andone-third of the country's population engaged in yacht-related industries. Compared to the downturn a decade earlier, the yacht market became more prosperous and active. In 2002, the sales volume of yachts in the United States reached a staggering US$30 billion, which exceeded 55% of the global yacht market, making the United States the leader in the global yachting industry.

In the 21st century, the rapid development of China's economy has attracted worldwide attention, and people's pursuit of quality of life has become increasingly high. Yachting has also become a fashion trend. It not only attracts the attention of some high-income groups, but also provides unprecedented development opportunities for many cities and promotes the development of new service industries.

Hong Kong is an important economic center in China, and its yachting industry is relatively mature. Here, there are dozens of yacht marinas with excellent conditions. Modern yacht clubs not only provide basic services, but also various entertainment and business activities, such as restaurants, bars, parking lots, maintenance centers, supply stations, and driving training centers. As people pursue fashion activities, yachts have become the first choice for people to relax. Typical yacht clubs usually have a variety of facilities, such as yachts, marinas, conference rooms, navigation systems, entertainment venues, and other activity venues.

Section 2: Yacht Clubs in Western Countries

Neva Yacht Club

This sailing club near the Neva River in St. Petersburg was founded in 1718 by Tsar Peter the Great, who was the most enthusiastic figure in water life in Russian history. In order to meet the operational needs of the club, Peter himself provided 141 small boats free of charge for the entertainment needs of club members. The club's current flag, which is still in use, was also designed by Peter the Great, inspired by the flag of the Russian Navy at that time. The Neva Yacht Club and its facilities, which are still in operation, were rebuilt on the original site in 1958. The original club ceased to exist after the death of its founder. and for this reason, the club's title as the "oldest yacht club in history" has been strongly challenged by the second ranked Royal Cork Yacht Club, which was established two years after Neva/

Royal Cork Yacht Club

The Royal Cork Yacht Club in Ireland was founded in 1720. The original site of the club was on the island of Howth, in the port of Cork, but now it is located in Crosshaven, near Cork City. The Royal Cork Yacht Club is a comprehensive club that provides services such as boat parking, repair, maintenance, rental, boat maintenance, social activities, leisure, and entertainment. The club has world-class facilities and services, providing members with the highest quality yacht experience. In the club's development history, it has undergone several name changes and relocations. It was originally called The Water Club of the Harbour of Cork. In 1831 King William IV of England officially renamed it the Royal Cork Yacht Club. At the end of the 19th century, the club moved to its current location in Crosshaven. Members of the Royal Cork Yacht Club can enjoy a variety of services and activities, including boat docking, repair, maintenance, rental, boat maintenance, social activities, leisure, and entertainment. The club also organizes various competitions and activities, such as the Spring Series, the Annual Dinner, and the Yacht Exhibition. This yacht club has maintained a high level of activity for nearly 300 years. Currently, there are about 1,600 members, and it hosts various world championships, European championships, and Irish championships throughout the year. The club offers a variety of small sailing projects, including youth OP sailing, Toppers, laser classes, and windsurfing, to meet the needs of different age groups. In the Irish sailing community, Cork Week is the most popular competition.

Royal Thames Yacht Club

The Royal Thames Yacht Club is located on the banks of the River Thames, adjacent to Hyde Park. In 1775, King George III, the Duke of Cumberland, and Prince Henry of Strathearn jointly organized a grand sailing competition, and then they formed the Cumberland Fleet, which opened the first professional yacht club on the banks of the Thames. All this brought an unforgettable experience to British yacht enthusiasts and provided them with a stage to showcase British yachting skills. With the accession of King William IV, the British Empire began to expand rapidly. The Royal Thames Yacht Club has also been renamed since the accession of King Charles III. Lord Louis Mountbatten had been in charge for 20 years. Now, Prince Andrew has taken on the new role of chair to manage the Royal Thames Yacht Club.

The Royal Yacht Squadron

The Royal Yacht Squadron is a prestigious club in the UK tha thas become the first choice for many tourists. In 1815, a group of British gentlemen who loved sailing jointly established this club, which holds two grand meetings in London and Cowes every year to explore the unknown parts of the world. Members in the early days of the club were required have a boat weighing no less than ten tons and be "gentlemen interested in yachting." After George IV inherited the throne in 1820, the club was renamed the Royal Yacht Club. In 1833, King William IV renamed the club the Royal Yacht Fleet Club to express his appreciation for the fleet and emphasize their close ties. The late Queen Elizabeth II was a patron of the club, and her husband Prince Philip was once the captain of the Royal Yacht Squadron, which shows the important connection of the royal family to the Royal Yacht Squadron Club. In 1826, the Cowes Week Regatta was successfully held, and its popularity and influence have spread all over the world. The club has played an important role in the history of sailing by contributing to the development of sailing regattas. In 1851, the first America's Cup was held between the New York Yacht Club and Cowes on the Isle of Wight. Every summer, more than 1,000 sailing boats and more than 8,000 sailors gather to participate in the world's largest sailing competition, which inspires much enthusiasm and vitality. During the Second World War, the Royal Yacht Squadron made important contributions to the British Navy. Many members of the club participated in the war and played an important role in it. After the war, the club resumed its daily activities and continued to provide high-quality services and experiences for its members.

Thanks to the support and encouragement of the British royal family, these yacht clubs have been able to grow rapidly and make great contributions to the progress of modern sailing sports. The yacht club culture also began to spread from the United Kingdom to the world.

Royal Northern & Clyde Yacht Club

The history of the Northern Yacht Club can be traced back to 1824, represented by the two fleets of Scotland and Ireland at that time. It was awarded the Royal title in 1830. The Clyde Model Yacht Club was founded in 1856 and received the title of Royal in 1863. The two yacht clubs provided services for yacht owners in Scotland at that time. In 1886, the Northern Yacht Club's sailing ship Galatea began to compete in the America's Cup sailing regatta. The following year, the Thistle from the Clyde Model Yacht Club also began to enter the America's Cup. In 1937, the Northern Yacht Club relocated to its current location in Rhu area; the Clyde Model Yacht Club also moved here and merged in 1978 to become the current Royal Northern & Clyde Yacht Club.

Royal Swedish Yacht Club

The Royal Swedish Yacht Club was founded on May 15, 1830. It is the oldest and largest yacht club in Sweden and the first yacht club on the European continent. In 1878, the Royal Swedish Yacht Club was born during a sailing competition. Since 1833, it has continuously held various sailing regattas and successfully launched the first Round Gotland Race in 1854. In addition, the club has participated in the America's Cup many times, and its Artemis team is also one of the best. Currently, the Royal Swedish Yacht Club has more than 5,000 loyal members.

Royal Yacht Association

The Royal Yacht Association is the largest yacht club in the United Kingdom. It was founded in 1835 and is headquartered in London. The club was originally formed by a group of people who loved sailing, aiming to promote the development of ocean navigation and sailing skills. In the early days of the club's establishment, the Royal Yacht Association participated in various oceanic competitions and activities, including sailing competitions and coastal navigation. In 1844, the club began organizing an annual canoeing competition, which was one of the earliest such competitions in the United Kingdom. In 1851, the club began participating in national-level sailing competitions and sent its own fleet to participate. Over time, the Royal Yacht Association gradually became the leader of the British sailing industry. In 1870, the club began hosting the Queen's Yacht Race, one of the earliest yacht races in the United Kingdom. In 1899, the club established the British Naval Recruitment Center, which made great contributions to recruiting naval soldiers for the country. In the 20th century, the Royal Yacht Association continued to participate in various sailing activities and competitions. In 1903, the club organized the first Queen Elizabeth Yacht Race, an international yacht race that attracted participants from all over the world. In 1920, the club established the Royal Yacht Squadron, which trained outstanding sailing talents for the country. During the Second World War, the Royal Yacht Association actively participated in rescue operations and assisted in evacuating wounded and refugees. After the war, the club continued to work on the development of the sailing industry and promote the development of various sailing activities and competitions. Today, the Royal Yacht Squadron has become an important organization and leader in the British sailing industry, with about 2,000 members. The club has performed well in various sailing competitions and has its own fleet and dock facilities.

Irish Yacht Club

The Irish Yacht Club in Cork, Republic of Ireland,was founded in 1836 and is one of the oldest yacht clubs in Ireland. The club was originally known as the Cork Yacht Club and was formed by a group of people who loved sailing. Its aim was to promote the development of ocean navigation and navigation skills. In its early days,, the Irish Yacht Club mainly participated in various sailing competitions and activities. In 1841, the club held the first Cork Yacht Race, an important sailing competition that attracted fleets from the United Kingdom and Ireland. Since then, the club has continued to host this race and gradually developed it into an international sailing competition. In the 1850s, the Irish Yacht Club underwent an important restructuring and was renamed the Royal Irish Yacht Club. This name has been used ever since, except for the period from 1921 to 1936, when the club temporarily cancelled the "royal" title for political reasons. During the late 19th and early 20th centuries, the Irish Yacht Club continued to grow and develop, not only increasing the number of members, but also expanding the scope of activities. In 1892, the club established the first women's sailing team in Cork City. In 1900, the club began participating in international sailing competitions, including the famous Irish Cup sailing competition. During World War II, the Irish Yacht Club actively participated in rescue operations and assisted in evacuating the wounded and refugees. After the war, the club continued to work towards the development of sailing and promote the development of various sailing activities and competitions. Today, the Irish Yacht Club is one of the largest yacht clubs in Ireland, with about 1,200 members. The club actively participates in various sailing competitions and activities, involving small sailing boats, large sailing boats, and rowing boats. In addition, the club has its own dock facilities for members and fleets to use.

Detroit Boat Club

On February 18, 1839, the Detroit Boat Club was officially established with unanimous approval at a meeting in E. A. Brush's office, becoming the oldest yacht club in North America. Georgiana was the first New York Clinker-built four-oared racing boat purchased by the club. After 1842, sailing yachts on the sea quickly became a popular recreational activity. In 1846, the club named a nearby island Belle Isle, which was the name of the daughter of club member Admiral Lewis Cass. In February 1996, the Detroit Boat Club left the island but remained committed to becoming a club with a long history of sailing and social activities.

The New York Yacht Club

On July 30, 1844, the New York Yacht Club was founded. Led by Commodore John Cox Stevens, nine gentlemen who loved sailing issued a call for crew members to set sail from New York to Newport, marking the official opening of the navigation exchange between the two port cities. The New York Yacht Club is famous around the world, thanks to its reputation with the America's Cup. In 1851, the first America's Cup regatta kicked off between the New York Yacht Club and the Royal Yacht Squadron Club. The America fleet led by John Cox Stevens fought its way through difficulties and finally won the final championship trophy. Since the event was held, the New York Yacht Club has remained the club with the most championships.

Société des Regates du Havre

In 1838, the Paris-Havre railway was connected, reducing travel time by train to only six hours, which prompted the establishment of this club. Afterwards, Monsieur Baudy began a sailing competition across the English Channel on the advice of the board members. On July 29, 1840, the first of these competitions was officially held, and this event has become a tradition ever since. In 1863, the Le Havre Yacht Club was given legal status by the government. Its original location was destroyed during World War II, but the club's supporters and members moved it to its current new address after the war.

Segel Yacht Club (Segel Club Rhe)

In 1855, the Segel yacht club was founded in Königsberg, East Prussia. At that time, its founder Ernst Burow, a high school student, received a fishing boat and decided to go out to sea with a group of like-minded friends. It was this group of young people who established this club. Since then, the club developed rapidly and achieved great success. In the summer, they hold various competitions in the Baltic Sea and surrounding waters. In the winter, they launch one sailing race after another. The Segel yacht club has made great contributions to the development of the German sailing industry. However, after the end of World War II, the Soviet invasion forced the Segel Yacht Club to relocate to the outskirts of Hamburg in Blanknesser. The club's move to a new address did not affect the development of its activities. The fleet often shuttled across the tranquil waters of the Alster Lake-Elbe River. The club's representative team participated in the America's Cup regatta, and the German United Internet Team was the first German team to participate. In 2007, the club became a member of the International Yacht Club Association.

French Cannes Yacht Club (Club Nautique de Cannes)

In 1860, the Cannes Yacht Club was established, becoming one of the oldest sailing clubs in France. In 1864, Duke de Vallombrosa generously donated a 3,000 square meter piece of land for the construction of its clubhouse, which is at the end of the Promenade des Anglais in Cannes. The vibrant Cannes Yacht Club is not only a domain for hereditary aristocrats, but also provides a more equitable platform for the entire society. Since 1928, it has hosted the French Royal regatta. At the end of September every year, dragon class sailing races and classical sailing races are held near Cannes. Meanwhile, the 12-meter yacht world championship is also held here.

Royal Belgium Yacht Club

In 1863, Gaston de Buisseret and Steenbecque de Blarenghien, two yacht enthusiasts, founded the Royal Belgium Yacht Club on the River Lehe in Ghent. In 1873, the club was given the royal title. The club has evolved into a large club with five bases, and with inland and coastal sailing. In 1963, the Prince attended a large naval parade and served as honorary president of the club to commemorate its 100th anniversary of the founding of the Royal Belgium Club. Today, the Royal Belgium Club has more than 2,400 members, including IOC Chairman Jacques Rogge and Belgian bronze medalist Evi Van Acker from the 2012 Olympics. The club is renowned for its numerous internationally influential sailing competitions, providing strong support for the organization of the regattas. The club actively invests in cultivating outstanding young yachtsmen, nurturing new forces for the yachting movement.

The Royal Melbourne Yacht Squadron

The Royal Melbourne Yacht Squadron is the number one yacht club in Melbourne, Australia. The Royal Yacht Club was established in 1870 and was granted the royal title by the British monarchy in 1924 after 53 years of construction and hard work. It is also the headquarters of the Olympic sailing competition and was the venue for the Olympics award ceremony in 1956. New members of the Royal Yacht Club of Melbourne must be invited and recommended by current members, and the conditions are very demanding

Yacht Club de Monaco

The Royal Yacht Club of Monaco (YCM) was founded in 1953 and is managed by His Serene Highness Prince Albert, the head of state. It has more than 1,200 distinguished members from 60 countries. Its yacht marina is home to top private custom yachts from all over the world. Members of YCM must meet strict standards, including the possession of classical sailing ships or vintage yachts, yachts over 40 meters, and super royal ships with a long maritime history. In addition, they must be recommended by at least two other members to become a member of YCM. It is considered to be a perfect global first royal club. YCM is a worldwide organization, and its members included Prince Albert's late mother, the world-renowned Princess Grace Kelly of Monaco, as well as members of British royalty.

The International Council of Marine Industry Associations (ICOMIA)

The British Yachting Association was founded in 1967 to explore the future direction of the yachting industry and provide support for its sustainable development through international cooperation and exchanges. The association is a national-level informal organization dedicated to providing professional guidance and advice to the yachting industry. Currently, ICOMIA includes more than 70 yachting associations in 40 countries and regions. The annual meeting held by the World Yacht Federation, also known as the World Yacht Congress and the Davos of the yachting industry, is hosted by member countries in rotation. Well-known figures in the global yachting industry will attend this event to discuss recent economic issues in the industry and its future direction. In 2009, China officially joined the World Yacht Federation as a member.

Section 3: Yacht Clubs in China

1. Overall Size and General Distribution of Yacht Clubs in China

In recent years, China's yachting industry has developed rapidly, but compared with Western developed countries, due to its late start, the domestic market is still in its infancy, with uneven distribution and a lack of agglomeration areas Most of China's yacht clubs are concentrated in the eastern coastal areas, but the degree of concentration is not very obvious. The development of China's yacht clubs has gradually improved in recent years. With the rapid development of the domestic economy and tourism industry, more and more people have begun to get involved in yachting.

On the one hand, the yachting industry in coastal cities such as Sanya, Shenzhen, and Guangzhou has developed rapidly, and yacht clubs have also been correspondingly strengthened. They not only provide services such as yacht rental, yacht sales, and driving training, but also hold various sailing events and activities, attracting a large number of tourists and investors. On the other hand, inland lakes and reservoirs have also become a new area for the development of yacht clubs, such as Liangzidao Yacht Club in Hubei province and Fuxian Lake Yacht Club in Yunnan province. These clubs mainly provide local yacht and boating services.

Currently, the most yacht clubs in China are located in Shanghai (22), Shandong (18), Guangdong (14), Zhejiang (12), and Jiangsu (11). In terms of China's urban areas, there are 22 in Shanghai, 10 in Tianjin, 10 in Qingdao, 8 in Xiamen, 6 in Shenzhen, 6 in Suzhou, 5 in Zhoushan, and 4 in Haikou and Sanya respectively.

2. Influential Factors of Yacht Club Layout in China

(1) Natural Resources and Environment

With the development of the economy, the number of Chinese yacht clubs is increasing. Most are in the eastern area, with its long coastline, vast sea area and beautiful islands, making it the best place for yacht sports. In addition, there are abundant biological resources such as coral reefs and mangroves here, which not only have important ecological value, but also have a unique landscape aesthetic value. Among them, mangroves are mainly distributed in Guangdong, Hainan, Zhejiang, and Fujian provinces. According to the Standard of Seawater Quality (GB3097 -1997), Hainan has the best water quality, Guangdong and

Shandong have good water quality, while Shanghai and Zhejiang have poor water quality. With the continuous improvement of the green ecological civilization index, the ecological environment in Hainan is becoming more and more perfect. In addition, the 5A-level scenic spots in Jiangsu, Shandong, Zhejiang, Guangdong and other provinces have excellent natural scenery and rich tourism resources, providing tourists with an excellent place for comfortable leisure and vacation. In addition to Yinghu Lake and Ankang in Shaanxi Province, many yacht clubs in inland provinces are also located insuch places as the Yangtze River in Chongqing, the Jialing River and the Three Gorges Reservoir area, the Xiangjiang River in Changsha, Hunan province, and Songya Lake, because they are all located in places with perfect water environment and fascinating natural scenery.

(2) Regional Economic Level

As a region's external economy continues to open up, the number and scale of private or foreign-funded enterprises are increasing, which will greatly enhance the local consumption level and encourage local residents to embrace new recreational activities, thus promoting the development of yacht clubs. In addition, a large number of high-net-worth individuals in a particular region provides good conditions for the development of yacht clubs.

(3) Yacht Manufacturing Industry

Yacht manufacturing plays a crucial role in the development of the yachting industry chain. It not only affects the development environment of yacht clubs, but also determines their target positioning. Some yacht clubs are striving to expand their business scope, with local yacht brands as the core, while also actively collaborating with yacht manufacturers to enhance their economic benefits.

(4) yachting industry Policy

The current policies for China's yachting industry have not been fully implemented for several reasons. There are many problems in current laws and regulations, such as the insufficient strictness of the inspection and registration procedures for yachts, the need to expand the scope of yachts' seaworthiness, and the lack of clear standards for the design, construction, and acceptance of clubs. In addition, some regions even prohibit night navigation and limit the maximum mileage of yachts, which hinder the normal operation of yachts, as well as the development of clubs and the popularization of yacht tourism. In order to promote the development of the regional yachting industry, Hainan, Tianjin, Shanghai, Guangdong and other provinces have introduced a number of policies, such as free trade ports, coastal new areas, water and land bonded warehouses, and free travel for tourists in Guangdong, Hong Kong and Macao. These policies can not only attract yacht clubs, but also effectively promote the development of the local economy and society. In addition, local governments have taken a series of measures to strengthen the safety management of the yachting industry, including upgrading the management of public security border defense, carrying out non-business yacht driver training, and mandating examination, evaluation, and certification management, in order to reflect its determination of macro-control and standardized management. Local fiscal policies, industrial planning, and coastal environmental construction can also provide effective support for club activities.

(5) Regional Marine Culture

Embracing an open and forward-looking maritime culture provides a favorable environment for the promotion of yachting and the development of clubs. The number of yacht exhibitions and competitions in 9 coastal provinces accounts for 81.82% of the national total, including various types of sailboats as well as provisions for such activities as windsurfing, rowing, kayaking, and canoeing, thus, providing yacht enthusiasts with a richer experience. The spread of marine culture is inextricably linked to the construction of seaside tourist attractions, which not only provide marine sightseeing but also provide bathing beaches,, thus providing a good social and cultural atmosphere for the development of yacht clubs.

3. Large-scale Well-known Domestic Yacht Clubs

The Royal Hong Kong Yacht Club

The Royal Hong Kong Yacht Club is the oldest yacht club in Hong Kong and the largest yacht club in China, with more than 10,000 members. In addition to its headquarters on Kellett Island, the Royal Yacht Club also has chapters in South Island, Ironwave Island and Shelter Cove in Saigon, offering visitors more options. The origins of the Hong Kong Yacht Club can be traced back to the Victoria Regatta Club, which first held a series of events in October 1849 and received widespread acclaim. In 1889, it was established as the Hong Kong Corinthian Sailing Club, and in 1893, the club board applied to the British Navy to change its name to the Royal Hong Kong Yacht Club. In 1997, when Hong Kong returned to China, the "Royal" title in the Chinese name was deleted, while the English name remained unchanged. The Hong Kong Yacht Club was originally located in the Yacht Club Clubhouse on Oil Street, North Point, Hong Kong. In 1938, the clubhouse moved to Kellett Island. After the end of World War II, on September 17, 1945, the clubhouse reopened. In 1951, a dam was built at the site to connect it with Hong Kong Island. In 1972, the opening of the Hong Kong Cross-Harbour Tunnel marked the formal inclusion of Kellett Island into Hong Kong. It is located at the exit of the tunnel and has become an important part of Hong Kong Island.

Shanghai Laiyue Yacht Club

Shanghai Laiyue Yacht Club, located in the center of the Bund, is an international yacht club. Established in 2006, it is meticulously led by an elite team from the China Laiyue Yacht Group, providing tourists with the best experience. Shanghai Laiyue Yacht Club Co., Ltd. has foreign connections, as in its commitment to promoting and spreading yacht culture in Australia and around the world. It has opened multiple clubs in China and serves as the general agent for Australian Sunrunner yachts. Laiyne has also imported yachts from the United States into China to meet the needs of yacht enthusiasts and provide the optimum experience for yacht enthusiasts. Its comprehensive services include membership services, dock construction and operation management, yacht sales and maintenance, dock planning, and yacht club project consulting. The club is committed to introducing internationally popular yacht leisure styles, high-quality products, and advanced club management models to China in order to enhance the quality and level of domestic yacht consumption and promote yacht leisure culture. It also provides a range of services including berthing, license application, inspection, channel application, insurance, and driving training.

Shenzhen Longcheer Yacht Club

In May 1998, Shenzhen Longcheer Yacht was established. It is the earliest membership-based yacht club in China, offering sea-view rooms, Chinese and Western restaurants, bars, conference rooms, entertainment rooms, seaview terraces, outdoor barbecue fields, and other services. It is deeply loved by high-end consumers on the South China coast and is known as the "high-end residential circle of the South China coast.". It enjoys a high reputation in society.

Dalian Xinghai Bay International Yacht Club

In May 2002, the Dalian Xinghai Bay International Yacht Club was officially established in the western part of the Dalian Xinghai Bay Business District. It has convenient transportation access, being only 5 kilometers away from Dalian Railway Station, 8 kilometers away from Dalian Port, 10 kilometers away from Zhoushuizi International Airport, and 12 kilometers away from the entrance to the Shenyang-Dalian Expressway. In addition, Xinghai Bay also boasts a series of exquisite tourism and cultural facilities such as Xinghai Park, Shengya Ocean World, Xinghai Bay Beach, Century City Carving, Modern Museum, Xinghai Convention and Exhibition Center, and World Expo Square. time, the club has made rapid progress in its development, and its infrastructure and supporting service facilities have reached an impressive level. The number and quality of moored yachts are among the greatest in China. It has become a perfect sightseeing destination, leisure resort, and fishing spot in the southern waters of Dalian, as well as being the largest and most well-equipped club in northern China.

Rhine Garden Yacht Club

The Rhine Garden Yacht Club is located on the Sha Jiao Island in Luoxi, Panyu District, Guangzhou. The facilities of the yacht club are very complete with a variety of restaurants representing both Chinese and Western cuisine, plus outdoor terraces, conference rooms, convenience stores, multi-function banquet halls, reading rooms, fitness centers, tennis halls, badminton halls, swimming pools, saunas, and luxury villas. In addition, Rhine Garden also provides a professional boat docking area, boat display area, boat driving training center and parking lot, making the function of this yacht club more complete.

Sanya Hongzhou International Yacht Club

Hongzhou International Yacht Club Co., Ltd. is located in Sanya, surrounded by mountains and rivers. It is located at the mouth of the Sanya River, facing the Luhuitou Mountain across the river. The sea here is wide and the climate is pleasant, making it possible to sail out to sea all year round. Hongzhou Group is a professional yacht operator that focuses on providing various types of yachts, including rental, sale, docking, exhibition, maintenance, and repair. It also provides various support services for customers, such as ship inspection and certification, yacht driving skills training, and ship insurance.

Nature International Yacht Club

The Nature International Yacht Club is located in the Kunshan sedimentation on the banks of the mountain lake, with a 12,000 square meter villa area that offers a high degree of luxury and dignity. This five-star private club is famous for its unique architectural design, exquisite appearance, and gorgeous interior decoration. It not only provides catering, accommodation, conference, leisure and entertainment, yachting and other services, but also has 27 luxury rooms and suites, as well as a well-equipped fitness center, outdoor swimming pool, wine and cigar bar, chess room and other leisure facilities.

Yinhai International Yacht Club

Qingdao Yinhai International Yacht Club, with 366 professional docking berths, is built according to international standards. . Yinhai is the first tourist attraction in China with a yacht club as its main body. The Yinhai Group began construction in March of 2003 with an investment of CNY¥300 million, and it opened in 2005. Provided by the Olympic Sailing Regatta with its excellent service, it has become one of the most influential yacht clubs in China. The club has the first-class facilities, including professional docks, yacht parking areas, sailing training grounds, athletes' residences, fitness and entertainment centers, Chinese and Western restaurants, and various standard guest rooms. It provides a perfect travel experience for tourists. Yinhai Haixing Convention and Exhibition Center is a professional yacht driving training and sailing training base, providing professional training services for domestic and foreign athletes. Every year, a series of exciting international maritime expositions, yacht and sailing exhibitions, conferences, and cultural performances are held here, which not only brings rich business opportunities to the yacht and sailing industry, but also creates a new brand of exhibition economy.

4. Conditions for the Development of Yacht Clubs in China

(1) Economic Strength

Yachts are high-end consumer goods, and yacht clubs needs strong economic backing to fulfill their roles as the agents of yacht consumption. As a rule of thumb, a per-capita GDP of US$3000 is generally required for optimum yacht sales in a country or region. Many cities in China such as

Guangzhou, Hangzhou, Qingdao, and Xiamen have reached the level of US$4000-$6000, whileShanghai, Beijing, Shenzhen have reached US$10,000 US. These figures indicate that China has become a player in the realm of yacht consumption.

In 2011, the Lin Guobao Wealth Management and Capgemini Consulting groups jointly published the Asia-Pacific Wealth Report, which showed that the total assets of the wealthy class (net assets exceeding US$1 million) in mainland China reached US$2.66 trillion, making it the second largest wealth market in Asia. According to the report, in 2010, only 0.5% of Chinese households owned more than 60% of personal wealth, and in the next few years, this proportion may further increase to 13%. In addition, in 2010, the total number of wealthy people in China with more than US$1 million reached 535,000.

With the continuous development of China's economy, the income of Chinese people is also increasing year by year, and buying or leasing a yacht is no longer a dream.

(2) Geographical Environment

China is rich in water resources, including 4.73 million square kilometers of ocean, more than 18,000 kilometers of coastline and 17 million hectares of inland waters, which provide an excellent external environment for the development of the yachting industry. Therefore, the government and enterprises in China should increase their investment to meet the development needs of the yachting industry, thus providing a solid foundation for the development of yacht clubs. Coastal cities such as Xiamen, Shenzhen, Zhuhai, and Sanya have vast sea areas and pleasant climate, making them ideal places for the development of yacht clubs. Cities such as Shenzhen and Sanya have also achieved remarkable results in yacht tourism and leasing, providing more development opportunities for yacht clubs.

(3) Infrastructure Support

With the continuous development of the economy, more and more yacht clubs have begun to enter China, with a variety of basic facilities such as marinas, clubs, hotels, and yacht parking areas to meet the needs of different tourists. Especially in coastal cities with prosperous economies, the infrastructure is more complete, and the activities of yacht clubs are also more frequent. Although the marine resources in second- and third-tier cities are relatively scarce, they can still be a focus for the future development of yacht clubs. Some cities may not be economically developed, but they have a good natural environment, convenient transportation, and well-developed infrastructure such as hotels and clubs, which enables them to make full use of and protect water resources so as to more effectively meet the needs of yacht clubs and promote the future development of the yacht tourism industry.

(4) Laws and Regulations

There are many factors to consider when building a yacht club, from the selection, purchase, operation, maintenance of yachts to the layout and size of the docks, all of which must meet certain standards. A sound legal system is an important foundation for promoting the healthy development of the industry. Although the laws and regulations of yacht clubs in China have not reached a perfect level in recent years, a series of measures have been taken to strengthen safety management. For example, on January 1, 2009, the Regulations on the Safety Management of Yachts were introduced, providing strict standards for the registration, operation and navigation of yachts. On March 18, 2010, the Haikou Municipal Government actively promoted the safety management of yachts and organized a national yacht club collaboration alliance to provide a safe and comfortable environment for yacht enthusiasts, promote the spread of yacht culture, and enhance the safety level of yachts.

Although China has the basic conditions for the development of yacht clubs, the development of the yachting industry has not yet reached the expected level, and the sales of yachts are far lower than that of luxury cars. According to statistics, an average yacht owner spends only about 15 days a year using the vessel, but they have to pay huge maintenance, parking and registration fees for it. Therefore, renting a yacht is attractive to most people, but if the club can effectively manage idle yachts, they can be promoted to the general public and become a fashion. There is a close relationship between yacht manufacturers and clubs, which jointly promote the development of the yachting industry.

5. Reasons for the Development of Chinese Yacht Clubs

Looking at the current development of domestic yacht clubs, the main limitations are as follows:

(1) Both Yacht Registration and Yacht Navigation Lack Regulations That Are in Line with International Standards

In 1971, the United States enacted the Federal Yacht Safety Act, which greatly facilitated the ownership of yachts, promoted the rapid development of the yachting industry in the United States, and brought great prosperity to the American economy. Although China has begun to make efforts to promote the construction of a yacht management system, there is still a lack of effective policies and regulations, especially for yacht-specific docks, waterways, active waters, maintenance, and driving guarantees. Moreover, there is also a lack of a fair and impartial recognition mechanism involving yachts in different administrative jurisdictions.

With the increase in yacht consumption, but lacking a unified management mechanism, yacht driving licenses can only be used locally, resulting in restrictions on yacht navigation between different regions, and the routes for cargo and yachts have not been completely separated. This situation greatly weakens the demand for yachts among the wealthy class and also hinders the development of the entire yachting industry.

At the 2005 Shanghai Boat Show, the first yacht in Shanghai, the Nun Man Er was put up for transfer. Its fate is a true reflection of the current situation of yachts in China and highlights the bottleneck of legal policies.

Chang Xiaolei, the owner of the Nun Man Er yacht, does not have a Chinese yacht license but holds a license issued by Australia. Therefore, he can only rely on the qualifications of river navigation boatmen to operate a yacht in China. He once drove a yacht with friends to Zhouzhuang, but when entering Jiangsu waters, he was blocked by the local maritime department because he did not apply in advance. According to China's current laws and regulations, the Nun Man Er yacht must be operated only in the Huangpu River and its surrounding areas in Shanghai. Navigation in mountains, lakes, the TaihuLake and other waters is not the same as in foreign countries, where you can drive freely throughout the whole country with your driver's license.

(2) Water Pollution

In countries with developed yacht economies such as Europe and the United States, beautiful water environments are important factors in the development of the yachting industry. Although China has abundant water resources, its water quality is worrying. The coastal areas of the Yangtze River Delta, Pearl River Delta, and Bohai Bay have high levels of marine pollution, making it difficult to travel by yacht and resulting in a poor tourism experience.

(3) Supporting Facilities Need to be Further Improved

With the advancement of technology, the number of yacht manufacturing enterprises is increasing, and their prices are relatively lower, but there are still certain challenges. In order to meet the development needs of yacht clubs, the government should increase investment in yacht ports and marinas to improve the operational efficiency of yacht clubs and provide them with more comprehensive services.

(4) The Market Needs to be Cultivated

With the development of the leisure industry, the yachting industry has become one of the most competitive high-end markets in China, and its development prospects are exciting. Even so, its underlying consumption potential is still difficult to fully realize. Therefore, it is necessary to explore the feasibility and potential of yacht tourism in depth. Fundamentally, there are significant differences between traditional Chinese culture and yacht culture. Chinese civilization is based on agriculture, while yachts represent ocean culture. Chinese people love the deep land, while yacht culture advocates the freedom and blue dreams represented by ocean navigation. In order to promote the development of China's yacht club industry, market leadership and cultivation are particularly important.

(5) The yachting industry Chain is not Perfect

China's yachting industry started late and still has significant differences compared to advanced countries in the world. These differences are reflected in, firstly, the lack of professional high-end enterprises to promote the construction and operation of the industrial chain, which cannot meet the needs of consumers. Secondly. the single business model and the failure to establish a sound industrial chain cannot achieve optimal benefits, which brings great difficulties to investors. Due to these factors, the development of the yachting industry in

China has been greatly impacted and has had a negative impact on the development of yacht clubs.

(6) Lack of Professional Talent

Few domestic universities have set up a yachting major. The lack of management, coaching, and maintenance skills is an important obstacle to the development of yacht clubs.

6. Countermeasures to Promote the Development of Yacht Clubs in China

(1) Improve the Laws and Regulations Related to the yachting industry and Yacht Clubs

On January 1, 2009, the Maritime Safety Administration of the People's Republic of China promulgated the Safety Management of Yachts and the Interim Provisions on the Statutory Inspection of Yachts, marking the formal implementation of China's first regulations for yachts. This has created a more rigorous legal environment to ensure the safety and legality of the yachting industry, promote its sustainable development, and build a more rigorous legal environment. The introduction of these regulations marks a major change in China's yachting industry. With the continuous development of technology, the cruise supervision of yachts in different waters has become feasible. Therefore, in order to promote the development of its yachting industry, China should refer to international advanced standards and formulate more suitable laws and regulations for the industry, as well as implementing effective supervision of yacht clubs to ensure their legal operation.

(2) Improve the Quality of China's Waters

According to statistical data in February 2006, among the 293 monitoring points in the coastal waters of the country, the proportion of Class I and Class II waters was as high as 67.3%, while the proportion of Class III and Class IV waters was 8.9% and 23.8% respectively. According to the latest survey results, in 18 marine ecological monitoring areas, more than 139,000 square kilometers of waters did not meet the water quality standards for clean waters, and a large number of waters were seriously polluted. The ecosystems of these bays, estuaries, and coastal wetlands are in a disadvantageous condition and may even be endangered. In view of the current shortage of water resources in China, the government must take more effective measures to improve the quality of water bodies to ensure that the whole people share a clean water environment, so as to provide a favorable ecological environment for the development of the yachting tourism industry.

(3) Reliance on the Guidance and Support of Government Policies

In order to promote the development of yacht clubs, the government should provide more support and assistance. y Reducing or waiving taxes and other preferential policies can help support the operation and management of yacht clubs. These measures can help yacht clubs achieve rapid growth in a short period of time.

(4) Promote Yacht Culture and Cultivate the Consumer Market

With the help of the yacht club platform, China can vigorously promote yachting culture and make the concept of "the wise enjoy water" deeply rooted in people's hearts. To this end, the club should take effective measures to enhance the public's awareness of yachts and create a good atmosphere for yacht consumption. Various strategies such as media, advertising, and exhibitions can be used to strengthen the public's understanding of yachts and related organizations and enhance the public's recognition of marine culture. At the same time, social media, mass media and social activities should be deployed to promote and develop a robust yachting culture. Through guidance and change, the yacht club can make potential customers feel the charm of yachting culture and turn it into actual business opportunities. In addition, the yacht club should adopt reasonable business strategies to meet the needs of different consumers

(5) Establishing a Strategic Alliance of Yacht Clubs

On March 18, 2010, Haikou officially announced the establishment of the National Yacht Club Collaborative Alliance. This initiative not only provides a strong support for the development of yacht clubs, but also helps promote exchanges and cooperation between yacht clubs, thus forming a mutually beneficial win-win situation. In order to promote the vigorous development of the yachting industry, yacht clubs and related industries around the country should work closely together to form similar strategic alliances and continue to improve the overall operational mode of the yachting industry.

(6) Cultivating Excellent Professionals

In recent years, ore and more educational institutions have established yachting majors to meet the needs of the market. However, as these majors are not yet perfect, the government should strengthen its support, integrate the teaching and research resources of major universities, and encourage educational institutions to create more yachting majors, including instruction on yacht design, manufacturing technology, and yacht tourism management in order to fundamentally solve the talent shortage problem in the yachting industry.

(7) Active Development of Yacht Club Projects

Although the scale of yacht clubs in China varies and their target consumers are also different, their business models are generally similar. In order to attract more consumers' attention and enthusiasm, yacht clubs should constantly try new projects and innovate to enhance their competitiveness. Yacht clubs are not only a place for yacht sightseeing, but also provide various entertainment programs such as sea fishing, sea weddings, and sea golf, and regularly hold various activities to increase the vitality and diversity of the yachting experience.

Chapter 7

Yacht Marinas and Yacht Destination Cities

Section 1: Planning layout, site selection, and design of yacht marinas

1. Influential factors of yacht marina layout

The development of the yachting industry in our China is still in its early stages, with the consumption of yachts mainly being dominated by enterprises and supplemented by private individuals. Compared with countries that have developed a relatively mature yachting industry, there is still a long way to go. Although yachts are still under the trend of long-term economic development in the future, the consumers of yachts will gradually shift to the middle class. The popularization of yacht consumption will be a historical inevitability, and this process of change has been slowly happening. As a result, there has been a recent demand for the construction of yacht marinas. The purpose of yacht marinas is to provide efficient, stable, safe, and convenient commercial services for the whole process of yacht consumption, so that operators can better create market-oriented products with more economic value. Here are some common planning considerations.

1. Number and type of berths

Operators need to determine the number and type of yacht berths based on projected demand and available space, which can include berths of different sizes to accommodate the docking needs of various sizes of yachts. They must also consider the access of channels and traffic flow lines to ensure that the owners and crew of the yacht can safely enter and exit the dock area.In addition to yacht berths, other necessary facilities and supporting equipment need to be considered, such as power supply facilities, water supply facilities, lighting equipment, safety equipment, and garbage disposal facilities These facilities should be planned according to actual needs and ensure compliance with relevant safety standards and environmental protection requirements.

2. Social and leisure areas

Providing social and leisure spaces for tourists and boat owners is an important part of the yacht marina, which can include restaurants, cafes, shops, and rest areas to meet people's various needs in the marina area. In order to effectively manage and operate the yacht marina, it is necessary to consider offices, concierge services, parking lots, and other necessary management and service facilities.

3. Environmental protection measures

Environmental protection measures should be considered in the planning process, including protecting the surrounding water quality, soil, and ecological environment. Sand basins, sewage treatment systems, and garbage classification facilities can be used to reduce the impact on the environment. The specific layout should be customized according to local needs, environmental conditions, and regulatory requirements.

2. Planning and design of terminal location selection

Ningbo can be used as an example here. This is an important port city on the southeast coast and the economic center of the southern fork of the Yangtze River Delta. The development of its terminal facilities illustrates the pattern of "one belt, one zone, and multiple points" based on the Xiangshan port coastline. Tourism resources in the three areas are used to build the core development zone of the yacht marina in Xiangshan Port and promote the development of yacht tourism and leisure on both sides of the Taiwan Strait The Sanmen Bay yacht marina functional area includes the Shipu Inner Bay yacht marina layout as its main part and surrounding developments as the supplements, creating a vibrant marine tourism gateway in southern Ningbo. The multiple points approach thus retains the existing LaiYue Yacht Club, relying on the existing yacht marina and island tourism resources.

1. Planning of yacht marina in Beilun District

An analysis of tourism and shoreline resources in Beilun District indicates that the development conditions at Meishan Bay Yacht Marina are good, being an important part of the core development zone of Xiangshan Bay Yacht Marina. In terms of development conditions, the Meishan Waterway Project is currently nearing completion and will be put into operation. This project is an important support for Meishan as it works to build a marine science and technology city and a coastal tourism resort. After its completion, a 10.85 km^2 "inner lake" water area will be formed, and the waterway will meet the environmental requirements of clear water, green shore, smooth waves, and flat tide. Two 500-ton locks will be set up at the western end of the waterway to facilitate the entry and exit of ships.

The tourism projects that have been developed on Meishan Island include the Gan Ao Leisure tourism area, the East China Sea Erxian Island scenic spot, the Meiyuan scenic spot, and a scenic tourism area on the west side of Yangsha Mountain. Therefore, Meishan Bay has good conditions for the development of yacht marinas. In terms of planning, combined with the analysis of the Ningbo Beilun District Meishan Bay Sea Area Utilization Plan and the Ningbo Binhai New City Spatial Development Strategy Plan (2012-2030), it is possible to build corresponding yacht marinas in the planned bay shore tourism area as well as the waterfront living and leisure area and the port marina area. Among them, the leisure tourism shoreline will be the site of yacht berths, and the urban living shoreline can, with proper land-use planning, be a site for large-scale yacht marinas, forming a large yacht base in eastern Zhejiang.

2. Planning of Fenghua District Yacht Marina

In terms of tourism and coastline resources, Fenghua District has excellent wind and wave protection conditions, clear water at the top of the bay, and dense vegetation on the mountains, which provide unique advantages for creating coastal tourist attractions. The development of yacht marinas for leisure tourism is also evident. In terms of development conditions, the total length of the coastline in the Fenghua area of Xiangshan Bay is about 63.7 kilometers. Some sections of the coast have excellent development conditions for yacht marinas, backing the Xian Provincial Forest Park. The park area includes Hongyan Waterfall, Huangxian Lake, Huanggong Tomb, and the Maritime Shanhai Pass. The scenic spot is an original ecological forest park integrating mountain scenery, coastal customs, and cultural relics. It faces the waters of Xiangshan Port, which is protected by the islands of Liuheng and other islands outside the port. The port is calm and the waters are rich in aquatic resources. In addition, there are several islands in the bay, including Xuanshan Island, Nansha Mountain Island, Fenghuang Mountain Island and Gangban Mountain Island.

The islands such as the Ningbo Island are beautiful and unique in scenery; in terms of planning, it is proposed to combine the analysis of the Ningbo-Zhoushan Port Master Plan (2014-2030), the Xiangshan Port Regional Space Protection and Utilization Plan, the Fenghua City Song'ao Town Area Master Plan (2015-2030), and the Fenghua City Coastal Line Utilization Planning Research while considering the actual utilization of the coastline. It is believed that the Song'ao Island can be developed into a tourism and leisure resort, which will not only benefit the local people, but also promote the overall development of the tourism industry in the region. The Song'ao yacht marina can be created within the 4.5 km living tourism coastline of Huangyantou-Nanshan. The Bodao Changlong Resort and Song'ao Fenghuang Town are also planning to settle in this area. Wuguitou Tsui has about 9 km of living and tourism coastline, which can be used for the construction of a yacht marina. The Sunshine Bay Tourist Resort is planned to be located in this area.

3. Planning of yacht marina in Ninghai County

Through analysis of tourism and shoreline resources in Ninghai County, the shoreline of Ninghai County is mainly divided into the Ninghai section of Xiangshan Bay and the Ninghai section of Sanmen Bay. The northern shoreline of Qiangjiao Peninsula on the Ninghai coastline of Xiangshan Port is difficult to develop due to the development of mudflats. Located between Qiangjiao and Dajiahe, Huangdun port and its surrounding islands are the core places of the Ninghai coastal tourism vacation area, which has rich tourism resources and can be used for the development of yacht docks. The coastline mudflats of Ninghai area in

Sanmen Bay are developed, but the conditions for developing yacht tourism are not very mature, though they can be developed to a small extent. In terms of development conditions, the north side of the Qiangjiao area coastline in Ninghai is industrial land, including the Ninghai Guohua Power Plant. The east side includes both industrial land and residential areas near the Guohua Power Plant. The south side is the Huangdun Port Sea Area.

The water depth of the north shoreline of Huangdun Port is relatively good, the coastal water depth beinga bout 2 ~ 4 m. To the south of the Jiajia Town shoreline, port construction conditions are poor, East of Huangdun Port are scattered small islands such as Tiesha Island and Tongshan Island scattered. The islands with larger areas include Hengshan Island, Zhongyangshan Island, and Baishishan Island. Except for some coastal reclamation and aquaculture, most of the islands are in a natural state, with dense vegetation and beautiful scenery, suitable for tourism development.

Planning is guided by documents that include the Xiangshan Port Regional Space Protection and Utilization Plan, the Ninghai County Overall Planning (2015-2030), and the Ninghai County Qiangjiao Town Overall Planning (2015-2030). It is believed that the west side of the coastline of Xiaoyuan Mountain is suitable for a yacht marina, and Ninghai Guanzun Yacht club has already built one here. Considering factors such as island size and waterway traffic, it is not recommended to built a yacht marina on other islands. Instead, it is possible to integrate with island development and built mooring points for pleasure boats (including yacht marinas).

4. Planning of yacht marinas in Xiangshan County

Xiangshan Sea covers a vast area and has unique marine resources, known as the "Oriental Immortal Island, the Fairy Kingdom of Sea Mountains". It marks the core area in which Ningbo can develop a marine tourism economy in the future. The local government will focus on building the Song Lanshan Mountain resort, a Chinese fishing village, and a Shipu fishing port near the ancient city of Tansan. Seven scenic spots, including Toushan Leisure Resort Island, have superior tourism resources, which are important prerequisites for the development of the yacht tourism industry in Xiangshan.

(1) Shoreline of Xiangshan Bay in Xiangshan

In terms of development conditions, through the above analysis, the shoreline available for yacht marina construction is mainly distributed in Xihu Port. The water depth in the inner section of Xihu Port is shallow, and shoals exist near Xihu and Xiasha waters. Considering the current spatial layout of coastal towns, the Yongtai Expressway, and the actual utilization of the coastline, the following areas are suitable for the development of yacht marinas: Xihu Port Huangbi, on the east side, Ao, the coastline near Dongta Village and Ligao Village in the township. Planning will be guided by the following documents: Analysis of Xiangshan Port Regional Space Protection and Utilization Planning, and Xiangshan Port Regional Tourism Development Planning (2014-2030). The tourist landscape resources and tidal flats in the North Gold Coast resort area can be used to guide the development of high-end leisure resorts, the construction of yacht docks, and form a north-south echo situation with the Sunshine Coast and Songao Phoenix Island to the north of Xiangshan Port. Therefore, a smallyacht marina utilizing 0.2 km of shoreline can be built at the port of Xihu.

(2) Xiangshan eastern coastline

In terms of development conditions the coastline in the eastern part of Xiangshan starts from Dwarf Mountain in Xiangshan County and extends southward to the east of Shipu Tongwamen. The overall port construction conditions in this section are poor and not suitable for the construction of large and medium-sized terminals. There are many islands in the east, which include the Waiganmen Island Group Dongyu Mountain Island, and Sanyue Mountain Island. Most of these islands are uninhabited, and a few of them have been developed into tourist sites. Some islands have unique scenery and can be developed for yacht marinas, but the investment is huge and it is not recommended to develop them. In terms of planning assumptions, combined with the analysis of the Overall Planning of Xiangshan County (2005-2020) and the Island Protection Plan of Xiangshan Count, it is believed that the above three sections of coastline that have been developed can be planned to accommodate yacht marinas. Other offshore islands such as Qiaomu Bay Island, Nanjiushan Island and Damoshan Island are tourism islands according to the Planning for Island Protection in Xiangshan County and can be combined with long-term development to build yacht marinas in a timely manner. Except for real estate and tourist attractions, it is not recommended to build separate yacht marinas along the remaining coastline, so as to avoid scattered and chaotic distribution of yacht marinas in the future, which would be difficult to supervise. Therefore, the planned yacht marina can utilize 0.62 km of coastline, which can be constructed around Songshan, Lanshan Mountain. Small yacht marinas will be built in the tourist resort area, 2.0 km away; atDayangyu, 0.2 km away; and Banbian Mountain Tourist Resort, 0.09 km away.

(3) Southern coastline of Xiangshan

In terms of development conditions, the southern coastline is mainly divided into the shoreline of Shipu Inner Bay, Baijiao Waterway and island shoreline. The shoreline of Shipu Inner Bay is mainly located in Shipu Town, Hepu Town and Gaotang Township. This section of coastline has good wind and wave protection conditions, with suitable nearshore water depth .The north shoreline of Tongqian Reef and the south shoreline of Zhongjie Mountain are close to the center of the town, with good supporting conditions. The Bai Jiao Channel shoreline of the island is an important anchorage for the fishermen of Xiangshan. The island shoreline mainly includes Tantou island, Huaao island, Nantian island and Gaotang island. The southern coastline of the islands faces the open sea, and the conditions for wind and wave protection are poor. The construction of the yacht marina needs to be equipped with breakwaters and other measures to improve the stability of the berth.

Planning is guided by the following documents: the Island Protection Plan of Xiangshan County, the Overall Planning of Huayao Island Tourism Development Zone in Xiangshan County, and the Construction Plan of Yushan Islands International Sea Fishing Base in Xiangshan County, It is believed that the layout of Shipu regional yacht marina can be centered on Xiangshan Shipu fisherman's wharf, and yacht marinas can be builton Chongtu Island and Huayan Island as the fulcrum to form a regional yacht marina distribution center and serve the development of Xiangshan marine tourism. Therefore, the planned yacht marina can utilize a shoreline of 0.6 km and a small yacht marina will be built within 0.2 km of each coastline of the island.

5. Other districts and counties

The coastline of Yinzhou District is situated in the waters of Xiangshan Port Gate, where the wave shielding conditions are relatively poor. The construction of a yacht marina there requires the construction of breakwaters and other facilities, which requires a large investment. In addition, there are relatively few tourist attractions nearby. Taking comprehensive consideration, it is not recommended to set up yacht marinas on the Yinzhou District coastline. Jiangbei District and Haishu District only have inland river shorelines. The Yongjiang River and Yaojiang River in this area are important components of the Beijing-Hangzhou-Ningbo Grand Canal. Since the river channel is narrow and the navigational density of ships is high, it is not recommended to expand the scale of Lai Yue Yacht Club, which retains the old Bund.

3. Key points and time sequence of yacht marina shoreline development

1. Development priorities

Taking into account the natural, transportation, and economic conditions of the planned shoreline, it is recommended to prioritize the construction of yacht marinas in Meishan Bay and Xiangshan Bay, while expanding the core development zone of the Xiangshan Bay yacht marina to form a cluster effect. Other areas that serve local tourism can be considered for construction, but the scale of construction should be controlled. For example, if the yacht marina is used as a supporting facility for real estate and is not located in the core development zone of the Xiangshan Bay yacht marina, consideration should be given to limiting its construction to avoid waste of shoreline resources, taking into account the functional positioning and management difficulties of the yacht marina.

The focus and timing of the development of the yacht marina shoreline can be considered based on the following factors: First, the focus should be on the construction of infrastructure along the shoreline, including piers, berths, fenders, and ramps. These facilities should meet safety standards and be able to accommodate yachts of different sizes and types. After the construction of infrastructure, attention should be paid to the development of supporting facilities. This includes such things as dining, shopping, and entertainment facilities, as well as parking lots and public toilets. The development of these facilities will provide better service experience and attract more tourists and boat owners. In the process of shoreline development, environmental protection is an important aspect. Appropriate measures should be taken to protect the marine environment, such as setting up sand basins, sewage treatment equipment, garbage classification and recycling facilities. With the advancement of technology, the development of yacht marinas can also be enhanced through intelligent technology to improve management efficiency and user experience. For example, by using intelligent parking systems, drone inspection, or electronic payment and reservation systems. After the development of the shoreline, brand building and market promotion are needed to enhance visibility and attractiveness. This includes promoting the yacht marina through publicity, marketing activities, and participationin relevant exhibitions, as well as collaborating with tourism agencies and yacht clubs.

Regarding timing, the specific development sequence of the shoreline may vary depending on the region and project. Generally, infrastructure construction will be the primary task, followed by the development of supporting facilities. Environmental protection measures should be fully considered throughout the development process. Technology and intelligent applications can be gradually introduced and improved at different stages. Brand building and market promotion can be carried out simultaneously with the development of the shoreline or initiated after the completion of infrastructure. In short, in the development of the yacht marina shoreline, it is necessary to determine the focus based on the actual situation and priority, and reasonably arrange the development sequence to ensure the smooth progress and successful operation of the project.

2. Time sequence

Based on the existing and under-construction marinas, in 2025 pre-development Meishan Bay. Shan Tourist Area, Meishan Bay Water front Living and Leisure Area, and Fenghua Chunhu Heng Lishanzhi turtle head, mouth, etc.The yacht marina shoreline has made the core development zone of the Yacht Marina in Xiangshan Bay take shape, forming about 2,000 yacht berths.

In the long term, a yacht marina layout compatible with the economic and social development of Ningbo will be formed, and yacht consumption will become an economic growth point of marine tourism. A yacht leisure and vacation tourism base with reasonable layout, complete functions, perfect facilities, outstanding characteristics, and efficient management will be basically established in the Yangtze River Delta.

4. Guarantee Measures for Terminal Construction

The construction and operation of yacht marinas involves multiple departments such as construction, land, transportation, port and shipping, tourism, maritime affairs, customs, oceanography, and economy and trade. It is suggested that the government and the port and shipping bureaus should take the lead in establishing a special coordination agency to be responsible for the construction and operation of yacht marinas. It is recommended that regulations on the planning, construction, and management of yacht marinas be formulated as soon as possible., and to ensure the planning and use of land and sea for yacht marinas through improved laws and regulations, strengthen environmental management requirements, and promote the healthy and sustainable development of yacht marinas. Public yacht marinas have social and public welfare characteristics, and the government should allocate special financial funds for the construction of public yacht marinas, increase investment in their construction, and broaden the investment and financing channels for the construction of public yacht marinas. A comprehensive information service platform for yacht marinas needs to be created, providing services such as supervision and management of yacht marinas, resource display and promotion of yacht marinas, and public information for the government, enterprises and individuals, so as to enhance the protection of the construction and development of yacht marinas through information technology.

Section 2: Construction and Development Trends of Yacht Marinas

1. The modern fishery industry upgrade brings opportunities for the development of the yachting industry

At present, domestic fishing ports are facing the problem of industrial transformation and upgrading. The fishing port industrial system and traditional service patterns fall short of meeting the requirements of the extension of the fishing port industry and are not in sync with the development needs of the rapidly emerging marine leisure tourism industry.

The construction of public yacht docks will have an undeniable and lasting influence on promoting the sales of yachts and yacht consumption. At this important juncture, it is important to takeadvantage of the current opportunities for fishing port transformation and industrial upgrading as the best shortcut to accelerate the construction of public yacht docks and promote the development of local yachting industry.

(1) Definition and connotation of fishing ports

A general fishing port is one that has the functions of shelter, berthing, loading and unloading of fish, processing of aquatic products, maintenance of fishing boats (equipment), management services, and living facilities for crew members. General fishing ports consist of three parts: basic facilities, public facilities, and general facilities.

1. Basic facilities

Basic facilities include fishing port embankments, dock waters, navigation networks, navigation assistance, pollution prevention, meteorological communication, and functional office facilities.

2. Public facilities

These include fish trading markets, laying grounds for fishing gear and net drying, and facilities for ship maintenance and fish unloading equipment. Also included are activity centers and rest facilities for fishermen.

3. General facilities

These mainly include water, electricity, oil and ice supply services, as well as fishery-related industrial facilities and auxiliary functional facilities such as ice plants, freezing plants, processing plants, shipyards, fishing associations, and offices of fishery groups.

4. Classified according to the classification standards of fishing port grades of the Ministry of Agriculture

Fishing ports can be divided into comprehensive fishing ports, sheltered fishing ports, and service fishing ports. They can also be divided into five levels according to their main functions and sizes, including central fishing ports, first- to third-level fishing ports, and non-level fishing ports.

(2) Impact of the fishery industry on the layout of yachts

1. The fishery industry is the cornerstone of the development of the yachting industry

As China's fishing ports are confronted by new challenges involving growth and sustainable development, it is crucial to implement a systematic set of fishing-port management services. From Nowadays, it is necessary to have the support of a business integration system which is suitable for the upgrading of fishing port industrialization and the development of a marine tourism market in coastal cities. As the status and role of fishing ports become more significant new and greater changes will occur in the integration and transformation of fishing ports.

2. The adjustments in the fishery industry are connected with the development of the yachting industry

The traditional backbone industries of the fishing port, such as shipbuilding, parts processing, and aquatic product processing, experienced a heyday in the 1970s and 1980s. More recently, their development has been greatly limited. Both these enterprises have idle land and occupy a large amount of water areas. The ship repair factories, cargo terminals, and aquatic trading markets located in the main port area have been subject to many restrictions involving the environment, safety, and sanitation, and have withdrawn from the main port area. It is necessary for the local governments to act to create new tourist opportunities in fishing-port areas.

The expansion of fishery areas to include recreational fishing boats has been raised to a higher level, and it is necessary to construct public service facilities such as a "Fisherman's Wharf" that includes specialty areas for shopping, bars, and restaurants. China's fishing ports have become an important platform for the development of modern fishery industry in coastal areas, an important carrier for the development of coastal tourism economy in coastal cities, and an important support for the construction of small towns and new fishing villages. New docks are needed to ensure the security of waterborne official boats, work boats, and emergency rescue boats.

(3) Opportunities and potential for the development of marine tourism

China's marine economic development strategy is being upgraded to a higher national strategic level, it will become a direct driving force for the development of coastal blue economic zones, marine economic development zones, and various marine and island development experimental zones. There is no lack of precedents in the world where fishing ports are also used as public marinas for yachts.

1. The example of Taiwan

In 2010, there were 225 fishing ports in Taiwan, including 9 first-class fishing ports and 216 second-class fishing ports. Based on the shore distance, there is an average fishing port for every 7.1 kilometers of coastline and 12 fishing boats. Since the mid-1980s, the overall environment of Taiwan's fisheries, including resources, has undergone many changes. The fishing ports there have entered a new period of transformation and development.

In recent years, the Taiwan Fisheries Agency has successively opened "fisherman's wharf" leisure and entertainment functions with public docks for yachts in 11 fishing ports such as Taipei Danshui, Kaohsiung Gushan, and Hsinchu, covering about 5% of the total number of fishing ports in Taiwan. The functional changes of these fisherman's wharf facilities have attracted a large number of tourists, changed the industrial structure of fishing ports, and marked the beginning of the transformation of traditional fishing ports in Taiwan into ports dedicated to leisure and recreation.

2. The example of Sanya

With the continuous improvement of infrastructure, the number of yachts in Sanya has continued to grow, from the initial "difficult to find a boat" situation to the current "city of thousands of boats." The mass consumption market of yacht tourism has entered a rapid development stage, and the yacht rental industry has also begun a period of rapid development. The Outline of the Development Plan for the yachting industry in Hainan Province (2021-2025) proposes that by 2025, the number of registered yachts on the island will exceed 2,446, the total number of yacht tourists will reach 1.36 million, and the industrial scale will exceed CNY¥10 billion.

Both the 2023 Sanya International Yacht Show and the International Wine Exhibition were held at the Sanya International Yacht Center, and the construction of the associated Nanbianhai International Yacht Marina project was accelerated. The berth will be the first to be unveiled in Hainan's cruise and yachting industry. The Sanya CBD is being planned using the Work Plan for Promoting the High-quality Development of Sanya yachting industry Chain. This plan proposes the overall goal of building Sanya into an Asia-Pacific yacht capital, and promotes the development of the whole yachting industry chain through global investment channels.

The development of the yachting industry has made great strides, bringing with it a continuous flourishing market demand for yacht marinas. By the end of 2022, Sanya had built 4 yacht marinas, forming about 960 berths on the water; 462 new yacht ownership registrations were added, up 43.03% from the previous year. The total number of registered yachts reached 1,137, up 20.32%. Duty-free cities, chain restaurants, and large-scale supermarkets near ports such as Hongzhou Times Coast and Banshan Peninsula Sailing Port have sprung up like mushrooms. Hongzhou Wharf tourism and leisure block was opened on July 26, 2005, located on a natural peninsula where the two rivers of Sanya meet at the entrance to the sea. The block is built along the mountains and water, facing the East China Sea Scenic Area to the east, the South Sea in the south, the Sanya Bay to the west, and facing the Luhuitou Mountain across the river with the lover's mountain. It has unique tropical marine resources and supporting resources. The block is centered on the Sanya River, and on both sides of the waterfront it has created a leisure resort integrating all-time yacht tourism, business office, catering and entertainment, and duty-free shopping. In 2023, it was successfully included in the second batch of national tourism and leisure blocks.

2. Trends and influencing factors of yacht marina construction and development

As an important component of water tourism and the yachting industry, the construction and development of yacht marinas present some obvious trends, as outlined below.

(1) Changes in tourists' consumption concept

With the improvement of people's living standards and the transformation of leisure concepts, yachts have become a popular way of leisure and entertainment. Customers' demand for yacht marinas has also become more diverse. In addition to the traditional yacht mooring function, customers also hope to enjoy more services and convenient facilities around the marina, such as catering, shopping, and entertainment. This requires yacht marinas to consider all-round customer needs as they are designed and constructed.

Environmental protection and sustainable development have become important issues in today's society. In order to reduce the impact on the marine ecosystem, the construction of marinas needs to consider the use of environmentally friendly materials, the proper treatment of wastewater and garbage, and the reduction of energy consumption. In addition, environmental protection and ecological restoration around the marina also need to be taken into account to ensure the harmonious coexistence of the yacht marina with the natural environment. Technological innovation plays an important role in the construction of yacht marinas. The application of intelligent systems can improve the management efficiency and service quality of yacht marinas, such as through the use of intelligent parking systems, drone inspection and remote monitoring to achieve a more convenient, safe, and efficient management model. Innovative technologies are also being applied to the construction of yacht marinas, such as solar power generation and seawater desalination, to reduce the dependence on traditional energy and reduce operating costs.

(2) The construction of yacht marinas often requires cooperation with relevant departments, enterprises, and social resources

A regional cooperation and coordinated development model can promote the expansion of the scale of yacht marinas and the extension of the industrial chain, and also provide more comprehensive services such as tourism, vacation hotels, and cultural entertainment, thus attracting more tourists and investors. With the rapid development of the global yachting industry, internationalization and overseas market expansion have become important trends in the construction and development of yacht marinas.

Some countries and regions have taken measures to attract the international yacht tourism market by providing competitive tax policies, high-quality services, and convenient entry procedures. This also provides more opportunities for yacht marina builders to carry out international cooperation and overseas investment. The construction of yacht marinas requires full consideration of local cultural characteristics and brand image. By combining local history, natural landscapes, and cultural elements, it is possible to create a unique yacht marina brand and enhance its popularity and influence. At the same time, it is also possible to attract more tourists and participants through various activities and events.

(3) Characteristics of yacht marina construction

The construction and development of yacht marinas are showing diverse trends such as environmental sustainability, technological innovation, regional cooperation and coordinated development, internationalization and overseas market expansion, as well as cultural characteristics and brand building. These trends will have a significant impact on the planning, design, and operation of yacht marinas, and builders and managers need to pay close attention and make corresponding adjustments and responses based on the actual situation.

1. Diversification

Yacht marinas are being constructed with diversified purposes in mind, not only providing docking services but also including catering, entertainment, conference and other supporting facilities to meet the diverse needs of tourists. Builders and managers need to consider how to provide diverse services in a limited space and enhance the experience of tourists.

2. Environmental protection and

sustainable development

With the increasing awareness of environmental protection, the construction and operation of yacht marinas should also focus on environmental sustainability. Measures such as using clean energy for power supply, garbage classification and treatment, and water quality protection should be adopted to reduce the impact on the surrounding environment and promote the sustainable development of the yachting industry.

3. Scientific and technological innovation

Technological innovation has a significant impact on the planning and operation of yacht marinas. Introducing intelligent management systems, drone patrols, intelligent parking systems, and other technologies can improve the safety, efficiency, and convenience of the marina. Builders and managers need to keep abreast of the latest technological trends and apply them to practical operations.

4. Regional cooperation and coordinated development

The success of a yacht marina requires cooperation and collaborative development with surrounding areas. Builders and managers should actively seek cooperation with local governments, tourism agencies, businesses, and other stakeholders to jointly promote the development of the regional yachting industry and achieve resource sharing and mutual benefits.

5. Internationalization and overseas market expansion

With the rise of global yacht tourism, yacht marinas also need to expand to the international market. Builders and managers should pay attention to international trends and the needs of yacht tourism, providing facilities and services that meet international standards and service levels, attracting tourists and yachts from all over the world.

6. Cultural characteristics and brand building

Each region has unique cultural characteristics and historical backgrounds, and yacht marinas can be designed and built in combination with local cultural elements to create a unique brand image. By providing activities, exhibitions, and products that integrate with local culture, yacht marinas can attract tourists and increase their popularity and reputation.

7. The development of yacht marinas requires more cooperation and coordinated development with surrounding areas

By linking tourism attractions, catering, accommodation and other supporting industries, a holistic tourism destination is created, enhancing the competitiveness and attractiveness of the region. With the rise of global yacht tourism, the development trend of yacht marinas is also moving towards internationalization and overseas market expansion. The marina operators should actively seek cooperation with international yacht clubs, luxury yacht manufacturers, and other related industries to attract international tourists and sailing enthusiasts. Each region has its unique cultural and historical background, and the yacht marina can be designed and built in combination with local cultural characteristics to form a unique brand image. By holding cultural events and exhibitions and promoting local special products, the popularity and attractiveness of the yacht marina can be enhanced. The yacht marina is no longer just a stopping point, but a place that provides social experience and comprehensive services. Builders and managers should closely monitor market demand and development trends and make corresponding adjustments and responses based on actual conditions to ensure the successful operation of yacht marinas.

Section 3: Management Mode and Operation and Maintenance Strategy of Yacht Marinas

Thanks to recent reforms, China's economy has taken off and developed, miraculously becoming the world's second largest economy, achieving world-renowned status, and comprehensively building a moderately prosperous society. The people's demand for quality of life is gradually increasing, and a yachting industry focused on leisure and entertainment is ushering in a great opportunity for vigorous development. Yacht marinas have become important infrastructure for coastal and river cities, and are key to the development of tourist cities. The marina management model, plus operation and maintenance strategies, have become an important boost to local economic development.

1. Development of yacht marinas

With the development of a social economy, the number of yachts continues to grow, and the facilities of yacht marinas are constantly improved. The mass consumption market of yacht tourism has entered a rapid development stage. The yacht leasing industry has also ushered in a period of rapid development . In 2022, China registered X new yachts, and the total number of registered yachts has reached X The number of yachts entering and leaving the port and the number of tourists received both maintained a rapid growth momentum. The total number of yacht tourists will reach X throughout the year.

Yacht marinas mainly consist of embankments, floating docks and positioning piles. They are infrastructure facilities along the rivers and coasts that provide berths and other services for yachts. Yacht marinas are mainly located in large cities along the coast and rivers, and the development of yacht marinas in tourist cities is particularly prosperous. Yacht marinas not only provide berths for yachts, but also integrate various functions such as catering, entertainment, accommodation, business, and so on, providing entertainment and leisure activities for high-end consumers, travel and vacation enthusiasts and even ordinary consumers.

2. The importance of yacht marina management

With the rapid growth in the number and scale of yacht entertainment consumption, the demand for yacht marinas is increasing, and the requirements for yacht marina services are becoming higher and higher. Yacht tourism has evolved from traditional self-entertainment to whole-boat rental business activities. At present, there is no standardized and mature practice in the management of domestic yacht marinas. The yacht marina market in China is still in its initial stage of development, with inadequate management and operation, and industry standards have not yet been fully established. There is a significant gap between the development level of yacht marinas in developed countries such as Europe and the United States, which has become an important factor restricting the development of local yachting industry and of tourist cities.

3. Major problems in yacht marina management

1. The number of yacht marinas is relatively small

At present, China is still a developing country, and the per capita GDP is far behind developed regions such as Europe and the United States. Although the construction of domestic yacht marinas has begun to take shape, the number of yacht marinas and berths is still relatively small. Compared with developed regions abroad, the number of yacht marinas in China is relatively small, and compared with the per capita consumption, the number of yacht marinas in China is even smaller.

2. The terminal hardware facilities are relatively poor

Yacht marinas not only require unique natural conditions, but also need to have fully equipped hardware infrastructure to facilitate the development of marinas handling cruises, cruise ships, and yachts.

3. There are relatively few regulations for yacht marinas

The management of yacht marinas lacks standards and the management system documents lack pertinence. Currently, the safety and pollution prevention management of yacht marinas is relatively backward and does not meet the actual needs. There are no regulations for using yacht marinas for other activities. The regulatory system of yacht marinas needs to be improved, including safety management regulations, service guidelines, yacht management measures, and industry promotion regulations need to be improved.

4. Some yacht marinas are not clearly located

Traditional marinas are relatively backward in terms of functionality, and some marinas have unclear positioning. The main business of traditional yacht marinas is to provide berthing and other management services for yachts, and there is a large gap between them and the emerging consumer demand.

5. The operation of the yacht marina is not clear

The comprehensive service platform for tourism at the yacht marina has not been confirmed by regulations, and the relevant departments are working in an uncoordinated fashion.

6. Industry self-discipline remains at the spontaneous level

While industry self-regulation has positive significance for the standardized management and high- quality development of yacht marinas, it is largely spontaneous and fails to play an effective role because of its lack of standardization.

7. The yacht marina industry chain is not complete

The development of the midstream of the industrial chain is relatively good, while the upstream industrial chain represented by design and manufacturing and the downstream industrial chain represented by infrastructure and supporting services are weak, even lacking certain functions.

8. Single service mode of yacht marina

Most marinas simply provide berthing services and other main businesses, lacking maintenance, supply, and other services. They also provide few value-added services, operate in a single way, lack service functions, and lack revenue sources. They have not formed a "brand" effect and lack of a good profit model.

9. Mismatch between O&M strategy and consumption

With the improvement of people's living standards, the rapid development of the yachting industry, and the increasing popularity of yacht consumption, the operation of yacht docks has become increasingly important. The operation and maintenance strategy of the marina does not match people's consumption needs. It is difficult for entertainment facilities to meet people's needs, and the resources and services provided by the marina do not match the needs of ordinary tourism consumption.

Suggestions for marina management and operation and maintenance strategies

(1) Optimize the management of yacht marinas

1. Promote the construction of supporting facilities for yacht marinas

It is suggested to promote the construction of public yacht marinas with supporting facilities for maintenance, safety, and environmental protection, to address the shortage of public infrastructure and service facilities and meet the general needs of yachting enterprises.

2. Strengthen the guarantee of industrial elements in the terminal

Yacht marinas should be built in a complex integrating yacht display, sales, training, cultural creativity, high-end catering, business offices, conference facilities, and exhibitions. They should be equipped with testing pools, dry berths for yachts, and public launching slides. The marinas should integrate a wide number of factors, including research and development, creative design, pilot service, achievement promotion, entrepreneurial incubation, exhibition and display, inspection and testing, standard consultation, and talent introduction, among others.

3. Optimize the management system of yacht marinas

Yacht marinas need to do a good job

in industrial services and data statistical analysis. They should provide efficient and high-quality customs clearance services for yacht enterprises, promote the construction of "smart ports" with digital border inspection. They should rely on information technology to oversee intelligent, automatic, and non-sensory management of yachts entering and leaving the port.

4. Steadily promote the "intelligentization" of yacht marinas

Yacht marinas should support projects devoted to the integration of industrialization and the new information media. These initiatives can be used to manage the replacement of workers with machines while promoting digital, green, and intelligent upgrading. Subsidies should be given to enterprises that support intelligent upgrading, cluster development, service-oriented extension, green transformation, and safety controls.

5. Strengthen the construction of the quality brands of yacht marinas

Yacht manufacturing enterprises should be guided to conscientiously implement international standards and improvequality assurance systems. These enterprises should be encouraged to carry out product promotion, enhance their corporate and brand awareness, and gradually establish a good image of Hainan yacht manufacturing brands. To this end, they should support product promotion and organize technical seminars, design competitions and other exchange activities to promote brand building and enhance market competitiveness.

6. Establish star-level classification management for yacht marinas

The spirit of the 20th CPC National Congress proposes to improve the social credit of the basic market economy system while and optimizing the business environment in general. In terms of yacht marina management, it is necessary to strengthen the level management and carry out grading management according to different service levels. Based on the comprehensive evaluation of management services, regular star-rating evaluation should be carried out to implement classified and grading management for yacht marinas.

7. Strengthen the management talents of yachting construction teams

Yachting terminals need to gather and attract high-level management talent. This can be accomplished by supporting universities, vocational schools, and technical schools in their efforts to provide targeted training for intellectual and human resources in yachting terminals.

8. Strengthen industry self-discipline via links with relevant associations

Full play should be given to the role of industry associations, classification entities, and other professional institutions and relevant think tanks in monitoring the demands of government departments and putting forward policy suggestions. This will strengthen the self-discipline of the yachting industry while safeguarding the rights and interests of enterprises.

9. Strengthen the supervision and man-

agement of yacht marinas

The basic requirements of the marina management system need to be clarified. This involves standardizing the management of yacht marinas and their operating personnel as well as improving the supervision, inspection, punishment, and exit mechanisms.

10. Build big data and command and dispatch centers

Yacht marinas should focus on creating a "one-stop yacht tourism service" driven by institutional innovation and centered on promoting the development of the yachting tourism industry. These efforts should include attempts to innovate the supervision and service mechanism of yacht tourism, promote a centralized display and promotion of yacht tourism products, and promote the construction of a yacht tourism service system.

(2) Innovating the operational and maintenance strategy of yacht marinas

1. Accelerate the cultivation and introduction of market entities

According to the policy guidance of the country, provinces, and cities, the construction of specific marketing entities in the yachting tourism industry should be promoted by China. In order to provide effective market supply for the industry, specific formats, projects, products, and services should be implemented. To meet the people's needs for a rewarding experience, public services are needed that ensure quality, quantity, and safety. Yacht consumers should be provided with channels and platforms enabling them to participate in innovative yacht experiences and that improve the overall level of tourism services. According to the model of "platform + chain leader + supporting enterprises," China should introduce well-known yacht manufacturing enterprises at home and abroad as the chain leader, gather a number of upstream and downstream supporting enterprises with high added value and low energy consumption, accelerate the cultivation and expansion of market entities, and form industrial agglomeration.

2. Assist the acceleration anddevelopment of the yachting industry chain

Efforts should be focused on the whole industrial chain of upstream innovation, including production, midstream sales, consumption, downstream support, auxiliary and other industries, building industrial chain innovation, public service, creative design, maintenance and remanufacturing platforms, gathering upstream and downstream unique competitive advantage ship supporting enterprises, and creating a yachting industry chain cluster.

3. Establish a yacht trading platform in the center

Based on the international market, big data should be mined to constantly improve the trading of yachts by verifying ship inspections and evaluations, as well as ship insurance and other services. High-quality second-hand ships can be locked up through financial means, and new boat trading, service, and management, can be improved, providing a low-cost, high-efficiency business environment for the development of industrial agglomeration.

4. Construct an industrial innovation and development platform

The Yacht Marina Industry Development and Innovation Association would strengthen the cooperation between industry executives and research institutions in the areas of design and manufacturing, information dissemination, and financial services to jointly explore institutional integration and innovation, accelerate the transformation of industrial achievements, develop industry standards, and improve the operational capacity of yacht marinas.

5. Enrich the service aspects of the yacht marina

Yacht rentals, yacht sales and other services can be established. These include the creation of a yacht commercial street, yacht hotel, yacht docking, member dedicated dock, yacht driving training schools, yacht maintenance facilities, multi-functional conference halls, plus entertainment venues and facilities for sailing and sports events.

6. Develop popular yacht consumption facilities

Some marinas are suitable for targeting the top-tier wealthy group, while others are suitable for targeting other elite groups. However, to create a profit point for the marina, yachts should not just be regarded as toys for the wealthy. The core of yacht marina operation is not to build a specific circle platform but also to emphasize yacht berthing and maintenance and optimize the service content of yacht marina as it applies to popular (ie, non-elite) consumption demand for yachts. These efforts can help the growth of yacht batch construction capacity, thus standardizing and optimizing the consumption of affordable mass-produced vessels.

7. Optimize the business environment of the yacht marina

This can be accomplished by establishing special routes and waterways to lead members to take self-driving yacht tours while cooperating with the Maritime Safety Administration to provide one-stop services for training yacht driving licenses and for such events as yacht weddings, water skiing, and other events.

8. Actively develop yacht rental business

Yacht leasing is facing a major development opportunity. Yacht marinas should establish leasing yacht clubs, independently operate yacht leasing and other related businesses, and make full use of the low utilization rate of personal yachts and the rise of popular water activities such as wake boarding.

9. Establish a supporting model of real estate business philosophy

With the construction of yacht marinas, land prices and housing prices will also increase accordingly. At the same time, a multi-functional real estate project cluster should be explored that integrates sea fishing, marine sightseeing, water activities, high-end dining, leisure and entertainment, and comprehensive supplies to promote the upgrading of tourism quality while, expand the water area and application scenarios for yacht sailing.

10. Strengthen the linkage between fiscal and financial policies

Take full advantage of preferential fiscal and tax policies, leverage investment funds, and provide financial support to yacht enterprises in a market-oriented manner. With the industrial chain as a link, China will actively carry out investment promotion activities, improve the level of international exchanges and cooperation in the yacht repair industry, and promote the construction of a yacht marina industry cluster.

11. Strengthen investment promotion and promote international exchanges and cooperation

Actively attract high-quality projects, funds, technology, management, brands and high-end talents from abroad to develop the yacht building industry in China. Introduce strategic partners, encouraging large foreign enterprise groups to invest in factories or cooperate with domestic enterprises to set up factories. With the industrial chain as a link, actively carry out investment promotion activities, improve the level of international exchange and cooperation in the yacht building industry, and promote the construction of yacht dock industrial clusters.

12. Build a brand of yacht events

Take full advantage of preferential policies, continue to expand and strengthen the yacht marina brand series activities, release strong development signals of the local yachting industry, gather attention from domestic and foreign yacht industries, hold a yacht marina festival, and form a unique new IP of port culture.

13. Build a solid advantage in differentiated industrial development

Do a good job in the marketing and promotion of cruise yachts and related water sports products and create via the Internet celebrity consumption projects. Yacht design competitions, new energy yacht competitions, and industrial innovation and development seminars should be held to support the creation of characteristic event brands, expand industrial influence, and help achieve goals such as "carbon peak" and "carbon neutrality." Using relevant policies, China will explore the implementation of policies such as night sailing of yachts, test rides of heat engines outside the bonded warehouse of imported yachts, and one-time visits of foreign yachts for 183 days so as to transform policy advantages into industrial advantages.

Section 4: International marketing of yacht marinas and promotion of yacht destination cities

This section explores the international marketing of yacht marinas and the promotional strategies of yacht destination cities. Yacht tourism was once a high-end and luxurious form of tourism that attracted an increasing number of wealthy individuals and tourists. Yacht marinas are important infrastructure for yacht tourism, and their international marketing and promotion by destination cities are crucial. By studying and analyzing international marketing strategies and the promotion practices of yacht destination cities, valuable references and effective suggestions can be obtained.

Yacht tourism has developed rapidly in the past few decades and has become an important part of the global tourism industry. The demand for luxury and unique tourism experiences among the wealthy class is growing, and yacht tourism is just the right solution to meet this demand. As an important part of yacht tourism, yacht marinas play a role in docking, maintenance, and service of yachts. However, having an excellent yacht marina alone is not enough to attract yacht tourists. International marketing and destination city promotion are crucial.

1. Overview of the development of the yacht tourism industry

In recent years, with the development of the global economy and the increasing demand for luxury travel, the yacht tourism industry has rapidly emerged and shown a strong momentum of development. Yacht tourism not only provides a unique luxury experience for wealthy people, but also becomes an important economic pillar and representative of the international image of many destination cities. Under the wave of globalization, the yacht tourism industry is experiencing further vigorous development, and the international marketing and promotion of yacht destination cities have become particularly important. The rapid development of the yacht tourism industry stems from the pursuit of luxury travel by wealthy people. With the concentration of global wealth and the increase in per capita income, wealthy people have higher demands for unique, luxury and private travel methods. Yacht tourism meets this demand, where tourists can enjoy personalized services, luxury facilities and spectacular sea scenery on luxury yachts and fully experience the fun of sea vacations. With the convenience of global transportation and communication, yacht tourism has become a borderless industry. Yachts can freely navigate the oceans around the world, and tourists can choose to expand their routes to destinations in every corner of the world. This global trend makes the yacht tourism industry more diverse and flexible, attracting tourists from different countries and regions, and promoting the development of the global tourism industry. In this context, the international marketing of yacht marinas and the promotion of yacht destination cities have become crucial. Yacht marinas are important infrastructure for the yacht tourism industry, and their destination cities are the starting point and end point of yacht tourism. In order to attract more yachts and tourists, marinas need to carry out international publicity and promotion activities, including participating in international yacht exhibitions, cooperating with maritime transportation companies, and carrying out overseas market promotion, in order to enhance their visibility and influence, and attract more yachts and tourists.

2. International marketing of yacht marinas

Yacht marinas are important infrastructural components in the yacht tourism industry, and their international marketing is crucial for attracting yachts and tourists. International marketing for yacht marinas includes brand building and market positioning, marketing channels and partners, as well as service quality and user experience.

(1) Brand building and market positioning

A yacht marina's unique design and architectural style can leave a deep impression on tourists and distinguish it from other marinas. At the same time, well-planned marina layout and advanced facilities are also important components of brand building. Through good marina layout and advanced facilities, the yacht marina can provide high-quality services and comfortable experience, allowing tourists to feel a distinctive treatment. The brand image should also highlight the commitment to quality and service. The yacht marina should pursue excellent quality and excellent service to meet the needs of high-end customers. For example, providing safe and reliable docking systems, a stable power supply, a clean water supply and other infrastructure, as well as comfortable rest areas, high-quality catering services and luxurious toilets and other value-added services can all demonstrate the commitment to quality and service. In addition, the yacht marina also needs to understand the characteristics and trends of the target market through market research and analysis. Different target markets may have different needs and preferences, so the marina can develop corresponding marketing strategies to meet the needs of different customer groups.

(2) Marketing channels and partners

The yacht marina can use digital marketing tools and social media platforms to expand its brand influence and increase its popularity. Through its website, the marina can showcase its unique charm, high-quality services and luxurious facilities, including information about the marina, docking services, facilities and equipment, and surrounding attractions. At the same time, the marina can publish attractive content, including beautiful photos, videos and tourism-related information to attract users' attention. By collaborating with tourism agencies, the yacht marinas can promote their identities as a part of luxury travel. The yacht marina can provide exclusive yacht tourism programs and collaborate with tourism agencies to promote them, attracting high-end customers. Collaborating with yacht brokers can attract more yachts to dock at the marina, increasing the marina's attractiveness and bringing more potential customers and business opportunities, which will bring more demand for yacht docking to the marina.

(3) Service quality and user experience

The yacht marina should provide safe and reliable docking systems, power supplies, water supplies, and other infrastructure. The improvement and stability of infrastructure can ensure the safe parking of yachts and provide necessary services for customers. At the same time, value-added services such as comfortable rest areas, high-quality catering services and luxurious bathrooms are also key to attracting customers. Yacht owners and tourists hope to enjoy high-quality services and a comfortable environment during their stay at the marina, which will increase customer satisfaction and loyalty. The yacht marina should alsofocus on providing personalized services and customized activities. Understanding the unique needs and interests of customers and providing them with customized route planning, special event planning, and other services can enhance customers' sense of participation and satisfaction. For example, providing private tour guides or translation services for customers, designing special activities according to their preferences and needs, and providing personalized experiences can increase their satisfaction and return rate. In addition, the yacht marina can organize exciting social events and theme parties to create unforgettable experiences for tourists. By holding various themed activities such as sea parties, theme dinners, and water sports competitions, the marina can bring unique entertainment and social experiences to its customers, which can not only increase customer loyalty but also attract more tourists through word-of-mouth promotion.

3. Promotion of yacht destination cities

The rapid development of the yacht tourism industry has brought tremendous opportunities to destination cities. The key to promoting yacht destination cities includes local characteristics and tourism resources, event and event planning, and tourism cooperation and promotion.

(1) Local characteristics and tourism resources

Yacht destination cities should fully display their unique culture and historical relics and showcase the unique charm of the city to tourists through cultural activities, art exhibitions, and traditional celebrations. For example, they can present local traditional music performances, art exhibitions, or historical and cultural lectures, allowing tourists to gain a deeper understanding of the city's cultural heritage and increasing tourists' interest and curiosity in the destination city. Yacht destination cities can also combine yacht tourism with local characteristic industries and cultural activities to create unique tourism experiences. For example, the cities can combine marine resources to carry out various sports and underwater exploration activities, such as sailing races or diving expeditions to attract tourists to experience the magnificence and mystery of the ocean. Organizing special parties, food festivals. parades, and folk performances during the festival can enrich the travel experience of tourists, allowing them to enjoy the fun of yacht tourism while also appreciating the unique cultural atmosphere of the destination city.

(2) Activity and event planning

By hosting yacht cruises, sailing competitions, fishing competitions, and other events, yacht destination cities can not only showcase the beautiful scenery and water resources of the destination city, but also increase the interaction and communication between tourists and local residents, enhancing the tourism experience. Destination cities can also plan and create brand activities to enhance the city's visibility and reputation, such as by hosting international yacht exhibitions, yacht culture festivals, yacht carnivals, and other activities. The cities can also establish partnerships with international yacht associations and yacht broker associations to jointly carry out promotional activities and publicity.

(3) Tourism cooperation and promotion

Yacht destination cities can establish partnerships with airlines, hotels, and travel agencies. Working with airlines can provide connecting flights and discount packages, making it convenient for tourists to arrive in the destination city from other cities or countries. Working with hotels can provide discounted accommodation and docking options, providing comfortable and convenient accommodation experiences for yacht tourists. Working with travel agencies can develop customized yacht tourism routes to meet the needs and preferences of different tourists. These partnerships can provide one-stop services for tourists and increase the attractiveness and competitiveness of yacht tourism. Yacht destination cities can also leverage opportunities such as tourism exhibitions and international conferences to promote the tourism advantages and charm of the destination city. Holding international conferences canattract the attention of professionals and the media. In addition to partnerships and promotional activities, destination cities can also cooperate with other yacht destination cities or tourism bureaus to carry out joint promotional activities. For example, cross-city yacht packages can be introduced to allow visitors to travel between multiple destination cities. This cooperation can expand the market share of the destination city and improve the overall competitiveness.

(4) International marketing of yacht marinas and the promotion strategies and practices of yacht destination cities

(I) Marketing strategy and practice of internationally renowned yacht marinas

Santorini Yacht Marina is located on the Greek island of Santorini in the Aegean Sea. It has become an internationally renowned yacht destination with its excellent marketing strategies and practices. Here are its successful marketing strategies and practices: First, Santorini Yacht Marina focuses on brand building and market positioning. It positions itself as the top yacht destination in the Mediterranean region and is committed to creating a high-end and luxury brand image. Through carefully planned marketing activities and brand promotion, Santorini Yacht Marina successfully connects itself with luxury and unique tourism experiences, attracting the attention and interest of many yacht enthusiasts. Secondly, Santorini Yacht Marina is adept at using a variety of marketing channels and partners to expand its brand influence. Digital marketing tools and social media platforms have become important means of promotion and promotion. By establishing professional websites and social media accounts, posting attractive content, and showcasing the unique charm and services of the marina, Santorini Yacht Marina has successfully built its brand awareness. In addition, it has established partnerships with local tourism agencies, yacht brokers, and other stakeholders to jointly promote the yacht tourism products of Santorini. These partnerships have brought more exposure opportunities to the marina and expanded its target customer base. In addition, service quality and user experience are key concerns for Santorini Yacht Marina. The marina provides high-quality yacht docking services and facilities, including a safe and reliable docking system, high-quality service personnel, and a luxurious docking area. By continuously improving and enhancing service standards, the marina has won praise from yacht owners and tourists. Finally, the marina focuses on customer experience and provides personalized services and customized activities. Visitors can enjoy customized route planning, special event planning, and other services to meet their unique needs and interests. This customer-centric business philosophy has made Santorini Yacht Marina stand out in the competitive yacht destination market.

(II) Successful promotion experience of yacht destination cities

As a unique yacht tourism destination, Miami, the destination city of yachts in the Americas, has accumulated rich experience in successful promotion. Here is a summary of its successful promotion experience: First of all, Miami is famous for its warm climate, beautiful beaches and unique cultural vitality. Miami successfully combines these characteristics with yacht tourism to create a stylish and luxurious yacht destination image. Visitors can enjoy sunny beaches, sea sports and luxury yacht experiences in Miami, fully enjoying the unique charm of the city. Secondly, Miami carefully plans and hosts a variety of high-profile events, such asthe Miami International Boat Show and Miami Yacht Week.Through hosting these events, Miami has successfully positioned itself as the center of the American yachting industry, attracting more yacht enthusiasts and professionals to the city. In addition, Miami has established close partnerships with airlines, luxury hotels, and travel agencies. These partnerships enable Miami to provide convenience and attractiveness through connecting flights, discount packages, and other means, improving the convenience of tourists.

International marketing of yacht marinas and promotion of yacht destination cities are key factors in the development of the yacht tourism industry. By adopting effective international marketing strategies, yacht marinas can expand their global market and attract more yacht tourists to visit. At the same time, yacht destination cities need to focus on uniqueness and differentiation, providing unique tourism experiences for yacht tourists. In order to achieve sustainable development of the yacht tourism industry, yacht marinas and destination cities need to work together to provide quality services and facilities to meet the needs of yacht tourists and create a better tourism experience.

Chapter 8

Promotional Policies for the Development of the Yachting Industry

According to the 2021 China Ocean Economic Statistical Bulletin, China's coastal tourism industry realized an added value of ¥1.5297 trillion for the whole year, an increase of 12.8% over the previous year. Yachts are an important part of coastal tourism and one of the most attractive industries in the marine economy. Moreover, with the general improvement of China's economy, people are more inclined to diversify their tourism methods. As an emerging tourism industry, yachts have broken the traditional mode of tourism transportation, allowing people to enjoy the fun of tourism during transportation. The yachting industry is known as the "golden fortress on the water," and it occupies an important market position abroad.

Although the development of the yachting industry in China is later than that in foreign countries, China has great potential in the development of yachts, and this strength is increasing year by year. In 2008, China launched the first regulation related to the yachting industry, the Regulations on the Safety Management of Yachts. in 2009, the State Council proposed to support the development of cruise ships, yachts and other emerging tourism industries in qualified areas, and required the improvement of yacht management tourism and yacht equipment manufacturing. In 2022, the Ministry of Industry and Information Technology and five other departments jointly issued the Implementation Opinions on Accelerating the Development of Cruise and Yacht Equipment and Industry, which proposed to promote the innovative development of the yachting industry, support coastal cities to encourage and guide the development of yacht events, and vigorously develop popular consumer yachts. It can be seen from these initiatives that China attaches great importance to the development of the yachting industry.

This chapter will delve into the current status of the yachting industry in major countries and regions, as well as the main policies and historical changes of the industry in order to understand the trends and context of industrial development in major yacht-owning countries.

Section 1: Development Status of yachting industry in Various Countries

(1) Development status of the yachting industry in Europe and America

1. Development status of the yachting industry in the United States

The development of the yachting industry in the United States mainly relates to yacht manufacturing. The USA is a pioneer in the yacht manufacturing industry. The rise of the yachting industry in the United States can be traced back to 1913. Its development process can be divided into four stages (as shown in Figure 8-1).

Figure 8-1 Number of yachts in the United States

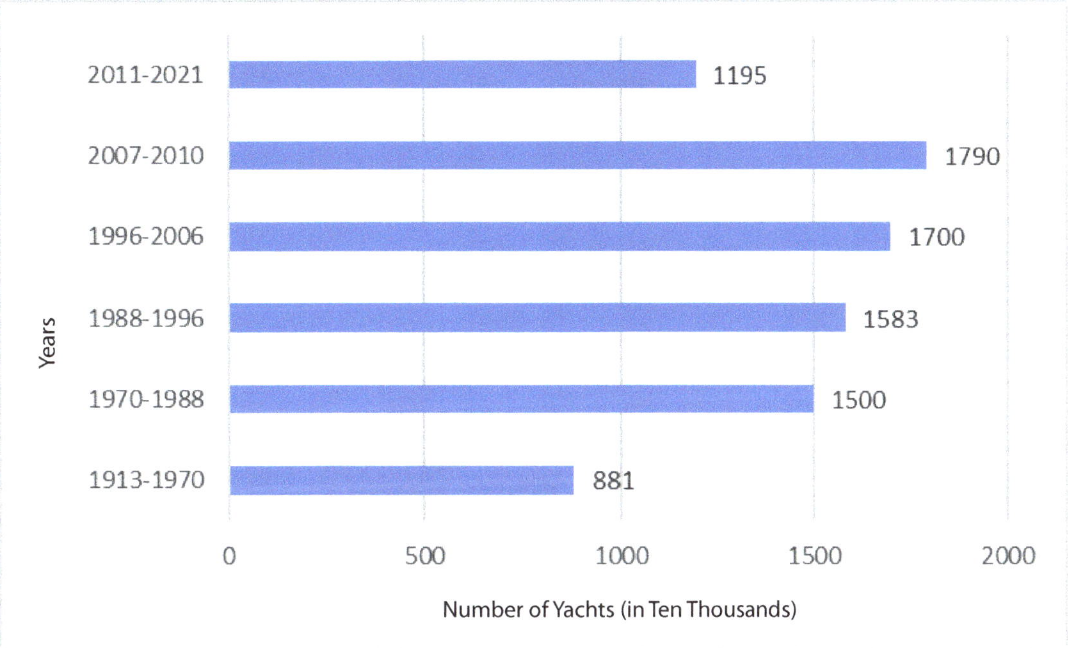

Source: Compiled from the World Yachting industry Report 2008, IBI International Yachting industry Magazine.

(1) The rise of the yachting industry. The yachting industry in the United States began to develop from 1913 to 1970. In 1913, when the yachting industry first emerged, the United States had 400,000 yachts. By 1970, the number of yachts had reached 8.81 million.

(2) The prosperous period. From 1970 to 1988, the yachting industry in the United States ushered in its first prosperous stage. In 1970, the United States' income from yachts reached US$3.44 billion. In 1988, the total sales of the yachting industry in the United States reached US$17.9 billion and the number of yachts was about 15 million. In 1992, the total sales of the yachting industry in the United States fell to US$10.3 billion, but the number of yachts was 15.83 million. From 1996 to 2006, the yacht market in the United States entered its second prosperous period. In 2002, the total sales of the yachting industry in the United States reached US$30 billion. In 2004, the total sales of yachts in the United States ranked first in the world. In 2006, the total sales of the yachting industry in the United States exceeded US$39.5 billion US dollars, with 17 million yachts in use.

(3) The more saturated stage. From 2007 to 2010, due to the impact of the financial crisis of 2008, the development of the yachting industry in the United States slowed somewhat. In 2009, the yachting industry only added 573,000 yachts, and the total sales fell to US$30.8 billion. By 2010, the number of yachts in the United States was about 17.9 million. During this period, the number of yachts did not increase significantly, and the yacht development market was in a relatively saturated stage.

(4) The decline stage. Due to the impact of the COVID-19 pandemic, the yachting industry has declined slightly since 2020, but the development and manufacturing of yachts in the United States have continued. According to NMMA data, sales in 2020 were nearly US$50 billion. In 2022, according to the U.S. Coast Guard, the number of registered yachts was 11.95 million.

2. Development status of the yachting industry in Europe

European yachts account for about 40% of the global yacht market. Among them, Italy, France, Germany, Britain and other countries of the yachting industry are very developed.

(1) Italy is in a leading position in the luxury yacht field and is second only to the United States in yacht production. Its manufacturers Azimut Benetti Ferretti and Sanlorenzolt rank among the top three in yacht manufacturing. In the Global Order Book 2019, it is noted that Italy's yacht manufacturing industry has the highest order volume in the world, accounting for more than 20% of the global share.

(2) France is a major producer and exporter of yachts. The yachting industry developed after 1960, and it exports almost 60% of the yachts produced domestically. France often holds yacht exhibitions, and at the 2019 Cannes Yachting Festival, it exhibited about 700 yachts. France's revenue in the yacht market is also increasing. In 2022, it increased by 38% after 2021 and successfully opened the Danish market.

(3) The development of the yachting industry in Germany ranks fourth in Europe. Germany is a major yacht consumer, and other well-known brands of yachts are sold on the German yacht market. Its yacht imports exceed exports.

(4) The UK is a pioneer in yacht racing. The UK is a major consumer of yachts and a pioneer in yacht racing. In the 17th century, the British were very fond of rowing, powerboat racing, and other activities. With favorable conditions, the development of the UK yachting industry has improved the level of economic development. In 2019, the UK had more than 400 yacht rental companies. In 2021, the UK's revenue from the yachting industry was about £4.23 billion.

Based on the above, the characteristics of the yachting industry development in Europe and the United States can be described as follows: The development level is high, the economic development is good, and the industrial technology is excellent. People's demand for yachts is considerable, and marine resources are abundant.

(2) Development status of the yachting industry in Japan

Although Japan has a small land area, it is rich in marine resources. Japan is a manufacturing powerhouse in the yachting industry and a leader in the development of the industry in the Asia-Pacific region. It is known as the kingdom of shipbuilding. Its development can be divided into the following stages:

(1) Rising stage

The yachting industry in Japan originated in 1950 and began to rise in 1950-1970. With the continuous improvement of domestic shipbuilding technology in Japan, yachts gradually penetrated into society.

(2 With the rapid post-WWII economic development of Japan and the increase of national income, the leisure culture of yachting on the sea began to become popular. By 1970-1980 Japan had developed into the Asia-Pacific yachting export powerhouse with low-cost and economical yachts as its development goal.

(3) Japan became a major yacht consumption country from 1980 to 2014. There are 440,000 yachts in Japan, and the number of yacht license holders exceeds 3 million. At the same time, the Japanese government has strengthened the strict training system for yacht drivers and established a yacht inspection agency, which has enabled the industry to develop in an orderly direction. The number of people obtaining yacht licenses is increasing.

(3) Development status of the yachting industry in South Korea

The yacht market in South Korea is one of the three giants in the Asia-Pacific region. The South Koreans began to enjoy leisure yachting in line with the South Korean government's goal of making the leisure yyachting industry a national prosperity strategy. Its development includes the following aspects:

(1) In the early stages of development, due to government support, the number of yacht registrations and yacht license applicants in South Korea showed a growing trend. From 2008 to 2013, a total of 15,285 yachts were registered in South Korea.

(2) Construction of marinas. Due to the increase in the number of yachts, South Korea has built a marina that can accommodate 90 yachts with a maximum length of 21.3 meters (70 feet). In the early stages of the development of the yachting industry in South Korea, the construction of marinas was used to attract yachts.

(3) Yacht rental. In 2012, more than 16,000 people rented yachts at the Seoul pier, and 93,000 people have used the services at the pier. The rental of yachts largely met people's needs and drove economic development.

(4) The economic environment in South Korea provides a good platform for the development of the yachting industry, and large-scale yacht exhibitions are held every year to attract enthusiasts from around the world. In 2023, the Seoul Yacht exhibition took place at 16th International Boat Show in South Korea.

(4) Development status of yachting industry in China

1 Development of Hong Kong yachting industry

Hong Kong is a special economic zone in China. It became the earliest region in China to develop yachts. Its development in yachts is mainly reflected in yacht consumption and yacht clubs. Its development includes the following aspects:

(1) Since 1849, Hong Kong began to introduce the production and consumption of yachts on a large scale. In 2003, Hong Kong began to introduce the most advanced yachts of different types from various countries. In 2021, according to the data released by the industry association, there were 10,269 yachts in Hong Kong, including powerboats accounted for 49%, outboard engine boats for 31% and sailboats for 20%. Hong Kong's per capital GDP is about US$60,000, ranking 12th in the world.

(2) In 2011, the development of yacht clubs in Hong Kong was very advanced. At that time, 12 yacht clubs had been established, in addition to some private marinas.

(3) In the early stages of yacht development in Hong Kong, its development targets were only local or foreign. However, since 2018, Hong Kong has cooperated with Guangzhou, Shenzhen and other places to support the development of cruise + yacht water leisure tourism.

2. Development status of the yachting industry in mainland China

The development of China's yachting industry is about 300 years behind that of foreign countries. China's yachting industry has become an emerging force in the Asia-Pacific region, and China's position in yacht manufacturing is second only to that of Japan and South Korea. At present, the yachting industry in mainland China is mainly concentrated in coastal cities such as Shenzhen, Shanghai, Zhuhai, Tianjin, and Sanya. Its development can be divided into the following three stages:

(1) The initial stage from 1980 to 1990: Economic reforms that promoted the development of tourism in turn promoted the start of the yacht ing industry. Enterprises in coastal areas such as Jiangsu, Shandong, and Fujian began to introduce foreign technology and began producing different types of yachts. In 1979, China exported yachts to foreign countries for the first time.

(2) The accelerated development stage from 1990 to 2008: With the growth of the tourism market, many manufacturers have emerged in China's yacht market, and companies have introduced a large amount of foreign technology and intelligence, greatly improving the design level and productivity of China's yachting industry. During this period, yachts began to diversify, gentrify and democratize.

(3) The rapid development stage from 2008 to 2022. According to the data analysis of the China National Shipping Association, there were 50 yacht enterprises with strong sales ability and outstanding design in China in 2010. By 2018, 8 more en-

terprises were added to the original list, and the output value of China's yachting industry from 2014 to 2018 was ¥5.5 billion.

Section 2: Changes in Yacht Policies in Various Countries

The previous chapter provided a detailed analysis of the current situation of the development of the yachting industry at home and abroad. The development of the yachting industry cannot be separated from the support of the government and policies. This chapter will focus on analyzing the development and changes of yachting policies at home and abroad, providing a solid foundation for the policy comparison in Chapter 4.

(1) Changes in the development policies of the yachting industry in Europe and the United States

The development of the yachting industry in Europe and the United States is very impressive. The earliest countries to start developing yachts in Europe and the United States include the United States, Italy, the United Kingdom, France, Croatia, and Greece. This section describes the yachting industry development policies of some countries in Europe and the United States through government official websites, literature, news, and other channels. See Table 1 and Table 2 below. From the tables, the changes in yacht policies in Europe and the United States can be summarized.

1. Changes in the policy of the yachting industry in the United States

(1) Changes in time: Taking the 1971 Yacht Rules and Regulations as the starting point and the 2022 Regulations for Reducing the Impact of Boats on Right Whales as the cutoff point, some US policies were collected to create Figure 1. From Figure 8-1, it can be seen that the years from 1971 to 1988 represented the main development stage of American yacht policy. During this period, the country's official yacht policy was promulgated rapidly, and several related policies were implemented together in the same year, which indicates the importance the US government attached to the yachting industry at that time.

(2) Changes in content: As a major yachting country, the United States has made comprehensive policy construction around yachting.

In the early stages of development, the focus of US policy was on yacht manufacturing and yacht management, which led to the birth of policies such as the Yacht Code and Regulations and the Yacht Manufacturer Qualification Regulations." These regulations covered the management of yacht manufacturers, the management of yacht driving, the management of ship noise, and the management of yacht standards. From this period, it can be found that the US government was more focused on the problems arising from yacht manufacturing. They hoped to provide the public with yachts that met standards.

In the middle stage of development, with the continuous growth of the US yachting market, the US refined the focus of itspolicy to include yacht safety, tariffs, yacht dock construction, ship emission standards, and ship coating standards, further regulating the yachting industry and market at that time. During this stage of development, the US government had higher requirements for yacht standards, hoping that the development of yachts could keep pace with changes in the social environment, thus forming a virtuous cycle and creating greater economic benefits.

At this stage, with the positive development of the yachting industry, people's demand for yachts is increasing. The US's policy on yachts has also added management of yacht immigration, management of yacht dealers, and management of yachts colliding with large marine organisms. The theme of adding immigration management indicates that the US's yachting industry has established good development relationships with other countries internationally. The management of dealers is due to the impressive sales of yachts and was designed to maintain a good development order in the market.

Table 8-1 Some yachting industrypolicies in the United States

Issuing unit	Date	Name	Theme
United States	1971	Yacht Rules and Regulations	The purchase registration of yachts, channel management, driving license examination, loan services.
United States	1971	Federal Yacht Safety Act	The minimum standards for yacht registration are specified in detail, including requirements for vessel number, navigation rules, personal life-saving, anti-pollution rules, and distress alarms.
United States	1972	Manufacturer Qualification Regulation	The manufacturers are managed uniformly and the qualification standards for manufacturers are clarified
United States	1972	Law on the Prohibition of Drinking and Driving Yachts	Drinking while driving yachts is strictly prohibited.
CaliforniaUSA	1972	Limits on Ship Noise	Strengthening the unified management of ship noise pollution.
United States	1977	International Convention on Regulations for Preventing Collisions at Sea	When a vessel under the jurisdiction of the United States is in foreign territorial waters, as long as the laws and regulations of the foreign country do not conflict with it, the regulations shall apply to the vessel and shall be observed by the vessel.

United States	1984	Ship Safety Law	Ensure that the ship can sail safely, normatively, and effectively.
US Department of Defense	1988	American Yacht Design Code	Standardized the design standards for yacht marina facilities.
United States	2000	Tariffs	Vessels entering or leaving a certain area shall comply with all laws of the United States, and vessels leaving an area and arriving at the customs territory of the United States shall comply with regulations that may be prescribed by the Secretary of the Treasury to protect revenue.
United States	2012	United States Standards for the Discharge of Living Organisms from Ships' Ballast Water in US Waters	Ensure that ships sailing in various waters meet the corresponding emissions within the specified period.
American Coatings Association	2015	Ship Coatings: Understanding the Requirements of US, State, and Local Copper-Based Anti-Fouling Regulations	A comprehensive ban on the use of copper-based anti-fouling coatings; requiring the use of soft pads and liners during hull cleaning, as well as switching to non-toxic anti-fouling coatings during normal vessel maintenance and repainting cycles.
United States	2019	Management of Entry and Exit Yachts	The United States' management of normal inbound and outbound yachts is mainly based on active declaration. If there is no declaration as required, fines will be imposed, and in extreme cases, the vessel may even be confiscated.
Federal Trade Commission	2022	Federal Trade Commission Act	Dealers of yachts, cars, recreational vehicles and motorcycles in the United States will face stricter regulations.
National Marine Fisheries Service	2022	Regulations on Reducing the Impact of Boats on Right Whales	The yachts are required to slow down in most areas of the East Coast to protect the endangered North Atlantic right whales from being hit by the boats.

Source: Collected from public information

2 Changes in European yacht policies

(1) Changes in time: The development of yachts in Europe ranks second in the world, so its yacht policies are also very rich. Table 2 collects some relevant policies starting with a UK decree in 1894 and ending with the Implementation Roadmap for the Circular Economy of Scrapped Ships issued by the European Union Ship Industry Association in 2023. The period from 1894 to 1996 was the initial stage of development, the period from 2006 to 2015 was an intermediary stage, and the period from 2017 to 2023 was the latest stage of development.

(2) In the European region, policy texts were mainly collected from the European Union, the United Kingdom, and Italy. In the early stage, taking the United Kingdom as an example, the policies at that time only imposed policy constraints on the Ministry of Defence's yachts. The focus of the development of British yachts from 1894 to 1992 was still only for the State Council's yachts. At that time, yachts were almost nevert open to the public. However, Europe as a whole paid more attention to the development of the yachting industry in terms of yacht norms and standards, yacht safety, yacht registration, and other aspects.

In the middle stage of development, other parts of Europe have also been constantly upgrading their yacht policies. During this period, the development of yacht policies mainly focuses on the ship tax rules, yacht leasing, and port management systems. Different regions have different tax standards, such as Malta's tonnage fee. As the environment changes, the yacht leasing industry is constantly expanding, so the demand for port parking is also increasing. Therefore, it is necessary to strengthen the policies on yacht leasing and port management.

At this stage, the EU has focused on the issues of yacht emissions, the construction and use of ship and yacht coatings, the creation of environmentally friendly yachts, and the recycling of abandoned yachts. At the same time, it has been increasing the benefits of the European yachting industry by strengthening cooperation with China and increasing the number of member states. The issues of yacht emissions, the use of ship coatings, and the creation of environmentally friendly yachts are mainly aimed at enhancing the performance of yachts, and only secondarily reducing the pollution of the marine environment, so as to achieve better sustainable development.

Table 8-2 European yachting industry policy table

Issuing unit	Date.	Name	Theme
United Kingdom	1894	The 1894 Act	The powers conferred by sections 530 to 534 (removal of sunken ships) may not be exercised by the Ministry of Defence yacht without the consent of the Secretary of State, except for lighting and buoyancy necessary for immediate protection of traffic.
Governments of EU signatories	1974	International Convention for the Safety of Life at Sea	Standards for the construction and operation of commercial ships. Other qualification standards applicable to commercial yachts.
Secretary of State, Department for Transport	1981	Merchant Shipping (Light Duty) Regulations 1981	For pleasure yachts kept or used outside any of the following countries and territories (including their territorial waters), namely the United Kingdom, the Isle of Man and the Republic of Ireland, a payment of £1.53 per 10 tons shall be made for each 30-day or shorter period of visit; (b) for tugs and pleasure yachts not included in paragraph (a) of this subsection, a payment of £18.36 per 10 tons per year shall be made.
Paris, France	1982	Paris Memorandum of Understanding	Regular inspections and supplementary inspections should include inspection of predetermined areas on each ship.
United Kingdom	1989	Merchant Shipping (Ministry of Defence Vessels) Order 1989	Neither the captain of the Ministry of National Defense yacht nor any seafarer employed on the yacht shall be liable for any fines, debts, or damages.
United Kingdom	1992	Merchant Shipping (Defence Yachts) Order 1992	The "Ministry of Defence Yacht" refers to government vessels serving the Ministry of Defence, whose main propulsion device is sails. It is stipulated that the registration application for the Ministry of Defence Yacht should be submitted in writing by an official of the Ministry of Defence to the Registrar of Ships in the UK.

United Kingdom	1993	Merchant Shipping (Commercial Vessels for Sport or Recreation) Regulations 1993)	"Recreation yachts" or the 'amusement vessels, as the case may be.
Italy 10	1996	Yacht Management Regulations	Regulate the process of registering Italian yachts and applying for navigation licenses.
RenatoSoru	2006	Local Law No. 4	The landing of private aircraft and the parking of foreign yachts will be taxed.
Malta	2006	Malta Commercial Yacht Code	Commercial yachts used for international passenger transportation are eligible for tonnage tax as long as they are registered as commercial yachts in Malta. They must engage in commercial transportation with a maximum of 12 passengers (49 passengers) and must comply with a set of strict safety and operational standards. Yachts certified as commercial yachts are considered equivalent to small passenger ships because they can navigate in international waters.
European Conference and Council	2009	Directive 2009/16/EC on Port State Control	Ensure the unified and effective implementation of the port State control system.
General Administration of Ship Registration	2012	2012 Internal Procedural Rules	About Malta's tax Internal rules for eligibility of the scheme ("Internal Procedural Rules 2012") (21). This includes restrictions on time charters
Malta	2013	Merchant Shipping Act	All ships registered in Malta, including fishing boats and yachts, are subject to tonnage tax.
European Union	2013	European Union Recreational Yacht Directive	Assessed the technical and economic feasibility of further reducing emissions from recreational yachts and their fuel systems. Assessed the appropriateness of existing yacht design categories and the impact of such categories on manufacturers and end users.
International Maritime Organization	2015	Tier III	For yacht manufacturers below 500GT, they must solve the problem of compliance.

Council of the European Union	2017	Amend Council Directive 98/41/EC on the Registration of Persons Sailing on Board Passenger Ships Arriving at and Departing from Ports in the Member States of the Community and Directive 2010/65/EU of the European Parliament and of the Council on the Procedure for Reporting Ships Arriving and/or Departing from Ports in Member States	Personal data collected in accordance with Directive 98/41/EC should not be processed or used for any other purpose, nor should it be retained for longer than necessary in accordance with Directive 98/41/EC, in accordance with the EU Personal Data Protection Act, without prejudice to other legal obligations that comply with data protection law. Therefore, once the safety of the ship's navigation is complete, personal data should be automatically deleted without undue delay, or, where applicable, after the investigation or judicial proceedings conducted after the occurrence of an accident or emergency have concluded.
European Union	2020	BAT Conclusion for Coatings of Ships and Yachts	The total emission of volatile organic compounds from the construction of materials for docks and slipways, as well as the coating of ships and yachts, is calculated using the solvent mass balance method. The unit is kilogram of volatile organic compounds per kilogram of solid mass input.
Daily news of international yachting industry	2023	Croatia Joins the Eurozone and Schengen Area	Croatia became the 20th EU country to use the euro and joined the visa-free travel zone of the 27th EU member state, which will boost the country's yacht tourism industry.
CCPIT, Business Associations of Central and Eastern European Countries, Ningbo Municipal People's Government	2022	2022 China (Ningbo) - Central and Eastern European Countries Business Association Business Cooperation Conference	Import environmental protection and energy-saving yachts and related products from Central and Eastern Europe to China; introduce advanced management experience in planning and construction of coastlines and public yacht marinas from Central and Eastern Europe to China; export small and medium-sized sailing boats, small and medium-sized fishing boats and the most advanced fishing equipment produced in Ningbo and China to Central and Eastern Europe.

European Union	2023	European Union Recreational Yacht Directive	Technical and economic feasibility of reducing emissions from leisure yachts and their fuel systems. Classification of yacht design categories based on meteorological standards
European Shipbuilding Industry Association	2023	Implementation Roadmap for Circular Economy of Scrapped Ships and Boats	Following the successful dismantling and recycling programs established in many European countries, the use of sustainable recycling solutions will be popularized and the problem of scrapped yachts will be comprehensively addressed.

(2) Changes in the development policy of Japan's yachting industry

By data obtained government websites, literature, news, and other aspects, the following table 3 summarizes the changes in the development of Japan's yachting industry policies.

(1) Changes in time: The data in Table 3 covers the period from 1975 to 2022, with many policies from 2019, 2022, and 2023. According to the table below, the time is divided into 1975-1996, 2002-2014, and 2018-2023. This reflects that the yachting industry is still an important development goal for Japan at this stage.

(2) Changes in content: The change of policy themes in different periods is increasing

In the early stages of development, due to the high frequency of accidents involving ships and yachts in the sea, Japan's local policies banning dangerous behaviors on yachts were constantly issued. Later, in 1979, Japan also introduced the Japan Port and Port Facility Technical Standards, which represented Japan's world-class knowledge compilation in port and port technology. It was a milestone in the development of Japan's yachting industry at that time.

In the middle stage of development, Japan divided the yachts into different grades, and the government's attention was allocated to various aspects such as ship docking and yacht rescue. However, the safety problem of yachts on the sea is still an issue. Pay attention to the classification of yachts, including the types, lengths, and tonnages. The focus of maritime rescue is on coastal areas that are vulnerable to maritime accidents, as well as the time and areas where cruise ships are active.

At present, the government's attention addresses a variety of yachting issues. various yacht policies. In addition to Osaka Kita-Kogyo Pier abolishing the rules of public management and liberating the yacht pier for yachts and other types of boats for marine sports, it also includes yacht port construction and management, yacht safety, yacht tourism, and the yacht economy. In the management and construction of yachts, new technologies are adopted and new discharge standards are formulated. In yacht tourism, super yachts are encouraged to visit Japan. In 2023, Japan revised the Regulations on the Administration of Vessel Navigation, setting the same level of fuel consumption standards as new ships according to the type and size of the vessel, withthe country of registry implcmenting inspection. For violations of the standards, it is stipulated that measures must be taken to meet performance requirements, including speed restriction and propeller improvement.

Table 8-3 Japanese Yachting Policy

Issuing unit	Date	Name	Theme
Port Authority	1975	Ship personnel and small ships law of business operators	Provision of regulations on dangerous behavior and drunken operation of small vessels including ships.
Provision of regulations on dangerous behavior and drunken operation of small vessels including ships.	1975		The user can be attributed responsibility. If the facilities or equipment of the yacht port are damaged or lost, they must be restored to their original state and compensated according to their original price.
Fukuoka City	1975	Regulations on Fukuoka City Yacht Port	The user can be attributed responsibility. If the facilities or equipment of the yacht port are damaged or lost, they must be restored to their original state and compensated according to their original price.
Mie Prefecture	1975	Regulations on the Prevention of Motorboat and Four-person Accidents in Mie Prefecture	Motorboats, yachts, and other dangerous behaviors are prohibited, as well as drunk driving.
Ministry of Transport and Tourism of Japan	1979	Technical Standards for Japanese Ports and Port Facilities	It represents Japan's world-class knowledge compilation in ports and port technology.
Japanese Cabinet	1996	Third Report of the Market Access Grievance Commissioner Committee	Revise the inspection system for the import of ships, marine engines, and propulsion devices.

Japanese government	2002	Small Craft Classification Act	Classification of yachts.
Hokkaido	2005	Regulations on the Prevention of Cruise Ship Accidents in Hokkaido	It is suggested that the country should formulate a maritime policy outline as soon as possible, improve the promotion system of the basic law of the sea, expand the national jurisdiction of the sea territory, and strengthen international cooperation.
	2003	Regulations on the Prevention of Cruise Ship Accidents in Hokkaido	It is prohibited to make the cruise ship approach the swimmer at dangerous speed.
Sea of Japan foreign policy research consortium	2005	21st Century Ocean Policy Proposal	It is suggested that the country should formulate a maritime policy outline as soon as possible, improve the promotion system of the basic law of the sea, expand the national jurisdiction of the sea territory, and strengthen international cooperation.
Japanese Cabinet	2006	White Paper on Traffic Safety in Japan	Strengthen the rescue capabilities of coastal areas vulnerable to maritime accidents, including more effective use of patrol boats and aircraft, as well as taking proactive measures to fully utilize the mobility, search and vertical rescue capabilities of helicopters, especially in areas and at times when cruise ships are active.
Japanese government	2007	Basic Law of the Sea	Establishing "building a country on the ocean" as Japan's new era maritime strategy and establishing the current maritime system.
Japanese government	2008	Draft Law on the Navigation of Foreign Ships in the Territorial Sea and Other Areas	Supervise suspicious foreign ships in Japan's territorial waters, and prohibit foreign ships from docking in Japan's territorial waters without legitimate reasons.
Rowing industry Public Relations Department	2014	Privatization of Osaka Kita-Kodo Wharf	Starting to accept yachts and motorboats. Now accepting windsurfing, SUP (standing paddle), kayaking, and canoeing. Starting to accept fishing boats and mini boats.
Ministry of Land, Infrastructure and Transport	2018	Japan Tourism White Paper	Take advantage of the rich marine resources to promote the development of yacht economy.

General Affairs Bureau	2018	Submission on the Third Basic Plan for the Ocean	Conducting ship inspections and supervision of foreign vessels, applying automation technology to terminal construction and shipbuilding.
Japanese government	2019	Table of Tariff Law	No tax on yachts.
Fujin City	2019	Regulations of Fujin City, Tsushima Yacht Port	In Tianjin Qi's Set up a yacht harbor and appoint directors and necessary staff to strengthen management.
Japanese classification society	2020	Latest Steel Ship Rules	Analyze, inspect, and modify the engine, power converter, etc.
Kobe, Japan	2020	Regulations on Port Facilities of Kobe City	It is prohibited to navigate vessels equipped with internal combustion engines or electric motors as propulsion engines.
Kobe City	2020	Regulations on the Protection and Cultivation of the Sea in Sumi	It is prohibited to use "motorboats, yachts, boats, windsurfing boards or equipment that expels gases or liquids that pose a danger to others" in the Amagi Coast area.
Japanese government	2021	Amend the regulations of "Foreign Registered Superyacht"	Make cruising on superyachts in Japan easier and encourage superyachts to visit Japan.
Akashi, Japan	2022	Mingshi City Regulations	Vessels are defined as boats, motorboats, yachts, windsurfing boards, etc. used for sports or entertainment, and cannot enter the swimmer safety zone.
Hyogo Prefecture, Japan	2022	Regulation on Prevention of Acts Causing Major Public Nuisance	No one shall sprint, turn or sew vessels or yachts propelled by motorboats or other prime movers through unnecessary speeding, sharp turns, sewing, etc.
Wakayama Prefecture	2022	Regulation on the Safety of Small Ships	Regulate the navigation of vessels and take measures to protect the safety of swimmers
Miyako Island, Okinawa	2022	Regulations on Promoting the Safe Use of Vessels in Miyako City	Ensure the safety of life and property on the water, prevent pollution caused by ships, and regulate the supervision and management of ship safety.

12 prefectures including Mie, Fukushima, Nagasaki, Hyogo	2022	Preventing Yacht Accidents	To prevent accidents of motor boats, yachts and other vessels used for sports and entertainment, and to regulate the operation of cruise ships. Regulations and prohibition.
Osaka	2022	Regulation on the Prevention of Violent Acts that Cause Major Troubles to the Public	Regulate the use of yachts by anyone on the water where people swim or row boats and other small boats move.
Japanese classification society	2022	Code for Inspection and Construction of Steel Ships	Support the use of innovative technology for more flexible hull structure design.
Japanese government	2023	Regulations on the Administration of Navigation of Ships	Based on the type and size of the ship, set a fuel consumption standard equivalent to that of new ships country of registry investigate the actual fuel consumption every year, and require the ship managers to submit improvement plans for any measures that are not in place.

Source: http://www.rilg.or.jp/htdocs/ and Cruise Yacht Service and Management

(3) Changes in the development policy of the yachting industry in South Korea

The macroeconomic environment in South Korea provides a good platform for the development of the yachting industry. Table 4 below summarizes the changes in South Korea's yachting industry policies based on information from official websites.

(1) Changes over time: The yachting policy of South Korea can be divided into three periods: 1970-2008, 2010-2015, and 2018-2022. The policy of 2018-2022 represents the main development stage.

(2) Changes in content: Affected by developments in the environment, South Korea's yachting policy is advancing with the times and is constantly updated.

Since 1970, the main goal of South Korea has been to build a world-class comprehensive marine leisure terminal by expanding mooring capacity, reinforcing breakwaters, and building yacht maintenance facilities. The world-class terminal will attract the parking of yachts and thus promote the development of the industry. During the period from 1970 to 2008, South Korea mainly focused on developing docks and competitions. In 2008, the Ministry of Land, Infrastructure and Transport, the Ministry of Administration and Security, and the Marine Police Department jointly issued the Rationalization Plan for Marine Leisure Industry Regulations, which greatly relaxed the restrictions and regulations on marine leisure boats. The yachting industry in South Korea officially entered the development stage.

Since 2010, South Korea has begun to regulate the standards for yachts and yacht ports. Later, South Korea also introduced the Master Plan for the Development of the Yachting Industry, the Amendment Act on Marine Recreational Vessels", and the Countermeasures for the Development of the Cruise Industry and Support for the Yacht Port Industry to comprehensively promote the development of the industry. In 2015, the South Korean government and the Chinese government jointly cooperated to develop high-end sightseeing boats and harbors as key commercialized projects, and looked forward to high-end and friendly yachts.

From 2018 to 2022, South Korea's yacht development policy has undergone detailed modifications, especially in local yacht policies such as those in Tongyeong City, Fu'an County, Lishui City, and Mokpo City. Local governments have proposed policy updates for the development of yacht management regulations to facilitate social development, promote the revitalization of the local economy, and promote the low-end diffusion of the yachting industry.

Table 8-4 Development Policies of the Yachting Industry in South Korea

Issuing unit	Date	Name	Theme
Busan Metropolitan City Hall	1970	Redevelopment of the private investment project of the swimming bay yacht arena	Expanding the mooring capacity, reinforcing the breakwater, yacht maintenance facilities and other facilities, strengthening the competitiveness of marine tourism.
Department of Cultural Tourism and Sports	2004	Guidance on the Implementation Plan for the Training and Qualification Certification of Sports Instructors in 2004	Sailing, rowing, canoeing and other sports events need to consult with relevant research institutes and submit materials.
Cultural Tourism Bureau	2006	2-year Fund Management Plan	The total cost of the yacht accommodation project is W600 million, with a burden rate of 33% and a non-burden rate of 66%.
Ministry of Land and Resources, Ministry of Administrative Security, Marine Police Department	2008	Rationalization Plan for Regulations on Marine Leisure Industry	Significantly relaxing the restrictions and regulations on marine leisure boats.
South Korean government	2010	Basic Planning for the First Yacht Port 2010-2019	The standard for planning yacht ports, stipulating the parties of yachts surface standard.

Marine Leisure Tourism Department	2013	Special Development Plan for Yacht Mooring Field and Marine Leisure Beach in Gyeongsangnam-do	Specially developed yacht ship, boatfield and surfing attractions.
Korean Warlords	2013	Master Plan for the Development of yachting industry	Matters related to the medium- and long-term policy orientation for the development of the yachting industry, the yachting industry cultivation plan by year, the development plan for the Zhenjun marina, and other necessary matters for the cultivation of the yachting industry.
Korean National Assembly	2014	Marine Recreational Vessels Amendment Act	All yachts begin to be officially rented at reasonable prices.
Ministry of Oceans and Fisheries of South Korea	2015	Countermeasures for Developing Cruise Industry and Supporting Yacht Marina Industry	It was decided to fully support the development of the yacht marina industry.
Korea Maritime and Fisheries Development Institute, Chinese government	2015	Global Daily - South Korea Pushes for Yacht Port	The development of high-end cruise ships and harbors has been highly valued by the South Korean government as a key "commercialization" research area. It is expected that high-end and friendly yachts will travel between China and South Korea.
Ministry of Oceans and Fisheries of South Korea	2018	Law on Marine Spatial Planning and Management	Preparation and implementation of marine spatial planning and comprehensively regulates the utilization and development of the land.
Ministry of Administration and Security	2018	Regulations on the Cultivation and Support of yachting industry in Gyeongsangbuk-do	Promotes and supports various measures to cultivate the yachting industry.

Xin'an County Culture Sightseeing Division, Administration and Security Department	2019	Regulations on the Establishment and Operation of Xin'an County Yacht Tourism Co., Ltd.	The company shall engage in the following businesses: tourism and sightseeing boat industry, coastal tourism industry, tourism accommodation industry, catering industry, and other tourism-related businesses, as stipulated in the articles of association.
Gyeongnam Province, Geoje City (Marine Port Division), Administration and Security Department	2019	Regulations on the Cultivation of yachting industry in Geoje City	Systematically cultivate and support the yachting industry, promote the expansion of the low-end yacht population and the revitalization of the yachting industry, and promote Jukjeon City, south and the development of the central marine tourism city in the coastal area.
Ministry of Ocean and Fisheries (Department of Marine Leisure Tourism)	2020	Regulations on the Use of Yacht Berth Facilities in Trade Port	Use and management of yacht berthing facilities in trade ports.
Ulsan Metropolitan City Marine Fisheries, Administration and Safety Department	2020	Regulations on the Cultivation and Support of the yachting industry in Ulsan City	Establish consensus, create and popularize the content required by the demand of the yachting industry.
The Korean government	2020	The Second Basic Planning for Yacht Ports 2020-2029	In the Second Basic Plan, three major promotion strategies and 10 policy issues have been established, including yachts that are popular with the public, yachts that integrate with the region, and yachts that promote industrial growth.
South Korea New Wanjin Development Office, South Korea Yacht Association	2020	Memorandum of Understanding on Cooperation	Ocean space will be introduced into yacht projects and yacht berths will be constructed.

South Korean government	2020	Basic Planning for the First Phase of Environmental Protection Vessels	Through the localization and advancement of core raw material technologies such as LNG, electricity, and hybrid power, we have developed low-carbon ship technologies such as hybrid fuel.
Gyeongsangnam-do system Yingshi (Sightseeing Division), Administration and Security Department	Issued in 2019, revised in 2021	Regulations on the Management and Operation of Yacht Facilities in the Marketing City	Establish a unified marketing system for yacht-type facilities in order to stimulate marine leisure tourism in the city, and stipulate the necessary matters for their management and operation.
North Jeolla Dao Fu'anCounty, Administrative and Security Department	Issued in 2011, revised in 2021	Detailed Rules for the Implementation of the Regulations on the Management and Operation of the Yacht Club Facilities in Fu'an County	Fuan County yachting facilities management and operation necessary regulations to promote the revitalization of the local economy and the low-end diffusion of the yachting industry.
Yeosu City, Jeollanam-do (Marine Policy Division), Ministry of Administration and Security	Issued in 2015, revised in 2022	Regulations on the Management and Operation of Yacht Marina Facilities in Lishui City	To promote the cultivation of the yacht and other dock industries and the development of marine leisure sports, through the development and efficient utilization of docks, ports and related facilities, the management and operation of the yacht dock facilities in Lishui City.
Mokpo City, Jeollanam-do (Marine Port Division), Ministry of Administration and Security	Issued in 2009, revised in 2022	Regulations on the Management and Operation of Yacht Quays or Facilities in Mokpo City	Anyone who wishes to use a yacht or facility must obtain permission from the Mokpo Market, set daily entry and exit times for the yacht marina, operate the yacht, and pay the usage fee for the yacht marina or facility in full from the date of use permission until the start of use.

Mokpo City, Jeollanam-do (Marine Port Division), Ministry of Administration and Security	Issued in 2009, revised in 2022		The professional custodian of the Marina yacht facilities must arrange forWater Recreation Safety ActThe prescribed general driving license (level 1 and level 2) or yacht driving license;
Department of Administration and Security	2022	Detailed Rules for the Implementation of the Regulations on the Management and Operation of Yacht Marina Facilities in Mokpo City	When operating yacht education, lectures, and yacht club training programs, it is possible to entrust some or all of the projects to yacht schools, continuing education colleges of universities within the province, or yacht-related organizations (including legal persons, hereinafter referred to as "yacht-related organizations").
Department of Administration and Security	Issued in 2012, revised in 2022	Gyeongsangbuk-do Commissioning Regulations Operating Rules for the Yacht School in Uijin County	The opening hours of the yacht school are throughout the year, and children, students, ordinary people, etc. who are interested in marine leisure sports such as yachting are recruited as students of the yacht school.

Source: https://cllk.nanet.go.kr/potal/search/searchList.do

(4) Changes in China's yachting industry policies

1. Changes in Hong Kong's yachting industry policy

Hong Kong has the longest history of yacht tourism development in China. This section identifies relevant yachting development policies in Hong Kong via the official website of the Hong Kong government, the Marine Department, and news websites. Regulations, notices, plans, and plans are selected as samples, and the following table 5 has been obtained through sorting.

(1) Changes over time: Hong Kong yachting policy was examined from 1978 to 2022. With the changes in national conditions and time, Hong Kong has strengthened its cooperation with the yachting industry in coastal cities in mainland China since 2018.

(2) Changes in content: Hong Kong's policy development is good

In the early days, Hong Kong made changes to its ship registration system in terms of policy. Initially, the regulations stipulated that all vessels in Hong Kong waters must be licensed. Later, the Merchant Shipping (Safety) Regulations also emphasized the safety of ship registration.

In order to strengthen the management of yachts, actively guide the public's attention and love for navigation, and support the healthy development of the yachting industry, the Maritime Safety Administration of Hong Kong's Ministry of Transport issued the Notice on Strengthening the Management of Yachts in 2006. This notice greatly increased the popularity of yachts in people's lives. However, it still did not clearly propose specific methods and strategies to guide the public.

From 2007 to 2010, Hong Kong implemented a consumption tax on yachts, standardized the rationality of yacht driving licenses, and regulated yacht safety management.

In the period from 2017 to 2022, Hong Kong strengthened cooperation with Shenzhen, Hainan, Guangdong and other regions in the development of yacht policies and standardized the entry and exit management of yachts. First, the State Council proposed a cooperation plan between Hong Kong and Shenzhen and Guangdong, an important strategy for building a new pattern of opening up to the outside world and promoteing the reform of international ship registration and supporting systems. Afterwards, it gradually strengthened cooperation with other places to jointly develop the yachting industry economy and tourism. At the same time, it also standardized the entry and exit management mechanism and operational guidelines to make the management mechanism more convenient.

Table 8-5 Hong Kong Yachting Policy

Issuing unit	Date	Name of	Theme
Hong Kong Government	1978	Shipping and Port Control Ordinance (Cap. 313)	The Regulation completely changed the ship registration system in Hong Kong, stipulating that all vessels in Hong Kong waters must be licensed.
Hong Kong Government	1981	Merchant Shipping Safety Regulations(Chapter 369)	Regulations governing the safety of Hong Kong registered vessels.
Hong Kong Government	2004	Protection of the Harbour Ordinance	Reducing reclamation works.

Maritime Safety Administration of the Ministry of Transport	2006	Notice on Strengthening the Management of Yachts	Actively guided the public's attention and love for yachts, supported the healthy development of the yachting industry, enriching citizens' water activities, ensuring water traffic safety, and preventing yachts from polluting the marine environment.
Hong Kong Government	2007	Marine Parks and Marine Reserves Regulation	Regulating the operation of glass-bottomed yachts in marine parks.
Hong Kong Government	2009	Provisional Regulations on Consumption Tax	Imposing a consumption tax on yachts.
Hong Kong Maritime Department	2009	Maritime Regulations for Two-level Yachts	Standardize the relevant regulations on yacht safety management and the rationality of yacht driving licenses.
Shenzhen Bureau of Culture, Sports and Tourism, Hong Kong Tourism Commission	2018	Cooperation Plan for the Development of Yacht Tourism between Shenzhen and Hong Kong	Focus on solving the problems connected with yacht manufacturing planning, yacht club and yacht marina construction planning, waterway design, route development, talent cultivation, and management standard formulations, all while improving the cooperation level of yacht tourism between Shenzhen and Hong Kong, deepening the cooperation field of yachting industry development, and jointly build the yacht tourism market in Hong Kong.
Hainan Province	2019	Implementation Plan for the Free Tourism of Hong Kong, Macao and Qiongdao in China (Hainan) Pilot Free Trade Zone	Standardizing a clear and easy-to-operate management system for yacht traffic between Hong Kong and Macao.

Hong Kong Maritime Department	2021	Merchant Shipping (Prevention of Air Pollution) Regulations	Strengthening environmental protection management systems, improving the service of collecting and cleaning up marine garbage, coping with oil spill accidents, implementing international conventions to prevent marine pollution, and enforcing relevant environmental protection laws and regulations on ships.
the State Council	2021	Comprehensively Deepening Reform and Opening-up Plan for Qianhai Shenzhen-Hong Kong Modern Service Industry Cooperation Zone	An important measure to support Hong Kong's economic and social development, enhancing the level of cooperation between Guangdong, Hong Kong and Macao, and building a new pattern of opening up to the outside world, and promoting the reform of international ship registration and supporting systems.
Hainan Maritime Safety Administration, Ministry of Transport, Hong Kong Maritime Department	2022	Work Arrangements on Facilitating Travel by Yachts between Hainan and Hong Kong	Holders of certificates for Grade I and Grade II operators of pleasure vessels issued by the Maritime Department of the Hong Kong Special Administrative Region Government can drive corresponding Hong Kong registered or licensed yachts in designated and announced yachting waters in Hainan Province.
Hong Kong Maritime Department	2022	Notice for Captains of Visiting Yachts/ Pleasure Boats	Standardizing the entry-exit management mechanism and operational guidelines to make the management mechanism more convenient.
Hong Kong Maritime Department	2022	Merchant Shipping (Local Vessels) (General) Regulation	Allowing yachts and pleasure boats from outside to navigate in Hong Kong's waters.

Source: Hong Kong Maritime Department, China Government Network

2. Changes in the policy of yachting in mainland China

This section describes yachting industry policies in mainland China as found in the official website of the Chinese government as well as those of Guangdong, Hainan, Shanghai, and other local governments. Also included here are some of their yachting industry policies from 2008-2022, as found in laws, regulations, plans, opinions, notices, and other materials.

(1) The Chinese government's support has led to a continuous increase of yachting policies since China officially opened the yachting industry market in 2008.In 2016, the yachting industry received full support, and 2016 was the year with the most yacht policy releases. Although the development of the yachting industry was affected by the COVID-19 pandemic from 2020 to 2022, the country still attaches great importance to the development of the yachting industry.

(2) Affected by China's environment, the content of policies is being refined and increased

China's policies on yachts initially focused on yacht construction, regulations, safety management, and encouraging yacht development.

Afterwards, according to the developmental needs, the core issues in China's yacht policy shifted to tax rates, yacht tourism, yacht immigration management, and yacht operation.

At present, yacht consumption, yacht economy, maritime rescue, cruise + yacht linkage, and yachting industry cluster innovations are also being incorporated into policy development.

Figure 8-2 Distribution of Chinese yacht policy texts from 2008 to 2022

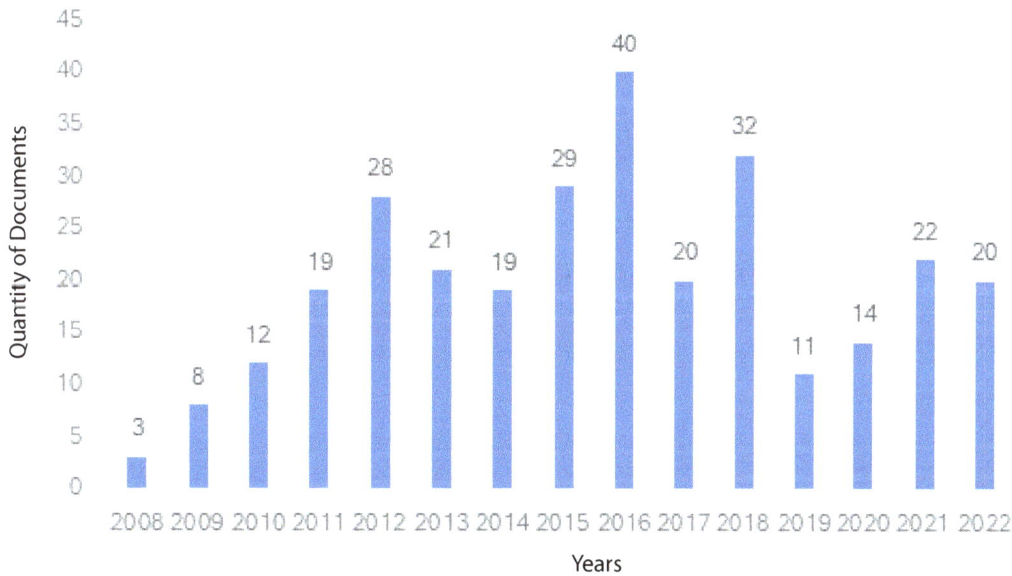

Table 8-6 China's Yacht Policy

Issuing unit	Date	Policy name	Policy theme
Ministry of Transport	July 2008	Regulations on the Safety Management of Yachts	The first set of policies and regulations on yachts in China. It aims to standardize the safety management of yachts and promote the healthy development of the yachting industry.
China Classification Society	August 2008	Yacht Building Code 2008	China's first yacht construction code. For non-commercial motor yachts under 20 meters, the inspection mode and technology are different from those for commercial ships.
the State Council	November 2008	Provisional Regulations of the People's Republic of China on Consumption Tax	The consumption tax rate for yachts is 10%.
the State Council	December 2009	Opinions of the State Council on Accelerating the Development of Tourism	For the first time, it proposed to support the development of emerging tourism industries such as cruise and yacht in regions with conditions.
the State Council	December 2009	Several Opinions of the State Council on Promoting the Construction and Development of Hainan International Tourism Island	It is pointed out that it is necessary to study and improve the management of yacht tourism, and cultivate and develop yacht equipment manufacturing.

the State Council	July 2010	Notice of the General Office of the State Council on Printing and Distributing the Plan for the Division of Labor of Key Work on Implementing the Opinions of the State Council on Accelerating the Development of Tourism	We will include the cruise and yacht tourism equipment manufacturing industry in the national list of encouraged industries. We will support the development of cruise tourism in regions where conditions permit.
Maritime Affairs Bureau	August 2010	Opinions on the Implementation of Yacht Safety Management	The inspection of imported yachts, the approval of electromechanical equipment installed on yachts, and the registration of yachts.
Standing Committee of the National People's Congress of the People's Republic of China	February 2011	Draft Vehicle and Vessel Tax Law	It is proposed to levy vehicle and vessel tax based on the length of yachts, and to delete the provision of surcharge for "high energy consumption and high pollution" vehicles and vessels.
Maritime Affairs Bureau	May 2011	Measures of the People's Republic of China on the Training, Examination and Certification of Yacht Pilots	Safeguarding the safety of yacht drivers.
Ministry of Transport	September 2011	Announcement on Strengthening the Management of Imported Yachts	Promote the integration of China's yachting industry with the international market.
Maritime Safety Administration	March 2013	Interim Provisions on the Statutory Inspection of Yachts	It belongs to the technical specifications supporting the Regulations on the Safety Management of Yachts. The regulations have undergone significant changes in terms of scope of application, design categories, inspection categories and intervals, and drawing review requirements.

General Administration of Quality Supervision, Inspection and Quarantine of the People's Republic of China	July 2013	Administrative Measures for Quarantine of Entry-Exit Yachts in Hainan	The conditions for applying for telecommunication quarantine for yachts have been relaxed, and those who do not hold relevant certificates can be subject to telecommunication quarantine.
Ministry of Transport	March 2014	Code for Design of Yacht Dock	It is a mandatory industry standard.
the State Council	August 2015	Several Opinions of the General Office of the State Council on Further Promoting Tourism Investment and Consumption	
General Administration of Quality Supervision, Inspection and Quarantine	May 2018	Administrative Measures for Quarantine of Entry-Exit Yachts in Hainan	Promote the construction of dock berths, streamline the approval procedures for yachts, reduce the entry threshold and the total cost of yacht registration, navigation, tourism, parking, and maintenance.
the State Council		Several Opinions on Improving the System and Mechanism for Promoting Consumption and Further Stimulating the Potential of Resident Consumption	In order to prevent the spread of epidemic diseases and standardize the quarantine of entry and exit yachts in Hainan.
the State Council	September 2018	The 14th Five-Year Plan for National Economic and Social Development of the People's Republic of China and the Outline of the Long-term Vision for 2035	Support the development of mass consumption of cruise ships and yachts, and strengthen the construction of related public supporting infrastructure.

Ministry of Industry and Information Technology and other four departments	2021	Opinions on Accelerating the Development of Cruise and Yacht Equipment and Industry	Clearly propose to improve the yacht development policy.
Maritime Safety Administration of the Ministry of Transport	August 2022	Notice on the Implementation Plan for the Issuance of Inspection Certificates for Imported Yachts in Pilot Cities for Optimizing the Business Environment and Innovation	It is proposed to promote the innovative development of the yachting industry, support coastal cities to encourage and guide the development of yacht events, and vigorously develop mass consumption yachts.
the State Council	October 2022	"14th Five-Year Plan for Tourism Development"	Optimize the inspection and certification process for imported yachts, continue to optimize the business environment, and actively and steadily carry out the optimization of the inspection and certification of imported yachts in the first batch of pilot cities for business environment innovation.
......	2022	......	It is proposed to promote the development of yacht consumption popularization and support the innovation of yachting industry in coastal cities such as Dalian, Qingdao, Weihai, Zhuhai, Xiamen and Sanya.
Guangdong Provincial People's Government	......	Implement the policy division plan announced at the 2011 High-end Forum on Cross-Strait Emerging Industry Cooperation and Economic Transformation and Upgrading	......

People's Government of Guangdong Province	November 2011	Notice on the Outline of Tourism Development Planning of Guangdong Province (2011-2020)	Promote exchanges and cooperation between Guangdong Province and Taiwan yachting industry associations, so as to gradually introduce Taiwan investment to develop the yachting industry.
Zhongshan Municipal People's Government	July 2012	"Zhongshan yachting industry Development Plan 2012-2020"	Support the development of cruise and yachting industry, and accelerate the introduction of management regulations and measures in line with international standards to promote the development of yacht tourism in Guangdong.
People's Government of Guangdong Province	January 2013	Notice of the General Office of the People's Government of Guangdong Province on Issuing the "Implement the key tasks of the Pearl River Delta Planning Outline in 2014"	Accelerate the expansion of the yachting industry cluster, accelerate the improvement of the yachting industry chain, accelerate the expansion of the yachting industry space, and accelerate the construction of the yachting industry system.
the State Council	April 2014	Overall Plan for China (Guangdong) Pilot Free Trade Zone	Formulate province The management measures for yachts, taking Guangzhou, Shenzhen, Zhuhai and Zhongshan as pilot cities, will promote the innovative cooperation of yacht tourism among Guangdong, Hong Kong and Macao.
Guangdong Provincial Free Trade Office, Guangdong Provincial Tourism Bureau, Guangdong Maritime Safety Administration	April 2015	Implementation Plan for Guangdong Free Trade Zone Yuegangao Yacht "Free Travel"	It is clearly stated that "the facilitation measures for yachts entering and exiting Guangdong, Hong Kong and Macao will be formulated", which indicates the dawn of the "free travel" of yachts in Guangdong, Hong Kong and Macao.

People's Government of Guangdong Province	June 2016	Measures for Optimizing Port Business Environment and Promoting Cross-border Trade Facilitation in Guangdong Province	Promote the "free travel" of yachts in Hong Kong and Macao in the Pilot Free Trade Zone, and further promote the development of yacht tourism in southern Guangdong.
the State Council	February 2019	Overall Plan for Deepening Comprehensive Cooperation between Guangdong, Hong Kong and Macao in the World in Nansha, Guangzhou	We will study and improve the mechanism and operational norms for the entry and exit of yachts from Hong Kong and Macao. We will promote the establishment and improvement of the guarantee methods for the entry and exit of yachts from Hong Kong and Macao. We will study and explore innovative yacht supervision models, further simplify the customs clearance procedures for yachts. We will support all regions to further promote and improve the construction of supporting facilities, promote the opening up of yacht marinas, and delimit the water areas for yacht activities.
......	June 2022	......	Deepen cooperation in the fields of shipping logistics, water-water transfer, iron-water intermodal transportation, shipping finance, maritime services, cruise ships and yachts.
Hainan Provincial People's Government	......	Administrative Measures for Yachts in Hainan Province	......
the State Council	February 2016	Overall Plan for the Construction of Hainan Free Trade Port	In order to strengthen the service and management of yachts, maintain national security, and promote the development of yacht economy.

Hainan Provincial Department of Transport	June 2020	Detailed Rules for the Implementation of the Measures for the Administration of Yacht Leasing in Hainan Province	Set up a yachting industry reform and development innovation experimental zone.
Hainan Provincial Department of Transport	November 2021	Regulations on Promoting the yachting industry in Hainan Free Trade Port	In order to further strengthen the behavior of the yacht rental industry in Hainan Province, maintain the order of the yacht rental market, cultivate new forms of yacht tourism consumption, and promote the sustainable and healthy development of the yacht rental industry.
Hainan Provincial People's Government	March 2022	Implementation Plan for the Reform, Development and Innovation Experiment Construction of Hainan yachting industry	Propose high-quality development of the yachting industry, yacht inspection, registration and navigation, yacht leasing, yacht services and supervision, etc.
Shanghai Municipal People's Government, Shanghai Municipal Bureau of Culture, Tourism and Sports	July 2022	Shanghai Tourism Industry Reform and Development Plan for the 13th Five-Year Plan	It is proposed to become an attractive regional yacht tourism destination and a vibrant new yachting industry by 2025.new business model. A pilot area for reform and innovation of the yachting industry system and mechanism with inclusiveness and openness.
Shanghai Municipal People's Government, Shanghai Waterwork, business bureau	November 2016	Shanghai Maritime "13th Five-Year Plan"	Promote the cluster development of cruise, pleasure boat and yacht industries.

Shanghai Municipal People's Government	January 2018	Reply to the Comprehensive Utilization Planning of the Huangpu River Shoreline - Core Section (Yangpu Bridge-Xupu Bridge)	Strengthen the marine tourism industry, accelerate the development of cruise and yacht economy, and support the pilot policies of cruise and yacht entry and exit management.
Shanghai Municipal People's Government	April 2018	Several Opinions on Promoting the High-quality Development of Shanghai Tourism and Accelerating the Construction of a World-renowned Tourist City	On the premise of ensuring the safety of navigation in the Huangpu River waterway and not affecting the connection and opening of public space along the river, the 11 yacht marinas are planned and arranged based on the principles of total quantity control, decentralized layout, and moderate development. The layout of the yacht marinas will be optimized and improved in the future in combination with regional development needs.
Shanghai Municipal People's Government	August 2018	Several Opinions on Promoting the Deepening Development of the Cruise Economy in Shanghai	We will accelerate the development of tourism equipment manufacturing industries such as yachts, cruise ships, caravans, low-altitude flights, and amusement facilities.
Shanghai Municipal People's Government	October 2018	Regulations of Shanghai Municipality on Tourism	Promote the coordinated development of cruise ships, yachts and pleasure boats.

Shanghai Municipal People's Government	May 2020	Opinions on Promoting Smart Weather to Ensure City Refined Management in Shanghai	The city promotes the development of cruise, cruise ship, yacht and other water tourism, increases the investment and construction of water tourism public facilities, promotes the development of water tourism routes and products, and strengthens the publicity and promotion of water tourism.
Shanghai Municipal People's Government	May 2021	Opinions on Strengthening the Construction of the Water Search and Rescue System in Shanghai	The maritime department and the meteorological department cooperate to carry out research on cruise ships, pleasure boats, yachts, urban ferries and the three islands of Chongming Island. International transportation is based on meteorological monitoring, forecasting and early warning of navigation conditions, and emergency support for severe weather such as heavy fog and strong winds on water is strengthened.
Shanghai Municipal People's Government	January 2021	Procedures for the Administration of Public Security in Shanghai Waters	Strengthen the emergency support for cruise ships and yachts in water search and rescue.
Shanghai Municipal People's Government, Standing Committee of the 15th Shanghai Municipal People's Congress	February 2021	Regulations of Shanghai Municipality on Search and Rescue on Water	Yacht clubs or other enterprises and institutions responsible for yacht management should implement security and safety management measures for yachts in accordance with relevant laws and regulations, and keep records of yacht navigation and occupant information; if they discover any illegal or criminal activities using yachts, they should report them to the public security organs in a timely manner.

Shanghai Municipal Transportation Commission	October 2021	Notice on the Implementation Measures for Shanghai Port Operation and Management	According to the emergency plan for water search and rescue, the search and rescue center and sub-center shall regularly organize and carry out water search and rescue for cruise ships, yachts, ferries, pleasure boats, dangerous chemical ships, aircrafts, etc., special search and rescue drills and comprehensive exercises.
	January 2022		For port operators engaged in providing dock facilities for yacht rental business (hereinafter referred to as yacht dock), the yacht dock facilities shall not be used for engaging in port passenger transportation services for individual tourists.

Source: China Government Network, Local Government Network

Chapter 9

An Exploration of the System of Yachting Industry Talent Training

With the recent rapid rise and development of the Guangdong-Hong Kong-Macao Greater Bay Area and the construction of free trade ports, China's yachting industry is also full of vitality, and China has become an emerging market for the industry. Since China plays an increasingly important role in the world, it is urgent that professionals be trained to meet the developmental needs of the yachting industry. This chapter mainly focuses on how training is constructed and evaluated as well as the dilemmas faced in the training process by both educational and commercial institutions.

Section 1: The construction and evaluation of training modes in the yachting industry

(1) Analysis of the current situation of talents in China's yachting industry

Entering the 21st century, China's shipbuilding industry is facing a new historical opportunity for development. The next ten years will be a critical period for China's shipbuilding industry to surpass Japan and South Korea and leap to the forefront of the world's yachting sector. However, China's yacht output value accounts for only 1% of the world's total, about CNY¥ 4 billion yuan, but the profit margin is as high as 40%.It is a typical "three high and one low" (high technology, high growth, high efficiency and low consumption) industry. Yachting is not only an important part of the shipbuilding industry, but it is also an important part of tourism industry and enterprises dealing with navigation movement, marine culture, and marine ecological protection. The promulgation of the State Council's Opinions on Promoting the Reform and Development of Tourism will bring great opportunities for the development of China's yachting industry in its infancy. The development and growth of the yachting industry is conducive to the optimization of China's industrial structure and the stimulation of domestic demand. However, as the yachting industry has just emerged in China, there is a shortage of professionals. Domestic yacht professionals are generally transferred from other professions. Such "halfway out" yacht talents cannot meet the future needs of China's yacht market, which demands specialization and internationalization. Therefore, it is very important to build a training mode and evaluation mechanism that is international and future-oriented and that promotes the sustainable development of the yachting economy.

(2) Yacht talent training mode, training mechanism and evaluation mechanism

Personnel training mode refers to the training of talent under the guidance of certain modern educational theories and ideas, in accordance with specific training objectives and personnel specifications. Education must be carried out as part of a process that includes a relatively stable teaching content and curriculum system, management system and evaluation methods.

The mechanism of yacht professional training refers to the coordinated system of talent training. The main elements of the specific professional talent mechanism include the internal changes and future laws of yacht talent development, the external factors and ways of realizing the development of yacht talent, and other external factors.

Yacht talent evaluation mechanism is neither a yacht talent evaluation system, nor a general yacht talent evaluation activity. It is a systematic and scientific development form of yacht talent evaluation. The characteristics and functions of yacht talent evaluation mechanism lie in its sociality, structure, circularity and linkage.

Improve the mechanism of yacht talent flow. Universities and scientific research institutes are allowed to set up mobile technical posts and employ and recruit entrepreneurs and technical representatives with successful practical case experience as consultants or part-time research work.

(3) Constructing a talent training mode and evaluation mechanism that adapts to the development of the times and faces the future

1. Defining the training objectives of yacht talents

The marine attributes of the yachting industry require that the talent training of this industry should be professional, safe, scientific while offering future technological empowerment,

The yachting sector is a new industry in China, which provides infinite vitality for stimulating domestic demand and serving domestic and foreign markets in the future. At a time when the global economy is facing a recovery, the authorities should seize the opportunity and follow the trend. The instructors who will be training talent in this industry should have a solid theoretical foundation, outstanding practical ability, good humanistic quality, strong cross-cultural communication skills and a high degree of social responsibility and innovative spirit. These training modes are suitable for ports, yacht clubs, yacht companies, hotels, travel agencies, tourist attractions and other tourism enterprises.

2. Establishing the training type of yacht talents

There is a diversity of talent training types as determined by the attributes of the yachting industry. Among them, technical talents, service talents and management talents are the main types, which are specifically subdivided into yacht driving, repair, design, assembly, education, training and other technical factors. Personnel also need to be trained for yacht sales, leasing, operation, planning, catering, brokerage and other service-oriented tasks, as well as for jobs in market development, financial credit, administrative human resources, and other management areas.

3. Formulating the training contents and plans for yacht talents

It is necessary to formulate a multi-dimensional and multi-level training system for yacht talents that issuitable for higher vocational colleges, ordinary institutions of higher learning, scientific research institutes, and for purveyors of continuing education and vocational education. China is committed to improve and perfect the system and mechanism for the assessment and promotion of the curriculum, the combination of production, teaching and research, the allocation of teachers, as well as the provision of vocational certificates, and job certificates. Strategies are designed too enrich and improve the multi-level teaching levels of undergraduates, postgraduates and doctoral students.

4. Constructing a yacht talent evaluation mechanism suitable for present and future needs

It is necessary first to establish a dual-track evaluation system for professionals and managerial personnel. Professionals are different from managerial talents, especially in the yachting industry. Different evaluation indicators and systems determine different promotion channels. Establishing a differentiated and step-by-step evaluation mechanism is conducive to the healthy development of talent within the yachting industry.

Second, it is necessary to establish a comprehensive mutual evaluation mechanism for the industry as a whole.

As the yachting industry involves many industries and formats, the interaction and linkage between them directly affect the economic benefits of the industry. As a whole, For example, the services provided by yacht drivers and yacht brokers directly affect the performance of yacht operation, leasing and even sales. Yacht designers and yacht brands also directly affect the performance and market value. Therefore, these mutual linkages should also be taken into account while creating the yacht talent evaluation mechanism.

In addition, a flexible evaluation mechanism should be established for talents in production, learning and research. China should encourage yacht enterprises to cooperate with scientific research institutes, general higher and vocational colleges (including technical schools) in running schools and in jointly building a yacht talent training base. In order to promote the improvement of a yacht talent training system, a flexible evaluation mechanism for industry-university-research talents should be established. This would have a far-reaching influence on the promotion of the economic development of the yachting industry.

Section 2: Research on the training strategies for foreign yacht talents

The origin and development of tourism theory and education originated as a

Western paradigm. Therefore, this section surveys four typical countries and regions as the focus of analysis. It aims to extract insights and wisdom from their rich knowledge systems .

(1) Successful experience of foreign yacht talent training modes

The development of domestic tourism has led to the development of a marine tourism economy and provided a broad space for the development of yacht tourism. However, in the context of the development of yacht tourism, China is still in its infancy. Considering that China's marine tourism education, especially in the field of yacht tourism, appeared relatively late, it will inevitably take time to create a talent-development model. Therefore, at this stage, the most important thing is to realize that the talent training mode must embody the dual principles of innovation and expediency. At the same time, China's efforts should be adhering to the key dimensions of quantity and quality in talent development. This section will explore the talent-training experiences of the United States, France, Britain, South Korea, Japan, Thailand, and Australia.

1. European and American model

The talent training model of European and American countries reflects a comprehensive approach. The impact of European tourism is enormous, generating a staggering annual revenue of €800 billion, equivalent to 5% of the region's GDP. At the same time, it has promoted the creation of 3 million jobs every year. The wide influence of the industry covers a range of social aspects, including sustainable development, urban mobility, rural and cultural tourism, peace tourism, sport-centered tourism and health-oriented tourism. Therefore, in response to the growing demand for experienced tourism professionals with a global perspective and multi-faceted management capabilities, the European tourism sector has taken a pioneering position in the development of general and strategic talent development models. This strategic approach not only extends to Europe, but also resonates globally. The strategy includes many aspects: most importantly, the integration of the learning process with practical work applications so as to establish a seamless synergy between theory and practice. The European model also demonstrates a wise implementation of the tutorial system to guide and cultivate emerging talents. These strategies include strong attention paid to students' career path planning and an unwavering commitment to a passionate and engaging learning environment. This collaborative effort ensures that students are seamlessly integrated into the learning process, where they quickly absorb and apply knowledge. The multifaceted nature of these strategies highlights the role of European and American countries in shaping a team of excellence, innovation, and perseverance in the dynamic field of global tourism.

At the same time, with the vigorous development of such phenomena as short-distance tourism, elderly tourism, health tourism, and business tourism, Germany has also made a clear commitment to actively train tourism professionals. These needs include online travel operators, travel planners, representatives specializing in customer relations, business travel planners and managers, and other indispensable intermediaries in the tourism support system.

In the trajectory of tourism development, Canada acknowledges the lack of high-level talent and inadequate incentives in the industry. It also notes a lack of corresponding educational prerequisites, along with the low barriers to entry for many positions. As a result, a comprehensive strategy has been developed for Canada to address these shortcomings, and targeted talent training initiatives have been planned.

In addition, the French tourism industry, taking advantage of its unique development advantages, has tailored a special talent development framework for the culinary industry. It's well known that the food industry is one of France's major tourism resources. Taking into account the complexity of online roles in the culinary sector. a detailed training plan has been developed for each role, covering skill mastery, interpersonal and social communication skills, and proficiency in organizational management and collaboration.

On a broader scale, European and American countries have properly recognized the lack of highly skilled professionals in the tourism industry. Accordingly, a series of countries in these regions have carefully constructed a comprehensive talent training model in order to cope with the scarcity of high-level expertise in the dynamic field of tourism. These include initiatives such as TEFI (The Tourism Education Futures Initiative) and SOTL (The Scholarship of the Teaching of Learning). These programs have been developed on the basis of careful consideration and in accordance with the unique characteristics of local tourism development. Among these models, TEFI is regarded as the cornerstone, since it provides an indispensable framework for training tourism talents. TEFI focuses on highlighting the complex challenges and reforms unique to the field of tourism. This value-driven approach provides guidance for promoting major changes in tourism education and its practical application. The core of this talent training model lies in the recognition of a subtle value orientation embodied through the skilled pedagogies of tourism educators. This implicit value needs to be quantified and expressed through corresponding customized measurement tools for precise implementation. In particular, the instrumental model needs to be quantitatively measured and improved.

Specifically, the rationale for TEFI is based on the general recognition that higher education, especially tourism and hospitality education, must change to meet new challenges. Thus, TEFI is largely organized around a process that is both proactive and action-oriented. The focus is on the transformation of tourism theory into practice in order to make fundamental changes in tourism and hospitality education. The TEFI-based evaluation process develops a set of principles based on five values: ethics, management, knowledge, professionalism, and mutuality. Because of the interconnectedness of these values and their permeability, they are portrayed as interrelated principles of value. TEFI proponents envision that educators could use a subset of the five values to integrate into their curricula, as appropriate.

A more comprehensive definition of these five values is set out below.

(1) Code of Ethics: Ethical conduct is based on the principles and values of honesty, acknowledging that people strive for behavior that is perceived as "good." Good behavior does not happen in a vacuum, but comes from a particular value system. These value systems further require understanding and respect for behavior based on authenticity and the true self.

(II) Management Duties: Management duties relate to the activities a person does when involved in sustainable development, responsibility, and service to the community. Sustainability requires managing resources to mitigate the impact of tourism on future generations. Linked to sustainability is the concept of responsibility. Sustainability can only be achieved if individuals and organizations acknowledge their responsibilities and act accordingly. If all stakeholders are to take responsibility for the future of the planet in tourism, it is necessary to empower those who are currently powerless, and it is necessary to restrain the power of other groups. Finally, serving the community is a way for stakeholders to demonstrate their commitment in taking responsibility.

(III) Knowledge: Knowledge can be described in several ways. It can refer to professional knowledge and skills acquired by a person through experience or education, relating to a theoretical or practical understanding of a subject. Knowledge also refers to the specific facts and information in a particular field. It also can mean awareness or familiarity acquired through the experience of a fact or situation. Knowledge is created through a process of selection, connection, and reflection. Knowledge always presupposes existing knowledge, which means that knowledge involves interpretation and contextualization. When appropriate, tourism professionals are encouraged to acknowledge the knowledge of others and question existing knowledge that may be taken for granted.

(IV) Professionalism: Professionalism is defined as the ability to align personal and organizational behavior with ethical and professional conduct. Professionalism is defined as a combination of leadership, practicality, a focus on service, partnership-building skills, and initiative.

(V) Mutuality: Within the framework of TEFI, mutual respect was initially defined as a relationship-based value that requires an evolving, dynamic attitude. Mutuality is an evolving and dynamic process, emphasizing that the achievement of mutual respect is a long-term or even lifelong learning process. It can be developed at different levels, from the individual to the social and global levels. Mutuality is the development of respectful relationships between self and person through the sharing and understanding of values and attitudes. It includes open discussion and appreciation of different opinions.

Many European and American countries have translated the TFEI model into practical action. This training plan has been realized by setting up a variety of courses and cooperative methods, including the Cornell Model in the United States, the Lausanne Model in Switzerland and the Surrey Model in the United Kingdom.

The model of Cornell University in the United States attaches great importance to improving students' abilities, and the curriculum revolves around different structures. A distinctive feature of this model curriculum is its strong focus on skill development. It is worth noting that at Cornell University School of Hotel Management, students must complete the designated internship period. This is a prerequisite for graduation and promotes real-world experiential learning.

By contrast, Switzerland's Lausanne model is known for its innovative industrial and academic integration. Educational ideas and teaching objectives tend to be consistent. Faculty members maintain close ties with the industries they educate, aligning the curriculum with contemporary trends and international benchmarks. This strict adherence to standardized teaching practices ensures that the instructional curriculum stays current with the evolving landscape of the field. Course design essentially emphasizes the integration of theory and practical application, and creates an environment conducive to practical learning.

The Surrey model, based in the United Kingdom, demonstrates a comprehensive and mature master's training structure for the field of tourism. The University of Surrey has a strong faculty and a rich reserve of teaching resources, emphasizing the cultivation of students' abilities. Using a holistic approach, the model equips students with comprehensive skills and a deep understanding of the multifaceted complexities of tourism. Through a careful combination of theory and practice, the Surrey Model provides students with the tools they need to excel in the dynamic field of tourism.

The results of their cooperation fully affirm the key role of TEFI teaching mode in training tourism talents. This synergy between academia and industry, the so-called industry interaction model, has also become a symbol of teaching methods for training skilled tourism professionals in European and American countries. This approach is rooted in the considerable support provided by prominent European and American travel industry associations. It promotes a strong interaction between educational institutions and the industry as a whole.

2. East Asian model

In the past few years, the yachting industry in Southeast Asia has gradually emerged and become an important growth point in the global yachting market. With the extension of the coastline of Southeast Asian countries, the vigorous development of tourism, and the increasing importance of marine culture, the prospects of the yachting industry in the region are increasingly promising. As a region with rich marine resources and unique marine characteristics, Southeast Asia has great development potential in yacht manufacturing, navigation operation, marine tourism, and other fields. The background of yachting talent training in Southeast Asia benefits from the multiculturalism and diversity within the region. At the same time, it has been continuously expanded by the international yacht market. Southeast Asian countries are actively cultivating talents to meet the needs of the industry.

As Southeast Asian countries gradually realize the contribution of the yachting industry to the regional economy and the importance of yacht tourism in attracting high-end tourists. Because of the importance of regional image, yacht talent training has gradually been incorporated into the strategic planning of regional development. In this context, more and more universities and training institutions have begun to offer professional courses related to yachts. Among them, in East Asia, including Japan and South Korea, the yacht talent training strategy obviously revolves around the promotion of practical skills.

These East Asian models are carefully designed to train yacht talents in the vast East Asian region: (1) through intermediary training, graduates of vocational education enter foundational positions in cruise lines; (2) After in-house training, general education graduates enter the basic work of a yacht company; (3) Graduates of general education majors enter the management of the company after internal training and secondary promotion training; (4) Graduates of general education go directly to work in yacht companies.

This Southeast Asian model clearly distinguishes itself from mainstream practice by combining its priorities with a practical approach that focuses on practical expertise. As exemplified by these four different training models, the Yacht Talent Development Strategy for Southeast Asia emphasizes the region's commitment to developing professionals who are fully proficient in the field of yacht tourism. Based on these training paths, many countries have established talent training programs that are more in line with their national conditions.

In Japan, the mode of "cooperation between industry, government and university" is the mainstream way to train tourism talents in Japan. In this model, there is a concerted effort that "society as a whole collaborates to train the next generation of technical professionals." Students contribute their expertise to enterprises, and companies and government agencies respond positively to impart technical expertise and social necessities to students, thereby creating a robust hands-on educational environment. As a bridge between educational institutions and the wider society, the Government of Japan has a key role to play in promoting such synergies. Schools actively look for suitable enterprises to organize student internships, improve students' practical ability, and alleviate employment pressure. They have also promoted close alliances between universities and the tourism industry. The demand for talents in tourism enterprises should be taken as the guiding principle for training in relevant professional skills. The establishment of comprehensive tourism curriculum emphasizes the principle of "solid foundation and wide scope," which is a multi-faceted approach that not only enriches students' enthusiasm for their chosen fields, but also enhances their mastery of core disciplines. Therefore, the orientation of universities is to contribute versatile talents to society. Japan Tourism University is noted for its high-quality teaching staff. The educational landscape is further enhanced by state-of-the-art teaching facilities. At the same time, tourism education in Japan has highlighted an international trajectory. Given the relatively late emergence of tourism education, internationalization has raised the level of education in the country. The cooperative teaching exchange between Japanese and foreign universities has made great progress in the field of tourism education in Japan, pushing the discipline to a new height.

Correspondingly, the training mode for Korean tourism talents obviously emphasizes the strengthening of tourism education. Since the 1990s, the Korean tourism industry has experienced exponential growth, and with the development in the early 21st century, the Korean tourism industry has developed rapidly. International tourism is gaining momentum. This evolution has promoted the simultaneous development of higher education and personnel training in tourism. The main features of its curriculum framework are as follows: (1) The clear educational vision highlights the universities offering tourism-related courses in Korea. The course design is derived from the professional reality of the field, with priority given to the teaching of basic theory and practical skills. It tailors training pathways to students based on their chosen employment trajectory, closely aligned with the needs of their future roles. (2) The integration of vocational education and academic education makes Korea's tourism curriculum system different from others. In order to comprehensively address the prerequisites of professional competence and acumen of tourism professionals, the system integrates a series of internships, practical modules, and theoretical courses. This synthesis goes beyond theoretical understanding and covers applied practice exercises, bringing theory and practice together in harmony. (3) The curriculum framework demonstrates flexible subject settings and is closely related to growing trends in the tourism industry. In order to better adapt students to the needs of tourism landscape and future careers, the course includes 32 subjects. At the same time, interdisciplinary fields such as psychology, statistics and management are intertwined to provide students with a richer knowledge base.

3. The Australian model

As a country with vast sea areas and rich marine tourism resources, Australia presents a unique background in the training of yacht tourism talents. The country's yacht tourism talent training focuses on practical education and close industry cooperation. Many educational institutions work closely with yacht enterprises and organizations to provide internship and training opportunities that enable students to accumulate valuable experience in a real working environment. In addition, Australian yachting industry associations and industry organizations are actively involved in personnel training by providing professional training and information exchange platforms to promote the skills upgrading of students and practitioners and in-depth understanding of thc industry.

In this training mode, TAFE (Technical and Further Education) plays an important role. Australia's TAFE model has attracted worldwide attention and is considered to be the representative of advanced and exemplary vocational education. The key factor behind its success lies in its unique characteristics, which distinguish it from other vocational education models. The innovative approach of the TAFE model emphasizes the integration of theoretical knowledge and practical experience to develop comprehensive skills with strong industry resonance. Through a strong partnership with industry, TAFE ensures that courses are always up to date with the development needs of the dynamic tourism industry. This close connection with the actual industry has greatly promoted the docking between academic and practical expectations, thus cultivating graduates with strong adaptability and willingness to accept innovation. TAFE also focuses on tailoring personalized learning paths according to individual abilities and interests, which improves the pertinence of education. It has trained a group of well-prepared professionals and made positive contributions to the development of Australian tourism in many aspects. This comprehensive talent training model plays an important role in promoting the development of yacht tourism in Australia.

Specifically, TAFE includes the adoption of four flexible and effective vocational education and training models:

(1) Virtual internship company training guided by teachers and supported by the industry. Students organize and manage their own companies that simulate a real business environment. Other business activities include customer visits, equipment financing, information feedback, receiving, sending orders, invoicing, financial management, and salary payment. In this way, students can improve their skills and ability to coordinate work processes. To better improve students' ability to solve problems via interpersonal communication and teamwork, this non-real environment allows them to make mistakes. It is also conducive to their continuous learning and improvement.

(2) Project teaching: After the students absorb the theoretical knowledge in class, they are divided into several groups and provided with an instructor. Students then need to complete the development and management of a project independently or cooperatively in a specific working environment. This teaching mode is conducive to consolidating and applying the knowledge learned and enhancing the ability of teamwork.

(3) School-enterprise cooperation: TAFE colleges and enterprises jointly undertake the training work, and students go to relevant enterprises for training and work.

(4) Industry training: During the period of study and training in TAFE College, students must complete the required courses in the relevant enterprises.

While many Australian suppliers have on-site campuses overseas, education and training can also be provided through partnerships with local training organizations. The Australian education and training system also provides flexibility to meet the varying characteristics and needs of students. The wide range of training products offered by the tourism industry enables providers to tailor training to students at different levels of literacy and numeracy. Training can also be provided in languages other than English. Australian education and training institutions also regularly provide assistance in overseas markets through the development of in-house training courses;. They also provide professional development and training to staff of local education and training institutions to enhance their skills. Overseas delivery of Australian education and training programs includes both higher education through universities and the vocational training sector. Often, pathways can be established between vocational training and university resources.

In addition, employers place a strong emphasis on practical skills, and this workplace learning is a key feature of the TAFE system. It helps to train graduates who are ready for employment. Many campuses, particularly in the area of vocational learning, have on-site trade training facilities that reflect the business environment and provide students with access to a simulated workplace training environment. Online platforms can provide cost-effective training when working with regional students. Hybrid delivery models that combine classroom training with online delivery are also common because they facilitate access through the use of technology. However, the personal contact and information transfer brought about by face-to-face training have been maintained. Market training providers have the opportunity to work with Australian education and training providers. One of the objectives of Australia's National Strategy on International Education 2025 is to strengthen overseas partnerships. Australian universities and training organizations are good at cooperating with international education and training organizations to establish training alliances and partnerships. The country's raining and education personnel are highly skilled and highly sought after in overseas markets. Australian training and education staff often also provide professional development opportunities for "tourism trainers" for local trainers to improve their education. This can be of great benefit, as it not only contributes to the continued sustainability of the tourism training market in the country while ensuring that the training provided is relevant.

4. Thai model

Tourism education in Thailand is closely related to the needs of the industry. In both public or private university settings, the training objectives of tourism education in Thailand focus on applied talents with practical professional skills and competitiveness in society. Thailand's tourism industry has become a pillar industry of the country's economy.

A study has found that tourism majors in Thai universities focus on cultivating students' practical abilities and internship experience. Most institutions partner with tourism businesses and related industries to provide students with hands-on experience in the actual work environment. This empirical study highlights the key role of Thai universities in designing tourism professional courses. Emphasis is placed on developing hands-on skills through an immersion internship program. The close cooperation between educational institutions and tourism enterprises has expanded the influence of this teaching mode, which creates an atmosphere for students to truly participate in the work environment. This connection with an actual practice environment allows students to gain a deeper understanding of the complexities of their future careers.

In addition, Thailand's tourism talent training focuses on multi-level and diversified development. It covers a wide range of courses on all levels, including doctoral, master's, bachelor's, associate's, college degrees as well as short-term training.

The talent training process includes the diversification of curriculum, the diversification of teaching process, and the diversification of professional practice. In the teaching process, instructors change the traditional classroom teaching mode by creating new teaching methods that include case studies and project learning. Schools are encouraged to take the working process as the main line and break down the original content of the chapters in the textbooks, allowing students to learn relevant knowledge through simulated or real projects in campus or off-campus training bases, and professional companies. In this way, students' ability to integrate knowledge with practice can be enhanced, and their working abilities can be improved. Through course study and practical training, they can obtain various vocational skills certificates related to their major before graduation. The competitiveness of employment has been greatly enhanced.

(1) Diversification of curriculum. The diversification of curriculum is the concrete embodiment of the goal of personnel training. At present, schools in Thailand usually divide the courses of tourism-related majors into three categories: public basic courses, subject basic courses, and majors. Each type of curriculum can be further subdivided into compulsory courses and elective courses, forming a highly homogeneous curriculum system. In order to construct curricula based on working ability, reduce the number of redundant courses, and improve the quality of education in general, schools have implemented effective measures. Special attention is paid to cooperation with enterprises and industry experts. When formulating their curricular systems, schools cooperate with private enterprises to align the curricula with industry standards and work processes. In this process, schools can increase professional required courses or provide more elective courses.

(2) Diversification of teaching process. This refers to the fact that teachers change the traditional classroom teaching mode by creating new teaching methods, applying case study, project learning, and other methodologies to the classroom. In this way, students' ability to integrate knowledge with practice can be enhanced, and their working ability and quality can be improved. Through course study and practical training, they can obtain various vocational skills certificates related to their major before graduation. The competitiveness of employment has thus been greatly enhanced.

(3) Diversification of professional practice. Practical teaching systems play a vital role in personnel training. However, there is a common phenomenon of attaching too much importance to theory and neglecting practice in the process of training tourism talents. Usually, students have only a few months of exposure to practical opportunities during the whole study process. The rest of the time, there is little opportunity for practical internship. As a result, students have a relatively shallow understanding of the jobs in the industry, and it is difficult for them to adapt to the increasingly complex and changeable demand for talent. Therefore, it is necessary to pay attention to the strengthening of practical links in the personnel training system. Through the establishment of closer cooperation between schools and industries, more practical internship opportunities can be provided. This may include establishing partnerships with tourism enterprises, hotels and scenic spots to provide more practical opportunities for students so that they can get in touch earlier with the specific operation and needs of the industry.

Schools need to ensure that the students trained have excellent professional loyalty and qualifications. In this process, schools need to provide students with appropriate career planning guidance. Specifically, schools should help students understand their major and possible career positions in the future and show them their employment prospects after they enter school. For this reason, it is particularly important to arrange internship programs, which can enable students to better understand and recognize their professional direction. Career planning is a long-term process, and schools need to ensure that it provides four years of classroom teaching and internship experience throughout the students' university years In this context, there is a close synergy between Thailand's tourism talent training model and the tourism industry. This synergy has been cleverly integrated into the university's curriculum blueprint, consolidating all aspects of higher education so as to ensure the rapid satisfaction of the diverse needs of different students.

Section 3: China's yacht talent training mode, dilemmas and future developmental prospects

1. China's Yacht Talent Training Model

(1) China's yacht talent training objectives

The goal of training personnel for yacht tourism positions requires a high level of theory and scientific research, but importantly, yacht tourism talents with strong practical service ability are needed.

China's yachting industry aims to cultivate individuals with firm ideals and beliefs, all-round development, and a certain degree of scientific and cultural literacy. The training objectives emphasize the craft-like spirit of the profession, , encouraging excellence, and giving students a firm grasp on details and quality. In addition, attention should be paid to cultivating students' employment competitiveness and sustainable development abilitiesThe training of yacht talents will continue to encourage students to develop in their careers and realize their own value. At the same time, it also contributes to the sustainable growth of yachts and ships. Therefore, the specific objectives students should have are as follows: good moral character, humanistic attitude, and sense of social responsibility; excellent professional qualities in the field of marine tourism; mastery of the qualitative and quantitative analysis of marine tourism, and certain scientific research ability; strong team cooperation and cross-cultural communication abilities; innovative spirit; and the possession of a certain skill qualification certificate.

(2) Orientation of Yacht Talents Training in China

The cultivation of yacht tourism talents first needs to be clearly defined and classified in detail. In the process of training, it should be ensured that the relevant talents have a wide range of knowledge, including yacht construction, design, inspection and other professional and technical fields.

Based on the different classifications of yacht tourism talents, they need to be classified and trained horizontally. At present, the training of yacht tourism talents in China is usually included in one direction of tourism management specialty. However, there is no independent specialty for yacht tourism personnel training. Considering the current demand for various types of talents in the yachting industry, it is necessary to set up an independent yacht tourism talent training specialty. Further branch training is carried out according to different types of talents. This adjustment will help to better meet the needs of the yacht tourism industry for diversified and professional talents.

(3) China Yacht Talent Training Specifications

Professionals in the yachting industry should meet the following requirements in terms of quality, knowledge and ability.

1. Quality (Q)

Q1: Have correct world outlook on life and values.

Q2: Have good professional ethics, professionalism, and legal awareness.

Q3: Advocate the Constitution, abide by the law and discipline, advocate virtue and benevolence, be honest and trustworthy, respect life, and fulfill moral standards and codes of conduct. Have a sense of social responsibility and social participation.

Q4: Have quality awareness, environmental awareness, safety awareness, information literacy, craftsmanship and innovative thinking. Respect and love labor, and have strong practical ability.

Q5: Have the courage to struggle, be optimistic, have the ability of self-management and the awareness of career planning. Have a strong sense of collective and team spirit.

Q6: Have a healthy body, psychology and sound personality, master basic sports knowledge and one or two sports skills. Develop good fitness and hygiene habits, and good behavior habits.

Q7: Have certain aesthetic and humanistic qualities and be able to form one or two artistic specialties or hobbies.

Q8: Strong communication skills, positive learning attitude, effective learning methods, courage to struggle, be optimistic and upward-looking. Have self-management ability, strong collective consciousness and team spirit.

2. Knowledge (K)

K 1: Mastery of the necessary ideological and political theory, have a basic knowledge of science and culture, and excellent knowledge of traditional Chinese culture.

K2: Familiarity with safety protection and psychological counseling, laws and regulations, and with environmental protection and other related knowledge related to the specialty.

K3: Familiarity with the basic knowledge of psychology such as common mental health, emotional regulation, and psychological problems and their prevention.

K4: Mastery of the basic knowledge of reading and creating mechanical drawings, electrical drawings and other engineering drawings.

K5: Mastery of the relevant knowledge of mechanics, mechanical parts, tolerance matching, machining, and other technologies.

K6: Familiarity with yacht design expertise such as hull line, hull structure, power plant, electrical control, styling, and interior decoration.

K7: Mastery of the operational knowledge of AUTOCAD, Rhino, KEYSHOT and other yacht design software.

K8: Mastery of the knowledge of lathe work, bench work, welding, and composite material production.

K9: Familiarity with yacht construction technology, mastery of WORD, EXCEL and other common office software.

K10: Familiarity with the relevant regulations and specifications of yacht design and construction, and familarity it with the relevant knowledge of yacht product inspection.

K11: Familiarity with the yacht construction process and yacht production logistics.

K12: Familiarity with the installation and commissioning of the main equipment of the yacht.

K13: Understanding of the modern shipbuilding mode, mastery of the basic concept of intelligent manufacturing, and an understanding of the relevant knowledge of pre-sale and after-sale service of yachts.

3. Competencies (A)

A1: Have the ability of inquiry learning, lifelong learning, problem analysis and problem solving.

A2: Have good language, written expression, and communication skills.

A3: Have the ability to adapt to life, the ability to regulate emotions, the ability of interpersonal communication, and the ability of self-psychological adjustment.

A4: Have professional dedication and professional ethics, and being realistic and innovative.

A5: Have the ability to read all kinds of mechanical parts and assembly drawings and be able to use computer-aided drawing.

A6: Have a certain specialty of preliminary yacht construction (hull, engine, electrical, interior decoration and modeling. Capability of scheme, submission for approval and production design.

A7: Have the ability to complete the processing and manufacturing of some simple yacht products according to the design drawings.

A8: The ability to use relevant software to prepare yacht construction process documents.

A9: The ability to complete the inspection of some simple yacht products

A10: The ability to prepare a yacht material procurement plan according to the yacht production design and process documents.

A11: The ability to complete the installation and commissioning of some simple yacht equipment.

A12: The basic ability to engage in yacht product sales and after-sales service technical support.

(IV) Training Mode of Chinese Yacht Talents in Colleges and Universities

At present, China's yacht talent training model mainly focuses on higher education. It aims to cultivate application-oriented yacht tourism compound talents with all-round development of morality, intelligence, physical fitness, beauty and labor. These talents not only need to master the basic knowledge of theory, management, and economics, but also should be familiar with laws and regulations, as well as having foreign language skills to meet the needs of international communication. They must have an international perspective and be able to examine the development trends of the yachting industry from a global perspective. At the same time, the spirit of innovation and practical ability are particularly important in this field. These talents need to be able to meet the constant changes and challenges in the industry and actively propose innovative solutions and put these schemes into practice.

1. Curriculum

The curriculum system is the main component of the talent training plan, which is to achieve the goal of talent training and shape the specifications of talent training. The curriculum is thus the main carrier of education and teaching that embodies the characteristics of personnel training. The traditional curriculum system is mostly composed of public basic courses, professional basic courses, professional knowledge courses, elective courses and practical courses. It can be subdivided into public basic course modules, professional compulsory course modules, professional elective course modules, foreign language ability modules, and practice modules. It not only takes into account the logic of knowledge, but also the interests and hobbies of students. According to the special requirements of employers and market demand for personnel training specifications, schools can set up a "directional" module that does not conflict with the school curriculum to ensure the employment of students to the greatest extent.

Based on this starting point, the curriculum module of tourism management specialty is not the same as the yacht tourism curriculum system. The adjusted curriculum also adds the course module of yacht design and manufacture. Moreover, some courses have been deleted if they are difficult to learn and master and whose application proportion is not high. It also makes special provisions for foreign language ability. Foreign language proficiency module is an important lever to select whether students have the opportunity to communicate and learn. Every student must learn English, and an elective module of language ability— a third foreign language—has been added.

In addition, the diversity of yacht tourism talents determines that the training time should be diversified and differentiated. The training duration and cycles of vocational education are quite different from those of systematic training in colleges and universities. According to the length of time, the nature of their certificates is determined by the credits students have completed, and the passing rate of examinations and skills tests. Regular undergraduate and specialist teaching still takes four (three) years of training time. However, it is necessary to control the length of theoretical teaching and increase the length of practical operation from the first year of university to the year before graduation. Every academic year includes two months of enterprise internship, and the last year of graduation internship must be spent in the enterprise. The total duration of the practice must be 600 hours.

2. Practice teaching

The task of application-oriented undergraduate education is to train high-level application-oriented professionals for production, engineering, management, and service. Therefore, practice teaching occupies a more important position in the talent training program. For yacht tourism discipline, it is different from other academic and research training objectives and should mainly focus on application. As an application-oriented specialty, the concept of practical teaching must run through the whole process of personnel training.

Practice teaching is an open teaching system with a wide range, which has the characteristics of diversified mode construction and functional mode expansion. Therefore, it is necessary to draw on the wisdom of the masses, make extensive contacts, and strive to open up a new teaching system for practical teaching. It helps students to develop steadily and spirally from a low-level to a high-level step by step in the practical teaching system. Teaching practice here is not a "supporting role" but an "equal" with classroom teaching. The practice part is mainly divided into the basic level of in-school training, the professional level of off-campus practice, and the comprehensive level of foreign practice. The main places of in-school training are the training laboratories and practice bases of the school; Off-campus practical teaching mainly relies on marine tourism enterprises and industry organizations; Foreign practice requires the school to establish cooperation with some internationally renowned countries with advanced training mode of marine tourism talents.

As shown in the figure, the practical teaching module is divided into three levels: the practical teaching system of in-school training, off-campus practice, and foreign practice learning. Each practical teaching module has the time and space to undertake and complement each other in function. Students can pursue their interests through practical experience on campus, so as to choose off-campus internship units. In turn, off-campus enterprises can select students for off-campus practice through the results of on-campus practice. Foreign practice is the third way of practice. Each practice module is connected and interrelated with the others.

3. Acquisition of professional skills and vocational certificates

In terms of professional certificates, the yachting industry in China has also created corresponding professional qualification certificates in order to promote the selection of yacht talents and the specialization of the industry. The acquisition of professional skills certificates is also emphasized in the training plan of colleges and universities. These professional certificates cover many fields from yacht design, manufacture, maintenance to management, ensuring that talents have comprehensive professional knowledge and skills. These certificates are widely recognized and important in the yachting industry, and have become one of the criteria used to measure the ability of talents. The main qualification certificates of China's yachting industry shown in Table 9.3 include but are not limited to:

(1) Yacht marina manager certificate: to verify the technical ability of the individual in the process of yacht construction, including material selection, process control, and quality control.

(2) Yacht repairman qualification certificate: It emphasizes the practical operational skills and problem solving ability of the repair staff who makes sure the yacht is kept in good condition during use.

(3) Yacht manager qualification certificate: covering yacht operation, marketing, customer service and other aspects of knowledge in order to cultivate talents with comprehensive management ability.

(4) Yachtsman qualification certificate: to confirm the ability of the driver in handling and managing the yacht while ensuring safe and smooth sailing and customer service.

These professional certificates not only help to improve the quality and overall level of yacht talents; they can also promote the improvement of technology and service level of the whole industry. Through certification, talents can obtain authoritative recognition and enhance their competitiveness in the employment market, thus injecting more vitality into the sustainable development of the yachting industry.

(5) Dilemma of Yacht Talents Training in China

At present, the training of talents in the field of yacht in China is facing a series of challenges. Therefore, China's yachting industry is facing many difficulties in talent training, which can be classified into the following points:

(1) A shortage of professionals

Yacht manufacturing, maintenance and design is a highly specialized and comprehensive field. It covers the knowledge and skills of ship engineering, material science, design and other disciplines. The manufacturing process of yacht involves not only the structural and aesthetic design of the hull, but also the comprehensive consideration of various factors. In ship engineering, it is necessary to understand the structure, stability and hydrodynamic principles of the hull to ensure the stability and smoothness of the boat in the water. In addition, material science is another key area, because yachts need to withstand the erosion of harsh environments such as sea water and climate. In addition, yachts need to integrate various electronic and mechanical equipment and systems, such as engines, communication equipment, and navigation systems Therefore, knowledge of electrical and mechanical engineering is also indispensable. In this regard, integration technology, control systems, and the ability of devices to work together are critical.

However, as the yachting industry is relatively new in China, the relevant professional education and training system may not be fully developed. Therefore, China's yachting industry needs to be more actively involved in the training of professionals. This includes strengthening the curriculum of universities and training institutions and encouraging students to study in depth in many related fields. At the same time, through the cooperation of industry associations, enterprises and academia, a more comprehensive talent training system can be established.

(2) Incomplete education system:

At present, most of the professional education related to yacht management in China is specialized education. However, the training level and knowledge structure provided by a college education are often unable to fully meet the needs of the future development of the yachting economy and industry. In addition, the yachting industry itself involves many fields and requires interdisciplinary knowledge. However, the training of related majors may not be comprehensive and perfect enough. Take the cruise major as an example. The curriculum still focuses on the traditional fields of tourism English, tourism catering management, tourism marketing and etiquette education. There are relatively few technical courses related to yacht operation management. This leads to the relatively narrow knowledge and lack of pertinence in yacht professional training programs.

(3) Low industry recognition:

China's yachting industry is a relatively new industry, however, due to its relatively new state of development, the public's understanding of the career prospects and development potential of the yachting industry may be relatively limited.

For one thing, a lack of in-depth knowledge about the boating industry can lead to misconceptions about career prospects in this field. People may generally think that the yachting industry is relatively small in China, and that relatively mature industries are more popular. Thus, the potential and development opportunities of the yachting industry may be ignored. This situation may have led people to be conservative in their career choices and unwilling to take risks in yachting related careers. Second, the unknown nature of the occupation may also exacerbate people's hesitation. As the yachting industry has not yet formed a clear career development path and successful track record in China, many people may lack confidence in the yachting industry. They are worried that they will not be able to find a stable career opportunity there or that their career development path in this field is not clear.

This limited understanding of career prospects in the boating industry can further contribute to brain drain and recruitment difficulties. The yachting industry needs to attract and train professionals in various fields, including ship engineers, designers, electronic engineers and so on. However, if the potential talent has limited knowledge of the field, they may be more inclined to choose a better-known field. They are unwilling to enter the relatively unfamiliar yachting industry, which leads to the loss of high-quality talents in the industry. On the other hand, recruiting talent may also face difficulties, as candidates may have doubts about career prospects in the boating industry. Hiring teams need to spend more time and effort explaining the potential of the Industry to candidates.

(4) Salaries and benefits are relatively low:

Relatively low salaries and benefits are a major challenge for any start-up industry, and the yachting industry in China is no exception. With the rapid development of social economy, people's expectations for the return of work and welfare benefits have gradually increased. This makes the salary levels and welfare benefits of the industry an important factor affecting the recruitment of talent. Because the development of the yachting industry in China is relatively new, its market scale and development stages are relatively basic. Start-up industries often face constraints in terms of resources, customer base and market share. This means that enterprises may be relatively limited in terms of financial investment. This constraint may make it difficult for industries to provide high salaries and benefits comparable to traditional industries. Thus, it is difficult to attract and retain high-level talent.

High-level professionals often take into account many factors in their career choices, including the stability of career development, working environment, salary, and benefits. Relatively low wage levels may make people more inclined to choose careers in more mature and competitive industries. As a result, it is difficult for the yachting industry to attract sufficient quantity and quality of talent. This may not only lead to the scarcity of employees but also affect the innovation ability and competitiveness of the industry. On the other hand, even if potential talents have a strong interest in the yachting industry, they may feel hesitant due to the low level of salary and welfare benefits. Lack of practice opportunities:

Lack of practice opportunities is another key problem facing China's yachting industry. Despite the progress made in theoretical training, the lack of practical operation and practical experience may have a negative impact on the training of talent in the industry. With the continuous progress of science and technology, practical operation and practical experience have become an indispensable part of various fields. Although some progress has been made in academic training in the boating industry, practical operation ability is still the key factor to ensure that professionals have comprehensive quality. Yacht manufacturing and maintenance requires engineers and technicians to master practical skills in a real environment. Only in this way can the nation better meet the challenges of diversification and improve the quality standards and innovation capabilities of the industry.

In addition, the lack of communication and cooperative opportunities within the industry may prevent professionals from benefiting from the practical experience of their peers. Compared with other traditional industries, the scale of China's yachting industry is relatively small. This may lead to insufficient channels of cooperation within the industry. It is difficult for professionals to obtain practical experience and successful cases from other enterprises, which limits the improvement of the overall technical level of the industry. More extensive opportunities for communication and cooperation will help to share best practices and solve problems within the industry and make greater breakthroughs in technological innovation. In particular, yacht building and maintenance is a highly practical field, requiring professionals with solid hands-on skills. However, some training institutions may face the challenge of providing adequate practice opportunities. Factors such as cost, equipment, and space may limit students' access to hands-on experience while in school. This means that they may not have enough practical application experience after graduation to quickly adapt to the requirements of the actual working environment. Lack of practical experience may have a negative impact on the actual ability and self-confidence of professionals, thus affecting their performance in their career.

In the competitive job market, candidates with practical experience are more favored by enterprises. However, recent graduates may not be able to meet this employment requirement due to a lack of hands-on opportunities. This may lead them to face greater competitive pressure in the process of job hunting, and may even miss the opportunity to enter the industry. This is a waste of resources for the industry, and may also limit the entry of outstanding talents.

4 Future development prospects

In the process of personnel training in colleges and universities, the nation should not only cultivate students who have a higher theoretical level and higher scientific research level but also students with a strong practical service ability. Policies should aim to cultivate the all-round development of morality, intelligence, physical fitness, beauty and labor. Talents need to have the basic knowledge of yacht science theory, management, economics, marine laws and regulations, and foreign language skills, combined with international vision, innovative spirit, and practical ability. After graduation, students are suitable for operation, management, service and professional technicians on islands, coastal tourist destinations, or in related enterprises and institutions. Therefore, the training of yacht talents needs to meet the following development goals.

1. Construct the integrated curriculum

system of "teaching, learning and doing" according to the requirements of the post

Yacht tourism is a new and cross-cutting discipline. In the early stage of its development, it faces many challenges and development prospects. Yacht tourism requires a broader and more professional background, one that includes a knowledge of ship engineering, material science, design and other fields. Therefore, when designing the yacht tourism curriculum,a more comprehensive and forward-looking vision is needed. From ship technology to tourism operation, it should be properly covered. Tourism colleges and universities should always pay attention to the development of yacht tourism and not build cars behind closed doors. In tourism teaching, the setting of each detailed specialty should keep up with the development trends of international tourism. A reasonable curriculum system for yachting should be designed, establishing an interdisciplinary specialty with theoretical and applied research of yachting industry and tourism. At the same time, tourism colleges and universities should constantly optimize the curriculum. Attention should be paid to the cultivation of students' practical operation abilities, adaptability and communication abilities. Elective courses such as public speaking, logic, psychology and communication can be offered as appropriate.

Although there are relatively few monographs and textbooks in the field of yacht tourism, educational institutions can creatively integrate and expand relevant curriculum materials with the help of the existing knowledge system and the developmental needs of the industry. Appropriate knowledge content from other related fields should be sought out in order to meet the needs of students for knowledge and skills in many aspects. In order to ensure that the education system is in line with the needs of the industry, it is important for industry associations, government departments, and enterprises to work together.

When training yacht tourism talents, universities and training institutions should screen and optimize the courses according to the actual needs of the industry. In addition, practical operation should be emphasized so that students can quickly adapt to the actual working environment after graduation .By integrating professional knowledge, practical skills and industry norms, educational institutions can provide students with a more competitive and adaptable education.

2. Take the demand of yachting industry as the center, take employment as the orientation, and expand the path of talent training

In addition to tourism colleges, enterprises in the cruise industry play a vital role in the follow-up stage of personnel training. To this end, cruise companies need to continue to expand the channels and ways of continuing education for practitioners. This can include internal training courses as well as professional lectures and seminars to ensure that employees keep their knowledge and skills up to date. In addition, enterprises should strengthen the development of soft power through professional training and training of employees, as well as the development of incentive mechanisms to improve the overall quality of employees.

When recruiting management and service personnel, enterprises should comprehensively examine the candidates' ideological and moral character, business ability, foreign language proficiency, appearance and other factors. Through comprehensive testing, they can find talents who meet the requirements of the post, so as to improve the management and service level of cruise ships. For example, enterprises can employ professional and senior foreign representatives stationed on ships to train experienced and knowledgeable escorts so that they have a helpful service attitude.

In addition, in the process of development, some cruise companies may consider setting up professional cruise colleges to meet their own talent needs. This has been a successful strategy employed by some overseas cruise companies. By establishing educational institutions independently, enterprises can train talents according to their own needs and ensure that they have the necessary skills and qualities. Cruise ship enterprises also need to actively shape a unique corporate culture to attract and retain high-quality talents. Corporate culture not only contributes to the growth of employees, but also promotes the sustainable development of enterprises. It is also very important to strengthen the professional quality training of practitioners, and to encourage them to love their posts and devote themselves to their work. Only when employees have good professional ethics can they really contribute to the development of enterprises.

3. Construction and improvement of an industry certification system to enhance the recognition of yachting industry

Establishing industry certification systems is an important measure for talent training in China's yachting industry. It can inject a higher level of talent quality and professional ability into the whole industry. Such a system can not only provide authoritative recognition for individuals, but also help them advance in their careers. It also has a positive impact on the technical level and service quality of the whole industry. The formulation of a certification system needs to consider the diversity and complexity of the industry and cover all aspects from yacht design and manufacture to maintenance and management. In the design stage, talents should have the ability to promote the innovative and continuous improvement of yacht design. In the manufacturing stage, talents need to master advanced manufacturing technology and technology to ensure the quality and safety of yachts. In terms of maintenance, talents need to have good repair and maintenance skills to prolong the service life and value of yachts. In the field of management, talents should have qualities such as project management and marketing to promote the efficient operation of their enterprises. The introduction of certification will provide practitioners with a clearer career development path and encourage them to continuously improve their knowledge and skills. At the same time, certification will also become an important basis for enterprise recruitment and talent selection and improve the transparency and efficiency of the talent market. Certification systems help to build a long-term mechanism for personnel training and encourage continuous learning and innovation of talents.

4. Promote the incentive system and improve the training mode of enterprise talents

Given the rapid development of the yachting industry, enterprises can improve the salary level and welfare benefits of employees. High salaries and generous welfare policies can be an important incentive for outstanding talents and can also enhance the loyalty and sense of belonging of employees to the enterprise. When formulating salary policies, enterprises can refer to the salary level and market standards in the industry to ensure that the salary is competitive. In addition, enterprises can also consider setting up a performance bonus system to motivate employees according to their performance thus promoting employee motivation and creativity. Generous welfare benefits, such as health insurance, annual leave, and training opportunities can not only meet the basic needs of employees, but also meet the needs of employers. It can also enhance the satisfaction and identity of employees to the enterprise.

In addition to salary and benefits, enterprises should also provide broad career development space and promotional opportunities that can help employees build a career path with potential for growth. Through continuous learning, accumulation of experience and hard work, employees can gradually be promoted from grass-roots positions to higher-level management positions. Planning a clear career development path for employees and setting up a clear promotion path can motivate them to work actively. This strategy also helps enterprises create a more stable and efficient talent team.

5. Construction and improvement of training courses inside and outside the school to achieve "zero distance" between students and vocational and technical posts

In order to create an the effective training program for yacht talents, it is necessary to pay attention to the actual production and management needs of industry enterprises. A professional and high-level yacht training base is needed to improve the conditions of practical teaching. Industry associations and enterprises play a key role in promoting personnel training by working closely with universities to provide internship and training opportunities for students. To help them understand the development potential and attraction of the yachting industry, trade associations can organize various exchange and cooperation activities, such as workshops, training courses, and seminars, thus providing a platform for professionals to share experience and knowledge. At the same time, colleges and universities can cooperate with enterprises to offer practical courses and internship projects that enable students to gain practical experience in a real working environment. Such a collaborative model helps to improve students' practical ability and enhance their competitiveness in the job market. At the same time, it can also train professionals who are more in line with the actual needs of the yachting industry.

In the whole process of talent cultivation, the cooperation and coordination between industry and education is the key. Such close cooperation combines theory with practice to provide students with more practical training and education so as to cultivate high-quality talents to meet the needs of the yachting industry. Such cooperation will help promote the development of the yachting industry, enhance the innovation ability of enterprises, and enhance the competitiveness of the whole.

Chapter 10

Laws, Regulations, and Policies in Systems of Yacht Safety and Management

This chapter will describe the relevant laws, regulations and policies of yachts in China on both the national and local levels. It will also focus on the management issues needing attention in the daily use of yachts, mainly including yacht safety management, yacht entry and exit management, and yacht operation management.

Section 1: Yacht Laws, Regulations and Policy Systems

The laws, regulations and policies related to yachts in China are very complex. The Regulations on Yacht Safety Management is the earliest and highest-level system document issued for yachts at the national level, while other documents mainly refine its relevant contents. The Hainan region has always been in the forefront of yacht development in China, having received institutional support from the General Administration of Customs as well as Hainan Province on the local level.

1. Relevant laws, regulations and policies related to yacht management

There are many laws, regulations and policies related to yacht management in China. They can be roughly divided as follows:: the relevant laws and regulations of the state regarding the planning, construction and operation management of the yacht terminal; the safety management of the yacht; the operation management of the yacht; and relevant regulations on yacht entry and exit management.

(1) Relevant national laws and regulations

The national laws related to yachts mainly include the following documents: the Port Law of the People's Republic of China; the Law of the People's Republic of China on the Administration of Exit and Entry, the Environmental Protection Law of the People's Republic of China; the Maritime Traffic Safety Law of the People's Republic of China; the Customs Law of the People's Republic of China; the Marine Environmental Protection Law of the People's Republic of China; the Law of the People's Republic of China on the Prevention and Control of Water Pollution, and the Law of the People's Republic of China on the Prevention and Control of

Water Pollution Frontier Health and Quarantine Law; the Law of the People's Republic of China on Import and Export Commodity Inspection; and the, Tourism Law of the People's Republic of China, among others.

The relevant laws and regulations on yachts mainly include: the Regulations on the Administration of Domestic Waterway Transport; the Regulations of the People's Republic of China on International Maritime Transport; the Regulations of the People's Republic of China on Seafarers; the Measures of the People's Republic of China on Vessel Registration; the Regulations of the People's Republic of China on the Administration of Foreign Vessels; the Regulations of the People's Republic of China on Exit and Entry Frontier Inspection, and the Regulations of the People's Republic of China on the Administration of Entry and Exit of Foreigners; Regulations of the People's Republic of China on the Administration of Marine Waste Dumping; Regulations of the People's Republic of China on the Administration of Inland River Traffic Safety; Regulations of the People's Republic of China on the Prevention and Control of Marine Environmental Pollution by Vessels; Regulations of the People's Republic of China on the Inspection of Vessels and Marine Facilities; Measures for the Inspection of Vessels on International Voyages Entering and Leaving the Ports of the People's Republic of China; Detailed Rules for the Implementation of the Frontier Health and Quarantine Law of the People's Republic of China; Rules for the Implementation of the Law of the People's Republic of China on the Administration of the Exit and Entry of Citizens; and Regulations for the Implementation of the Vehicle and Vessel Tax Law of the People's Republic of China, among others

(2) Yacht terminal planning, construction and operation management

The relevant provisions on the planning, construction and operation management of yacht terminals mainly include: Provisions on the Management of Port Operation, Provisions on the Management of Port Planning; Provisions on the Management of Port Engineering Construction; Provisions on the Maintenance and Management of Port Infrastructure; Provisions on the Safety Management of Port Dangerous Goods; Measures for the Management of Port and Ship Shore Power; Provisions on the Management of Foreign Ships in China's Territorial Waters; Regulations on the Use of International Maritime Satellite Ship Earth Stations in Inland Waters and Ports; Measures for the Examination and Approval of the Use of Port Shorelines; Regulations on the Construction and Management of Waterway Projects, among others.

(3) Yacht safety management

Relevant regulations on yacht safety management mainly include: Regulations on Yacht Safety Management; Training of Yacht Operators of the People's Republic of China; Measures for Certification and Certification; Rules for Safety Management of High-speed Passenger Ships of the People's Republic of China; Rules for Collision Avoidance in Inland Rivers of the People's Republic of China; Regulations of the People's Republic of China on the Prevention and Control of Environmental Pollution in Inland Waters by Ships; Rules for Competency Examination and Certification of Seafarers of the People's Republic of China; Special Regulations on Water Traffic Safety Management of the Yangtze River Trunk Line; Emergency Management of Transportation Emergencies Regulations; Regulations of the People's Republic of China on Minimum Safety Manning of Ships; Regulations of the People's Republic of China on Navigation Safety Management of Surface and Underwater Operations and Activities; Regulations of the People's Republic of China on International Ship Security; Regulations of the People's Republic of China on Ship Safety Supervision; Regulations of the People's Republic of China on Real-name Management of Waterway Passenger Transport; Regulations of the People's Republic of China on Marine Environmental Pollution Caused by Ships and Their Related Operations; Regulations on the Management of Environmental Prevention and Control; and Regulations of the People's Republic of China on Emergency Preparedness and Emergency Disposal of Marine Environmental Pollution by Ships, among others.

(4) Yacht management

The relevant regulations on yacht safety management mainly include: the Regulations on the Administration of Domestic Waterway Transport and the Detailed Rules for the Implementation of the Regulations of the People's Republic of China on International Maritime Transport.

(5) Yacht entry and exit management

The relevant provisions on the administration of entry and exit of yachts mainly include: Measures of the Customs of the People's Republic of China for the Administration of Temporary Entry and Exit Goods; Measures of the Customs of the People's Republic of China for the Supervision and Control of Entry and Exit Means of Transport; Measures for the Administration of Entry and Exit Inspection and Quarantine of Vessels on International Voyages; Provisions on the Administration of Pilotage of Vessels; Provisions on the Administration of Frontier Security of Coastal Vessels, and Provisions on the Administration of Health Quarantine of Special Goods on Entry and Exit , among others

2. Yacht Management Laws, Regulations and Policies at the National Level

Yacht laws, regulations and policies at the national level can be traced back to the Regulations on Yacht Safety Management promulgated by the Ministry of Transport in 2008, and the subsequent laws, regulations and policies mainly focus on yacht safety management. At the same time, Hainan Province, as one of the main regions for the development of China's yachting industry, has always been valued at the national level, and the relevant ministries and commissions of the state have issued a series of targeted policies to regulate and guide the development of Hainan's yachting industry.

(1) Management of the whole industry

1. Regulations on Yacht Safety Management

In 2008, the Ministry of Transport promulgated Regulations on Yacht Safety Management, which is the first national regulation on yacht management in China, aiming at addressing the issue that the regulations on water traffic safety supervision in China had been mainly formulated on operating ships. The concept of yachting is put forward for the first time in these regulations, which formulate a management system including yacht registration, inspection, navigation rules, yacht driver training, examination and yacht club operation mode. It is a guiding document for yacht safety management in China and is of great significance to the development of yachting industry in Hainan.

2. Interim Provisions on Statutory Inspection of Yachts

In order to implement the relevant requirements of yacht inspection in the Regulations on Yacht Safety Management, the Maritime Safety Administration of the People's Republic of China promulgated the Provisional Regulations on Yacht Statutory Inspection (2009) in 2008, which was be implemented from January 1, 2009. On March 11, 2013, the Maritime Safety Administration of the People's Republic of China revised the original technical specifications and promulgated the Interim Provisions on Statutory Inspection of Yachts (2013), which was implemented from September 1, 2013. According to the Provisional Regulations on Statutory Inspection of Yachts (2013), yachts are divided into vessels of less than 24 meters in length and those greater than 24 meters in length. For the smaller yachts, of which yachts of less than 24 meters include general rules; cabin layout, crew quota and escape measures; fire fighting; freeboard, stability and tonnage; safety equipment and environmental protection requirements; and sailing operation requirements. The section on yachts over 24m covers general items; construction; welfare and stability; freeboard and personnel protection; fire protection; safety equipment and environmental requirements.

3. Opinions on Implementation of Yacht Safety Management

In order to further improve the applicability of yacht laws and regulations and promote the healthy development of yachting industry and water tourism economy, the Maritime Safety Administration of the People's Republic of China issued the Opinions on the Implementation of Yacht Safety Management on August 18, 2010. This document covers the inspection of yachts, the approval of yacht mechanical and electrical equipment, the registration of yachts, the examination and certification of yacht drivers, the navigation and supervision of foreign yachts, and the export inspection of yachts manufactured in China.

4. Announcement on Strengthening the Management of Imported Yachts

In order to promote the healthy development of the yachting industry, improve the overall technical level of yachts throughout the country, protect the water environment, and ensure the safety of people's lives and property, the Ministry of Transport issued

Announcement on Strengthening the Management of Imported Yachts on September 15, 2011, which prohibits the import of yachts over one year old from abroad. Those who apply for importing yachts from abroad shall go through the formalities of filing with the Ministry of Transport; those who do not meet the requirements of the announcement will not be able to register imported shall imported yachts.

5. Measures of the People's Republic of China for Training, Examination, and Certification of Yacht Operators

In order to implement the relevant management requirements of yacht operation in the Regulations on Yacht Safety Management, standardize the management of yacht operators and improve the technical level of yacht operators, the Maritime Safety Administration of the People's Republic of China issued and implemented the Measures for Training, Examination and Certification of Yacht Operators of the People's Republic of China for the first time in 2011, and revised them in September 2021. This document divides yacht operators into two categories: offshore and inland, each of which is further subdivided into two grades according to the length of the yacht, and clarifies the application conditions, required materials, expiration and renewal of the Yacht Driver's License. In the revised version of 2021, some relevant provisions have been adjusted, including age requirements, training syllabus, examination syllabus, validity period of results, and renewal of overseas yacht driving licenses.

6. Implementation Opinions of the Ministry of Industry and Information Technology and Other Five Ministries and Commissions on Accelerating the Development of Cruise Yacht Equipment and Industry

In order to satisfy the popular development of cruise yacht consumption, this document upgraded provisions regarding the cruise yachting industry chain. It accelerated the formation of a cruise yacht equipment industry system, promoted the upgrading of domestic tourist passenger ship quality, cultivated and improved industrial ecology, created new advantages for development, accelerated the construction of a new pattern of industrial development, and promoted the general development of the cruise yachting industry. The document was jointly issued on August 17, 2022 by the Ministry of Industry and Information Technology, the National Development and Reform Commission, the Ministry of Finance, the Ministry of Transport and the Ministry of Culture and Tourism. Among the key tasks it advanced are the following: vigorously developing popular consumption yachts, promoting the construction of yacht infrastructure, strengthening public information services, promoting the innovation and development of the yachting industry, creating professional brand exhibitions, and improving policies, regulations, and standards.

(2) Yacht management in Hainan

1. Interim Measures of the Customs of the People's Republic of China for the Supervision and Control of Yachts Entering and Leaving Hainan Province and the Articles

Carried Thereon

The General Administration of Customs has this document, which came into effect on April 15, 2011, in order to regulate the customs management of yachts entering and leaving Hainan Province and clarify the customs clearance procedures for yachts and their articles. Its provisions specify hat yachts can enter and exit at approved yacht supervision wharfs in addition to berthing at open ports. It stipulates that the owner of a yacht or the yacht service enterprise shall submit a deposit equivalent to the amount of tax payable by the yacht to the Customs and go through the formalities of entry and exit declaration with reference to the means of transport. It clearly stipulates that overseas yachts can stay in Hainan for up to 30 consecutive days after entering the country, and can be extended twice after the expiration of the period, each time not more than 30 days, and that the total period of stay of overseas yachts in Hainan Province in each Gregorian calendar year shall not exceed 183 days.

2. Measures for the Administration of Entry-Exit Yacht Quarantine in Hainan

In order to prevent the spread of epidemic diseases and standardize the quarantine of entry-exit yachts in Hainan, the General Administration of Quality Supervision, Inspection and Quarantine of the People's Republic of China (AQSIQ) adopted these measures on April 23, 2013, and stipulated that they would come into effect on August 1, 2013. Subsequently, in accordance with Decree No. 238 of the General Administration of Customs on April 28, 2018 and Decree No.240 of the General Administration of Customs on May 29, 2018, the measures were amended twice. They are divided into six chapters and 41 articles, including general provisions and those for entry quarantine, exit quarantine, supervision and management, legal liability and supplementary provisions. Based on the principles of "first try" and "control and convenience", the measures provide a fast and convenient customs clearance environment for yachts on the basis of ensuring quarantine safety. Among them, the focus has been on relaxing the conditions for telecommunication quarantine and simplifying the quarantine procedures.

3. Announcement of the General Administration of Customs on Adjusting the Administration of Yachts Entering and Leaving Hainan

In accordance with the requirements of the Circular of the State Council on the Temporary Adjustment and Implementation of the Relevant Administrative Regulations in the China (Hainan) Free Trade Pilot Zone (State Letter [2020] 88), the General Administration of Customs issued this document on July 9, 2020. It was clarified that the owner of the yacht or its agent would be is exempted from providing guarantees to the Customs for the yacht entering the country by self-driving in the China (Hainan) Free Trade Pilot Area.

4. Measures for Customs Implementation of "Zero Tariff" Policy for Vehicles and Yachts in Hainan Free Trade Port (Trial Implementation)

In order to implement the requirements of the General Plan for the Construction of Hainan Free Trade Port, the General Administration of Customs promulgated these measures on January 5, 2021. It is pointed out that before the closure of the whole island, enterprises registered in Hainan Free Trade Port with independent legal personality and engaged in transportation and tourism shall import ships, aircraft, vehicles and other operational vehicles and yachts for transportation and tourism, and shall be exempted from import tariffs, import value-added tax and consumption tax.

Table 10-1 Sorting of Yacht Laws, Regulations and Policies at the National Level

Serial number	Classification	File name	Document number	Issuing authority	Date of issuance
1	Industry-wide management	Regulations on Yacht Safety Management	Decree No.7, 2008 of the Ministry of Transport of the People's Republic of China	Ministry of Transport	July 22, 2008
2		Opinions on Implementation of Yacht Safety Management	Maritime [2010] No.352	Maritime Safety Administration of the People's Republic of China	August 18, 2010
3		Announcement on Strengthening the Management of Imported Yachts	Announcement No.55, 2011 of the Ministry of Transport	Ministry of Transport	September 15, 2011
4		Interim Provisions on Statutory Inspection of Yachts (2013)		Maritime Safety Administration of the People's Republic of China	March 11, 2013
5		Measures of the People's Republic of China for the Training, Examination and Certification of Yacht Operators	Sea Crew [2021] No.163	Maritime Safety Administration of the People's Republic of China	September 3, 2021
6		Implementation Opinions of the Ministry of Industry and Information Technology and Other Five Ministries on Accelerating the Development of Cruise Yacht Equipment and Industry	MIIT LZZ [2022] No.101	Ministry of Industry and Information Technology, National Development and Reform Commission, Ministry of Finance, Ministry of Transport, Ministry of Culture and Tourism	August 17, 2022

7	Yacht management in Hainan	Interim Measures of the Customs of the People's Republic of China for the Supervision and Control of Yachts Entering and Leaving Hainan Province and the Articles Carried Thereon	Announcement No.15, 2011 of the General Administration of Customs	General Administration of Customs	March 11, 2011
8		Measures for the Administration of Entry-Exit Yacht Quarantine in Hainan	Decree No.153 of the General Administration of Quality Supervision, Inspection and Quarantine of the People's Republic of China	General Administration of Quality Supervision, Inspection and Quarantine	Deliberated and adopted on April 23, 2013, and amended twice in 2018
9		Announcement of the General Administration of Customs on Adjusting the Administration of Entry and Exit Yachts in Hainan	Announcement No.80, 2020 of the General Administration of Customs	General Administration of Customs	July 9, 2020
10		Announcement on Issuing the Customs Implementation Measures for the "Zero Tariff" Policy for Vehicles and Yachts in Hainan Free Trade Port (Trial Implementation)	Announcement No.1, 2021 of the General Administration of Customs	General Administration of Customs	January 5, 2021

3. Laws, Regulations and Policies on Yacht Management at the Local Level

As an important part of water tourism consumption, yachts have always been valued by coastal provinces and cities in China. In recent years, provinces and cities such as Hainan, Tianjin, Xiamen, Shenzhen, Zhuhai and Sanya have issued laws, regulations and policies to guide the development of yachts. Among them, Hainan Province has listed the yachting industry as one of the key industries in the province, and has actively promulgated a series of laws, regulations, and policies to regulate and guide the development of the industry, which has important reference significance for the development of the yachting industry in other provinces and cities.

The laws, regulations and policies related to yacht management in Hainan Province can be divided into six aspects: yachting industry management, yacht comprehensive management, yacht rental management, yacht club management, yacht traffic management and yacht tax management. Hainan, as a free trade port with independent legislative power, took the lead in introducing the first local legislation for the yachting industry in China, which filled the gap of the lack of superior law for the yachting industry, cleared the institutional obstacles for the development of the yachting industry, and also provided superior law support for the promulgation of relevant laws and policies for yachts. Therefore, Hainan's yachting management laws, regulations and policies are relatively perfect and more systematic.

(1) yachting industry management

1. Regulations on the Promotion of yachting industry in Hainan Free Trade Port
   In order to promote the high-quality development of the yachting industry in Hainan Free Trade Port, improve the service and guarantee level of the yachting industry, and build an innovative pilot area for the reform and development of the yachting industry in Hainan, the 35th meeting of the Standing Committee of the Sixth People's Congress of Hainan Province deliberated and adopted the Regulations on the Promotion of the yachting industry in Hainan Free Trade Port on March 25, 2022 to be effective as of July 1, 2022. The Regulations on the Promotion of yachting industry in Hainan Free Trade Port is an important regulation in the legal system of Hainan Free Trade Port, the first local legislation for yachting industry in China, and the first creative legislation in the province to promote industrial development. There are 7 chapters and 56 articles, including general provisions, industrial development, inspection, registration and navigation, yacht leasing, service and supervision, legal liability and supplementary provisions.
2. Implementation Plan for the Construction of Hainan yachting industry Reform and Development Innovation Pilot Zone
   This plan was created in order to implement the General Plan for the Construction of Hainan Free Trade Port, fully draw lessons from international experience, seize strategic opportunities, actively explore new ways for the development of

the yachting industry in line with China's national conditions and give full play to Hainan's unique advantages, as well as to comprehensively promote the construction of Hainan yachting industry Reform and Development Innovation Pilot Zone, and support the construction of Hainan Free Trade Port. On June 28, 2022, the Department of Transportation of Hainan Province issued this implementation plan, which proposed to optimize the layout of yachting industry development, build a modern yachting industry system, strengthen and consolidate the construction of yacht infrastructure, consolidate the development foundation of yachting industry, innovate the consumption mode of yacht tourism, and expand the consumption space of yacht tourism. It includes 21 specific tasks in six areas, including innovating the yacht policy and regulation system, optimizing the development environment of yachting industry, improving the yacht social governance system, improving the yacht social governance ability, accelerating the application of technological innovation, and promoting the development of intelligent, safe and green technologies.

3. Outline of Hainan yachting industry Development Plan (2021-2025)

   In order to implement the strategic plan of the CPC Central Committee and the State Council on building Hainan's international tourism consumption center, and promote the high-quality development of the yachting industry there, , this four-year development plan was issued on) on July 1, 2022 The plan includes six parts: planning background, overall requirements, industrial layout, main tasks, safeguarding measures, and annexes, all of which provide planning guidance for the development of Hainan yachting industry during the 14th Five-Year Plan period and into the future.

(2) Comprehensive management of yachts

1. Measures for Yacht Management in Hainan Province

   In order to strengthen the service and management of yachts, safeguard national security, and promote the development of yacht economy, the People's Government of Hainan Province promulgated these measures on February 5, 2016 in accordance with national laws, regulations, and relevant provisions. On the same day, a previous set of trial measures were abolished. The measures include provisions for yacht inspection, registration, security, entry and exit management, wharf management, club (yacht club) management and other aspects, effectively promoting the normative management of yachts in Hainan.

2. Interim Measures for Yacht Safety Management in Hainan Province

   In order to implement the spirit of the Regulations on Yacht Safety Management issued by the Ministry of Transport, Hainan Maritime Bureau issued and implemented these interim measures on December 29, 2010. They cover ten aspects, including yacht inspection, registration, drivers, entry and exit ports, navigation and berthing, yacht clubs, security, pollution prevention, supervision, and management. In addition, they cover the inspection procedures for imported yachts, the restrictions on the household registration of yachts and the proportion of foreign investment, the implementation of the national general yacht driver certificate system, the acquisition of yacht driver's license by foreigners in Hainan, the recognition of overseas yacht driver's certificate, the inspection procedures for overseas yachts entering and leaving ports, and the non-compulsory pilotage of foreign yachts.

3. Measures for Training, Examination and Certification of Yacht Operators in Hainan Free Trade Port

   In order to promote the development of the yachting industry in Hainan Free Trade Port, standardize the management of yacht operators, improve the technical level of yacht operators, ensure the safety of life and property on water, and protect the marine environment, Hainan Maritime Bureau promulgated these measures on October 29, 2021, and they came into effect on November 1, 2021. The measures consist of seven chapters and 37 articles, including general provisions as well as regulations involving yacht driver's licenses, yacht operator training, yacht operator examinations, supervision and management, and supplementary provisions.

4. Notice on Clarifying Relevant Measures for the Management of Imported Yachts

   In order to speed up the implementation of the policy of allowing the import of yachts under five years of age and promote the high-quality development of the yachting industry in Hainan Free Trade Port, the Hainan Provincial Department of Transportation, the Hainan Provincial Department of Commerce, the Haikou Customs and the Hainan Maritime Bureau jointly issued this notice on December 22, 2022. They deal with issues involving imported yachts, including confirmation of ship age; scope of administration of import licenses for mechanical and electrical products; clarification of customs clearance procedures, initial inspection, and initial registration.

(3) Yacht leasing management

1. Measures for the Administration of Yacht Leasing in Hainan Province (Trial Implementation)

   On December 8, 2019, the People's Government of Hainan Province promulgated the these measures. which came into effect on January 1, 2020 and were valid for three years. This is the first management measure for yacht leasing in China. They were designed to standardize yacht leasing behavior, safeguard the legitimate rights and interests of both operators and lessees of yacht leasing businesses, ensure the safety of water traffic, and promote the healthy and orderly development of the industry, according to the relevant laws and regulations such as the Safety Production Law of the People's Republic of China. The measures stipulate the responsibilities of administrative departments and trade associations such as transportation, maritime affairs, public security, market supervision and tourism, as well as the responsibilities of operators engaged in the yacht leasing business. . At the same time, it stipulates that yacht leasing passengers shall be subject to real-name management and that the yacht leasing business shall be subject to a credit management system.

2. Detailed Rules for the Implementation of the Measures for the Administration of Yacht Leasing in Hainan Province (Trial Implementation)

   In order to further strengthen and standardize the management of the yacht leasing industry in Hainan, according to the previously referenced measures, the Hainan Provincial Department of Transportation and the Hainan Maritime Bureau agreed to formulate these detailed rules effective on December 1, 2021. Both these measures unify the market access conditions of leasing operators, formulate the service standards for yacht leasing, implement the responsibility for safety and pollution prevention, manage the night voyage of leasing yachts, and build the market integrity system. They also deal with appropriate relaxation of the market access threshold, clarify yacht rental night sailing conditions, strengthen the main responsibility of market security, strengthen the new regulatory mechanism and promote the identification of rental yachts and other aspects of innovation.

3. Interim Provisions of Hainan Province on Inspection of Yacht Leasing

   In order to further improve the inspection of leased yachts and promote the healthy and orderly development of the yacht leasing industry, the Hainan Provincial Department of Transportation promulgated these interim provisions on November 4, 2021, which took effect on December 1, 2021. They are divided into three parts: general regulations, inspection and certificates, and technical standards for inspection. The interim provisions clearly define the inspection technical standards of sailing, stability, navigation and navigation equipment, fire safety, life-saving equipment and layout, crew quota and cabin equipment and pollution prevention.

(4) Yacht club management

1. Measures for Examination, Registration and Filing of Yacht Clubs (Yacht Clubs) in Hainan Province

   In order to speed up the development of the yachting industry in Hainan Province and further standardize the management of yacht clubs the Hainan Provincial Coastal Defense and Port Office, the Hainan Provincial Department of Transportation, the Hainan Provincial Department of Commerce and the Hainan Provincial Administration for Industry and Commerce jointly issued these measures on January 21, 2012. These measures are divided into 5 chapters and 16 articles, including general provisions for examination, registration, filing and supplementary provisions, focusing on the registration and filing procedures of yacht clubs.

2. Opinions of Hainan Maritime Safety Administration on Further Strengthening

the Record Management of Yacht Clubs

In order to further standardize the record management of yacht clubs and give full play to their role in issues yacht safety and pollution prevention, the Hainan Maritime Bureau issued these opinions in September 2020. Some 23 standards and requirements were implemented that established system of yacht safety and pollution prevention, improved the ability of safety and pollution prevention management, and strengthened the construction of emergency response capacity.

(5) Yacht traffic management

1. China (Hainan) Pilot Free Trade Zone Hainan, Hong Kong and Macao Yacht Free Travel Implementation Plan

   In order to implement the General Plan of the State Council on the Issuance of China (Hainan) Free Trade Pilot Zone and accelerate the free travel of yachts in Qiongzhou, Hong Kong, and Macao in line with several other official promulgations in 2018, the General Office of the Hainan Provincial People's Government issued this implementation plan on June 18, 2019. It mandated that Hong Kong-Macao Yachts should implement facilitation supervision measures in terms of entry and exit, navigation, berthing and tourism in Hainan Free Trade Zone. The measures were based on the notion of "bringing the yacht entry formalities into a single window" and implementing the port management mode of "fixed-point docking, joint inspection nearby." The plan also cancelled cancellation of the requirement of yachts reporting to the maritime administration before launching. This policy is the first of its kind in China.

2. Announcement on Implementing Convenient Travel Arrangements for Yachts in Hainan and Hong Kong

   In order to further implement the above plan and promote the opening of the yachting industry in Hainan Free Trade Port to the outside world, several government agencies have been involved. These include the Maritime Bureau of the People's Republic of China (the Maritime Bureau of the Ministry of Transport) and the Maritime Department of the Government of the Hong Kong Special Administrative Region. On September 9, 2022, the Hainan Maritime Safety Administration of the People's Republic of China issued the Notice on the Implementation of Convenient Travel Arrangements for Yachts in Hainan and Hong Kong, proposing that holders of Class I and Class II operator certificates for pleasure vessels issued by the Marine Department of the Government of the Hong Kong Special Administrative Region may drive corresponding Hong Kong-registered or licensed yachts in the waters designated and announced for yacht activities in Hainan Province.

(4) Yacht tax administration

In order to implement the General Plan for the Construction of Hainan Free Trade Port and effectively manage "zero tariff" imported vehicles and yachts in Hainan Free Trade Port, the General Office of the

Hainan Provincial People's Government issued the Measures for the Administration of "Zero Tariff" Imported Vehicles and Yachts in Hainan Free Trade Port (Trial Implementation) on December 30, 2020. Included in this document 7 chapters and 31 articles that mainly focus on the import, use, supervision and management of "Zero Tariff" vehicles and yachts. The measures look at the issues from the five aspects of import subject, registration, use and operation, supervision and management, and legal liability. They clarify the specific management responsibilities and boundaries of the competent departments in order to facilitate enterprises to clarify the identification criteria, scope of use and operation process of the policy. At the same time, two other notices were issued: the Notice on the Qualification of "Zero Tariff" Vehicles and Yacht Import Enterprises in Hainan Free Trade Port and the Notice on the Management of "Zero Tariff" Imported Ships and Yachts.

Table 10-2 Yacht laws, regulations and policies at the local level (Hainan)

Serial number	Classification	File name	Document number	Issuing authority	Date of issuance
1	yachting industry Management	Regulations on the Promotion of yachting industry in Hainan Free Trade Port	Announcement No.116 of the Standing Committee of the Hainan Provincial People's Congress	Standing Committee of the Hainan Provincial People's Congress	March 25, 2022
2		Implementation Plan for the Construction of Hainan yachting industry Reform and Development Innovation Pilot Zone		Department of Transportation of Hainan Province	June 28, 2022
3		Outline of Hainan yachting industry Development Plan (2021-2025)		Department of Transportation of Hainan Province	July 1, 2022
4		Interim Measures for Yacht Safety Management in Hainan Province		Hainan Maritime Safety Administration	December 29, 2010
5		Measures for the Administration of Yachts in Hainan Province	Qiongfu [2016] No.19	People's Government of Hainan Province	February 5, 2016
6		Measures for Training, Examination and Certification of Yacht Operators in Hainan Free Trade Port		Hainan Maritime Safety Administration	October 29, 2021

7		Notice on Clarifying Relevant Measures for the Administration of Imported Yachts		Hainan Provincial Department of Transportation, Hainan Provincial Department of Commerce, Haikou Customs and Hainan Maritime Bureau	December 22, 2022
8	Yacht charter management	Measures for the Administration of Yacht Leasing in Hainan Province (Trial Implementation)	Qiongfu Office [2019] No.35	General Office of Hainan Provincial People's Government	December 8, 2019
9		Detailed Rules for the Implementation of the Measures for the Administration of Yacht Leasing in Hainan Province *(for Trial Implementation)*		Department of Transportation of Hainan Province	November 4, 2021
10		Interim Provisions of Hainan Province on Inspection of Yacht Leasing		Department of Transportation of Hainan Province	November 4, 2021
11	Yacht club management	Administrative Measures for Examination, Registration and Filing of Yacht Clubs (Yacht Clubs) in Hainan Province		Hainan Provincial Coastal Defense and Port Office, Hainan Provincial Department of Transportation, Hainan Provincial Department of Commerce, Hainan Provincial Administration for Industry and Commerce	January 21, 2012
12		Opinions of Hainan Maritime Safety Administration on Further Strengthening the Record Management of Yacht Clubs		Hainan Maritime Safety Administration	September 30, 2020
13	Yacht traffic management	Implementation Plan for Free Yacht Travel in Hainan, Hong Kong and Macao in China (Hainan) Pilot Free Trade Zone	Qiongfu Office [2019] No.16	General Office of Hainan Provincial People's Government	June 18, 2019
14		Announcement on Implementing Convenient Travel Arrangements for Yachts in Qionggang	No.1 of 2022	Hainan Maritime Safety Administration	September 9, 2022

15	Yacht Tax Administration	Measures for the Administration of "Zero Tariff" Imported Vehicles and Yachts in Hainan Free Trade Port (Trial Implementation)	Qiongfu [2020] No.60	People's Government of Hainan Province	December 30, 2020
16		Announcement on the Qualification of "Zero Tariff" Vehicles and Yacht Import Enterprises in Hainan Free Trade Port		Department of Transportation of Hainan Province	February 8, 2021
17		Notice on Clarifying the Management of "Zero Tariff" Imported Ships and Yachts		Department of Transportation of Hainan Province	July 23, 2021

Section 2: Yacht Safety Management

Yachts are private and non-operational leisure ships that are mainly used for sightseeing, leisure and entertainment, and business receptions. Their construction style is individualized, and they do not participate in public transport. Because of these non-operational attributes of yachts, it is difficult to apply the relevant laws, regulations and to restrict them. Therefore, in 2008, the Ministry of Transport promulgated the first national yacht safety management regulation directed toward the yachting industry in China. Combined with the content of this regulation, this section will focus on the introduction of yacht inspection and registration, yacht operator training, examination and certification, yacht navigation and berthing, and yacht safety and security.

1. Yacht Inspection and Registration

Yachts, as non-conventional ships, do not have uniform safety and anti-pollution requirements specifically for them, and their inspection and management are stipulated by the domestic laws of various countries. Some countries and regions have strict yacht management, such as the European Union and the United Kingdom. Some countries and regions have more relaxed management of yachts, such as Canada, New Zealand, and Hong Kong.

(1) Yacht inspection

The Regulation on Yacht Safety Management requires that the yacht shall be inspected by the ship inspection agency in accordance with the regulations approved or recognized by the Ministry of Transport, and that the yacht can be used only after obtaining the corresponding ship inspection certificate. The yachts are also required to apply for additional inspection. for additional inspection.

As a supporting policy for yacht inspection in the Regulations on Yacht Safety Management, the Maritime Safety Administration of the People's Republic of China promulgated the Provisional Regulations on Yacht Statutory Inspection 2009, and the China Classification Society compiled the Rules for Yacht Construction 2008 as the basis for yacht inspection. Among them, the Provisional Regulations on Statutory Inspection of Yachts 2009 give statutory inspection requirements for non-commercial small yachts (excluding sailboats) with a length of less than 20 meters. This regulation defines 20 meters as the limit, which is coordinated with the limit of other domestic ship regulations and specifications for large and small ships. However, this classification standard was different from the international general standard at that time. For yachts with more than 12 passengers, the statutory inspection requirements of the Maritime Safety Administration for passenger ships should be met; for yachts with relevant valid documents and certificates issued by the institutions recognized by the Maritime Safety Administration, the approval and reference of relevant drawings and can be exempted when applying for the initial inspection.

On August 20, 2010, the Maritime Safety Administration of the People's Republic of China issued the Opinions on the Implementation of Yacht Safety Management, which further clarified the inspection regulations for imported yachts. According to this document, imported yachts with CE and ABYC certificates and marks can be exempted from the examination of drawings and data during the initial inspection. It should be specially noted that the exemption of drawings and data in the notice is attached to the Interim Provisions for Yacht Statutory Inspection 2009. Once the Interim Provisions for Yacht Statutory Inspection 2009 has been replaced by the Interim Provisions for Yacht Statutory Inspection 2013, this part of the notice will be invalid.

On March 11, 2013, the Maritime Safety Administration of the People's Republic of China issued the Interim Provisions on Statutory Inspection of Yachts 2013, which came into effect on September 1, 2013. The scope of application, design category, inspection category and interval, and drawing review requirements of the Interim Provisions on Statutory Inspection of Yachts 2013 are quite different from those of the Interim Provisions on Statutory Inspection of Yachts 2009. Among them, the Interim Provisions on Statutory Inspection of Yachts 2013 divides yachts with a length of 24 meters and has different inspection requirements.

In 2012, in order to meet the rapid development needs of the yachting industry, and in line with the relevant technical requirements of the Interim Provisions on Statutory Inspection of Yachts 2013, the China Classification Society compiled and issued the Yacht Classification and Construction Regulations 2012 and the Yacht Inspection Guidelines 2012. The specification adjusts the design categories and other requirements and provides classification services for yachts of 24 meters and above. The China Classification Society has also issued corresponding classification standards for yachts below 24 meters.In view of the characteristics of yacht, such as ballast keel, sail, and rigging, the China Classification Society has compiled the Yacht Inspection Guide 2012 on the basis of the Yacht Classification and Construction Rules 2012 so as to make the yacht rules more perfect.

Based on the development of yacht technology, China Classification Society has upgraded the Yacht Classification and Construction Rules 2012 and compiled the Yacht Classification and Construction Rules 2020, which came into effect on July 1, 2020, by comparing and analyzing foreign advanced yacht standards. These rules were issued after feedback from the industry and an analysis of the characteristics of domestic yacht use and the trend of large- scale development. Compared with the Yacht Classification and Construction Specification 2012, the Yacht Classification and Construction Specification 2020 added comfort (noise and vibration); clarified stability and fire protection as classification conditions; added relevant requirements for lithium-ion battery packs; added relevant requirements for propulsion of yachts in pure battery shops; and clarified relevant requirements for multi-hull boats.

(2) Yacht registration

Different countries or regions also have different attitudes towards yacht registration: some are relatively relaxed, while others are relatively strict. Some require registration, while others do not. Taking Hong Kong, China as an example, the registration of ships and the application for licenses are carried out separately, and yachts, as a kind of ship, also follow the above rules. Among them, the application for a license is a statutory requirement: that is, yachts operating in the waters of Hong Kong, China (excluding temporary berthing) must obtain a license, but only individuals with Hong Kong identity cards or Hong Kong companies can apply. Registration follows the principle of voluntariness. Ships whose ownership has been confirmed by registration can sail under the Hong Kong flag. At the same time, they have the nature of proof of property rights. Registration imposes no restrictions on applicants.

Yacht registration in China is basically equivalent to the management system of merchant ships. According to Article 5 of the Regulations on Yacht Safety Management, yachts can only be used after obtaining the corresponding ship inspection certificate. However, in fact, yachts cannot sail in the waters under the jurisdiction of China immediately after obtaining the inspection certificate. According to Article 6 of the Regulations on the Safety Management of Yachts, yachts sailing and berthing in the waters under the jurisdiction of China shall

obtain certificates of ship nationality. The so-called "three certificates" are the ship's inspection certificate, ownership certificate, and ship's nationality certificate. According to the provisions on yachts in the Regulations on the Safety Management of Yachts, yachts are not commercial transport vessels, so they are not subject to the restrictions on the proportion of Chinese investment in the Regulations of the People's Republic of China on Ship Registration.

2. Training, Examination, and Certification of Yacht Operators

The yacht inspection and registration system is mainly aimed at whether the yacht itself is seaworthy, while the training, examination, and certification of yacht operators mainly involve personnel operation. If the yacht operators do not have the ability of yacht operation and safety emergency response, this will impact safe navigation. The Regulations on Yacht Safety Management put forward requirements for the main qualifications and professional qualities of yacht operators, while the Regulations on Training, Examination and Certification of Yacht Operators of the People's Republic of China clarify the implementation rules.

(1) Management of training, examination, and certification of yacht operators

In May of 2011, in order to standardize the management of yacht operators and promote the healthy development of the yachting industry, in accordance with the relevant requirements of the Regulations on yachting industry Management, the Maritime Bureau of the People's Republic of China issued the Measures for Training, Examination and Certification of Yacht Operators of the People's Republic of China. The document aims to refine the relevant contents of "training, examination and certification of yacht operators" proposed in the Regulations on Yacht Safety Management, and further clarify the management requirements. In September 2021, the Maritime Safety Administration of the People's Republic of China revised and issued a new edition of these measures. This revision has not changed the overall framework, but mainly revised the age requirements of yacht operators, the application, renewal and reissue of yacht driving licenses, the renewal of overseas yacht driving licenses, and the training examination and practical evaluation outline of yacht operators.

(2) Classification of Yacht Driving License

When sailing a yacht in the waters under the jurisdiction of China, the yacht operator shall hold a valid Certificate of Competency for Yacht Operators of the People's Republic of China or an equivalent electronic certificate (hereinafter referred to as the "Yacht Driver's License") issued by the maritime administration and accept the supervision and inspection of the maritime administration. Yacht operators are classified into two categories and four grades. Among them, two categories are marine yacht operators and inland river yacht operators. The four grades are based on the above two categories, and each category is sub divided into two grades, the first grade and the second grade, totaling four grades. Specifically, offshore yacht operators are divided into two classes based on the length of the yacht. Among them, first-class yacht operators can drive all lengths of yachts at sea; second-class yacht operators are limited to driving yachts at sea with a length of 20 meters or less. Inland yacht operators are divided into two classes according to whether they are closed waters or not. Among them, first-class yacht operators can drive yachts in any navigable waters of inland rivers; second-class yacht operators are limited to driving yachts in closed waters of inland rivers. Therefore, the yacht operator should drive the yacht within the scope of application specified in the "yacht driver's license".

(3) Training and examination of yacht operators

The Measures for Training, Examination and Certification of Yacht Operators of the People's Republic of China have made detailed provisions for the training and examination requirements for yacht operators. Among them, the institutions providing training for yacht operators shall have certain conditions and be approved by the Maritime Safety Administration of the People's Republic of China; the examination for yacht operators shall be organized by the maritime administration authorized by same body. Therefore, not all training institutions and maritime management agencies can carry out the training and examination of yacht operators.

In 2019 and 2021, the Outline of Competency Training and Examination for Inland River Ship Seafarers and the Outline of Training for Seafarers have been revised and implemented successively, and the outline of training for yacht operators has been added to the above. Therefore, the above two documents have also become important learning materials for the training of yacht operators and important standards for the examination of yacht operators.

The yacht operator examination is divided into two parts: theoretical examination and practical operation evaluation. Among them, the total score of the theoretical examination is 100 points, and 70 points are the passing grades The actual operation evaluation includes such activities as berthing and leaving the wharf, bypassing the mark, rescue of people falling into the water, and chart identification.

Because yacht operators are not professional crew members, they do not need to register and manage in accordance with the provisions of the Regulations of the People's Republic of China on Seafarers, but only need to obtain a "yacht driver's license".

3. Yacht sailing and berthing

In the process of yacht navigation, yacht operators are the main responsible persons for safety management and bear the relevant legal consequences. For this reason, Article 14 of the Regulations on Yacht Safety Management clearly states that yacht operators should do a good job of safety inspection before sailing to ensure the seaworthiness of yachts.

(1) Yacht sailing

Yacht sailing needs to be supervised by the maritime department. In addition to carrying relevant navigation information with the ship, it is also necessary to carry radio communication tools to ensure that contact can be made with maritime management agencies and yacht clubs. At the same time, yacht operators should carry the certificate of competency of yacht operators when driving yachts.

Yachts are affected by their own size, endurance and other factors, and there are differences in the seaworthiness of yachts. Therefore, Article 17 of the Regulations on the Safety Management of Yachts stipulates that yachts should sail within the seaworthiness scope determined by their inspection certificates. At the same time, before the first voyage, the yacht owner or yacht club shall report the navigation waters to the local maritime administration for the record; if the navigation waters exceed the scope of the record during the subsequent voyage, it shall be reported to the maritime administration in advance. The above requirements are mainly due to safety considerations.

The entry and exit management of yacht navigation will be introduced in the third section of this chapter.

(2) Yacht berthing

Yachts should be berthed in the special berthing waters or berthing points announced by the maritime administration, which is conducive to daily supervision on the one hand and the navigation safety of yachts on the other. For the temporary berthing of yachts during navigation, they shall be berthed in waters that do not hinder the navigation, berthing, and operation of other ships. At the same time, it is not allowed to berth in the main channel, anchorage, prohibited navigation area, safe operation area, near the ferry and in the prohibited waters announced by the maritime administration. The owner of the yacht will bear the corresponding responsibility for the failure to berth as required.

The construction of yacht berthing points is mainly divided into two categories: the yacht club wharf which now occupies the dominant position in China, and the public yacht wharf. The main difference between the two lies in the original intention of construction and the main body of service. Among them, the yacht club wharf is generally a subsidiary product of real estate development, providing parking services for club members, and the parking fees are relatively expensive. The public yacht wharf is similar to the public parking lot, is generally funded by the government, with public service attributes, and the parking fees are more affordable.

According to Article 22 of the Regulations on the Safety Management of Yachts, the builders of yacht berthing wharfs, breakwaters and mooring facilities in port waters shall apply for corresponding permits in accordance with the provisions of the Port Law of the People's Republic of China. However, there is no uniform requirement for the construction of yacht berthing terminals in non-port waters.

4. Yacht Safety Guarantee

The owner of the yacht shall be responsible for the safety and pollution prevention of the yacht. Specifically, the owner of the yacht shall be responsible for the daily safety management and maintenance of the yacht, ensure that the yacht is in good safety and technical condition, and ensure the safety of the yacht navigation, berthing and the personnel on the yacht. However, when the yacht is entrusted to the yacht club for safekeeping, the owner of the yacht should sign an agreement with the yacht club to clarify the responsibilities of both parties.

Therefore, the yacht club needs to assume two responsibilities, one agreement with the yacht management client, and the other from the relevant provisions of the maritime administration. However, when there is a contradiction between the former and the latter, the latter shall prevail, that is, the responsibilities and obligations of the yacht club will not be transferred by the agreement signed with the owner of the yacht.

Article 30 of the Regulations on Yacht Safety Management clearly adopts a reporting system for dangerous situations water traffic and pollution accidents that may be encountered during the use of yachts. The reporting subjects are divided into three categories: the yacht operators and other passengers; the yacht clubs; and the ships and personnel who have found dangerous situations or accidents. At the same time, the yacht club should start the contingency plan immediately, and the people on the yacht should actively take self-rescue measures.

The contents related to the operation and management of yacht clubs in the yacht safety guarantee will be introduced in the fourth section of this chapter.

Section 3: Entry and Exit Management of Yachts

In the entry and exit management of yachts, the vessels actually have dual attributes, namely, the attributes of commodities and goods and the attributes of means of transport. Therefore, he entry and exit management of yachts shall comply with the Customs Law of the People's Republic of China, the Frontier Health and Quarantine Law of the People's Republic of China, the Law of the People's Republic of China on Entry and Exit Animal and Plant Quarantine and other laws and regulations, as well as the Measures of the Customs of the People's Republic of China for the Administration of Temporary Entry and Exit Goods, the Measures of the Customs of the People's Republic of China for the Supervision of Entry and Exit Means of Transport, and the Measures for Inspection of the Entry and Exit of International Sailing Vessels at Ports of the People's Republic of China. This section will focus on the four aspects of customs declaration and filing management, guarantee policy, inspection and quarantine, and domestic and foreign period management.

1. Customs Declaration and Filing Management

According to the Measures of the Customs of the People's Republic of China for the Administration of Temporary Inbound and Outbound Goods, yachts, as self-driving vehicles for tourism and their supplies, are temporary inbound and outbound goods. It is necessary to submit the Application for Confirmation of Temporary Inbound and Outbound Goods to the competent customs to apply for verification and confirmation of whether the relevant goods are temporary inbound and outbound goods. At the same time, the consignee or consignor of the goods temporarily imported or exported under the non-goods temporary import permit document shall provide a guarantee to the competent customs in accordance with the relevant provisions.

According to the Measures of the Customs of the People's Republic of China on the Supervision of Inbound and Outbound Means of Transport, inbound and outbound yachts, persons in charge of inbound and outbound yachts and inbound and outbound yacht service enterprises shall file with the Customs directly under the General Administration of Customs or the Customs directly under the General Administration of Customs authorized by the General Administration of Customs. When filing, it is necessary to submit the Filing Form for Entry and Exit International Navigation Vessels, the Filing Form for Persons in Charge of Means of Transport and the Filing Form for Service Enterprises of Means of Transport, and to submit the materials listed in the column of documents attached to the above-mentioned filing forms. The Customs shall implement the national customs network management for the above-mentioned filing. When the record information is changed, the yacht holder and the yacht service enterprise shall, within the time limit prescribed by the Customs, go through the formalities for the change of the record with the Record Change Form and the relevant documents.

2. Guarantee Policy

According to the relevant provisions of the Regulations of the People's Republic of China on Customs Affairs Guarantee, foreign yachts need to go through customs affairs guarantee formalities before entering the country. Due to the complicated procedures and relatively large amount of guarantees, the demand for overseas yachts entering China for tourism consumption has been restrained to a certain extent. In recent years, Guangdong Province and Hainan Province have explored and implemented institutional innovation, and have actively carried out the policy of entry exemption from guarantee formalities.

(1) Yacht entry guarantee

Because yachts have dual attributes, namely, the attributes of commodities and goods and the attributes of means of transport, yacht entry and exit also involves personnel inspection and ship characterization. In order to better supervise and avoid tax evasion, the Customs of China has established a yacht entry guarantee system according to a certain tariff ratio in accordance with the relevant provisions of Article 5, Paragraph 1, Item 2, of the Regulations of the People's Republic of China on Customs Affairs Guarantee and Article 42 of the Regulations of the People's Republic of China on Import and Export Tariffs. Among them, the guarantee fund is related to yacht price, yacht depreciation and exchange rate, and can be guaranteed by CNY, convertible currency, or a guarantee letter issued by domestic financial institutions and other methods.

Table 10-3 Administrative Regulations on Yacht Guarantee

Serial number	Name of regulation	Specific terms
1	Regulations of the People's Republic of China on Customs Affairs Guarantee	Where the party concerned in Item 2 of Paragraph 1 of Article 5 applies for handling the following specific Customs business, it shall provide a guarantee in accordance with the provisions of the Customs: (2) Goods and articles temporarily entering or leaving the territory;
2	Regulations of the People's Republic of China on Import and Export Duties	Article 42. For the following goods entering or leaving the country temporarily, if the taxpayer pays a deposit of an equivalent amount to the duties payable or provides other types of guarantee to the customs at the time of entry or exit, duties may not be paid temporarily, but the goods shall be transported out of or into the country within 6 months, starting from the day of entry or exit. In cases where the time limit for re-shipment out of or into the territory needs to be extended, the taxpayer shall, in accordance with the provisions of the Customs General Administration, go through the formalities for extension with the Customs: (1) Goods displayed or used in exhibitions, trade fairs, conferences and similar activities; (2) performance and competition supplies used in cultural and sports exchange activities; (3) Instruments, equipment and articles used in news reporting or in the production of films and television programs; (4) instruments, equipment and supplies used in scientific research, teaching and medical activities; (5) Means of transport and special vehicles used in the activities listed in Items (1) to (4) of this paragraph; (6) Samples of goods; (7) instruments and tools for installation, commissioning and testing of equipment; (8) containers for goods; (9) Other goods used for non-commercial purposes. In cases where temporarily imported goods listed in the first paragraph fail to be transported out of the country within the specified time limit, or temporarily exported goods fail to be transported into the country within the specified time limit, the Customs shall levy duties on them in accordance with the law. Import duties shall be calculated and levied on other temporarily imported goods listed in the first paragraph of this article, except for those that may be temporarily exempted from customs duties, on the basis of the customs value of the goods and the proportion between the time of their detention in China and the time of depreciation. The specific measures shall be formulated by the General Administration of Customs.

(2) The entry of yachts is free of guarantee.

On June 28, 2017, the Ministry of Transport, the Ministry of Public Security, the General Administration of Customs and the General Administration of Quality Supervision, Inspection and Quarantine jointly issued a letter agreeing in principle to the Implementation Plan of "Free Travel" for Yachts in Guangdong, Hong Kong and Macao in the China (Guangdong) Pilot Free Trade Zone. According to the implementation plan, we will explore the implementation of the form of general guarantee provided by trade associations or other third-party organizations to the Customs for entry and exit yachts and assume corresponding legal responsibilities. This implementation plan has become the first exploratory policy document in China to propose free yacht guarantee exemption. On June 18, 2019, the General Office of the People's Government of Hainan Province issued the Implementation Plan for Free Travel of Yachts in Hainan, Hong Kong and Macao in the China (Hainan) Free Trade Pilot Zone, proposing that "the policy of tariff-free entry for Hong Kong and Macao yachts that go through entry formalities through free travel." On July 9, 2020, in conjunction with the construction of the China (Hainan) Pilot Free Trade Zone, the General Administration of Customs issued the Notice on the Adjustment of the Management of Yachts Entering and Leaving Hainan, proposing that the owner of the yacht or the agent entrusted by the owner of the yacht shall be exempted from providing guarantees to the Customs for the yacht entering the China (Hainan) Pilot Free Trade Zone. So far, Hainan has taken the lead in realizing the full coverage of the entry guarantee exemption policy.

Self-driving yachts do not need to pay high guarantees to the Customs, which can not only shorten the time spent on entry and exit formalities, but also, more importantly, reduce the large amount of funds occupied by the entry yacht guarantee to the yacht owners, reduce the cost of entry yachts due to guarantee, and add vitality to the development of entry self-driving tours.

3. Inspection and Quarantine

Foreign yachts entering and leaving China's frontier ports and Chinese yachts sailing on international routes are all international navigation ships, which should comply with the relevant requirements of the Measures for the Administration of Entry-Exit Inspection and Quarantine of International Navigation Ships. According to the relevant regulations, China has strict requirements for the inspection and quarantine of entry and exit yachts. Among them, entry yachts must be quarantined at the first port of arrival.

(1) Entry inspection and quarantine

The person in charge of the entry yacht or the entry yacht service enterprise shall declare at the Customs 24 hours before the arrival of the yacht at the port and fill in the entry quarantine declaration. Customs shall, in combination with risk assessment, carry out anchorage quarantine, telecommunication quarantine, berthing quarantine or on-board quarantine on entry yachts. Among them, the person in charge of the yacht may apply to the Customs for telecommunication inspection and quarantine if he holds a valid Vehicle Health Certificate issued by the Customs of China and there is no major epidemic situation. However, if the yacht is from a quarantinable infectious disease epidemic area, or from the animal and plant epidemic area, the state has specific requirements; if there are infected patients, suspected infected patients, or people who died due to non-accidental injury and the cause of death is unknown, or if there are abnormal deaths of rodents, the person in charge of the yacht shall take the initiative to report to the Customs, and go to the anchorage or designated place for quarantine.

Yachts subject to entry quarantine shall hang quarantine signals in accordance with regulations, and may lift quarantine signals, board and leave yachts, load and unload luggage and other articles only after the Customs has issued the Ship Entry Quarantine Certificate. Yachts that do not have the conditions to hang quarantine signals should wait at the quarantine place when entering the country and notify the Customs to carry out quarantine.

During their stay at ports and designated berthing wharfs, the crew shall not remove any animals and plants, animal and plant products, or other quarantine objects from the yacht. If it is really necessary to take them away, they shall apply to the Customs for inspection. If the yacht is loaded with such quarantined objects that are prohibited from entering the country, the Customs shall seal them up or destroy them. Necessary quarantine treatment shall be carried out under the supervision of the Customs for household garbage, swill, animal and plant wastes and their storage sites and containers.

The Customs shall issue the Certificate of Vessel Entry Health and Quarantine to the entry yachts that are judged to be free from epidemic diseases after quarantine. For entry yachts that have been judged to be infected with epidemic diseases, suspected of being infected with epidemic diseases, or come from epidemic areas of infectious diseases and should be subject to sanitary and disinfestation treatment or have other restrictions, the Vessel Entry Quarantine Certificate shall be issued after the corresponding sanitary and disinfestation treatment has been carried out, or the sanitary and disinfestation treatment items that should be accepted have been indicated.

(2) Exit inspection and quarantine

When a yacht leaves the country, it shall declare to the inspection and quarantine authority at the exit port three hours before leaving the country and go through the exit quarantine formalities. If a yacht stays at the port for less than 24 hours, the person in charge of the yacht or the yacht service enterprise may, with the consent of the inspection and quarantine authority, go through the exit formalities while going through the entry formalities. If the yacht fails to leave within 24 hours after the completion of the exit formalities, the yacht returns for some reason after leaving the country, or if there are personnel changes, it is necessary to go through the exit formalities again.

4. Management during domestic and overseas period

Yachts shall enter or leave the country through ports with Customs or approved yacht supervision wharves and shall be subject to Customs supervision. Time limit for entry and exit of yachts under customs supervision; The supervision of foreign yachts' stay after entering the country and the supervision of their continuous driving in China have always attracted much attention. This section mainly focuses on these three aspects.

(1) Management of time limit for entry and exit

As temporary entry and exit goods, entry and exit yachts should still comply with the regulatory requirements of "temporary entry" or "temporary exit", but there has been a lack of targeted regulatory measures for a long time. On March 11, 2011, the General Administration of Customs issued the Interim Measures of the Customs of the People's Republic of China on the Supervision of Entry and Exit Yachts and Their Articles in Hainan Province, in which the time limit for the entry and exit of yachts was clarified for the first time, providing an important reference for the management of the time limit for the entry and exit of yachts nationwide.

According to the Interim Measures of the Customs of the People's Republic of China on the Supervision of Entry and Exit Yachts and Their Articles in Hainan Province, foreign yachts should return to the country after 30 days of entry, and domestic yachts should return to the country after 30 days of exit. Without the consent of the Customs, it shall not be detained in or outside the territory beyond the time limit, nor shall it be transferred or used for other purposes without authorization. If the time limit needs to be extended due to special circumstances, the owner of the yacht or the yacht service enterprise entrusted by him shall apply to the Customs at the place of entry or exit for an extension. It can be extended only after approval, and each extension period shall not exceed 30 days, and it can be extended up to 2 times. Foreign yachts shall not stay in China for more than 183 days in a Gregorian calendar year.

(1) Stay supervision

According to the Regulations of the Customs of the People's Republic of China on the Supervision of Inbound and Outbound Means of Transport, yachts should be subject to customs supervision and inspection when they arrive at the port. Customs will focus on checking basic information such as the hull of the yacht, the articles carried, the personnel on the yacht and their personal belongings, inspecting the appearance of rooms, warehouses and other parts, and quarantining areas or parts that may be at risk of infection. During the inspection, the person in charge of the yacht shall be present to cooperate with the inspection, accept inquiries, provide various materials, open or dismantle some parts, and cooperate with the removal of corresponding articles according to the needs of the customs, so as to facilitate the customs inspection. After the customs inspection is completed, the person in charge of the yacht shall sign the Inspection Record after confirmation.

(3) Domestic driving supervision

When an inward or outward yacht moves from one place with a customs office to another place with a customs office within the territory, the person in charge of the inward or outward yacht shall go through the formalities for its departure in accordance with the relevant provisions. Without the consent of the customs at the place of departure, the entry and exit yachts shall not be diverted to other destinations. Those who have not gone through the customs formalities shall not be allowed to change to foreign countries.

When a foreign yacht has an accident or mechanical failure during its stay in China, which affects the seaworthiness of the yacht, it may go to the shipyard for maintenance by itself with the approval of the Customs, and the enterprise undertaking the yacht maintenance shall go through the customs declaration formalities with the Customs in the form of "repair articles". Foreign yachts shall be monitored by the Customs through the information system before going through the exit formalities after the entry declaration. After going through the exit formalities, the yacht will be monitored by the Customs through the information system until it actually leaves the country.

Section 4 Yacht Management In the yacht economy, the matters related to yacht management are relatively scattered. From the perspective of the existing management system and policy system, it is mainly divided into three aspects: imported yacht management, yacht club management and yacht rental management. Among them, yacht leasing is a new form of business in China, and the relevant management system has just begun to be formulated and mainly concentrated in Hainan Province. Therefore, the yacht management system will be introduced around the first trial of Hainan Province in the management of imported yachts, yacht clubs and yacht rental management.

1. Management of imported yachts

Due to the relatively late start of China's yachting industry, imported yachts have always occupied an important position in China's yacht consumption. The Regulations on Yacht Safety Management promulgated in 2008 provide guidance for the management of imported yachts and put forward specific requirements for the inspection and age of imported yachts.

(1) Inspection of imported yachts

After the promulgation of the Regulations on the Safety Management of Yachts in 2008, the Maritime Safety Administration of the People's Republic of China promulgated the Provisional Regulations on the Statutory Inspection of Yachts in 2009, which standardized the safety management of yachts. In order to further improve the applicability of yacht laws and regulations and promote the healthy development of the yachting industry and water tourism economy, the Maritime Safety Administration of the People's

Republic of China issued the Opinions on the Implementation of Yacht Safety Management in 2010, which simplified the inspection of imported yachts to a certain extent.

As a temporary measure, the Maritime Safety Administration of the People's Republic of China recognizes CE and ABYC certificates and marks as "other recognized standards accepted by the Administration" and "relevant valid documents and certificates recognized by the Administration" as stated in Article 1.1.2.4 and Article 1.2.5.1 of the Interim Provisions for Statutory Inspection of Yachts. Imported yachts with the above certificates and marks will not be required to provide drawings during inspection, but their certificates or inspection certificates shall be checked for conformity with the actual ship. Imported yachts that do not hold the above certification certificates and marks are required to provide or supplement ship drawings and stability calculation data during inspection, and after passing the examination, they can be inspected for conformity.

(2) Age of imported yachts

In order to further strengthen the management of imported yachts, the Ministry of Transport issued a notice prohibiting the import of yachts from abroad with an age of more than one year and requiring maritime administrations at all levels and ship inspection departments to strictly implement the provisions of the notice, and not to go through the formalities of registration and inspection of imported yachts that do not meet the requirements of the notice.

On the one hand, the announcement did not specify the calculation method of the age of imported yachts, referring to the Notice on Clarifying the Measures for the Management of Imported Yachts issued by the relevant departments of Hainan Province in 2022. For a yacht that needs to obtain an import license, the age of the yacht refers to the period from the date of completion specified in the technical data (the certificate of the builder or the ship inspection certificate issued by the builder) to the date of issuance of the import license. For a yacht that does not require an import license, the age of the yacht refers to the period from the date of completion specified in the technical data (the certificate of the builder or the ship inspection certificate issued by the builder) to the date of import (the date of import recorded in the customs declaration). Among them, if the construction factory certificate does not specify the specific date of completion, the date of issuance of the construction factory certificate shall prevail.

On the other hand, the age of imported yachts is strictly limited to less than one year, which reduces the demand of Chinese consumers for second-hand yachts abroad, which is not in line with the prosperous second-hand yacht market abroad. To this end, Hainan Free Trade Port, in its Regulations on the Promotion of yachting industry in Hainan Free Trade Port, proposed that "the age of yachts purchased from abroad or obtained through other legal channels and intended to apply for registration can be relaxed to five years."

2. Yacht Club Management

Yacht clubs, as organizations providing yacht storage and use services for their members, have developed along with the yacht economy. As an entity with legal personality, yacht clubs provide relevant services while assuming relevant responsibilities and fulfilling corresponding obligations.

(1) Yacht club filing

Yacht clubs in China need not only to have legal personality, but also to implement the relevant requirements of record management. The object of record is the local Maritime Bureau or the provincial local Maritime Bureau. Although the filing requirements are not clear in the Regulations on Yacht Safety Management at the national level, the document points out the safety and anti-pollution capabilities that yacht clubs should possess and the safety obligations that they should fulfill, which has also become an important reference for the local government.

(2) The responsibility of yacht clubs for safety and pollution prevention

According to the Regulations on Yacht

Safety Management, yacht clubs should have the required safety and pollution prevention capabilities and assume the responsibility for yacht safety and pollution prevention. Specifically, the yacht club shall establish a management system for yacht safety and pollution prevention, provide corresponding full-time management personnel, have corresponding safe berthing waters, provide facilities for yacht safety and pollution prevention, provide water safety communication facilities and equipment, and have facilities and capabilities for yacht daily repair, maintenance and maintenance. The facilities should also have the ability to recycle yacht waste, residual oil and garbage; have safety and anti-pollution measures and contingency plans; and also have the corresponding emergency rescue capabilities.

(3) Safety obligations to be fulfilled by yacht clubs

The safety obligations of the yacht

club mainly include: to carry out publicity, training and education on yacht safety, environmental pollution prevention and emergency response for yacht operators and passengers; to urge yacht operators and passengers to abide by the regulations on water traffic safety and pollution prevention and control, and implement corresponding measures; to ensure the safety of yachts in the berthing waters or berthing points; to check the certification of yacht and yacht operators to ensure that the yacht and yacht operators hold the corresponding valid certificates; too provide information services such as meteorological and hydrological conditions required for navigation issued by maritime administrative agencies to yachts; to stop yachts from sailing and notify yachts that have sailed to return when they are not suitable for sailing under bad weather conditions or when they are warned by maritime administrative agencies that they are prohibited from sailing; to master the sailing, return sailing and crew conditions of the yacht, and make records for future reference; to maintain smooth communication with the yacht and the maritime administration; to regularly organize emergency drills for internal management and yacht members in accordance with the contingency plan filed with the maritime administration.

III. Yacht leasing management

According to the definition of yacht in the Regulations on Yacht Safety Management, yachts are classified as non-commercial ships. However, when a yacht is engaged in commercial transportation, it shall go through the formalities of ship inspection, registration and ship operation licensing in accordance with the relevant regulations of the State on the management of operating ships. However, yacht rental, as a new form of the tourism consumption market in China, has gradually become the mainstream. Hainan Province has taken the lead in formulating and promulgating rules and regulations for yacht leasing in China and leads the standardized development of yacht leasing.

(1) Concept of Yacht Leasing

Yacht leasing refers to a kind of leasing activity in which the business operator provides yachts to the lessee for the purpose of sightseeing, leisure and entertainment, business and other activities, and provides supporting yacht driving and security services. It does not include any off-board water activities arranged by the yacht charter operator for the crew. If the leased yacht changes its use to engage in waterway transport business activities, it shall go through the formalities of ship inspection, registration and ship operation license in accordance with the relevant provisions of the State.

(2) Qualification requirements for the filing of yacht leasing business operators

Enterprises engaged in yacht leasing business must apply to the competent transportation departments of the cities and regions where they are located for filing in accordance with requirements. The competent transportation departments of cities and regions shall publish the list of approved operators and the list of yachts to the public in an appropriate way and manage them dynamically. The specific filing materials mainly include the following items: there are yachts and berths suitable for the scope of leasing services; the yachts shall obtain valid ship registration certificates and seaworthiness certification documents, as well as inspection; there are safety management personnel and yacht operators with qualified and valid certificates that are suitable for the scope of business services and the number of yachts applied for; having a sound business management systems, service procedures, safety management system and contingency plans, as well as the ability to ensure safety and prevent pollution as required by relevant regulations.

(3) The main responsibility of the operator of yacht leasing business

The operators of yacht leasing business shall assume the responsibility for safe production and pollution prevention, standardize the responsibility for operation and service manufacturing, and establish the responsibility system for safe production and pollution prevention. They must also formulate and implement safety operation procedures, emergency response plans, and safety production responsibility systems for all employees of the enterprise. The operators are also required to abide by the principles of operation according to law, honesty and trustworthiness, fair competition, and standardized operation.

(4) Subject obligations of yacht leasing business operators

The operator of yacht leasing business

shall sign a non-transferable lease contract with the lessee to clarify the service content, service standards, rights and obligations of both parties. The main obligations of the operator of the yacht leasing business include: the daily maintenance of the yacht, the repair and maintenance of the relevant facilities and equipment on the yacht; the inspection before sailing to ensure the seaworthiness of the yacht; the provision of qualified yacht operators and relevant staff in accordance with the regulations; the completion of relevant entry and exit reports or reports; the navigation of the leased yacht within 20 nautical miles from the shore; having insurance in accordance with relevant regulations; and truthfully recording the relevant information of each voyage.

(5) Inspection of leased yachts

In order to implement the Measures for the Administration of Yacht Leasing in Hainan Province (Trial Implementation), ensure the safety of life and property of yachts and their personnel, and prevent environmental pollution in waters, the Department of Transportation of Hainan Province has formulated the Provisional Regulations on the Inspection of Yacht Leasing in Hainan Province. The document specifies the technical standards for inspection of rental yachts, such as sailing, stability, navigation and navigation equipment, fire safety, life-saving equipment and layout, crew quota and cabin equipment, and pollution prevention. In addition to the initial, renewal or special periodic inspection and temporary inspection in accordance with the Provisional Regulations on Statutory Inspection of Yachts and the Code for Classification and Construction of Yachts, an initial inspection and annual inspection shall also be carried out.

Chapter 11

Yacht Technology Innovation and Future Development Prospects

The future of yacht technology innovation is full of hope. The use of new materials, cutting-edge designs and innovative propulsion systems has transformed the yacht experience and made it more enjoyable and accepted by a wider audience. Emerging trends such as autonomous yachting, green technology and personalized yacht design will revolutionize the industry. At the same time, the yachting industry is also facing potential challenges and opportunities, such as increased competition, changing consumer preferences, and new demands.

This chapter will explore the innovative results of yacht technology and its impact on the industry, the economy, and the visitor experience. Included here will be role of new technologies such as new materials, electric and hybrid propulsion systems, as well as navigation, communications, and entertainment systems. Also discussed will be the challenges faced by yacht manufacturers in protecting intellectual property through patents.

Due to the industrial ecosystem of yacht technology innovation, material suppliers, technology providers and service providers also play a vital role in the future development of yachts. Therefore, analyzing and solving the challenges and opportunities presented by these entities will also promote the development of the yachting industry.

In addition, the potential impact of yacht technology innovation will be examined, with a focus on analyzing the potential challenges and opportunities that the industry may face in the next few years.

Section 1: New Yacht Materials

Yachts are complex and sophisticated vessels that require the use of multiple materials for construction, maintenance, and operation. The materials used in the construction of yachts play a vital role in determining the performance, safety, and sustainability of these vessels. This has become a key factor in the innovation and development of the yachting industry.

From fiberglass and aluminum to carbon fibers and composites, yacht builders and designers can choose from a variety of materials when building these boats. The development of new materials has changed the behavior choices of yacht designers and enthusiasts. The choice of material depends on a variety of factors, including cost, strength, weight, and corrosion resistance. The development and introduction of new materials in the boating industry thus has the potential to greatly impact the design, performance and sustainability of yachts. Compared with traditional materials such as wood or steel, composite materials are lighter, stronger and more resistant to corrosion. This increase in strength and durability means that yachts can become lighter, improving speed and performance while reducing fuel consumption.

In addition to composite materials, yacht manufacturers are also incorporating new materials such as glass fiber reinforced plastic (FRP) and high-density foam into their designs. These materials are lighter, more durable, and provide better insulation than traditional materials, making them an ideal construction material for marine vehicles.

Another significant development in yacht materials is the use of 3D printing technology that can produce cumbersome and complex parts that are difficult or impossible to produce using traditional manufacturing techniques. The use of 3D printing not only saves time, but also opens up new possibilities for yacht designers, enabling them to create yachts that are lighter, stronger, and more aerodynamic.

1. Materials commonly used in yacht construction

(1) Glass fiber

1. Glass fiber and its types

Glass fiber is a kind of inorganic non-metallic material with excellent performance. It is one of the most common materials in yacht manufacturing. It is made up by using six minerals of pyrophyllite, quartz sand, limestone, dolomite, borocalcite, and szaibelyite as raw material through the processes of high-temp melting, wire drawing, weaving and the like. The diameter of the monofilament is several microns to more than twenty microns, which is equivalent to 1/20-1/5 of a hair, with each bundle of fibers composed of hundreds or even thousands of monofilaments.

There are many kinds of glass fibers, including alkali-free, chemical resistant, high alkali, medium alkali, high strength, high elastic modulus and alkali-resistant materials. Among them, alkali-free glass fiber, also known as E-glass, is a kind of borosilicate glass. It has good electrical insulation and mechanical properties and is the most widely used material in the construction of sailboats, especially for the hull of a mass-produced cruising sailboat. Non-alkali glass fiber is widely used in yacht construction, usually as a reinforcing material combined with resin. It can be used to make hull, deck, interior and other parts, and can also be used in yacht maintenance and modification.

2. Advantages and disadvantages of glass fiber

(1) Advantages of glass fiber

Light weight and high strength. Fiberglass is a lightweight material, but its strength is very high, which makes it one of the ideal materials for yacht construction.

Resistance to corrosion. Glass fiber has strong corrosion resistance, which can resist the erosion resulting from the natural environment such as sea water and sunshine.

Easy to process. Fiberglass is easy to process and shape and can meet the needs of yachts of different shapes and sizes.

Low cost. Compared with other materials, the cost of glass fiber is lower, which can reduce the cost of yacht construction.

(2) Deficiencies of glass fiber

The stiffness is low. Although the strength of glass fiber is very high, its stiffness is relatively low, and it is easy to be deformed by external impact.

It is easily damaged by ultraviolet rays. Although it has certain anti-ultraviolet ability, long-term exposure to sunlight will gradually age and yellow glass fibers, affecting its appearance.

Not suitable for high-temperature environments. Glass fiber has poor heat resistance and is not suitable for yacht construction in high-temperature environments.

3. Application Prospects of Glass Fiber

In terms of manufacturing process, with the continuous improvement of glass fiber manufacturing technology, new production processes can improve the performance, strength and durability of glass fibers. In addition, the application of new technologies may improve the efficiency and sustainability of glass fiber production. With regard to the development of fiberglass composites, fiberglass can be used in combination with other materials, such as polyamide or carbon fiber. These combinations result in stronger, more durable materials while maintaining the lightweight benefits of fiberglass.

In the aspect of glass fiber recovery and reuse, due to the requirements of environmental protection and sustainable development, the recycling and reuse of glass fiber has become a research hotspot. Researchers are exploring ways to recycle waste fiberglass and reuse it in new yacht- building projects.

All in all, with the continuous progress of technology and the emergence of innovative designs, the application of glass fiber will be more extensive. In the future, there may be more fiberglass parts in yacht design, so as to keep the vessels lightweight and provide better performance, aesthetics and practicality.

(2) Aluminum alloys

1. Aluminum alloys and their varieties

Aluminum alloys have aluminum as the matrix element and a certain amount of other alloying elements, such as copper, zinc, manganese, silicon, or magnesium.

Aluminum alloys used in yacht construction industry are mainly aluminum- copper alloy, aluminum-magnesium alloys, and aluminum-silicon alloys. The poor corrosion resistance of the aluminum- copper alloy in seawater limits its wide application in the shipbuilding industry. The aluminum-magnesium alloy is mainly used for hull shells, water pump conduits, pump shells, engine base brackets and the like, and the models are distinguished according to the magnesium content, such as 5083, 5086, 5456, and 5466.The aluminum-silicon alloy has moderate structural strength, good fluidity and strong filling capacity, and is easily used to produce parts with high density and complex structures, such as high-pressure valves, cylinder bodies, pumps, reduction gearbox shells, turbine blades and the like.

2. Advantages and disadvantages of aluminum alloys

Lightweight: Aluminum is a lightweight metal. Boats with hulls and superstructures made of aluminum alloy are strong and lightweight, which can reduce fuel consumption and increase the speed and distance.

Corrosion resistance: Aluminum alloys will not rust, corrode or rot, have good corrosion resistance, and can withstand temperatures of 200 below zero. They can effectively resist seawater, oxidation, and bad weather.

High strength: Aluminum alloys have excellent strength and anti-strike abilities, which make aluminum ships more resistant to foreign objects than composite ships. They can also ensure the stability and safety of the yacht in high-speed navigation and harsh sea conditions.

Plasticity: The aluminum alloy hull is easy to process and repair, for example, it can be customized with a higher degree of freedom. It is relatively easy to splice and patch the hull using aluminum plates.

There are some disadvantages to an aluminum hull, though. For example, the price is relatively high, compared with traditional materials such as glass fiber. Aluminum hulls also require special protective measures to avoid electrolytic corrosion.

3. Application Prospects of Aluminum Alloys

In the future, the application of aluminum alloy materials in yacht construction will continue to develop and innovate. With the continuous progress of technology, the performance and process of aluminum alloy materials will be continuously improved. Aluminum alloy materials with higher strength and lighter weight will be more widely used. At the same time, with the increasing attention of yacht consumers to environmental protection and sustainability, the use of renewable resources such as recycled aluminum to manufacture yachts will also become a trend of the future. In addition, the development of digital design and manufacturing technology will also help to improve the accuracy and efficiency of aluminum alloy materials, thus bringing more opportunities for the development of yacht construction industry.

(3) Carbon fibers

1. Carbon Fibers and Their Application

Carbon fiber refers to a high strength and high modulus fiber with carbon content of more than 90%. They are made of acrylic fiber and viscose fiber by high temperature oxidation and carbonization, and its high temperature resistance ranks first among all chemical synthetic fibers. The characteristics of carbon fiber, such as high stiffness, high strength, light weight, high chemical resistance, high temperature resistance and low thermal expansion, is widely used in aerospace, rail transit, military industry, sports equipment, medical equipment, automobile manufacturing and other fields.

It has also been rapidly popularized in the yachting industry.

Carbon fiber is commonly used in masts, blades, and structural components of yachts, which can improve their speed and durability. At the same time, carbon fiber is also used in interior parts of yachts, such as panels, ceilings, floors and furniture. Because of the unique appearance and texture of carbon fiber, the yacht looks high- grade and fashionable.

2. Advantages and disadvantages of carbon fiber

Carbon fiber has certain advantages as a construction material in yacht manufacturing:

High strength. The strength of carbon fiber is much higher than that of steel and aluminum alloy, which can ensure that the structure of the yacht is strong and stable.

Lightweight. Carbon fiber is lighter than traditional materials, which can reduce the weight of yachts and improve speed and fuel efficiency.

Corrosion resistance is good. Carbon fiber is not easy to corrode, which can prolong the service life of yachts.

However, carbon fiber is an expensive material, and the cost of building a yacht using carbon fiber is high. At the same time, once the carbon fiber is damaged or damaged, it is difficult to repair.

In a word, carbon fiber has a broad application prospect in the field of yacht construction. With the continuous development of science and technology and the continuous improvement of carbon fiber manufacturing process, the cost of carbon fiber will be gradually reduced. The scope of application is also gradually expanding. Carbon fiber is expected to become one of the mainstream materials in the field of yacht construction in the future.

Table 11-1 Comparison of Common Materials for Yacht Construction

Material	Advantages	Shortcomings	Uses	Applicable scenarios
Aluminum Alloy	Lightweight, strong, corrosion-resistant, durable and easy to repair	It is expensive; it is easy to have chemical reaction when contacting with other metals; it has a low melting point and is not suitable for use in a high- temperature environment.	Hulls, decks, masts, frames, fittings and other structural elements	Suitable for yachts requiring high strength, light weight and corrosion resistance
Glass Fiber	Light weight, easy to process, economical, good impact resistance, good insulation	It is easy to penetrate and absorb water; its strength is not as good as other materials; its rigidity is low, and it is easy to crack under stress; it is not resistant to wear and tear.	Hulls, decks and other non-structural parts	Suitable for yachts of moderate size and speed

Carbon fiber	Very strong and rigid, lightweight, corrosion resistant, fatigue resistant, impact resistant	Expensive, fragile, difficult to repair, not suitable for use in a high- temperature environment.	Masts, masts, rigging and other high-performance structural components	Suitable for yachts requiring high strength, light weight, corrosion and wear resistance

2. New Materials for Yacht Construction

Compared with the commonly used materials, the new materials for yacht construction have certain advantages, such as increased strength and durability, reduced weight, and improved corrosion and weather resistance. In addition, the production of new materials promotes the progress of yacht technology. Many of the new materials being developed and tested have the potential to transform the yachting industry in terms of manufacturing technology and design. Some of these materials include advanced composites, titanium alloys, polymer nanocomposites, and degradable composites.

(1) Advanced composite materials

Advanced composites refer to the combination of two or more different materials to form a new material, with better performance and advantages such as better strength and durability. They are resistant to mechanical and chemical damage and have been used in the aerospace and automotive industries for many years. In yacht construction, advanced composite materials can reduce weight and improve fuel efficiency, such as carbon fiber reinforced plastics, glass fiber reinforced plastics, and high density foams. The following describes the application of several common advanced composite materials in yacht construction.

1. Carbon fiber reinforced plastic

Carbon fiber reinforced plastic (CFRP) is a kind of reinforce material with carbon fiber and resin (usually epoxy resin) as the matrix composition of high strength, lightweight composite materials. Carbon fibers are made of carbon elements. They demonstrate extremely high strength and rigidity, while being very light. The composite material formed by the composite material and the resin has different performance, and some of the composite material has good rigidity and poor toughness. The composite materials formed by single resin and compound resin and carbon fiber also have different performances. Among them, carbon fiber reinforced plastics with high strength, high stiffness and light weight are widely used in the field of high performance, such as aerospace, racing, ships, and sports equipment.

The application of carbon fiber reinforced plastics in yacht construction is becoming more and more common. Due to its high strength and stiffness, light weight, good corrosion resistance, excellent durability, and good appearance carbon fiber reinforced plastics can be used to manufacture the hull, deck, mast, tiller and other parts of yachts.

By using carbon fiber reinforced plastic materials, yachts can greatly reduce weight, improve speed and fuel efficiency. In addition, because of its high rigidity and strength, the yacht can adopt a larger hull design, providing more internal space. In addition, carbon fiber reinforced plastic can also make the design of yachts more flexible, making it easier for designers to achieve complex curves and shapes. However, the cost of CFRP is relatively high, requiring higher production and maintenance technology. This is also one of the factors that limit its application.

Carbon fiber composites have excellent properties and play an important role in the high-tech field, and the future development is bound to change with each passing day. With the development and progress of carbon fiber manufacturing technology, its production costs will be greatly reduced, and its application will expand in the yacht manufacturing industry.

2. Kevlar composites

Kevlar is ahigh-performance, lightweight, and high-strength synthetic fiber material developed by DuPont Company, Widely used in aerospace, automotive, sports equipment, body armor, and other fields. Kevlar has a very high tensile strength and modulus while also providing excellent resistance to impact, erosion, and abrasion. Compared with carbon fiber, the elastic modulus and strength of Kevlar are relatively low. But it has better impact resistance and can absorb more energy. Therefore, Kevlar is usually a better choice in some situations that need to withstand high impact loads.

In the field of yacht construction, Kevlar composites can achieve the ideal balance of strength, stiffness and weight. Usually, Kevlar composites are used to reinforce the hull, which can make it lighter, stronger and more resistant to damage. At the same time, it can also improve the speed and stability of the yacht and enhance the performance under hydraulic fatigue load. Kevlar composites can also be used to make decks, bridges, masts and other components that improve the durability and reliability of yachts. Kevlar composites are currently used in recreational yachts as well as racing boats, sailboats and speedboats.

Compared with traditional materials such as wood, steel, and aluminum alloys, Kevlar composite materials have many advantages in yacht construction. First of all, Kevlar composites have high strength and stiffness, so they can make lighter yacht structures, reduce overall weight and improve speed and fuel economy. Secondly, Kevlar composites have excellent waterproof properties, which can prevent water penetration and reduce maintenance and repair costs. In addition, Kevlar composites have good corrosion resistance and are not easily affected by seawater, sunlight and climate. The service life of the yacht can thus be prolonged. However, the cost of Kevlar composites is high and the production is difficult, which requires advanced technology and equipment for production.

3. Glass fiber reinforced plastic (GFRP or FRP)

Fiberglass reinforced plastic (GFRP or FRP), also known as glass fiber reinforced plastic, is a composite material composed of glass fiber and thermosetting resin. During the manufacturing process, glass fibers are usually soaked in liquid resin and then cured to shape. The ratio of fiberglass and resin can be adjusted as needed to achieve the desired mechanical properties and cost effectiveness. Glass fiber reinforced plastics have excellent properties, such as high strength, light weight, corrosion resistance and low maintenance cost. They have a wide range of applications, such as in ships, aircraft, automobiles, construction, and other fields.

In yacht construction, glass fiber reinforced plastics are often used to manufacture the hull, deck, interior, and other parts. Fiberglass reinforced plastics are lighter, more durable, and easier to maintain than traditional materials such as aluminum and steel. The advantages of GFRP in yacht construction include its light weight, durability, and insulation properties. Its light weight can enable the yacht to sail more quickly and be more amenable to handling. GFRP's durability means it will not corrode, deform, or be damaged by UV light. GFRP's good sound and thermal insulation properties can help provide a more comfortable sailing experience; Finally, the processing and maintenance of GFRP is relatively easy, and any damaged parts can be repaired or replaced quickly.

Although GFRP has many potential advantages in yacht construction, there are also some limitations. GFRP is less strong than some other composite materials and is prone to cracking or cracking. The fire resistance of GFRP is relatively poor, and the production process in making GFRP items may produce some harmful chemicals.

4. Honeycomb structure composite material

Most yachts are made of glass fiber reinforced plastic. The fabrication process is usually done using an accurate negative mold for the hull, deck, and other modules. When making the hull, a thick layer of gel coat (a colored, high-quality, shiny resin) is applied to using an abrasive tool coated with a release agent. After the gel coat has solidified, layers of glass fiber cloth can be added. Fiberglass is very strong, but it must be laid in multiple layers to be most effective, which will undoubtedly increase the weight of the hull and affect the performance of the vessel. In order to solve this problem, honeycomb composites have been applied in yacht construction.

Honeycomb composites are composed of two face sheets (skin) and a sandwich layer (honeycomb structure). Honeycomb structures typically consist of a honeycomb core, which is typically a lightweight material made of aluminum or cardboard, and a panel layer, usually made of a high strength material such as fiber reinforced plastic or metal. This makes the hull, deck, or other parts stronger, but also lighter than components using fiberglass reinforced plastic alone.

In yacht construction, honeycomb composites are often used to make parts such as hulls, decks and interiors. The lightweight design of honeycomb structure makes the yacht more energy-saving and environmentally friendly, and improves the speed and maneuverability of the vessel At the same time, the high stiffness and strength of the honeycomb structure make the yacht more durable and capable of withstanding greater force and torque. In addition, the honeycomb structure composite material also has good energy absorption capacity and can absorb energy during collision and impact, reducing damage to yachts and passengers. In addition, the design of honeycomb structure can also improve the sound insulation and heat preservation effect of the yacht, providing passengers with a more comfortable sailing experience.

(2) Titanium alloys

Titanium is a metal that is both strong and lightweight, making it ideal for yacht construction. It is also highly resistant to corrosion and weathering, making it an excellent choice for use in harsh marine environments. Titanium alloys are composed of titanium and other elements (such as aluminum, vanadium, magnesium, or iron. They have the advantages of high strength, corrosion resistance, high temperature resistance, sound transmission, non magnetism, and elasticity resistance, and are widely used in aerospace, automotive, medical, energy, marine and other fields.

Among the countries in the world, Russia is the most advanced in the practical application of marine titanium alloys and has a large number of specialized marine titanium alloy systems. A series of marine titanium alloy products with high strength have been manufactured there, including the hull, the ship's engine and the power plant. The technology used in material manufacturing is also very mature. Although there is a certain gap between China and foreign countries in the application of marine titanium alloys a series of marine titanium alloys with independent intellectual property rights have been independently developed, such as Ti75, TiB19, Ti70, Ti80, and TA5.

Because of the high strength and light weight of titanium alloys, their use in yacht parts can reduce the overall weight of the vessel, thereby improving its speed and fuel efficiency. At the same time, titanium alloys have good corrosion resistance, which can prolong the service life of yachts in harsh environments such as seawater. For example, if copper or stainless steel is used to make the pumps, valves and piping of ships, these components usually have a life span of only 2 to 5 years. If they are made of titanium alloys, their service life will be far more than 5 years. However, due to the high cost of titanium alloy materials, they are mainly used to manufacture more important components in yachts.

The performance of titanium alloys is not perfect, and the cost of its application in ships is relatively large. Many countries are beginning to develop new titanium alloys with lower cost and higher performance. At present, the new progress in titanium alloys at home and abroad is mainly reflected in high temperature titanium alloys, titanium-aluminum compounds, high strength and high toughness β types, and flame-retardant types.

(3) Polymer nanomaterials

Polymer nanomaterials are composite materials composed of polymer materials and nanomaterials such as nanoparticles or nanotubes. Nanoparticles or nanotubes are typically between 1 and 100 nanometers in size. The new composite material can combine the rigidity, dimensional stability and thermal stability of inorganic materials with the toughness and processability of polymer materials. The perfect combination of dielectric and dielectric properties opens up a new era of composite materials. This is because basically, polymer materials have the characteristics of light weight, corrosion resistance, wear resistance, and good plasticity. Combining them with nanomaterials can further improve the performance of materials and expand their application scenarios.

Polymer nanomaterials can be subdivided into nanotubes, nanoparticles, nanoplates, and nanofibers. Depending on the material, further subdivisions can include inorganic polymer nanomaterials and organic polymer nanomaterials, the latter of which are widely used in yacht construction.

The application of polymer nanomaterials

in yacht hull manufacturing is mainly used in the selection of hull materials and the manufacturing process itself. On the one hand, the use of polymer nanomaterials can produce lighter, stronger, and more durable hulls, thus improving the speed and comfort of the yacht. On the other hand, the use of polymer nano-coatings can improve the corrosion resistance, wear resistance, and ultraviolet resistance of the materials, effectively prolonging the service life of yachts and reducing maintenance costs. In addition, the application of polymer nanomaterials in yacht equipment can improve the performance and stability of the equipment, such as lighter and stronger masts and ropes.

Polymer nanomaterials are lighter and stronger than traditional materials, which can greatly reduce the weight of yachts. Their use improves the speed and fuel economy of yachts. The materials also have excellent corrosion resistance to the effects of seawater and solar radiation. In addition, polymer nanomaterials can be produced and recycled through sustainable development methods, making them environmentally friendly. However, compared with traditional materials, polymer nanomaterials are expensive, difficult to maintain, and are easily deformed at high temperatures.

Polymer nanomaterials can also be used to manufacture various smart materials, such as smart coatings and smart ceramics. These materials can change their morphology and properties independently depending on different environments and needs.

(4) Biodegradable materials

Biodegradable materials refer to substances that can be decomposed into non-toxic and harmless substances after a certain period of time in a specific environment. Environmentally friendly composite materials are usually composed of one or more natural or synthetic polymer materials and biodegradable additives. This material can be broken down by microorganisms and eventually converted into water, carbon dioxide and other natural components, which have less impact on the environment. Biodegradable composites have a variety of applications, such as in packaging materials, consumer durables, and as soil covers.

In the construction of yachts, biodegradable materials can reduce the impact of yachts on the ecology of the marine environment. Among these things, bio-based materials, starch-based materials, and biodegradable polyesters have been applied in yacht construction. These composites are usually made of natural fibers and bio-based synthetic resins, so they are environmentally friendly. The main application of biodegradable composite materials in yacht construction is to make interiors, decorations and lightweight structural parts.

Biodegradable composites can also achieve the goal of sustainability and environmental protection, which is compatible with the future development trends of the yachting industry. However, biodegradable composites also have some disadvantages, such as high cost, short service life and low durability, which therefore require more frequent maintenance and replacement.

Although the application of biodegradable composite materials in yacht construction is relatively limited at present, in the future, the application of degradable materials in yacht construction will be more and more extensive, asin yacht coatings and antifouling agents.

Section 2: New Yacht Technology

As yachts have become more popular, so has the demand for new and innovative techniques in yacht design and construction. In recent years, the development of new materials, propulsion systems and shipboard technology has made significant progress and revolutionized the yachting industry. This section will provide an overview of some of the most promising and innovative new technologies currently in use in the boating industry, and the potential impact these advances could have on the industry as a whole.

One of the key areas of concern for yacht technology is the development of more sustainable and environmentally friendly yacht designs. This is reflected in the growing interest in hybrid and electric propulsion systems, and the use of lightweight, high-strength composites that are more durable and energy efficient than traditional materials. The development of these new technologies not only helps to reduce the environmental impact of yachts, but also reduce fuel consumption, improve performance, and improve passenger comfort.

Another area of innovation for yachts is the increasing use of automation and digital technology on board. From advanced navigation and communication systems to fully integrated smart automation systems, these technologies are changing the way yachts are operated and maintained. These technologies enable better control and customization of on-board systems, as well as improved safety and efficiency.

In addition, the yachting industry has begun to change to a more versatile and adaptable yacht design. This is due to the use of advanced computer-aided design (CAD) and 3D printing technology. These technologies allow rapid prototyping and testing of new designs and components. This in turn has led to the development of more modular and easily interchangeable components that can be swapped out and replaced as needed to provide greater flexibility and functionality.

This section explores some of the most promising and innovative technologies for a more comprehensive look at the state of the art in yacht technology.

I. Electric propulsion technology

With increasing global concern over environmental issues and climate change, there is also a rising demand for more environmentally friendly technologies and equipment. In the shipbuilding industry, electric propulsion technology is regarded as an important technological innovation. It can improve the fuel efficiency of ships and reduce carbon emissions. At present, the application of electric propulsion technology has been widely promoted and applied. Many yacht manufacturers have begun to develop and produce electric propulsion systems and apply them to the design and manufacture of yachts. Among them, the most representative brands are Silent Yachts in the Netherlands and Torqeedo in Germany.

Silent Yachts is a company specializing in the manufacture of electric yachts. All of its yachts use solar power generation and electric propulsion systems. In addition, Silent Yachts also uses renewable and environmentally friendly materials.

Torqeedo is a company specializing in the research and development of electric propulsion technology. Its electric propulsion systems can be applied to different types of vessels, such as yachts, sailboats, kayaks and inflatable boats. Torqeedo's electric propulsion system uses efficient motors and intelligent control systems to improve the efficiency and performance of yachts while reducing their noise and vibration.

In addition to Silent Yachts and Torqeedo, many other yacht manufacturers have begun to apply electric propulsion technology in order to improve the competitiveness and environmental protection of its products.

(1) Basic principles of electric propulsion technology

Electric propulsion technology uses electric energy to drive the propeller to produce propulsion and realize the forward movement of the ship. Normally, the electric propulsion system of a yacht includes several main parts, such as the battery pack, electric motor, controller, and propeller.

The battery pack is the core component of electric propulsion technology, which is used to store electric energy. Modern yachts generally use lithium-ion battery packs, which have high energy density and stability and can provide long-term power support. The electric motor is the core component that converts electric energy into mechanical energy. The motor is usually composed of multiple electric components designed and configured according to the size and needs of the yacht. The controller is the center of the electric propulsion system, responsible for controlling the speed and thrust of the electric motor and manage the charging and discharge of the battery pack. Propellers convert the mechanical energy of electric motors into propulsion, usually in the form of blades or water jets.

Compared with the traditional internal combustion engine propulsion mode, the electric propulsion technology has the following advantages:

1. Zero emissions

Yachts using electric propulsion technology do not produce any exhaust gas and wastewater emissions, greatly reducing the impact on the environment.

2. Quiet sailing

Electric propulsion technology can minimize noise and is quieter than traditional internal combustion engine propulsion technology. It brings a more comfortable sailing experience to yacht passengers.

3. Low maintenance cost

Compared with traditional internal combustion engine propulsion technology, the maintenance cost of electric propulsion technology is lower. Since electric motors do not have the same moving parts as traditional internal combustion engines, it is not necessary to change oil and other wearing parts regularly.

4. High efficiency and economy

Electric propulsion technology has higher conversion efficiency, which can convert more electric energy into mechanical energy and reduce energy waste. It also improves the yacht's endurance.

(2) Application of Electric Propulsion Technology in the Yachting Industry

1. The electrification of yachts More and more yachts have begun to use electric propulsion technology to realize their electrification. Electric propulsion technology can be used in the main propulsion system or the auxiliary propulsion system of a yacht. In the main propulsion system, the electric power can directly drive the ship forward or backward, while in the auxiliary propulsion system, it can help yachts dock or adjust their direction by turning side thrusters or underwater thrusters.

In view of the advantages of yacht electrification, electric propulsion technology has been widely used in various types of yachts, including sailboats and motorboats. For example, Silent 55, a pure electric yacht designed by Vripack, a Dutch shipyard, is powered by solar panels and a large battery storage system; t has a maximum speed of 20 knots and a maximum range of 100 nautical miles. In May 2023, the first 62-foot pure electric catamaran yacht designed by Kanghe Shipping and Italian Ship Design Team was built in Hainan, China. The boat is 19.27 meters long and 9 meters wide, can carry 29 people, and is mainly used for water sightseeing. It is characterized by small draft, small power propulsion resistance, zero emissions, silence, and comfort.

Electric propulsion technology is currently facing some development bottlenecks: battery life is limited, and charging needs to be completed in a limited time. The electric propulsion systems are costly and need more investment; traditional fuel propulsion systems have a richer history and technology accumulation. Therefore, yacht designers and users need to accept and adapt to the new electric propulsion technology, whose problems will be solved through continuous technological innovation.

2. Yacht Hybrid Power

Hybrid yachts combine two power systems: the internal combustion engine and the electric motor. electric propulsion technology is one of the core technologies toward realizing the electrification of hybrid yachts.

In a hybrid yacht, a conventional internal combustion engine and fuel system are combined with an electric propulsion system that can be used to accelerate the yacht and provide additional power when cruising at low speeds. With the traditional fuel power system, the electric propulsion system can also be used to assist in controlling the position and attitude of the yacht.

Hybrid yachts can also improve their efficiency through energy recovery technology. For example, when braking or decelerating, an electric propulsion system can convert kinetic energy into electrical energy for later use or storage. This way of recovering energy can reduce dependence on traditional fuels and reduce fuel consumption and emissions.

In addition to reducing emissions and improving efficiency, electric propulsion systems can provide a quieter and smoother sailing experience. Because the electric propulsion system is almost free of noise and vibration, the yacht can be quieter and cruise more comfortably. For example, the Italian superyacht Wider brand pioneered the application of hybrid technology to superyachts. At the 2016 Monaco Yacht Show, the Wider 150, the first superyacht to combine series hybrid propulsion with azimuth propulsion, ranked first in the world. The superyacht has won numerous awards. Wider's newest superyacht, the Wider 210, is the largest yacht in the Wider family at 62 meters. The serial hybrid propulsion system of the yacht can limit consumption and emissions by reducing the use of traditional engines.

2. Intelligent control systems

Intelligent control systems monitor and control yachts through computer and sensor technology. They have been widely used in yacht design and manufacture. Through the intelligent control system, the yacht driver can easily monitor and control the yacht, which can be automatically driven and parked, thus improving safety and comfort. For example, yacht designers can use intelligent control systems to automatically adjust the attitude of the hull.

(1) Navigation control systems

Through the use of sensors, controllers, and actuators, these systems can automatically manage the power, manipulation, electricity, air conditioning and other aspects of the yacht by controlling its speed, steering, and inclination angle. The automatic control systems can also monitor the environmental parameters of the yacht, such as water temperature, air temperature, and humidity.

(2) Energy management systems

Intelligent energy control systems can manage engines, batteries, and solar panels to achieve efficient use of energy and energy conservation and extend the endurance of the yacht.

(3) Intelligent entertainment systems

The intelligent control system can also integrate various entertainment facilities on the yacht, enabling drivers and passengers to operate audio, television, lighting and other equipment through touch screen or voice control.

(4) Safety monitoring systems

Intelligent control systems can also be used for the safety monitoring of the yacht via infrared cameras, ultrasonic sensors, water depth sensors and similar devices. They can monitor the environment around the yacht in real time so as to predict any potential safety hazards.

Generally speaking, the intelligent control systems can improve the operational efficiency, safety, comfort and environmental protection of the yacht by reducing manual operation and human error. Especially in large yachts, these systems can help the crew quickly and accurately grasp the yacht's operational status and maintenance issues.

3. Virtual Reality Technologies

Virtual Reality (VR) is a computer technology that simulates the real environment. Through human-computer interaction, the user's immersive sensory experience is realized, and the technology can be applied to a wide range of applications, such as games, education, and medical treatment. VR technology is beginning to be used more widely.

(1) Application of Virtual Reality Technology in Yacht Design

Through the use of 3D modeling technology, designers can quickly and accurately construct three-dimensional models of theyachts, which can be quickly modified and optimized. Thus, manufacturing costs can be reduced and manufacturing efficiencies can be improved. Using virtual reality technology, yacht designers can design yachts in a virtual environment, including their shapes, interior spaces, and equipment layouts. Virtual reality technology can also simulate the operation of yachts in different environments, such as wind, waves, and currents.

(2) Application of Virtual Reality Technology in Yacht Manufacturing

1. Yacht manufacturing simulation tests Virtual reality technology can help design teams and manufacturers conduct simulation tests and optimize designs in the early stages of manufacturing. By using virtual reality technology, manufacturers can create and test digital prototypes of yachts before real physical manufacturing. This helps to find design flaws, eliminate errors and improve the performance of the yacht. For example, in a virtual reality environment, manufacturers can simulate the marine environment and check the sailing performance of yachts.

2. Yacht manufacturing training

Through virtual reality technology, manufacturers can train yacht operators in a safe virtual environment, where they can learn how to install and maintain the yacht's systems and components. This technology thus helps to improve work safety and reduce accidents. In addition, virtual reality technology can also help manufacturers to train and share knowledge across different factories and production lines, thereby improving the production efficiency and quality of the whole yacht manufacturing industry.

3. Optimizing the manufacturing process Through virtual reality technology, manufacturers can analyze the production line in

a digital environment and identify bottlenecks and problems. This information can be used to improve the production process to improve efficiency and quality. For example, a manufacturer may simulate a yacht assembly line in a virtual reality environment to find and eliminate any problems that may cause assembly delays or assembly errors.

(3) Application of Virtual Reality Technology in Yacht Sales

In traditional yacht sales, consumers need to go to an exhibition hall in person in order to actually observe the exterior and interior of the yacht. Using virtual reality technology, consumers can observe and experience yachts directly at home through head-mounted virtual reality devices. The technology can also create a high-fidelity yacht model to simulate the operation of the yacht in different environments, such as wind and waves, sunshine, or moonlight, providing consumers with a simulated visual and auditory experience.

Through virtual reality technology, yacht sellers can communicate with potential customers at different geographical locations and time points. It reduces the cost of marketing and time, and at the same time, it enlarges the potential customer base. In addition, virtual reality technology can also be used for yacht customization and design. Customers can try different interior decoration, materials and colors in the virtual environment, as well as change the layout of the cabin so as to obtain the most satisfactory scheme.

At yacht exhibitions, virtual reality technology can provide potential customers with a more realistic yacht display experience. Through virtual reality technology, yacht manufacturers can display virtual models of yachts in exhibition halls or on websites. It also allows customers to interact through VR headsets or other devices. Customers can realistically understand the shape, interior space and equipment configuration of the yacht in the virtual environment and better understand the performance and characteristics of the yacht, thereby improving sales conversion.

Generally speaking, the application of virtual reality technology in yacht sales not only provides consumers with a better shopping experience. It also improves the sales efficiency and competitiveness of yacht sellers.

4. Sustainable technologies

Sustainability technology is a hot spot in yacht technology innovation, which can significantly improve the environmental impact and sustainability of yachts. Its application in the yachting industry is gradually being valued and promoted. In addition to the electric propulsion technology, intelligent control system and virtual reality technology mentioned above, the application of sustainable technology in yacht technology innovation includes renewable energy technology, equipment miniaturization technology and material lightweight technology.

(1) Solar and wind energy technologies

Renewable energy technologies such as solar energy and wind energy can reduce carbon emissions and environmental impacts during the use of yachts while also providing enough energy for the yacht.

Solar energy technology is widely used in the energy supply system of yachts. It mainly provides power for ships by collecting and converting solar energy from solar panels usually installed on the deck or roof of the yacht, including lighting, communication, navigation equipment and so on. Solar panels are used, which can maximize the absorption of sunlight and generate enough electricity. In addition, some high-end yachts are equipped with solar photovoltaic sails and other solar devices, which can collect more solar energy, thereby further increasing the energy source of the yacht.

Wind energy technology has been used relatively infrequently in yachts, but it has also received attention. Wind energy technology generally collects and utilizes wind energy by installing wind turbines or sails to provide power and energy for yachts. Wind turbines can collect wind energy and convert it into electricity to provide power for yachts. In addition, some yachts are equipped with special sails, which can capture more wind energy to power the yacht.

In general, the application of solar and wind energy technology in yachts has high potential and development prospects. With the continuous progress of technology and the continuous reduction of cost, solar and wind technologies will become an integral part of yacht design, construction and use. It is expected to realize the real greening of yachts.

(2) Wastewater treatment systems

Wastewater treatment systems are being more widely used in yacht technology inno vations. This is due to the growing concern about the impact of wastewater discharge from pleasure craft on the marine environment. The wastewater treatment system can effectively reduce the pollutants discharged by the yacht, thus minimizing the impact of the yacht on the marine environment.

Wastewater treatment systems generally consist of three major components: pre-treatment, main treatment, and post- treatment. The pre-treatment stage is mainly to screen and precipitate the wastewater to remove larger impurities and suspended solids; In the main treatment stage, the pollutants in the wastewater are treated and decomposed by biological and chemical methods. The post-treatment stage is to disinfect and adjust the pH value of the treated wastewater and ensure that the treated wastewater meets the relevant national and regional discharge standards.

There are two ways to treat wastewater in yachts, Small yachts are equipped with a sewage collection device, and the sewage produced must be sent ashore. Wastewater treatment systems generally use physical and chemical methods, such as ultrafiltration, reverse osmosis, ozone oxidation, or ultraviolet disinfection. These technologies can effectively remove harmful substances such as suspended solids, organic matter and microorganisms in wastewater. The wastewater reaches the specified discharge standard and can be recycled.

The application of wastewater treatment systems can not only protect the marine environment, but also improve the comfort and sustainability of yachts while contributing to the sustainable development of the yachting industry.

(3) Miniaturization technology

Miniaturization technology refers to the technology of miniaturizing traditional large-scale equipment and components, mainly to improve the performance of yachts, reduce their size and weight, and improve energy efficiency.

1. Miniaturization of hydraulic control systems

The hydraulic control system is a very important part of the yacht, which directs the power, steering and docking of the vessel. Conventional hydraulic control systems typically require a lot of space and weight. The use of a miniaturized hydraulic control system can greatly reduce the volume and weight of the system and improve the performance and maneuverability of the yacht.

2. Miniaturized sensors and controllers Yachts require a large number of sensors and controllers to monitor and control various parameters. Traditional sensors and controllers are usually relatively large. Their volume and weight can be greatly reduced by using miniaturized sensors and controllers, and accuracy and response speed can also be improved.

3. Miniaturized engines

The use of miniaturized engines can reduce the weight and space of yachts, while improving fuel efficiency and performance. Miniaturized engines usually use superalloy materials, turbocharging, and other technologies to achieve high power output in a small volume.

4. Miniaturized gas turbine generators Gas turbine generators represent a new type of power generation equipment. Their miniaturized design can reduce the volume and weight to less than half of the traditional generator while also improving power generation efficiency and reliability.

5. Miniaturized air conditioning systems Yachts need air conditioning systems to maintain a good indoor environment in hot weather. Traditional air conditioning systems are bulky and heavy. Miniaturized air conditioning systems can greatly reduce their volume and weight, while improving its efficiency and cooling capacity.

Section 3: Yacht Standards and Patents

Yacht standards refer to a series of regulations and guidelines for the design, construction, maintenance and operation of yachts. These standards cover all aspects of yachts, including but not limited to material selection, construction regulations, equipment installation, safety measures, environmental protection, and communication equipment. The formulation of yacht standards aims to improve the quality and safety of yachts and promote the healthy development of the yachting industry.

Yacht standards are applicable to yacht manufacturers, shipyards, designers, accessories manufacturers, dealers, owners, crew members and other relevant personnel. It has certain restraint and guidance. Compliance with these standards is important to yacht manufacturers because it allows them to sell their products in the global market. Standards also provide consumers with a baseline level of safety and quality, which is essential for building industry trust. At the same time, standards can also promote industry innovation and technological progress. Through the provisions of the standard, yacht designers and manufacturers can understand the best practices and technological development direction of the industry. Innovative yacht design and manufacturing technology to improve the performance and market competitiveness of yachts.

The main international yacht standards organizations include the International Maritime Organization and the European Yacht Standardization Committee. The International Maritime Organization is a specialized agency of the United Nations, it is responsible for promulgating and regulating international conventions and guidelines for maritime safety, ship design, construction and maintenance. The European Yacht Standardization Committee is one of the European standardization organizations, which is responsible for the formulation and publication of European yacht standards. In addition, many countries and regions will also develop their own yacht standards.

Patents play an important role in the boating industry by protecting the intellectual property of companies and individuals who develop new technologies and innovations. A patent gives the holder the exclusive right to use and sell the patented technology for a limited time. This can incentivize companies to invest in R & D because they are able to protect their investments and benefit from their innovations. On the other hand, patents may also create barriers to entry for smaller companies and limit market competition.

In general, yacht standards and patents play an important role in shaping the yachting industry. They affect innovation by balancing the need for safety, quality, and intellectual property protection with the need for improvements in new technologies and products.

1. International Standards Organization and its normative standards

International Yacht Standards Organization refers to the organization that formulates yacht standards worldwide. These standards include yacht design, manufacturing, testing, inspection, safety and environmental protection.

(1) Standards of the International Maritime Organization (IMO)

The International Maritime Organization (IMO) is a specialized agency under the United Nations. Founded in 1948 and headquartered in London. The responsibility of IMO is to promote and coordinate the development of international navigation and maritime affairs. It is committed to the formulation and promotion of international conventions, guidelines, standards and recommendations related to shipping. Among them, IMO has also formulated and promoted the standards for yachts.

IMO's standards in the field of yachts mainly include:

1. International Yachting Code (In-

ternational Code of Safety for High-speed Craft, HSC Code, which applies to high-speed craft and pleasure craft with speeds exceeding 20 knots and includes various safety requirements such as fire prevention and escape.

2. Guidelines for the Safe Construction and Operation of Yachts and Small Commercial Vessels): This standard establishes safety requirements for small commercial vessels and yachts. including construction, installation equipment and operation specifications.

3. The International Regulations for Preventing Collisions at Sea, (COLREGs): These standards are developed by the International Maritime Organization for the avoidance of collisions between ships and are applicable to all types of ships, including yachts.

4. Code of Practice for the Safe Operation of Small Commercial Vessels). This standard applies to small commercial vessels and pleasure craft. These include requirements and guidelines for design, construction, and operation.

In addition to these norms and standards, IMO has also formulated a series of international conventions on ships and yachts, such as the International Convention for the Safety of Life at Sea (SOLAS) and the International Convention for the Prevention of Pollution from Ships (MARPOL).

In addition, IMO has published several guidelines related to yacht design and construction to help yacht builders and designers meet the requirements of IMO regulations. These guidelines cover ship structural design, fuel consumption and emission control, mechanical and electrical systems, and emission and blowdown control guides in this area.

Generally speaking, the formulation and implementation of IMO regulations and guidelines provide a global standardized framework for the yachting industry, enabling yacht builders and designers to follow the same standards, To ensure that the safety, environmental protection and performance of yachts meet international standards. In addition, these regulations also promote the innovation and progress of yacht technology, making the yacht manufacturing industry more sustainable and competitive.

These international standards and conventions provide uniform guidelines and requirements for yacht design, construction and operation. They have played a positive role in promoting the development and innovation of the yachting industry.

(2) Standards of the International Association of Classification Societies (IACS)

The International Association of Classification Societies (IACS) was founded in 1968. It is a technology-based non- governmental organization currently composed of 11 classification society members. It is one of the most influential classification societies in the world.

IACS is recognized as the principal technical advisor to the International Maritime Organization (IMO), Through its teams, expert groups and project teams, it has developed minimum technical standards and requirements for ship safety and marine environmental protection. Through technical support, compliance verification and R & D, The classification standards developed by its member associations cover more than 90% of the world's cargo ship tonnage. Its standards cover ship design, construction, inspection, certification, maintenance and navigation. It is one of the most authoritative and credible standards in the field of international shipping. It mainly includes the following aspects:

1. Yacht structure design

It includes the specifications of yacht structure design, material selection, processing technology and so on. To ensure that the safety, strength and stability of the yacht meet the relevant standards and regulations.

2. Yacht construction

It includes the specifications of yacht construction technology, construction quality and equipment selection. To ensure that the construction of the yacht meets the relevant standards and regulations.

3. Yacht Inspection and Certification

It includes yacht class certification, safety Inspection, environmental protection certification and other specifications. To ensure that the safety and environmental protection of yachts meet relevant standards and regulations.

4. Yacht maintenance and repair Including the maintenance, repair and modification of yachts, to ensure that the yacht is in good condition and performance during use.

5. Yacht operation and management

It includes yacht operation rules, crew training, navigation safety and other specifications. to ensure that the yacht is safe, reliable and efficient in operation.

6. Environmental protection and energy efficiency of yacht

Including yacht pollution prevention and control, energy management, emission limits and other aspects of the norms. To ensure that yachts meet international standards in terms of environmental protection and energy efficiency.

Table 11-2 Main IACS Standards

Serial number	Standard name	Standard content
1	Common Structural Rules (CSR)	The standard provides structural design and construction requirements for bulk carriers and oil tankers.
2	Unified Requirements (UR)	The standard provides technical requirements for the design, construction and maintenance of various types of vessels, including passenger ships, container ships and offshore vessels.
3	Procedural Requirements (PR)	The standard provides procedures and guidance for the certification and inspection of ships, including new ships, in-service ships and ship dismantling.
4	Classification Rules (CR)	This standard provides technical requirements for the classification of ships and offshore structures, including materials, equipment and systems.
5	Environmental Notation (EN)	This standard provides criteria and guidance for assessing and certifying the environmental performance of ships and offshore structures.
6	Quality Management System (QMS)	This standard provides the requirements for a classification society to implement and maintain a quality management system.

(2) Standards of the International Organization for Standardization (ISO)

The International Organization for Standardization (ISO) is a global non-governmental organization. Headquartered in Geneva, Switzerland, it is the largest international standardization organization in the world. Its international standards are widely used in various fields. ISO has also developed a series of specifications and standards related to yachts to ensure their safety, reliability and quality. ISO standards for yachts mainly cover the following aspects:

1. Yacht Design and Construction

ISO has developed a series of standards for yacht design and construction, including standards for yacht hull structure, materials, construction and testing. These standards are designed to ensure the safety and quality of yachts.

2. Yacht operation and maintenance

ISO also develops standards for the operation and maintenance of yachts, including standards for yacht operators and standards for yacht maintenance. These standards are designed to ensure that yachts are kept in good working condition during use and that breakdowns and accidents are reduced.

3. Yacht safety

The yacht safety standards developed by ISO include those related to yacht life- saving equipment, marine fire-fighting equipment, navigation signal equipment and emergency communication equipment. These standards are designed to ensure that yachts can provide the necessary protection and rescue materials in the event of an accident.

4. Yacht environmental standards

The environmental standards developed

by ISO include standards for yacht wastewater, exhaust gas and noise emissions. These standards are designed to reduce the environmental impact of yachts and protect the health of marine and coastal ecosystems.

Table 11-3 ISO Certification Standards for the Yachting Industry

Serial number	Standard number	Standard content
1	ISO 8666	The measurement standard of yacht length and width stipulates the size of yacht, which is convenient for yacht manufacturers and consumers to have a unified understanding.
2	ISO 12215	The structural standards for yacht construction include the requirements for strength, stability and waterproofing of the hull.
3	ISO 15085	Yacht design standards, including yacht appearance, interior space design and layout, power systems, piping systems and other requirements.
4	ISO 6185	Requirements for the size, material, strength and stability of inflatable boats.
5	ISO 10240	Standards for the transportation and storage of yachts, specifying the size, weight, and storage requirements for yachts.
6	ISO 12217-2	Assessment requirements for stability and buoyancy of sailing craft.
7	ISO 12217-1 ISO 12217-3	Requirements for assessment of stability and buoyancy of non-sailing craft.
8	ISO 21487	Inspection criteria and requirements for permanently installed fuel tanks on pleasure craft.
9	ISO 14509	Inspection standards and requirements for noise emission of yacht engines.

The yacht standards of ISO play an important role in yacht manufacturing and sales. They provide a recognized and common norm and standard for the industry, thus making yacht products more comparable, reliable, and sustainable. At the same time, these standards also promote the innovation and development of yacht technology and promote the overall prosperity of the global yacht market.

(4) CE certification standard

The CE (Conformité Européenne) is a compulsory safety certification mark in the EU market, even for products manufactured elsewhere. The CE mark shows that the product meets the basic requirements of the EU's Directive on the New Approach to Technical Harmonization and Standardization. This is a mandatory safety requirement for products under EU law, not a general quality requirement.

The European Commission issued its Yacht Directive in 1998.The directive stipulates that all yachts sold in the European Economic Area must meet European standards for safety, health, and environmental protection. The yacht manufacturer must affix the CE mark on the yacht and provide a yacht operation manual that meets the CE standard. These standards include requirements for yacht hulls, equipment and systems such as hull structures, fuel systems, electrical systems, fire protection equipment, marine toilets and drainage systems. These standards ensure the safety and environmental performance of yachts and protect the interests of consumers.

The CE standard is a mandatory one for the manufacture and sale of yachts in the European Union. The continuous upgrading of CE standards has also promoted the innovation and progress of yacht technology and the development of the yachting industry.

2. Yacht Standard Organizations in China

(1) National Standardization Management Committee (NSMC)

The National Standardization Management Committee (NSMC) is a specialized agency authorized by the State Council to manage the national standardization work in a unified way. The relevant national standards are approved and issued by this agency, which also has the right to carry out compulsory national standards for external notification.

As of May 1, 2023, the national standards for the yachting industry are summarized in Table 11-4.

Table 11-4 yachting industry National Standards Approved by Standardization Administration of China (Current)

Serial number	Standard number	Standard Chinese name	Centralized unit
1	GB/T 35558-2017	Yacht Management Service Specification	TC 264 (National Service Standardization Technical Committee)
2	GB/T 35353-2017	Large yacht deck machinery anchoring equipment	TC 12 (National Technical Committee for Marine Ship Standardization)
3	GB/T 38312-2019	Rules for mooring and sea trials of large yachts	TC 12 (National Technical Committee for Marine Ship Standardization)

4	GB/T 35384-2017	Requirements for strength and weathertightness of doors for large pleasure craft	TC 12 (National Technical Committee for Marine Ship Standardization)
5	GB/T 33485-2017	Safety requirements for main and auxiliary diesel engines of large yachts	TC 12 (National Technical Committee for Marine Ship Standardization)
6	GB/T 33486-2017	Ships and Marine Technology Large Yachts FRP Boat Structural Fire Protection	TC 12 (National Technical Committee for Marine Ship Standardization)
7	GB/T 37438-2019	Basic requirement and evaluation method of production conditions for yacht manufacturers	TC 12 (National Technical Committee for Marine Ship Standardization)
8	GB/T 31885-2015	Ships and marine technology-Measurement and evaluation of the appearance of coatings for large pleasure craft	TC 12 (National Technical Committee for Marine Ship Standardization)
9	GB/T 35354-2017	Ships and marine technology-strength requirements for large pleasure craft deck cranes and boarding ladders	TC 12 (National Technical Committee for Marine Ship Standardization)
10	GB/T 40528.1-2021	Specification for structural scantlings of multi-hull yachts-Part 1: Composite materials	TC 12 (National Technical Committee for Marine Ship Standardization)
11	GB/T 19322.1-2021	Small craft-Motor yachts-Airborne noise-Part 1: Passage measurement procedure	TC 241 (National Technical Committee for Small Craft Standardization)
12	GB/T 19322.2-2017	Small craft-Motor yachts-Airborne noise-Part 2: Noise assessment using reference craft	TC 241 (National Technical Committee for Small Craft Standardization)

13	GB/T 19322.3-2017	Small craft-Airborne noise of motor yachts-Part 3: Noise assessment by calculation and measurement procedures	TC 241 (National Technical Committee for Small Craft Standardization)
14	GB/T 33196.1-2016	Large pleasure craft-Visitor windows-Strength, watertightness and weathertightness-Part 1: Design criteria, materials, framing and testing for free-standing view windows	TC 12 (National Technical Committee for Marine Ship Standardization)

(2) China Classification Society

China Classification Society (CCS) is the only state-level accreditation organization with independent legal authority in China, specializing in the work of classification societies. Its technical backbone includes senior professional and technical personnel in the fields of shipbuilding, marine engineering and maritime technology. In 1988, the China Classification Society joined the International Association of Classification Societies (IACS) and became one of the 11 formal members of the association. CCS is mainly responsible for the inspection, identification, certification and technical consultation of ships, and has a high international reputation and influence.

CCS's standards for yachts mainly include the Code for the Construction and Inspection of Offshore Yachts (2020). The specification provides specific technical requirements and inspection methods for yacht manufacturing and inspection according to the size of the yacht. It includes provisions for the design, construction, installation and inspection of yachts.

In addition, CCS has developed a series of technical specifications, industry standards and guidelines related to yachts. They include the Code for Construction of Fiber-Reinforced Plastic Ships (2015), the Code for Certification of Ship Safety Management Systems (2018), the Green Ecological Ship Code Specification (2022), the Specification for Battery Power for Marine Applications (2023), and the Specification for Intelligent Ships (2023). These standards and norms provide a strong guarantee for the technological innovation and sustainable development of the yachting industry.

(3) Large Yachts Sub-Technical Committee of the National Marine Ship Standardization Technical Committee

The Large Yacht Sub-Technical Committee of the National Oceanographic Ship Standardization Technical Committee is a national professional standardization technical committee established and guided by the National Standardization Management Committee.

More than 300 national standards have been issued, including its number TC12/SC9, which is responsible for the standardization of yachts with a length of more than 24 meters. Examples are shown in the table below.

Table 11-5 Some National Standards Issued by Large Yacht Sub-Technical Committee of National Oceanographic Ship Standardization Technical Committee

Serial number	Standard number	Standard Chinese name
1	GB/T 42055-2022	Ships and marine technology-Shipboard machinery-Data format
2	GB/T 30007-2022	Ships and marine technology-Guidelines for the evaluation of speed and power performance by analysis of tachometric sea trial data
3	GB/T 42054-2022	Ship and Marine Technology Shipborne Marine Shared Data Server
4	GB/T 41888-2022	Ship and Marine Technology Ship Launching Technology with Air Bag
5	GB/T 41887.1-2022	Ships and marine technology-Guidelines for private maritime security companies (PMSC) for private armed security personnel (PCASP) on a contractual (pro forma contract) basis-Part 1: General
6	GB/T 41893-2022	Basic requirements for logistics management of digital workshop for hull parts manufacturing
7	GB/T 41892-2022	Guide for information integration and coding of intelligent marine machinery and equipment
8	GB/T 41517-2022	Ships and marine technology--Ventilation of cargo spaces of vehicles with internal combustion engines--Theoretical calculation of total air demand
9	GB/T 40788-2021	Ships and Offshore Technology Offshore Wind Energy Port and Offshore Operations
10	GB/T 40528.1-2021	Specification for structural scantlings of multi-hull yachts-Part 1: Composite materials

(4) National Small Craft Standardization Technical Committee

National Technical Committee for Small Boat Standardization is another national professional standardization technical committee established and guided by the National Standardization Management Committee. Its standard number TC241 is responsible for the equipment and structure of yachts with a length of less than or equal to 24m and other small boats with similar equipment. As for the standardization work, dozens of national standards have been issued. See the following table for examples In addition, the industry standard involved is the Calibration Power Classification of

High-speed Diesel Engines for Ships (CB/T 4369-2014).

Table 10-6 Some national standards issued by the National Technical Committee for Small Craft Standardization

Serial number	Standard number	Standard Chinese name
1	GB/T 34315.1-2022	Small craft-Inflatable life rafts-Part 1: Type I
2	GB/T 41721-2022	Small craft-Navigation lights-Performance of led lights
3	GB/T 40884-2021	Small craft-Electric propulsion system
4	GB/T 19322.1-2021	Small craft-Motor yachts-Airborne noise-Part 1: Passage measurement procedure
5	GB/T 40787-2021	Small craft-Mounting and arrangement of navigation lights and visibility
6	GB/T 19314.3-2019	Small craft-Hull construction and scantlings-Part 3: Materials: Steel, aluminum alloys, wood, other material
7	GB/T 38340-2019	Small craft-reciprocating internal combustion engines-exhaust emission measurements-test-bed measurements of gaseous and particulate emissions
8	GB/T 19314.4-2019	Small craft--Hull construction and scantlings--Part 4: Workshop and fabrication
9	GB/T 19314.2-2019	Small craft-Hull construction and scantlings-Part 2: Materials: Core, embedment materials for sandwich construction
10	GB/T 37419-2019	Small craft-Electric or electronic control systems for steering, gear shifting and throttle

3. Yacht Patents and Development

Yacht patents cover different types of patents, including authorized inventions, utility models and designs.

Internationally, there are a large number of high-value patents for yachts in the United States, Europe and Japan. Some well-known yacht manufacturers and design companies also own many yacht-related patents, such as Feadship, Benetti, and Lurssen. In addition, some international organizations have actively promoted the development of yacht technology and supported the protection of yacht patents, such as the International Yacht and Sailing Federation (ISAF).

(1) The importance of yacht patents

Yacht manufacturing is constantly evolving, with new technologies and materials being developed to improve their design, performance, and sustainability. One of the ways yacht manufacturers protect their innovations is by obtaining patents. A patent is a legal document that grants an inventor exclusive rights to an invention for a limited period of time. This is usually 20 years from the date of application.

Obtaining a patent can bring many benefits to yacht manufacturers. First, it gives the exclusive right to make and sell their inventions, preventing others from copying or using their ideas without permission. This can provide a competitive advantage and help maintain a manufacturer's market share. Secondly, patents can also provide a source of revenue for yacht manufacturers, who can license their inventions to other companies or sell their patent rights, generating additional revenue. This helps offset the costs associated with developing new technologies and materials. However, obtaining patents can also pose challenges for yacht manufacturers. The process of obtaining a patent can be complex and time-consuming, requiring significant legal and financial resources.

In addition, the process of obtaining patents can be competitive, since other companies are also seeking to protect their innovations. This can lead to disputes over ownership of ideas and technology, leading to lengthy and costly legal battles. When developing new technologies and materials for the boating industry, yacht manufacturers must consider the potential benefits and challenges associated with patents.

(2) General trend of yacht patent application in the world

Based on the core retrieval elements such as keywords, patentees, and IPC classification numbers, Boolean logic operators were used to construct the retrieval search in the Smart Bud Global Patent Database from January 2004 to July 2023. After screening, 563 patents related to yacht design were obtained, including 274 utility models, 200 invention applications, and 89 authorized inventions; From the perspective of legal status, there are 294 valid patents and 26 patents in the substantive examination stage.

Table 11-7 Core search elements

Retrieve the dimensions	Retrieve features
Key words	Yacht cabin, atrium, radar mast, superstructure, passenger ship, HVAC, air conditioning, ventilation
IPC classification number	B63 Ships or other waterborne vessels; Equipment associated with ships

From the overall trend of global patent applications (see Figure 11-3), the number of yacht patent applications generally shows a fluctuating upward trend. Since 2006, the growth rate has accelerated, which is due to the continuous innovation of yacht design and technology, and the introduction of more environmentally friendly and energy-saving yachts. Many countries and regions have provided support and encouragement to the yacht manufacturing industry to promote its development, and yacht patent applications have increased accordingly. It reached its first peak in 2008 because of the Beijing Olympic Games and the Shanghai World Expo. Since that time, yachts have received more attention in competitions and exhibitions, the Chinese yacht market has gradually expanded, and the demand for small and medium-sized yachts has also increased. These factors undoubtedly speeds up the process of yacht patent applications.

Figure 11-3 Global Yacht Patent Application Trends

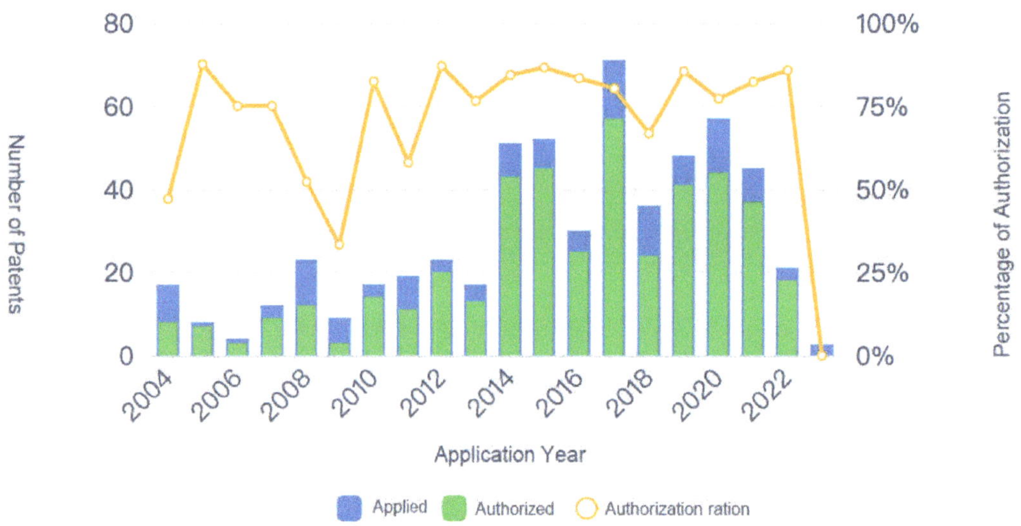

From 2013 to 2015, global yacht patent applications grew substantially. This is because the Internet and intelligent technology have been further integrated into yacht design and management to promote the development of intelligent ships. The yachting industry welcomes more investment and cooperation to promote technological innovation and market expansion. At the same time, the customized yacht market is growing rapidly, and the demand for personalized yachts is increasing. In 2013, the Chinese government issued its report Several Opinions on Promoting the Development of the yachting industry. To further support the evidence of this development and growth, China's yacht market is growing rapidly, and annual sales are gradually increasing. In 2015, China's yachting industry showed diversified development, involving luxury yachts, leisure yachts, official yachts and other types. Some yacht manufacturers began to export yacht products and expand overseas markets.

In 2017, the global yacht patent application entered a peak period, and foreign patent technology entered its mature period. Yacht manufacturers are committed to improving the sustainability and environmental protection of yachts, reducing carbon emissions and environmental impact. On the one hand, yacht products and services for the younger generation have received more attention. On the other hand, yacht rental and sharing modes are gradually rising to meet the needs of different users. At this stage, China's yachting industry continued to expand, domestic yacht manufacturers launched more new yacht products, and the yacht market grew rapidly. It is gradually expanding to the middle classes and the younger generation of users, and more people are choosing to rent yachts for vacation.

After 2020, the global outbreak of COVID-19 had a negative impact on the yachting industry. Although yacht manufacturers continued to promote innovation and create more intelligent, environmentally friendly and comfortable yacht products, it is undeniable that patent applications had declined.

(3) Distribution of Yacht Patentees in the World

In Figure 11-2, the top 10 patentees in terms of the number of patent applications are analyzed.

Figure 11-4 Ranking of Major Yacht Patentees in the World

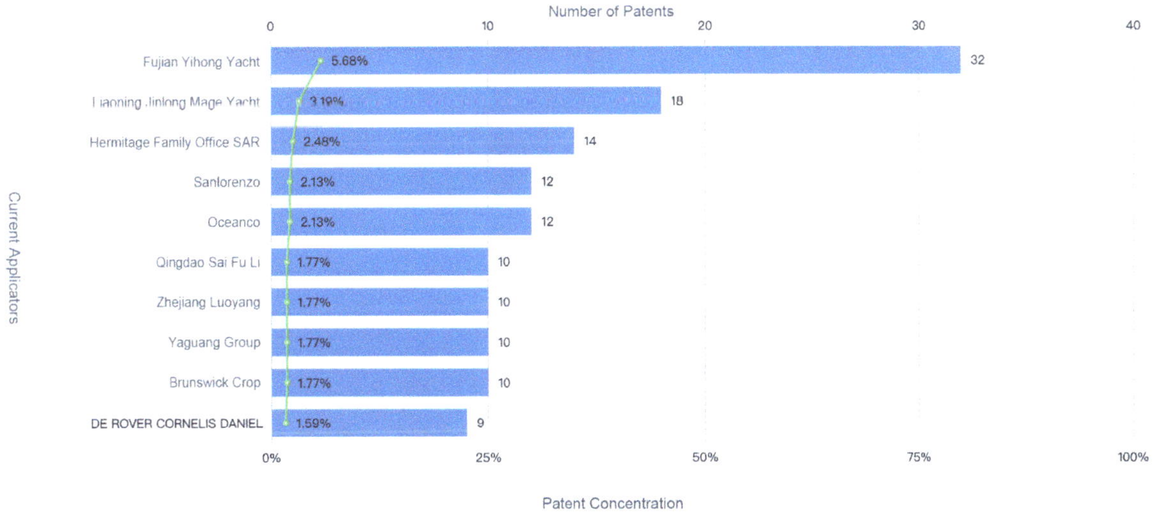

(1) Regional distribution of yacht patent technology in the world

After years of development, especial-ly since the 18th National Congress of the Communist Party of China, China's yacht patent application work has developed rapidly. The number of yacht patents, software copyrights and well-known brand trademarks continued to increase. The total number of patent applications in the whole industry in China now exceeds half of the total number of global applications, ranking first in the world (see Figure 11-3). However, it should be noted that although the total number of domestic yacht patent applications has increased rapidly, most of the patented products or technologies are concentrated in the development of conventional ship types and general products. This indicates that the distribution of high-value patents is still in its infancy. The creation and reserve of independent intellectual property rights in basic and forward-looking fields need to be strengthened. In the future, China should fully understand the strategic significance of intellectual property policy by developing the cultivation of high-value patents in key areas and by building core competitiveness.

Figure 11-3 Distribution of Global Yacht Patent Application Receiving Offices

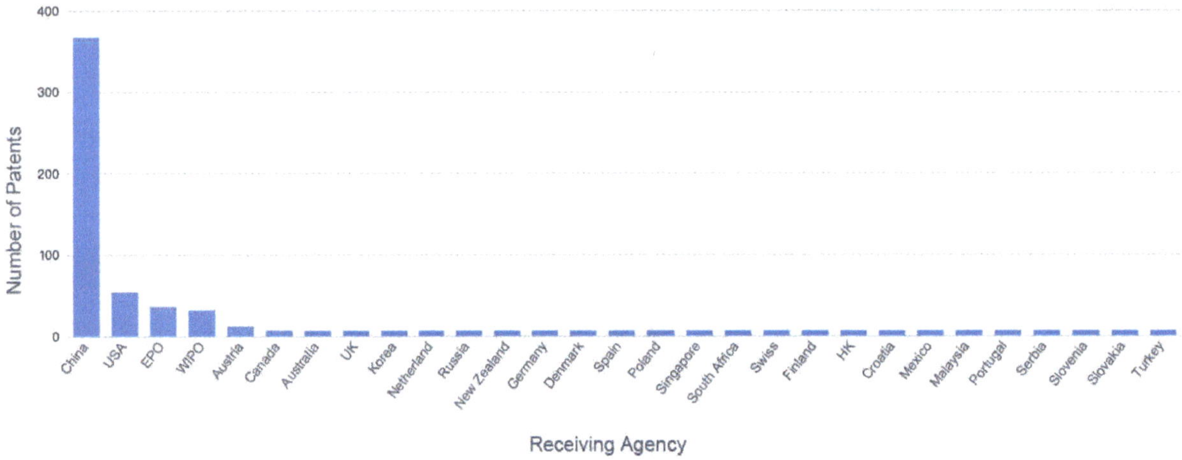

Section 4: Future Outlook for the Yachting Industry

The yachting industry faces challenges in such areas as environmental protection, sustainability, safety, and trade policy. But at the same time, with the continuous innovation and application of technology, the industry also has many opportunities. For example, digital technology, intelligent technology, lightweight material technology and renewable energy technology are being widely used. In the future, the yachting industry will continue to develop and innovate to promote green and sustainable development. China needs to adapt to the changing global policy and market environment, seizing opportunities and meeting challenges.

1. Challenges and Opportunities Facing the yachting industry

In recent years, with the upgrading of consumption and the recognition of yacht tourism, the development prospects of the yachting industry are bright. However, the yachting industry also faces some challenges. A major challenge is environmental sustainability:

The operation and manufacture of yachts generate large amounts of carbon emissions and wastewater, which negatively affect the environment. The yachting industry is required to meet the requirements of various safety and environmental regulations governing discharge standards, wastewater treatment, and waste management. To solve these problems, yacht manufacturers need to adopt more environmentally friendly technologies and materials.

At the same time, greener technology and materials can put economic pressure on yacht manufacturers. With the high cost of yacht production and economic instability, yacht manufacturers need to find new market opportunities too ensure long- term profitability. In addition, they need to cope with changes in consumer demand. For example, some consumers may prefer simple, small and affordable yachts to large, luxurious ones. Manufacturers need to understand and adapt to changes in consumer demand in order to remain competitive in the market.

In short, the yachting industry is facing many challenges, but there are also many opportunities for development, such as the emergence of new technologies, including sustainable technology, lightweight technology, intelligent technology, and digital technology. Yacht manufacturers and service providers can improve the performance and comfort of their yachts while reducing costs and environmental impact. For example, yacht manufacturers can use virtual reality and augmented reality technology to design and produce their vessels, thereby reducing the time and cost of prototyping. Yacht maintenance and service providers can use the Internet of Things and sensor technology to monitor the state of their vessels, forecasting maintenance needs and provide remote support to improve maintenance efficiency and customer satisfaction.

The growth and diversification of market demand also provide new opportunities for the yachting industry. Emerging markets such as China, India, and Brazil, have large populations and a growing affluent class, providing a growing demand for luxury goods. Also relevant is the growth of the yacht rental market. As more and more people seek unique travel experiences, yacht chartering becomes a popular option. This trend is likely to continue to grow in the future, especially among high-net-worth individuals. This will drive yacht manufacturers to continue to innovate and produce more competitive products to meet consumer demand. Finally, the increase of personalized demand has also brought new developmental changes to the industry. As consumers pay more and more attention to personalized experience, yacht designers and manufacturers can develop different types and styles of yachts to meet the needs of consumers.

2. Future prospects of yachts

With the rapid development of global tourism, yachts, as high-end tourism products, will continue to receive attention. In the future, with the enhancement of sustainability and environmental awareness, the yachting industry will also pay more attention to green environmental protection. It is expected that in the next few years, more yachts will adopt renewable energy technologies, such as solar and wind energ to reduce dependence on fossil fuels and reduce carbon emissions from yacht use. Specifically, it includes the following aspects.

First, yachts will be more environmentally friendly. Yacht manufacturers will invest more in sustainable technology to reduce the negative impact of yachts on the environment. For example, more yachts will use lightweight materials, bio-based materials, solar and wind power generation systems, At the same time, technologies such as wastewater treatment and garbage disposal will also be improved to protect marine ecosystems.

Yachts will also be more efficient. On the one hand, more efficient yacht designs will provide comfort and efficiency in the future. For example, more streamlined design and more efficient propulsion systems will be adopted to improve the speed and fuel efficiency of yachts. Yacht builders have also begun to use 3D printing technology, which will greatly shorten the manufacturing cycle and reduce costs.

Yacht manufacturers will also strive to produce more digital and intelligent yachts and provide more personalized and intelligent products. With the development of artificial intelligence and Internet of Things technology, yachts will adopt more digital and intelligent technologies. To improve efficiency and convenience, such technologies as intelligent navigation, automatic control, and virtual reality will make the control of the yacht more convenient, and also provide more entertainment and safety functions. At the same time, the ports that are destinations for yachts are becoming "smart ports" by adopting intelligent methods that provide more services and convenience. These include intelligent parking, intelligent charging, and intelligent maintenance.

Generally speaking, the yachting industry will continue to be modernized by new technologies, new materials and new designs. These technologies and designs will make yachts safer, more environmentally friendly and more intelligent, and will also bring more opportunities and challenges to the yachting industry. In the future, the yachting industry will continue to develop and innovate along these lines to meet people's demand for high-quality life at sea.

www.ingramcontent.com/pod-product-compliance
Lightning Source LLC
LaVergne TN
LVHW070908210926
848482LV00017B/1018